Crusader Warfare against islam from 634-2021

By Gregory Heary

The key to knowledge and teaching is to know what to teach, to who, in the right way, at the right time. From this I've learned an important lesson in that sometimes by teaching history for religious reasons we are teaching ignorance despite removing historical ignorance. Usually a teacher can justify teaching good useful information due to their arrogance when in reality they are teaching ignorance by misprioritizing and over-teaching. Yes, it is possibly for a book to have "too much information" even though it all might be good and useful. Sometimes sharing too much good useful information defeats the very purpose for sharing any good useful information. The prophetic method is to share the right amount that pleases God, not everything that you can. Commonly history lessons, while part of religion, detract from the very message of religion which we try to teach even though the entire history lesson may be framed in a religious context. At the beginning, middle and end of the day we are soldiers fighting against Satan and while knowing his history of waging war against the truth is beneficial sometimes learning such information instead of other information makes us lose the present and future religious wars. Consider neither God nor the prophets taught the full history of every prophet ever, even though such a history is the best history to know and most useful to us. Instead God and his prophets taught us what we needed to know and stressed practicing it. It is hard for any to remain a "Muslim fundamentalist" in practice. The ignorance and arrogance of an extremely intelligent layman or "student of knowledge" or even a genuine scholar can lead many smart sincere people to think teaching knowledge is wisdom when over-teaching good things actually equals anti-teaching. The truth does liberate one from Satanic slavery, however learning too much truth before one can handle it can enslave one despite the truth itself being liberating. Thus truth alone cannot set one free from Shaitan or give one victory, only God can. Truth is a great medicine, but must be given in proper doses.

Ultimately, I think it is important to know the following information. This is because whenever an author writes a book or a chapter they must ask themselves at least 4 questions, after ensuring the attention is sincerely for God's sake and according to the prophetic method. 1. Is the work adding anything of lasting value? 2. Has it got anything original, interesting or perceptive to say about certain aspects of its subjects? 3. Will the reader learn anything valuable from the book/chapter? 4. Or is it simply ideas and information readily available elsewhere? So whether what follows in this book should be written or not, I'm not 100% sure. History will not be the judge of my decision, as would be cliche to say, but God will judge this decision and God is a much more severe and fair judge than history. Whereas perhaps the best lesson in this dilemma is that in judging history (commenting on history) we forget God and his knowledge of the matters we write/talk about and that God will judge us based on our judgement of others. Hence while it is prudent to only speak/write of that which concerns you, sometimes things must be shared and explained because they do concern us and others. May God forgive us all for what we write/say/think/do. Good intentions are one of the things that lead us to make mistakes and good intentions also can cause us to fail to do good deeds as well. History is made by our intentions, actions and inactions.

462 years after the first Muslim conquest of Jerusalem, in 1099 CE when the Christian crusaders conquered Jerusalem they slaughtered nearly everyone inside Muslim, Jew, man, woman, child

(and I only say nearly because a few escaped the slaughter and fled to tell Muslims in other cities so they could prepare themselves). Yet if you read the Christian records, according to the Crusaders there were no Muslim survivors. So Muslim records actually make the Crusaders seem better than the Christian records do. As unlikely as it seems today, Jews in Jerusalem actually fought alongside the Muslims against the Christians because the crusaders came with the slogan of *"Embrace the Cross or die!"* Pope Urban II misinformed them that all the Christians had been slaughtered by the Muslims and prohibited from practicing their religion when motivating them to crusade, despite the Christian Hospitaler knights having operated a hospital in Jerusalem since 1050 CE. Regardless the crusaders decided they would kill as many non-Christians as they could. It is reported that when the crusaders captured Jerusalem the streets were flooded with blood that reached up to the knees of their horses. The Jews were burned alive in their synagogue. After the crusaders entered Jerusalem, on the 15th of July 1099 CE more than 70,000 dead bodies of Muslim children and women were found just in the Qibley Masjid alone. The Dome of the Rock had a cross put on it and was turned into a church, the

Qibley Masjid became a palace and the rest of Masjid Al-Aqsa became stables for the crusader horses, later a tiny portion of space was allotted to the Knights Templar to be their headquarters next to the Dome of the Rock. The few Muslims who survived the initial bloodbath when discovered were brought to the Masjid Al-Aqsa and would be killed via a long agonizing crucifixion on a large cross. Muslims were then banned from being in all cities under crusader control and got turned into slaves to work the land now owned by the crusader knights. Most masjids got demolished except for the ones which were converted into Christian churches or palaces. The athan would not be called in Jerusalem for the next 90 years. But why did this brutal invasion happen if Christians had peacefully lived in Jerusalem under Muslim rule and been allowed to practice for over 400 years? Keep in mind I'm referring to the Muslim rule, not Shia rule. You see at the time the middle east was even more divided than it is today with nearly every city being almost like its own nation state. Honestly if you think Muslim nations today are weak and divided, back then they were even weaker and more divided than they are now. The Khilafah was a shell of it's former self because of Muslim disunity and infighting, which allowed Shia to gain power in North Africa and spread as the Fatimid empire reaching from Algeria to Palestine and Yemen. In 1009 CE the Shia ruler Al-Hakim, who was leader of the Fatimid empire, destroyed the church of the holy sepulchre in Jerusalem and persecuted Christians. Then in 1016 CE this Shia, Al-Hakim, claimed he was the incarnation of God on earth and founded a cult within Shiism that became what is known as Ismai'ilism. One night while wandering alone in the hills, Al-Hakim went missing and was never heard from again; leading Ismai'ilis to further split off into different sects in doctrinal deviance like the famed Assassins of Masyaf who taught a doctrine later adopted by the Bavarian Illuminati. After this tragedy of Shia oppression, the church of the holy sepulchre was nearly completely rebuilt by 1048 CE except for it's western parts which were still ruins when Christian pilgrims returned to visit the city. Eventually the Seljuk Turks recaptured Jerusalem in 1073 CE from the Shia Fatimids. But rebels took over Jerusalem in 1077 CE which led to the Seljuks reconquering the city, with more drama in 1091 CE when the governor of Jerusalem died and his 2 sons disputed with each other. In 1092 CE the Seljuk Empire fractured after the death of the

Sultan when the four sons of the Sultan and his brother all fought each other carving out their own mini states. In the midst of this mess in 1095 CE Pope Uban II gives his famous speech telling the Christian world to kill Muslims launching the "first crusade" claiming they were persecuting Christians preventing them from visiting Jerusalem and destroyed the church of the holy sepulchre. Whereas in reality it was the Shia who did that 86 years earlier. Then ironically in 1098 CE, 3 years after the "first crusade" began and a year before the crusaders took Jerusalem, the Shia Fatimids recaptured Jerusalem from the Abbasid Khilafah, who had it gifted to them by the Seljuks, and the Shia expelled the Christians again. When the crusaders arrived at the gates they met the Shia and were completely clueless that their crusade against the Muslims throughout Seljuk Turkey directly helped the Shia oppressors from Egypt retake Jerusalem and oppress Christians, which the Shia expelled just before the crusaders got to Jerusalem thereby acting as a confirmation for the lies the crusaders had been told about Muslims. So the whole problem of the first papal crusade comes down to the Western World believing Shias are Muslims when they aren't, then as a result attacking

Muslims because of their hatred for Shias and the lies their Christian leaders told them. In short, Shias started oppressing Christians and the Muslims did jihad and stopped them, then when the problem was nearly resolved and forgotten with the wounds healed, the Pope comes and blames Muslims for having caused a problem they were innocent of and the Pope orders that the Muslims are to be killed. So crusaders attack the Muslims because of what they were told about Muslims even though the Shia were the real bad guys, and by attacking the Muslims they helped the Shia criminals regain power so they could oppress again so that when the crusaders see the Shia oppression upon reaching Jerusalem they thought the Pope was right. Upon defeating the Shia, they say, *"See, we told you those Muslims were evil and God is on our side"*. Meanwhile most Western crusaders never looked into Islam or what actually happened and just believed they were the good guys because the Pope told them so and they "had a feeling" along with circumstantial "evidence". Thus they fought Muslims because they mistake Shia for Muslims and equate them. So then when they later unjustly oppressed and murdered Muslims and the Muslims did jihad and fought back, the crusaders didn't realize that they were actually evil oppressors who were, are and to this day continue to be in the wrong. But was it just a simple mistake by Pope Urban II or did he know the Muslims were innocent and that the Shia were of a different religion? Unfortunately it doesn't appear to be accidental. Politically the "first crusade" was designed to aid the Byzantine emperor Alexios I, who's army was too weak to fulfill his desire to recapture the land his ancestors had once brutally ruled over, which the Muslim Seljuks had recently liberated. Past Shia actions simply provided Pope Urban II the excuse the Church was looking for to attack Muslims, that's why it didn't matter that the crimes used to justify the papal crusades were done 86 years beforehand or by people who weren't even Muslims. To show how wrong the first official crusade was imagine if the leader of the U.N. today said "*86 years ago X building was destroyed in Y country and innocents were killed by S people. Therefore even though X building has been rebuilt and Y country is now ruled by M people let's invade Y country and kill all M people!*" This was what Pope Urban II did and it worked because he didn't say anything about 86 years ago or the difference between S people(Shia) and M people (Muslims). He knew better though and was 86 years behind when it came to world politics. It was because there was no oppression or injustice under Islamic Shariah in any of the Muslim territories that the Shia crimes of the distant past had to be cited as reasons to motivate crusaders to go slaughter. This doesn't seem familiar does it? Historically that's what happened. If such things are still happening then perhaps we're still in the "Dark Ages", with our time just being a different shade of dark.

There are 5 versions of Pope Urban II's speech that launched the first papal crusade, the version as related by Fulcher of Chartes is as follows:

Most beloved brethren: Urged by necessity, I, Urban, by the permission of God chief bishop and prelate over the whole world, have come into these parts as an ambassador with a divine admonition to you, the servants of God. I hoped to find you as faithful and as zealous in the service of God as I had supposed you to be. But if there is in you any deformity or crookedness contrary to God's law, with divine help I will do my best to remove it. For God has put you as stewards over his family to minister to it. Happy indeed will you be if he finds you faithful in your stewardship. You are called shepherds; see that you do not act as hirelings. But be true shepherds, with your crooks always in your hands. Do not go to sleep, but guard on all sides the flock committed to you. For if through your carelessness or negligence a wolf carries away one of your sheep, you will surely lose the reward laid up for you with God. And after you have been bitterly scourged with remorse for your faults-, you will be fiercely overwhelmed in hell, the abode of death. For according to the gospel you are the salt of the earth [Matt. 5:13]. But if you fall short in your duty, how, it may be asked, can it be salted? O how great the need of salting! It is indeed necessary for you to correct with the salt of wisdom this foolish people which is so devoted to the pleasures of this -world, lest the Lord, when He may wish to speak to them, find them putrefied by their sins unsalted and stinking. For if He, shall find worms, that is, sins, In them, because you have been negligent in your duty, He will command them as worthless to be thrown into the abyss of unclean things. And because you cannot restore to Him His great loss, He will surely condemn you and drive you from His loving presence. But the man who applies this salt should be prudent, provident, modest, learned, peaceable, watchful, pious, just, equitable, and pure. For how can the ignorant teach others? How can the licentious make others modest? And how can the impure make others pure? If anyone hates peace, how can he make others peaceable ? Or if anyone has soiled his hands with baseness, how can he cleanse the impurities of another? We read also that if the blind lead the blind, both will fall into the ditch [Matt. 15:14]. But first correct yourselves, in order that, free from blame , you may be able to correct those who are subject to you. If you wish to be the friends of God, gladly do the things which you know will please Him. You must especially let all matters that pertain to the church be controlled by the law of the church. And be careful that simony does not take root among you, lest both those who buy and those who sell [church offices] be beaten with the scourges of the Lord through narrow streets and driven into the place of destruction and confusion. Keep the church and the clergy in all its grades entirely free from the secular power. See that the tithes that belong to God are faithfully paid from all the produce of the land; let them not be sold or withheld. If anyone seizes a bishop let him be treated as an outlaw. If anyone seizes or robs monks, or clergymen, or nuns, or their servants, or pilgrims, or merchants, let him be anathema [that is, cursed]. Let robbers and incendiaries and all their accomplices be expelled from the church and anthematized. If a man who does not give a part of his goods as alms is punished with the damnation of hell, how should he be punished who robs another of his goods? For thus it happened to the rich man in the gospel [Luke 16:19]; he was not punished because he had stolen the goods of another, but because he had not used well the things which were his.

"You have seen for a long time the great disorder in the world caused by these crimes. It is so bad in some of your

provinces, I am told, and you are so weak in the administration of justice, that one can hardly go along the road by day or night without being attacked by robbers; and whether at home or abroad one is in danger of being despoiled either by force or fraud. Therefore it is necessary to reenact the truce, as it is commonly called, which was proclaimed a long time ago by our holy fathers. I exhort and demand that you, each, try hard to have the truce kept in your diocese. And if anyone shall be led by his cupidity or arrogance to break this truce, by the authority of God and with the sanction of this council he shall be anathematized."

After these and various other matters had been attended to, all who were present, clergy and people, gave thanks to their deity and agreed to the pope's proposition. They all faithfully promised to keep the decrees. Then the pope said that in another part of the world Christianity was suffering from a state of affairs that was worse than the one just mentioned. He continued:

"Although, O sons of God, you have promised more firmly than ever to keep the peace among yourselves and to preserve the rights of the church, there remains still an important work for you to do. Freshly quickened by the divine correction, you must apply the strength of your righteousness to another matter which concerns you as

well as God. For your brethren who live in the east are in urgent need of your help, and you must hasten to give them the aid which has often been promised them. For, as the most of you have heard, the Turks and Arabs have attacked them and have conquered the territory of Romania [the Greek empire] as far west as the shore of the Mediterranean and the Hellespont, which is called the Arm of St. George. They have occupied more and more of the lands of those Christians, and have overcome them in seven battles. They have killed and captured many, and have destroyed the churches and devastated the empire. If you permit them to continue thus for awhile with impurity, the faithful of God will be much more widely attacked by them. On this account I, or rather the Lord, beseech you as Christ's heralds to publish this everywhere and to persuade all people of whatever rank, foot-soldiers and knights, poor and rich, to carry aid promptly to those Christians and to destroy that vile race from the lands of our friends. I say this to those who are present, it meant also for those who are absent. Moreover, Christ commands it.

"All who die by the way, whether by land or by sea, or in battle against the pagans, shall have immediate remission of sins. This I grant them through the power of God with which I am invested. O what a disgrace if such a despised and base race, which worships demons, should conquer a people which has the faith of omnipotent God and is made *glorious with the name of Christ! With what reproaches will the Lord overwhelm us if you do not aid those who, with us, profess the Christian religion! Let those who have been accustomed unjustly to wage private warfare against the faithful now go against the infidels and end with victory this war which should have been begun long ago. Let those who for a long time, have been robbers, now become knights. Let those who have been fighting against their brothers and relatives now fight in a proper way against the barbarians. Let those who have been serving as mercenaries for small pay now obtain the eternal reward. Let those who have been wearing themselves out in both body and soul now work for a double honor. Behold! on this side will be the sorrowful and poor, on that, the rich; on this side, the enemies of the Lord, on that, his friends. Let those who go not put off the journey, but rent their lands and collect money for their expenses; and as soon as winter is over and spring comes, let hem eagerly set out on the way with God as their guide."*

Aside from it being an opportunity to massacre Muslims who he hated because they weren't Catholics, Pope Urban II saw the first crusade as an opportunity to bring the Eastern Orthodox Church into the Roman Catholic faith. They had first split when Emperor Leo III prohibited statues and images of Jesus pbuh and Mary, correctly citing that the 2nd commandment prohibited images of any animate beings from being made, whereas Pope Gregory II disagreed with the Eastern Orthodox Church's ban on images. The son of Leo III, Constantine the Adoptionist, declared at the 7th synod of Constantinople in 774 CE that image veneration was a corruption of Christianity and a renewal of paganism, he ordered all images to be destroyed. Although later at the 2nd council of Nicaea in 787 CE images were once more endorsed and allowed. Today the Catholic Church has many images inside and outside of church, disobeying Jesus' position pbuh and even that of the famous Catholic "saint" and scholar Thomas Aquinas who said: "*It is always illicit to make use of images.*" As if that weren't enough the New Testament prohibits images and says people who make them deserve death! The English translation of the New International Version of the bible says in Romans 1:20-32, "*For since the creation of the world God's invisible qualities – his eternal power and divine nature – have been clearly seen, being understood from what has been made, so that* **people are without excuse.** 21 *For although they knew God, they neither glorified him as God nor gave thanks to him, but their thinking became futile and their foolish hearts were darkened.* 22 **Although they claimed to be wise, they** *became fools* ²³ *and exchanged the glory of the immortal God for images made to look like a mortal human being* and birds and animals and reptiles. ²⁴ Therefore God gave them over in the sinful desires of their hearts to sexual impurity for the degrading of their bodies with one another. ²⁵ **They exchanged the truth about God for a lie, and worshiped and served created things rather than the Creator** – who is forever praised. Amen. ²⁶ Because of this, God gave them over to shameful lusts. Even *their women exchanged natural sexual relations for unnatural ones.* ²⁷ *In the same way the men also abandoned natural relations with women* and were inflamed with lust for one another. Men committed shameful acts with other men, and received in themselves the due penalty for their error. ²⁸ Furthermore, just as *they did not think it worthwhile to retain the knowledge of God,* so God gave them over to a depraved mind, so that they do what ought not to be done. ²⁹ *They have become filled with every kind of wickedness, evil, greed and depravity. They are full of envy, murder, strife, deceit and malice. They are gossips,* ³⁰ *slanderers, God-haters, insolent, arrogant and boastful; they invent ways of doing evil; they disobey their parents;* ³¹ *they have no understanding, no fidelity, no love, no mercy.* ³² Although **they know God's righteous decree that those who do such things deserve death**, they not only continue to do these very *things but also approve of those who practice them."* Incidentally the things listed here as capital offenses in the New Testament are committed by Christians. Specifically making God into an image of a mortal human being and worshipping created things rather than the Creator. The New Testament of the bible says disbelievers do this and deserve death. In the Vatican there is even a depiction of God as an old white bearded naked man extending his finger to touch the finger of an image of Adam pbuh. How the Church justifies a painting of God as an old nude white man, I cannot comprehend. If that is not against the 2nd commandment then nothing is. Surely the Creator of all cannot be condensed into a 2 dimensional fresco image. It is a blasphemous slander that such an image was ever created. Where did they get the idea that God looked like that? It's a hypocritical sinful satanic depiction which every prophet would destroy if they had the chance. The Eastern Orthodox Church also disagreed with the Catholic view that Jesus pbuh created the holy spirit in the trinity, they thought the father created the holy spirit, despite the fact that not one version of the bible has the word trinity in it anywhere. Biblically they were both wrong on that point and it's illogical to say

God is a trinity or that one part of God created the other part of God. This would mean some of the trinity is Creator and some is created therefore they cannot be considered equal parts, the trinity contradicts itself. The word "trinity" originates from Tertullian who ironically coined the term refuting the strange new doctrine as a heresy which Jesus pbuh was entirely unfamiliar with. Meaning the word "trinity" was first used by Christians to label/denounce what was a false belief. In the 2nd-3rd century the Christian Scholar Tertullian wrote: *"Common people think of Christ as a man"*.

Before becoming a Muslim I was afflicted with a crusader mentality and thought the crusades were the greatest time period in Christen history, since from a papal perspective they were because the Church was at its apex of power. After becoming a Muslim I essentially "switched sides" and currently hold a different opinion on the crusades. This has given me a very interesting experience of learning how personal perspective can distort one's historical point of view. Since I studied that time period in depth as a Catholic and later as a Muslim, I learned both sides of history from both perspectives and saw how different versions of the same events can exist with both versions having "historical" evidence. It is extra interesting when both sides think they are divinely correct and their opponents are satanic; it makes for quite an intense historical disputation. Looking at it from a military perspective, the "first official crusade" was the only one to have been successful in obtaining its goals. Although the first official crusade would have utterly failed at Antioch if it were not for a traitor called Firuz betraying the city. Coincidentally this traitor had the same name as the man who assassinated the 2nd Khalif Umar bin Khattab, which makes one wonder whether he was a Shia because it would be extremely unusual for a Sunni Muslim to name their child after Umar's assassin. Not one person with a crusader mentality would disagree on the point that had it not been for a Muslim traitor the first papal crusade would have been unlikely to reach Jerusalem, let alone succeed. This is because as soon as Antioch was conquered by the crusaders they were then besieged inside of it by the Muslims who came to fight the crusaders at Antioch and arrived days after it had fallen. The genocidal tactics of the crusaders also had a strong impact on how they were perceived. The crusaders practiced cannibalism intending to frighten the Muslims. The crusaders would eat the Muslims they killed in plain view, roasting the corpses on skewers. Such tactics developed a reputation for Christian ruthlessness *"Not only will they kill you, but they'll eat you as well"*. The logic of the crusader cannibalism is difficult to understand from a religious perspective. Crusaders thought that by eating Jesus pbuh, whom they considered God, during the Eucharist purified their soul, so what did they think eating the bodies and blood of Muslims, whom they considered disbelievers, would do?

The 2nd crusade was sent after Edessa was retaken during the Jihad of the Muslim leader Imad ad-Deen Zengi on December 24, 1144 CE. Although this crusade would've been considered an utter failure had the crusaders not captured territory in the Iberian Peninsula in what is modern day Portugal. But if the crusades were about the Holy Land what did Portugal have to do with crusaders? Well it was because Muslims lived there and the papal crusades were not about the Holy Land but were about spreading Christianity via the sword by killing non-Christians or forcing them to convert. Christians know this is true, that's why some today apologize for the crusades whereas Muslims never have and never will apologize for waging jihad against the crusaders because the Muslims were justified in doing so. There are many instances where Crusaders would desecrate Qurans in front of besieged Muslim cities purposely taunting them. The Crusaders would also kill, rob and rape unarmed Muslim pilgrims on their way to Mecca. The Crusaders even tried on several occasions to steal the prophet Muhammad's body pbuh from Madinah. The knight Reynald de Chatillion, famous for mocking the prophet Muhammad pbuh, even brought an army into Arabia trying to capture Madinah and Mecca before it was defeated at Tayma, which is 249 miles north of Madinah. This is a very important aspect of the official Crusades that get completely hidden by the non-Muslim historians. The Crusaders actually tried to conquer Mecca and Medinah. They preached this in churches all over the world that the Crusaders would conquer Mecca, kill the Muslims, destroy the Kaba and end Islam. All in the name of Jesus Christ their Deity and Saviour who would surely help them destroy Islam and Muslims once and for all. That's a pretty big goal and they came within 249 miles of it before being physically prevented from achieving that goal. It was a clearly religious goal for a military campaign thus making it a religious war. Yet when have you ever heard non-Muslims admit that, "*Oh yeah and the Crusaders planned to go to Mecca and Medinah to completely destroy Islam and all Muslims and steal the body of Muhammad but they lost the battle on the way.*" How can they leave that battle out? Truly not knowing that battle or the reason for it distorts one's whole view of the crusades. I'm not saying the crusades were 100% about Christianity vs. Islam and that every soldier on both sides fought for religious reasons but clearly it is a lot more religious than the non-Muslim world currently believes it to have been. Let's face it, the Christians failed to capture Mecca so that's probably why today they fail to report they ever tried to capture it. However when we discuss propaganda wars, that such details are very well hidden from the non-Muslim world has the effect of deep propaganda and indicates the crusades might not really be over since most of the non-Muslims aren't yet ready to mention all that happened during them. Typically after wars end both sides are ready to discuss all the evil they did honestly so they can receive closure and heal. How can the religious wounds the Muslims received when Christians tried to conquer Mecca and Medinah be healed when the majority of the non-Muslim world ignores them? Could there be any possible benefit in not mentioning the Crusader plan to conquer Mecca and Medinah and it's failure? Truly there is no benefit when the truth is buried during war and never returned to the surface. Lasting Peace is not built upon lies. Censorship is done during wartime to help the military efforts. Hiding history or crimes does not lead to justice nor lasting peace. If we are to live on earth together in peace we can't lie about when, where, how or why we fought. Don't we know this from our families how if we misremember past fights that causes more? We are supposed to fix our relationships with others not fix our historical records. The truth is simply a mirror, it is never ugly. How can we trust our leaders today to tell us the truth about ongoing wars when we aren't even being told the full story about wars that happened thousands of years ago? If the truth of the past is too hard for us to handle then what about the truth about the present? Are we following leaders or liars? People did not die in wars so that lies could be told about them later. So while the general rank and file Crusaders themselves weren't the most religious or Christianesque of people and the majority were crusading for economic or political reasons, the leaders and promoters of the Crusades were religious fanatics who explicitly defined their wars as being Christianity vs. Islam. While today most leaders and teachers pretend the wars had nothing to do with either. Yet it was an era of religious warfare, even though the majority of Crusaders weren't primarily motivated to crusade for religious reasons. Many might say today's wars have nothing to do with religion and aren't against Islam at all, but keep in mind the majority of Crusaders fighting a religious war designed to be against Islam weren't fighting for that reason exclusively. So don't confuse the motives of the soldiers who fight in wars as being the reason and purpose for the wars. It's a common historical pattern in that the biggest lies in warfare are about what the wars are really for and why they are being waged. Soldiers are just pulling triggers, to know the reasons why they're really fighting you have to know the motives of those who raised the armies and sanctioned the hostilities. Frequently the reasons the soldiers are fighting have nothing at all to do with the reasons the wars are being waged. They follow orders for their own reasons not knowing the true reason for why the orders are being given, because if they knew then they might not obey those orders. Sometimes a person could fight for side A intending to do so for reason X not realizing that the reason side A is fighting is for reason Y. Such a person would in reality be fighting for reason Y even though it's their intention to fight for reason X. So just to make the record clear, the Crusades were fought for religious reasons even though the individuals fighting acted immorally and may have personally fought for secular reasons. People today may try to claim otherwise but that's because of the other pattern of history in that future generations give different reasons for why they fought wars in the past. The modern reasons historians and politicians give for past wars are rarely ever the true reasons since everyone who wins always wants to portray themselves as the underdog good guys who won miraculously against all possible odds despite never ever ever wanting to go to war. Nobody ever wants to admit they went to war for unjust reasons or based on lies. For all the allegations enemies of Islam spread about Muslims in the past cutting people's heads off if they didn't convert, the Christians were the ones who did this. In Evora, Portugal there is even a statue of a Christian knight called Geraldo "the fearless" with a sword in one hand and a decapitated Muslim head in the other publicly glorifying this Christian practice. Today if you go to Portugal you can see this statue in public, it's very famous since there aren't many statues with decapitated heads as a prop for the "*fearless hero*" to hold. The Muslims don't have any statues like that, they never have and Godwilling never will. While Christians not only built such statues showing the head of a decapitated Muslim but they still have them saying they're lovely works of art which should be cherished and something tourists pay money to visit. Thus giving such Christian war criminals praise, glory and honor. Is that statue indicative of tolerance or intolerance? Does the fact that there are statues with Christians holding Muslim heads "prove" that Christianity is a more intolerant religion than Islam? If we have to say one of the religions is one spread by the sword which teaches "convert or die", which would the "bad faith" be based on the statue? Is the statue considered statutory evidence? What kind of doctrine do we learn today from such a statue? Is it radical violent extremism to have or want the statue up? Is it radical fanaticism or extremism to want the statue destroyed? History is history, the truth is important to remember so it really is a difficult decision for some as to what to do with the statue.

I'm just mentioning it for it's historical and present relevance. We should know that such statues were made and still exist. Everyone can agree that ignorance is dangerous for all of us. History is bloody primarily because people don't learn from it. If you want to save lives then spend a lot of your life learning.

Pope Gregory VIII launched the 3rd crusade just days after becoming pope, after the famous battle of Hattin wherein the "true cross" was lost. Having once been a deeply devout Catholic I had obtained and held in my possession what was supposedly a relic of the true cross. This was a very expensive pendant with verified authentic seals from long dead christian bishops as certification. Allegedly it contained two splinters in the shape of a cross from the alleged cross Jesus pbuh was said to have been crucified on. The splinters are believed to have special powers that have been active since first discovered, allegedly. The story goes that Constantine's Trinitarian mother Helena searched for Christian relics. She found 3 wooden crosses after demolishing a pagan temple devoted to either Venus or Jupiter, scholars differ as to which, then a sick person touched one of the crosses and they later recovered from their illness, so people started thinking the cross that she touched had powers and that it was "the one" Jesus pbuh was allegedly crucified on. This discovery is thought to have happened between 326-328 CE, about 300 years after Christ pbuh. It is important to note that the cross was only found AFTER the council of Nicaea when Christianity became a legal religion of the Roman Empire by decree. As pilgrims went to visit the relic they would kiss the cross and take splinters home between their teeth. At other times pieces would be broken off of it and given to prestigious people as gifts. During the crusades Christian armies would take this cross into battle with them thinking it gave them victory. Prior to the 3rd crusade the Muslim leader Yusuf ibn Ayubi known as "Salah Ad-Deen" and his army defeated the army of the crusader kingdom of Jerusalem at the battle of hattin on July 4th, 1187 CE. The Christians lost the cross and it went into Muslim possession and has disappeared from history ever since. When the news of this battle came to Pope Urban III he instantly died from shock. This used to make me very angry every 4th of July, especially when American Christians are typically ignorant of such history. I couldn't figure out why God would let the "true cross" fall into Muslim hands allowing it to be forever lost. If Christianity were true and we all had to believe in it to be saved, surely God could have prevented it and the cross could've been used today to revitalize the Christian faith. It also made me suspicious of the American government, why would they make the fourth of July the day to party when the "birth of the nation" according to the declaration of independence and President John Adams was on July 2nd, 1776 CE? It seemed as though they distinctly wanted to avoid the embarrassment of Christianity having lost the "true cross" in a "holy war" to Muslims. I thought if people knew the history it would anger Christians and they could then be manipulated to start another crusade, hoping to re-capture the cross after all these years. Having learned America's founding fathers were not Christian they couldn't have wanted to spare Christians any embarrassment. Rather they likely changed the date to make the memory of the Muslim victory fade away. Also on July 4th, 1863 CE the Confederate States surrendered at Vicksburg, Mississippi. Making it a cruel twist of irony for southerners to celebrate the 4th as "Independence day" when it was the day their Confederacy surrendered to the Union.

An example of Crusades for the cause of relics or tourist sites is the "true cross" and famous "Church of the Holy Sepulchre" in Jerusalem. The official history of the "Church of the Holy Sepulchre" states that it is both the place Jesus pbuh was biblically crucified and the same spot he was buried in a sepulchre to later rise from the dead 3 days later. Officially both events are said to have occurred at this spot and that's what they tell tourists. Yet the bible itself refutes this and says both locations were miles apart from each other. The Christian tourists who flock there don't care, even though they should know better. Most figure if it wasn't true then they wouldn't say it was, because they can't fathom such a blatant big time public lie. But it gets worse. This Church of the "Holy Sepulchre" did not exist until 325 CE. If you remember 325 CE is the same year the Council of Nicaea took place, during that year Constantine also established this "Church of the Holy Sepulchre in Jerusalem". What was there before? It was an ancient pagan temple devoted to the greek goddess Aprhodite. Yet in 325 CE it became a holy church. But it gets worse still. The famous event of Helena finding the true cross Jesus pbuh was alleged to have died on took place between 326-328 CE in a former temple devoted to

Jupiter or Venus; as has already been mentioned. What does that have to do with the Church of the Holy Sepulchre? Absolutely nothing, right? Well the Christians say that the place Helena found the true cross is the same place where the Church of the Holy Sepulchre is and that's why it was built there. However it is impossible for Helena in 326-328 CE to find the legendary "true cross" in a temple devoted to Jupiter or Venus in the same place a church was built the year earlier in 325 CE on a site formerly dedicated to Aprhodite. The legend of the true cross basically says Helena found the crosses in a church after the church was built but when she found these crosses in that church it wasn't a church, then she went back in time and built the church on the same spot years earlier; except Christians ignore the implied time traveling bit that is necessary for their stories of the Church being the site of the Sepulchre and the Crucifiction and the place the "True Cross" was found be true. Typically they only tell one story at a time, frequently without citing dates, names, or history so the contradictions are left unknown. Another such "holy site" Christian tourists visit is the "Church of the Nativity" in Bethlehem, which is alleged to be the spot Jesus pbuh was born. Who built this church?

Constantine's mother Helena did in 327 CE, again 2 years after the Council of Nicaea. This church in Bethlehem was formerly a temple devoted to the god Adonis, who was the greek god of beauty/desire, prior to being a temple to Adonis it was a temple dedicated to Tammuz. So by claiming that is the site Jesus pbuh was born Christians are unwittingly saying that Jesus pbuh was born inside of a pagan temple wherein a pagan son of god/man-god crucified savior idol was worshipped, except since Christians don't know the architectural history they insist it was a cave at the time ignoring the archaelogical facts. Even the famous Jerome who was a priest at the Church of the Nativity said that prior to it becoming the Church of the Nativity it was a consecrated heathen temple. Yet tourists today insist it's the birthplace of Jesus pbuh despite the priest who said mass there on a regular basis in the 400s CE saying it is not the birthplace of Jesus pbuh but the site of a pagan temple converted into a church. Anyone looking at the official stories of such Christian "holy sites" can see they are logistically and historically impossible folktales. Christian tourists are being lied to and scammed out of their money. Constantine's mother invented the Christian tourism and relic industries.

Even the famous Constantine and Helena Cathedral built in 326 CE, was previously a temple where Baal was worshipped. Simply put the Christian "holy sites" have no real connection to Jesus pbuh but are simply tourist traps created because Christians will pay to visit places to get told they are seeing spots Jesus pbuh once was, though they don't care to live how he preached for us to live. Millions of Christians flock to such "sacred sites" each year to get spiritually charged claiming such former pagan sites are proofs of Christian doctrine being true due to the placebo feeling of increased faith. The worst part about it is the Crusades were started because Christians were told these sacred tourist sites were endangered.

The 3rd Crusade had 3 main leaders: King Richard of England, Emperor Frederick Barbarossa of Germany and King Phillip II of France. The rulers were leading the armies themselves personally putting their own lives on the line for this campaign. Just imagine if the leader of your country were going to war thousands of miles away to do hand to hand combat with the enemy. This was a major military campaign of historical proportions, the likes of which has never been imitated again in military history. To raise funds for the war England and France instituted a special emergency tax of 10% on all revenue and movable property, while the few Jews who were too important to rob and kill had to pay 25%. This was a temporary emergency Crusade tax, meaning during the crusades most citizens were able to keep 90% of what they earned and there were no other taxes. Today most governments levy heavier daily taxes on their people than the zealous Crusaders did during the "Dark Ages", when they physically forced people to pay "temporary emergency taxes". Mathematically it's cheaper to be oppressed under medieval fiefdom than to have modern "freedom". Ironically historians say that the entire Western tax system can trace it's origin to the taxes levied during the Crusades. So it makes one wonder that if taxes were introduced to post-Roman Europe and the West as an emergency measure in order to pay for the Crusades then why do they still levy taxes today? Does that mean the Crusades haven't stopped yet? So many people "*took up the cross*" that there weren't enough boats in all of Europe to provide transportation, forcing Fredrick and his army to march on land. Frederick and his army entered the famous city of Tarsus (birthplace of Saul/Paul) and then history has conflicting accounts of what exactly happened next. Some say he fell off his horse and drowned, while others claim he got hit by a falling tree branch and drowned, some say he took a bath in the river and got a chill then died as a result, while still others say he had a heart attack and drowned. However all agree that Frederick died in Tarsus with the death having something to do with a river, thought to be the Saleph River. When I would read about the death of Frederick as a Catholic it seemed to be a tragedy that I couldn't explain. As a Muslim it is plain to see that God was not in support of Fredrick's cause and supernaturally killed him sending the angel of death to take his soul similar to how God killed the Pharaoh. Soon after his death, Frederick's remaining army fell sick and ill with many dying or deserting. Although Frederick had made an oath to the Christian concept of God that he would set foot in Jerusalem; thus his son wanted to have his father's oath fulfilled. The dead body of Frederick Barbarossa was boiled, stuffed and put in a barrel of vinegar pickling him so he didn't decompose. Yet for some inexplicable reason the body still rotted and the barrel actually exploded before they reached the Holy Land. About 95% of the German "holy army" never made it to the holy land. These are historical facts. Now if we look at this from a religious aspect and say God was either on the side of the Crusaders or the Muslims, then it would appear based on the humiliating demise of the Christian king and his army that God was against him. Especially when one considers Frederick took an oath to his version of God that was made impossible for him to fulfill, even as a corpse. The rest of the crusade went the same way with both Phillip II leaving and Richard "the Lionheart" leaving to return to England in order to save his kingdom. Yet on the return journey Richard became bankrupt and was imprisoned before reaching England, having to be ransomed for an astronomical amount that bankrupted England. Crusader historians depict Richard as a religious man, yet he refused to enter Jerusalem when offered the opportunity by Salah Ad-Deen. Richard said he only wanted to enter Jerusalem if he could conquer and keep the city. This reveals Richard to be more materialistic than religious, especially considering how he left a "religious war" in order to keep his earthly kingdom. Coincidentally the Muslim leader Salah Ad-Deen died months after Richard left. Many historians think that had Richard stayed a few more months until the death of Salah Ad-Deen and kept fighting the world today would have been a very different place. Although this is pointless speculation by historians, we know that God intended everything to turn out the way it turned out. The other official crusades also failed in unusual ways. The total number of medieval crusades numbers in the double digits. However not all of them were directed at Muslims exclusively, some were against Jews and what were considered heretics living in Europe. The 4th crusade actually ended up with the Roman Catholic crusaders slaughtering and looting the Eastern Orthodox city of Constantinople, despite the original intentions being to conquer Jerusalem. The 4th crusade involved Christians killing Christians in the name of Christianity in Christian land. Pope Innocent III planned the 5th crusade in 1208 CE but waited until the timing was opportune in 1213 CE to launch it with a new goal to conquer Egypt before Jerusalem. It took years to gather momentum and quickly failed nearly upon arrival. The end result of the 5th crusade being the Crusaders returned the city of Damietta in exchange for all the crusaders Muslims captured in battle after which an 8 year peace treaty, one of the many offered by the Muslim leader Al-Kamil, was agreed to in 1221 CE despite angry protests by the papal representative. Guess what happened next? 7 years later, with 1 year left on the peace treaty, the 6th crusade was launced in 1228 CE by the recently elected Pope Gregory IX, who was also the inventor of the Papal Inquisition. King Frederick II was the prime participant in this crusade mainly because the Pope excommunicated him for not going on the 5th crusade and said the only way to become a Christian again was to start/lead the 6th crusade. The Pope even launched a crusade against Frederick II because of his lack of will to crusade. It was a *"You're either with us or against us"* mindset. In 1229 CE Al-Kamil offered peace to the crusaders even giving them Jerusalem, Bethlehem and Nazareth, on the condition that they wouldn't rebuild any of Jerusalem's fortifications which had been demolished and that after the 10 year truce expired the territory would be returned to the Muslims. Well not only did the Christians kick the Jews out of Jerusalem and rebuild the fortifications, in violation of the treaty, but they didn't return the territory. More than 11 years after agreeing to the 10 year treaty, in 1240 CE the non-Muslim Tartars conquered Jerusalem from the Christians, which should've been returned to the Muslims the year before. The Christians retook Jerusalem in 1241 CE from the Tartars and kept it until 1244 CE when the Muslim Khwarizmis reconquered it, since by that time it was clear to the Muslim world that crusaders don't honor their treaties no matter how generous the terms are. What happened in response to the Muslims getting Jerusalem back? Why the 7th crusade was launched by Pope Innocent IV in 1248 CE. The 7th crusade managed to capture the city of Jerusalem, but within 48 hours the local Muslim tribesmen defeated the entire crusader army and drove them out, later on capturing and ransoming the Catholic "Saint" King Louis IX of France; who gained his fame for having went on multiple crusades and dying in Tunis as a result of fever during his last crusade.

When I had a crusader mentality I believed all these defeated official crusades were simply flukes, as a Muslim I think differently. Religion aside, if interpreted objectively the only successful official crusade depended heavily on a Muslim traitor in Antioch. All the others were drastic failures that are difficult to blame military reasons for. The one commonality most all "official" crusades from the 11th-15th century CE have is their endorsements by the Catholic Popes. Pope Clement V, even made it a sin to utter the name of Mahomet in Christian territories and Pope Callixtus III instituted the ringing of church bells at noon so that Christians remembered to pray for the Crusaders. Religiously the only reason Christians ring their church bells at noon is because in 1456 the Pope said to do so in order to remind people to pray for Crusaders fighting Muslims. That's the reason! Truly they never used to ring churchbells at noon until 1456 for that reason. Today Catholicism teaches that the popes were and are infalliable, meaning never wrong, meaning it's obligatory for Catholics to believe that all popes were free from errors. Yet recent popes have said crusader era popes were wrong; thereby not even believing in their own religious doctrines which they propagate. This makes it impossible to believe in papal infallibility. In a nutshell the popes are either intolerant liars or it's wrong to believe in Catholic doctrines; or both. Yet those church bells still ring at noon everyday in every Christian church all over the globe despite the claims of tolerance and alleged recantation of islamophobia. So if Christian noontime bell ringing started in 1456 as a crusader practice why do the church bells still ring at noon if they have stopped crusading and praying for crusaders? Either they must admit they are religious idiots who don't know why they do what they do but just follow blindly, and in such case they should research islam who has claimed such about them from the beginning or they must admit that they still hate Islam and are pursuing a crusader agenda against it til this day. Pope Benedict XVI who served as Pope of the Catholic Church from 2005 CE to 2013 CE said this in regards to Islam: "**<u>Islam has a total organization of life that is completely different from ours</u>**; *it embraces simply everything,...There is a very marked subordination of woman to man; there is a very tightly knit criminal law, indeed,* **<u>a law regulating all areas of life, that is opposed to our modern ideas about society</u>**. *One has to have a clear understanding that* **<u>it is not simply a denomination that can be included in the free realm of a pluralistic society</u>**."

    Many people today will say the Catholic Church teaches tolerance and has reformed, but I was training for the Catholic priesthood from 2006-2011. It is a historical fact that for hundreds of years the Catholic Church aggressively pursued a public policy of annihilating anyone who wasn't Catholic, in Europe and the rest of the world. There are groups within the Church today that are actively trying to restore power to the Church so it can oppress and exterminate again. Opus Dei is one such institution within the Catholic Church. Don't think the plot for Catholic domination is some paranoid conspiracy theory or anti-Catholic defamation; I use to be actively working towards it. Naively many Christians themselves think the various denominations preach tolerance towards other Christians. But not only have Christians killed Christians for thousands of years, the intolerance Christians have for other Christians extends even beyond humans. For example in 1685 CE after the revocation of the edict of Nantes in France, which in 1598 CE had previously allowed non-Catholic Christians to practice in France, a Protestant chapel in La Rochelle was demolished except for the expensive church bell. Although to expiate for the crime of having rang heretics to prayer, the bell was sentenced to be publicly whipped, afterwhich it was buried and disinterred so as to symbolize its "new birth" passing into Catholic hands. Then the bell was catechized and obliged to recant and promise everyone that it would never again relapse into sin. After the bell made this public atonement it was reconciled, baptized and sold to the parish of St. Bartholomew.

Yet when the governor sent the bill for the church bell to the parish's authorities they refused to pay for it, alleging that as a recent convert to Catholicism the bell desired to take advantage of a law passed by the King which allowed all converts to delay paying their debts for 3 years. This was a church bell! Christians claim other religions are intolerant, but the most intolerant people towards Christians throughout history have been Christians of other denominations. Every Christian nation that fought in WWI collectively thought it was Armageddon and called their living soldiers saints and their dead ones martyrs, both sides claimed angels fought for their side in the trenches and that it was a "holy Crusade" against heretical Christians. Although the Vatican actually denounced this crusade and called for peace, since they had no state at that time and saw that it wouldn't benefit their long term goals in any way. One of the biggest lies is that WWI had nothing to do with Christianity, whereas it was actually the most zealous Christianized warfare to have ever taken place. Politicians and preachers at the time on both sides said it was more important to wage war in Europe to save Christian land from secular Christians than to crusade to Palestine to kill Muslims. Although coincidentally in 1917 CE the British ended up taking Jerusalem from the Muslims during WWI as they conquered the Holy Land. Just research the war propaganda from each country during WWI, the sermons which were given, the movies produced, the books written, the soldiers' own diaries/letters and the politicians' statements. Nearly every Christian soldier carried a bible into battle, and wore religious medals as protective talismans particular to their denomination. After Jerusalem fell Christians said the Crusades were finally won but today they don't want Muslims or others to know about all the Crusader propaganda such as the books "*Khaki Crusaders*", "*The Modern Crusaders*", or "*The Last Crusade*" and the movie "*The New Crusaders*" all of which came out less than 3 years after Jerusalem and the Holy Land fell to the British glorifying the conquest of the Holy Land as a victory for Christians over Muslims. The French got their kicks in too. Such as when in July 1920 CE the French general Henri Gouraud was reported to have went to the grave of Salah Ad-Deen in Damascus and after kicking it he proclaimed, "*Awake, Saladin. We have returned. My presence here consecrates victory of the Cross over the Crescent.*" So clearly the WWI conquest of the Middle East was perceived as a religious Christian war against Islam by those doing the fighting. The world wars were also pivotal in the war between Christianity vs. Secularism. Throughout both the Christians on both sides were depicting them as great apocalyptical crusades. This was because at that time the States were the Churches and nationalism was essentially just a specific denomination of Christianity. It's possible the governments simply manipulated religion to wage war, but they both claimed and people thought the wars were primarily about Christianity. This is why during/after WWI the Communists took over Russia and were able to outlaw religion, because the Russians blamed Christianity for dragging them into poverty as a result of WWI. They blamed Eastern Orthodox Christianity for telling them to crusade all the way to the poor house. The whole idea of separation between Church and State only really gathered momentum after WWI when secularism began to flourish. Whereas since the Germans lost the religious crusade of WWI they searched for a reason of how to explain losing if their religion was right, thus they blamed German Jews for betraying the nation and separating Church from State in the new 1919 constitution.

Germans then revived the anti-Jew spirit of the German Martin Luther who was so virulent in his statements regarding Jews that the Nazi's would quote him fully without any edits or distortions. Martin Luther actually called for Jews to be forced to work in special labor camps. Yet what people aren't told is that the Nazis weren't the most radical anti-Jew German political party after WWI. Their rival until 1933 CE was the "Deutsche Christian" (German Christian) movement. These Christians had such hatred for Jews they taught that Jesus pbuh wasn't a Jew, that Paul should be rejected because he was a Jew and that the Old Testament should be removed from the Christian bible because it stems from Jewish texts and that Christians who were ethnically Jewish should be removed from churches. Politically Nazis were seen by Jews as the "lesser of two evils" so most German Jews voted for Nazis, and we know how that turned out. After the dust of WWII settled to reveal both the winners and losers were heartless mass-murderers, the evangelists of the Christian world decided to say Christianity was entirely innocent of the whole affair, both WWI and WWII, and decided to start preaching about a meek and mild Jesus pbuh instead of the Jesus pbuh they claimed was fighting in the trenches who wanted Christians to sacrifice their lives for the nation just as he allegedly did for them. The Nazis even quoted the bible as their reason for Jewish genocide, citing John 8:44 as their divine command for massacre. The German Nazi Holocaust was done in the name of the bible and for the sake of Jesus pbuh. WWII was a holy war both a Christian holy war and a Jewish holy war. Of which depending on your view the Jews might've started it when international Jewry declared war on Germany in 1933 CE. That's another thing history books fail to mention. Due to Nazi economic changes that decreased Jewish profits International Jewry united and instigated a global boycott of Germany in an attempt to change the Nazi economic policies.

The president of the World Jewish Economic Federation Samuel Untermyer explained what global Jewry intended by this boycott on August 7th, 1933 CE when he announced, long before WWII, over the American radio network, "***The Jews of the world now declare a Holy War against Germany.*** *We are now engaged in* *a sacred conflict* *against the Germans. And we are going to starve them into surrender. We are going to use a world-wide boycott against them. That will destroy them because they are* *dependent upon their export business .... Each of you, Jew and Gentile alike, who has not already enlisted in this sacred war should do so now and here. It is not sufficient that you should buy no goods made in Germany. You must refuse to deal with any merchant or shopkeeper who sells any German-made goods or who patronises German ships or shipping. . . we will undermine the Hitler regime and bring the German people to their senses by destroying their export trade on which their very existence depends."* So even though WWII was fought by some Christians for Christian reasons, it is unfair to say that Judaism and Jews had nothing to do with causing WWII. Let the record show that Jews did declare a "holy war" on Nazi Germany in 1933 CE. Don't think Jews were 100% innocent as the Zionist historians of today may lead you to believe. WWII was a religious war any way you look at it. After the genocide of WWII and the devastation of the atomic bomb came to be known, making both sides be seen as evil, the evangelists of Christendom decided to distance themselves from culpability. Thus the blame for the world wars was placed on secularism in an attempt to say Christianity was the solution and way to peace even though originally Christianity played a major role in the world wars. Consider the statement of Adolf Hitler when he said, "*It is always more difficult to fight against faith than knowledge."* Now do you think Hitler having such ideas about "faith" is not going to use religion and faith to bolster his fighting force? Seriously in an anti-Jew climate with a German nation that has an extensive anti-Jewish pro-Christian history and has International Jewry declare a "holy war" on it instigating a global boycott, Hitler would be a fool to not use Christianity to fight back. Only a faith that teaches "Jews killed God" could result in such massive Jewish bloodshed. Honestly if as the bible says a Christian believes the Jews killed God or the son of God and the blood is not just on the Jews who did it but all Jews for all time as the gospel of Matthew says then why can't Christians just kill all the Jews without mercy? Biblically no mercy exists for Jews. People kill people for insulting God or killing people but Christians literally believe the Jewish people are guilty of killing the Creator of the Universe and/or his son. That is an anti-Jew genocidal doctrine and it always will be no matter what people say. Even pagans would kill those who smashed their idols. So Christians do plan on killing all the Jews too, eventually, it's just that currently they've decided to use Jews to kill the Muslims. Either the Jews didn't suffer during

WWII as much as they claim, or Christianity is responsible for a large part of that Jewish suffering, both could be the case, but we must admit that Judaism and Christianity played a major role in the fighting of WWII. Unfortunately Jews and Christians have written many history books. They kill each other, then claim that their religions had nothing to do with it and that religion has nothing to do with the current carnage in Palestine. Instead of "agreeing to disagree" they have "agreed to distort" history. It's plain and simple Adolf Hitler was a Christian Crusader, not a classical one but a modern one; the modern ones can't use the ancient antique gimmicks. Economics and politics also played a part, but the Christian faith greatly influenced the buildup and continuance of the world wars and prevented the cessation of hostilities. Later historical and political spin was applied to make it seem that no teams were Christian and that the Churches didn't paint the world wars as holy wars but Secularism was to blame. Incidentally instead of the Western world becoming more Christian after the world wars as was hoped for by Christian Evangelists throughout the world, both during the wars and after the wars when they blamed the wars on secularism, the

Western world became more secular because the masses knew that in reality Christianity was involved and contributed to both world wars. People still alive from that time know that their country was represented as a bulwark of the Christian faith and their enemy was satanic, but the kids today are taught a different history. Seriously if people over 75 years old read school history books about what life was like when they were young and what people thought, they would be appalled and say their generation is being lied about. Currently instead of the States using religion to promote nationalism, secularism has decreased the religious denominational differences of nations and made nationalism the new State religion. Hence today war and savagery is even more likely because now nations are more supportive of their nation regardless of what religious differences exist amongst themselves and without any care for what religion the opposing countries follow. Whereas before the world wars could only go so far in human brutality because at the end of the day there was still a tinge of contradicting hypocrisy in Christians from X country fighting Christians from Y in the name of Christianity. Although today since nationalism is the religion of the era the next world war will likely have no holds barred whatsoever without any sense of leniency or mercy. Nationalism is simply tribalism on a massive scale and any historian knows tribalistic wars were the most deadly. This is because when fighting occurs due to people belonging to a different tribe, that always results in extinction of the losing tribe since they can never biologically stop being part of their tribe. The only type of war that could theoretically be less merciful would be an intergalactic war between humans and aliens, but that is what the whole globalization movement and space colonization is leading us towards. Anyways the reason Christians aren't oppressing each other today isn't because of the religion, it's because none of the various denominations has enough power to coordinate any violence on a major scale.(or at least they can't publicly coordinate religious violence) The inter-denominational wars during the 1500s-1700s between Catholics, Lutherans, Protestants, Calvinists, Baptists, Anabaptists and Methodists are some of the bloodiest in recorded history. Protestants were even more intolerant to the other denominations of Protestantism than the Catholics were. Historically Protestants and non-Catholics have actually harmed each other more than they have non-Christians. Heretics are always more harshly persecuted than infidels, for obvious reasons. While I've been rather critical of Catholicism in this book I really don't want any reader to get the wrong impression thinking Catholicism is the most intolerant version of Christianity, it's not. Catholics just had the longest run and more time to cause havoc than other denominations had. When given the opportunity the non-Catholics have displayed even greater intolerance. Ironically much Christian intolerance is directed towards Catholicism and Catholics and anti-Catholicism has been trending for sometime, albeit it's diminished over the centuries. However In the 1600s Protestants were adamantly anti-Catholic, they would forbid Catholic masses from being said in their vicinity, rebel against rulers on the basis of their Catholicism, and even attack Catholic parades. Protestants also forbid Protestants from attending Catholic ceremonies such as baptism, marriages, funerals, church services and their ministers would in effect excommunicate those who married Catholics. In France during 1620 CE the Catholic King of "Catholic France" was even shocked when visiting the city of Pau to discover no Catholic churches existed in the city because Protestants didn't tolerate non-Protestant forms of Christianity. Calvinists had a similar policy towards Lutherans and vice versa. One of the biggest deceptions of Christianity today is that Catholics are the violent intolerant ones and the Protestants are peaceful/tolerant. The only thing Christians hate more than non-Christians is other types of Christians who believe in the bible differently than them, or even dare to use different versions of the bible. Most Christian denominations teach that you don't turn the other cheek when it comes to other Christians with rival doctrines. They used to teach that you are supposed to hit their cheek first. Although as Americanism has spread, Americanist Christians are dominating most Christian denominations today so they rarely advocate hate or intolerance towards other denominations, publicly. Behind closed doors though all the various Christian groups hate each other. That's why they all have separate churches and different bibles. If any Christian denomination in the world today could logistically destroy the other denominations by force or other means they would, but since they can't they team up with Jews and Secularists to fight Muslims. Most Christian groups take the position of *"We'll kill each other after we kill the Muslims."* (typically completely forgetting about the Hindus and Buddhists) Whereas fundamentally speaking this modern Christian unity is exactly like how Catholic and Orthodox Christians teamed up for the first crusade. This was why NATO and the European Union was formed.

Since the 1930s CE the popes began calling for a "United States of Europe" as a prerequisite for the next crusade against Muslims and the charter for the European Union is the 1957 CE Treaty of Rome. Originally the EU flag was going to be a blue field, with a red cross inside an orange circle at the centre, but due to "Muslim sensitivities" they decided it'd be better not to use a cross on the flag. The one responsible for choosing the E.U. flag, Paul Levy, said he choose the design after seeing a statue of the Virgin Mary with a halo of stars and was "inspired" by the way the stars, reflecting the sun, glowed against the blue of the sky. Whereas the designer Arsene Heitz said he based the 12 golden stars on a blue background because of the biblical book of Revelation 12:1 mentioning a women (thought to be Mary) crowned by 12 stars depicted in blue garb. Regardless the flag's design was officially adopted on December 8th, 1955 CE coinciding with the Catholic feast day of Mary's Immaculate

Conception. So when the E.U. says they are combatting "radical Islam" know that it was a Christian Union from the beginning first called for by the Catholic popes in the 1930s CE. However is the EU truly a papist plot? No, it is not. Many will be shocked that despite all the facts I just shared linking Catholic designs with the EU decades before it was formed the EU is actually a Protestant plot. In 1609 CE King Henry IV of France and James I of England planned a "Grand Design" to unite the nations of France, England, Scotland, Denmark, Sweden, Holland, Germany, Switzerland and Venice to combat the Hapsburg alliance of Spain, the Netherlands, Italy, Savoy, Austria, Luxembourg, and other European principalities. Henry IV and James I (the same James famous for the King James bible) hoped this "Grand Design" would conquer all of Europe except Russia, Turkey, Italy and Spain and divide Europe into a federated "Christian Republic" of 15 autonomous states with free non-tariff trade amongst each other who submitted their foreign policies to a federal council armed with supreme military force. Ironically that's practically exactly what the EU tried to be, except it was larger than Henry IV and James I ever planned their "Grand Design" would be. So the EU was planned since 1609 CE and took 347 years to occur.

Although don't misinterpret this and think history was always an exclusive "The Western Christians vs. Islam" scenario. There was another non-Muslim non-Christian enemy, even more fierce in fighting the Muslims than the familiar Frankish Christian foes. In 1220 CE they conquered the city of Bukhara on a Friday. Be aware the city of Bukhara is/was the very same city where the famous scholar Imam Bukhari was born and died in, and Imam Bukhari authored perhaps the 2nd most religiously important and influential book in the post-Muhammad pbuh Muslim world. So in this famous Muslim city, in the autumn of 1220 CE, on a Friday, the Muslims masses gathered in the masjid; however the Muslim masses had not gathered in order to pray. Instead the Muslim masses flocked to the masjid that Friday, in Bukhara, to hear the speech of the man who conquered their city and was now their defacto ruler. He was a foreigner and they could not understand his speech, but to convey his decree he still insisted on doing it in person in the masjid on the pulpit while a translator would translate his message to the masses in real-time so the Muslims could understand what he said. The historic speech he gave that day, when translated into english was, "*O people, know that you committed great sins and that the great ones among you have committed these sins. If you ask me what proof I have for these words, I say it is because I am the punishment of God. If you had not committed great sins, God would not have sent a punishment like me upon you.*" After saying this he descended the pulpit and his soldiers began butchering the inhabitants, plundering the city burning all the flammable buildings to the ground, and as a final measure forcing the surviving inhabitants to besiege the citadel of their razed city wherein 30,000 Muslims had refused to surrender peacefully as the Bukharans had foolishly done days earlier expecting to be treated with mercy. Eventually the Bukharans themselves slaughtered their own Bukharan compatriots because of their subjugation to their conquerors was to such an extent that the majority of the Muslims of Bukhara murdered the other Muslims of Bukhara who tried to defend the city from the non-Muslims who were butchering the Muslims and burning all of Bukhara to the ground. That was the effect of the terror the Muslims of Bukhara had for their new non-Muslim conquerors. The terror and subjugation was so complete that after the citadel of Bukhara was destroyed the few survivors later agree to be arrow fodder on the front lines when besieging Samarkand since the non-Muslim foreigners also planned to conquer that famous Muslim city and slaughter the inhabitants. Now you may be wondering who were these non-Muslims that inflicted such a calamity upon the Muslim world and turned Muslims against Muslims for their sake? Who was their leader that gave such a blood-chilling religiously zealous speech in the masjid of Bukhara before butchering the Muslims for "their sins" for which "God sent him as a punishment". They were not "Crusaders". Though due to their speech and actions who then could these religious zealots of the 1200s CE have been if not Crusaders? The name of that conqueror who spoke at Bukhara was Chingiss Khan and he was the leader of the Mongols. Yes, the Mongols were "holy warriors" who fought for the sake of their religion, which is a fact often unmentioned by modern historians. In fact most people don't even know the name Chingiss Khan and ignorantly call him Gengis Khan, which if anyone ever does then know that they probably know nearly nothing about the Mongols, except what they learned from movies or fools like themselves. Calling Chingiss Khan by the name of Gengis is like referring to China by the name of Gena. Whereas anyone who thought China was called Gena and referred to it as such would be publicly treated by nearly everyody like they were clueless idiots regarding China and everything Chinese, yet when "history experts" use the word Gengis most people still look at these fraudulent copycat historical butchers with respect worthy of academic prestige. Now it's one thing for people to just not know and say Gengis because that's how they've always heard or read it, but the problem is those people acting like they know what they are talking or writing about when they don't and having others believe they are getting good information or respecting these ignorant instructors much more than they deserve, when they are guilty of such a simple easily avoidable error. If you ever hear anyone ever tell you "Genghis Khan" if they are respectable take them aside and ask them "Do you have a speech impediment that causes you to say Genghis when his name was Chingiss?" while if they are not respectable people then ask them point-blank, perhaps publicly if deserved, "Do you have a speech impediment that causes you to say Genghis when his name was Chingiss or are you simply an idiot who doesn't know even the name of the person whom they are talking about?" By "not respectable" in this situation I'm referring to the non-Muslim school teachers or historians who pretend to teach history accurately. Seriously, not to digress, but you have freaking professional teachers in schools and professional historians using the name Gengis instead of Chingiss and getting away with it. I find such a grievous error unacceptable for persons preaching at such a level and roundly condemn such "experts" who are paid to teach about Chingiss as incompetent historywhores who are screwing history and the minds of the masses while getting paid money to do so. Those people disgust me even more than the anti-Muslim Mongol murderers. The fact is Mongols fought the Muslims for religious reasons perhaps even more zealously than the Crusaders did. What most don't know is that many Mongols were Nestorian Christians and Buddhists, the Mongols had so many Christian tribes that in the 10th century Christianity became one of the Mongol state's official religions. Chingiss Khan's son even married a Nestorian Christian princess who gave birth to: Hulegu Khan who ruthlessly and infamously sacked Baghdad, as well as Kublai Khan who ruled China as emperor and a third son. (Also forgive me if I now misspell Mongolian names, I'm no official expert on Mongols so I hope for lenient criticism. Yet with Chingiss Khan, seeing as he is the most famous Mongol of all, I feel less leniency is allowed for such a basic core piece of information to be botched by people posing as experts.) It wasn't until the 14th century that Nestorian Christian influence diminished as the Ming dynasty arose. For centuries the Mongols ravaged the Muslim empire killing millions and destroying entire cities in the name of their Buddhist/Christian/Shaminist ideology. Chingiss Khan even boasted he was the "Scourge of God" sent to wreak havoc on Muslims and destroy them. In the 13th century the Mongols of Asia and the Crusaders of Europe tried to unite, join their territories and pincer the Muslims wiping them off the planet once and for all; as Pope Innocent IV proposed in his messages sent to the Mongols. However this anti-Muslim union was prevented when the Mamluk Muslim army gave the Mongols their first ever defeat at the battle of Ayn Jalut (Eye of Goliath) in Palestine in 1260 CE. At that time the Muslims were fighting the Crusaders attacking them from the West and the Mongols attacking them from the East. Both were defeated individually although the Mongols had deeply penetrated Muslim territory conquering/occupying entire countries. Yet one day Hulegu Khan's cousin Berke Khan decided to ask a Muslim what he actually believed, when he heard what Islam is he choose to become a Muslim. Afterwards many soldiers in his army and his citizens became Muslim as well after Berke explained Islam to them. Then Berke Khan used his share of the Mongol empire and army to fight against his cousin Hulegu Khan who was exterminating Muslims. Not all Mongols became Muslims though and their nation split apart as some did and some didn't. This was because those who didn't embrace Islam couldn't tolerate Islam or Muslims being amongst them even though many of the Muslims were their fellow Mongols. I've had similar experiences myself where Americans think I'm some type of foreigner who doesn't speak English because I'm Muslim. Seriously I've had American strangers ask "*Do you speak English?*" without them even being sarcastic about it, they legitimately assume that I don't speak english because I dress like a Muslim and they actually get surprised when I tell them I do speak english. Sometimes even my own family forgets and asks me "*Why do you Muslims come to our country and tell us to do things differently? If you don't like it why don't you go back to your desert Muslim hellhole, this is America! Why don't you Muslims assimilate like all the other immigrants who came here did?"* and it shocks me. Because these people are my flesh and blood who've known me my whole life yet because I'm Muslim sometimes they think I'm some foreign immigrant despite having been born and raised in America and being there most every day of my life. I've never even left the continent. One time my mother even told me that a distant cousin of mine, who didn't really know me before I became a Muslim, asked her, *"Where did you get him from?"* honestly thinking I had been adopted from some Arab country and wasn't really related to him. So this is like what happened when some Mongols became Muslims and the other Mongols thought that meant they changed races and nationalities automatically; so they were called Mughals. Later in Mongol history another Khan talked to a Muslim and embraced Islam, he was named Tughlugh Timur Khan and had more military successes against the anti-Islamic Mongols but unfortunately is consistently slandered by historians who frequently derogatorily call him Timur the lame. The Mongols are a unique example of recorded history in which the conquerors actually embraced the religion of the people they conquered. So when people say Islam is spread by the sword, ask them who put the sword to the Mongols neck after they had destroyed the Muslim empire and were oppressing millions of Muslims treating them as sub-humans? Nobody did. It was a simple peaceful conversation about religion. On the other hand we cannot find any other example of a religious group today, aside from Muslims, that can claim they were practically obliterated by disbelievers and then those disbelievers voluntarily embraced their religion after having killed and conquered them for centuries. It is because Islam spreads so easily and quickly through peaceful polite means that the enemies of Islam don't want peaceful religious dialogues, so they promote barriers of intolerance, stereotypes, paranoia, arrogance, misconceptions, lies and violence to prevent people from learning what Islam actually is and what Muslims are really like. I myself have read such material where anti-Muslims say the Mongols first mistake was that they stopped killing every Muslim man, women and child and allowed them to live amongst them as second class citizens. Then they say their second mistake was interacting with them. Honestly, do you think anyone on the side of truth or even sanity would make such a claim? You really have to be suspicious of someone and curious about Islam when the enemies of Islam say the only solution is to kill every Muslim and never let them have a chance to communicate with you. Yet more people than you think actually agree with the sentiment that the Muslim world should be bombed into oblivion. Yet the same people who believe and publicly preach such a doctrine, will then turn around and watch a science fiction movie about bad guys in space ruling an empire that builds weapons which they use to blow up planets in one shot and these people who believe the Muslim world should be blown up then condemn this fictional empire as evil when they are advocating the same exact policies. Thus when it's in a movie they are bad guys, but when it's America or some other nation blowing up the Muslim world they get called heroes. Yet what's even more ironic is that the "hero" in this science fiction saga comes from a desert planet who fights against the evil empire because they killed his relatives. Today Muslim desert dwellers fighting against an empire that killed their family get called terrorists. The worst part is the masses don't even make this connection where fictional evil deeds in space become good deeds on earth. The average person isn't that insanely intolerant of Islam, but the non-Muslim so-called "experts on Islam" promote total Muslim genocide to the most influential and dangerous people on the planet. It's sad because the American revolutionaries at the battle of Bunker Hill in 1775 CE were allegedly told by their Freemason General Israel Putnam, "*Don't shoot the redcoats until you see the whites of their eyes.*", similar to how Frederick told the Germans in 1757 CE "*no firing till you see the whites of their eyes*" and how Charles of Prussia in 1745 CE said "*Silent until you see the whites of their eyes.*" and as Cavemen millenia ago probably told their hunters when hunting animals not to use their range weapons which had limited ammunition until they saw the whites of the targeted animal's eyes. But today with the drones, artillery, and airstrikes, the U.S. government as well as the Russians, French, Germans and many others don't even want their soldiers to see the Muslims they kill but simply drop the bombs on Muslims while they are inside their homes or vehicles. They literally kill Muslim masses without even seeing them or hearing them. The enemies of Islam treat Muslims like we were the mythical Medusa combined with Harpies. The Greeks thought if you look at Medusa you'll be turned to stone and if you heard the Harpies you'll be seduced into insanity and devoured by them. Islam tells Muslims violence is a disliked last resort, yet the enemies of Islam publicly say violence is the first and only resort that has any effectiveness. Now why would that be unless Islam is true? Seriously if one religion were true with 100% irrefutable proof then how do you think Satan would try to stop it from spreading? Why else do you think Pharaoh and his army chased after the Muslims who left Egypt? What did the "righteous" Pharisees say was the only way to counter Jesus pbuh?

The history of Spain is another interesting era which I've learned and believed different versions of at different times in my life. When Muslims conquered Spain the region flourished and was a beacon for tolerance. Muslims, Christians and Jews peacefully coexisted. Jews even served the Muslim government, the year was 709 CE. Before religious tolerance was even a concept Muslims practiced it. In the 7th century CE more than 90% of Jews lived in Muslim lands under the Khilafah, without suffering persecution as a result of disbelief. Jewish scholars have said: *"never in the history of the world have Jews been more tolerated than in Muslim Spain"*.

Compare this to the Visigoth Catholics in neighboring Portugal. In 709 CE they were forcing Arian Christians and Jews to either convert to Catholicism or die. In mainland Europe as of 781 CE the "Saint" Emperor Charlemagne required everyone in Saxony to get baptized and become a Christian, those who didn't were put to death. Ironically the "conversions via the sword" which Christians accuse Muslims of doing didn't happen, but they did happen in the Christian territories when pagans were forced to convert or die. Historically Chirstians have falsely accused the Muslims of doing what the Christians were guilty of even though the Muslims were innocent of such religious crimes. Doing any sin is bad enough, but blaming innocent people for the sins you are guilty of is even worse. Later when the Spanish Reconquista drove the Muslims out, the Catholic conquerors set about killing all the other Christians, Jews and Muslims in what is known as the Spanish inquisition. The problem the Catholic inquisitors had wasn't just with those of a different religion, rather they had to change the population's perception that different religious groups could peacefully co-exist. The reconquista wasn't a final crusade as it's frequently portrayed to be. It was actually called for by Pope Gregory VII in 1073 CE in a papal bull ordering all Christians to remove Muslims from Spain. Which was 26 years before the "first crusade"! This means even before the wars commonly called crusades Popes were saying, *"kill the Muslims wipe them off the face of the earth."* After the inquisition the population of Spain changed from Muslim, Christian, Jew and Other to being strictly 100% Catholic, by force. I don't want to turn this into a gory horror book by mentioning what took place during the Inquisition in these pages, but I do strongly encourage you to research it on your own in depth. Nazis were harmless compared to the Catholic inquisitors. Although while Nazi's are famous for their death camps, in Spain during Franco's dictatorship from 1939-1975 CE, Catholicism was again made the only legal religion via State force and non-Catholics were persecuted and sent to concentration camps to die, as Franco killed more Spaniards than Hitler killed Germans when Spain was Catholicized again. In 1933 CE a Spanish priest Juan Tusquets Terrats, who later collaborated with Franco, even visited Hitler's concentration camp in Dachau and remarked, *"they [Nazis] did it [issue the invitation] to show what we had to do in Spain"*. The world mostly ignores the recent Spanish genocide because nobody stopped it. During Spain's 20th century re-Catholicizing period, people were even killed for not attending Catholic Church services; of course this was a temporary policy not implemented throughout the entire country but still in the 1930s CE you could get killed in Spain for not attending a Catholic Church Service. So when Catholics dismiss the inquisition as a distant past, it's not, officially it still continues. The office of the inquisition was renamed the "*Supreme Sacred Congregation of the Holy Office*" in 1908 CE by Pope Pius X and relabeled by Pope Paul VI in 1965 CE as the "*Congregation for Doctrine of the Faith*". Anyways the first bloody post-Muslim Catholic occupation of Spain sent the country back in time to the point where in 1566 CE King Phillip II forbid everyone in Spain from using the Arabic Language or bathing. Why bathing? Because Allah taught Muslims to bathe routinely and made bathing a part of Islam, therefore bathing was considered disbelief in Christianity since it meant believing the Islamic teachings of Allah were correct and practicing them. Christians actually said it's forbidden to bathe because that's what Islam tells people to do. Similarily Muslims introduced Europeans to toothbrushes and encouraged them to brush their teeth, yet because that's what Muhammad pbuh told people to do the Christians taught that you can't brush your teeth either because that'd be following Islam, thus they delayed brushing their teeth until the 17th century until they saw Chinese monks use a tooth brush too. Yet even to this day the tooth brushes and tooth pastes the West has invented are still scientifically inferior to the Islamic sewak. Even the World Health Organization has stated the organic Islamic sewak/miswak used by Muhammad pbuh in the 7th century is scientifically better to brush with than any toothbrush and toothpaste combination used in the world today, it's much more convenient and cheaper too. So when people refer to the "Dark Ages" they were only "Dark Ages" in Europe and the Americas because people weren't living under Islam or practicing Islam, and morally speaking the West is still in the "Dark Ages". Today people bath and brush their teeth thinking it's "common sense" or hygiene because they don't want to say "*Islam was actually right all along and us non-Muslims were wrong for saying the Islamic religious practices of the Muslims were satanic.*" To this day due credit still isn't given to Muhammad pbuh for teaching us to bath and brush, they say it's "modern medicine" when it's actually an ancient Islamic religious practice. It was part of Islam until it became popular amongst the non-Muslims. Ironically the gold Spain took from the Americas, destroyed the Spanish economy due to the increased supply causing excessive inflation. Despite the alleged enmity between Jews and Muslims today, at the time Jews fled the persecution of Catholic Spain and settled in the Muslim Ottoman Empire. Had Jews remained in Spain they would have suffered miserably under the Inquisition. Then in 1492 CE, the very same year the last Muslim city in the Iberian Peninsula fell to Spain, Catholic Spain's royalty Ferdinand and Isabella officially banned Jews from the country and legally forbid them to enter Spanish territory. A similar decree was also passed in 1492 CE decreeing that the entire Muslim population of Granada, that final Muslim city, had to either convert or be expelled. Portugal enslaved the Jews who sought asylum and in 1497 CE decreed that Jews had to either convert to Christianity or leave without their children. Whilst just to cover any possible legal loopholes in 1502 CE Queen Isabella declared conversion to Catholicism compulsory within the Kingdom of Castile and King Charles V did the same in the Kingdom of Aragon in 1526 CE. Meaning you would not be allowed to exist unless you were Catholic. Many Christian and Secular countries have exiled Jews and banned Judaism before and since, such as England in 1290 CE, but never in all of history has any Khilafah governed by the Islamic Sharia law ever exiled Jews, let alone forced them to convert. 500 years ago Jews fled Christian Europe in order to live in Muslim lands so they could be safe and practice their religion. The Catholic extermination of Muslims was so complete that today it's nearly inconceivable to imagine that for practically 800 years Islam dominated Spain causing an intellectual golden age in the region that started the renaissance. Math, Science and modern technology as we know it today would be unfeasible without Muslim contributions such as Al-Jabr which is known as Algebra, or Algorithms which are named after the latin name of its inventor Muhammad Al- Khwarizmi; who also invented algorisms. Likewise the world today wouldn't function without the Islamic societies contributions in aeronautics, medicine and trigonometry. While the scientific method was invented by Ibn Al-Haythem in the eleventh century. Islamic civilization produced the very methodology for all modern sciences and math. But why aren't Muslim inventors and geniuses taught to non-Muslims in school when they are using the very formulas and scientific theories which were first discovered in Islamic civilizations? They teach kids about the pagan contributors like Pythagoras, Ptolemy and philosophers. Do the teachers simply not know of the Muslims who made the subjects and theories they teach? If so, then why don't they know? Students get taught about those pagans whose teachings exist today because the Muslims translated their writings but teachers skip over the Muslims themselves as if they didn't exist. Not only do they ignore the contributions of Muslim societies, they credit Europeans like Leonardo Da Vinci (twice arrested for homosexuality), Isaac Newton(freemason) and Albert Einstein (atheist Jew who invented the atomic bomb) for intellectual breakthroughs made in Muslim lands centuries earlier. Why? Do people not want great Muslims to be modern role models? Is a non-Muslim tolerant if they have zero Muslim role models?

Many know the story about Christopher Columbus sailing from Spain to America in 1492 CE, but few know the reason why. School textbooks will say it was for trade reasons. Although after the crusades had failed and Muslims occupied Constantinople renaming it Istanbul, trade from Asia had increased dramatically. The prices of spices dramatically decreased and flooded Europe with cheaper goods, since they no longer had a high Byzantine tax levied on them. Economically there was less reason to find an alternate trade route with Asia than before. The reason is directly related to the failure of the crusades and the Christian invasions into Muslim Africa having been repulsed. The Muslims had already been to America and maps exist proving it. Christopher Columbus had access to some of these maps. Records specifically say Columbus used an estimate from a Muslim geographer al-Farghani for the circumference of the earth, but because he didn't understand the difference between Roman miles and Muslim miles Columbus' estimate of the earth was 25% too small. Contrary to what many are told about Columbus being the genius who first learned the earth was round, he wasn't. Muslims had known the earth wasn't flat for centuries; the Quran specifically states that the earth is spherical and that the moon, earth and sun move in orbits and rotate. The reason Galileo and Copernicus were condemned by the Catholic Church was because if they were right it would mean the Quran was right nearly 1,000 years before Christendom. Also the reason only 4 gospels were chosen to be in the bible was because the proto-Old Testament texts said the world had 4 corners, thus if earth didn't have 4 corners and wasn't flat then how would they be able to explain including only 4 gospels in the bible and burning all the rest; which they claimed they did under divine inspiration when the bible was created. If the earth did not have 4 corners they would have to admit that the Church wasn't divinely inspired when picking the material to include in the bible, which would then mean that men had compiled the book based on their own human desires and were wrong to burn thousands of gospels and might have picked the wrong gospels to put in the bible. Therefore if the earth did not have 4 corners then the way the Christian bible was created would have to be wrong, but if the bible was created in the wrong way based on false assumptions about the earth being flat then the Holy Spirit would not have allowed that to happen. If the earth was not flat and did not have 4 corners then it would mean the Christians were not divinely guided, their biblical books were not written, translated or selected via divine inspiration and that would mean the religion had no guarantee for being right and the bible would not be trustworthy nor could we trust those who passed it down. As a result the Church did not want the world to be anything but flat and persecuted those who said it wasn't, since if earth wasn't flat then the bible and Christianity would have lost it's claim on being a divine religion guaranteed to be correct forever being constantly guided by a Holy Spirit, Jesus and/or God. Yet now it is known that earth does not have 4 corners. Thus people proclaimed the bible is wrong but then the Church said how the bible never said that earth was flat. While people checked and saw that it doesn't say that completely forgetting that even though the bible doesn't say earth is flat those who made it picked 4 gospels for the New Testament saying the reason was because earth was flat and had 4 corners and God inspired them to do so just as God inspired them to pick the 4 gospels of Mark, Matthew, Luke and John. Thus the bible in itself isn't' wrong because the earth isn't flat but those who picked the 4 gospels and burned the rest were wrong and mistaken when they said God inspired them to select the books they selected to be a part of the Old and New Testament. Although most people just checked to see if the bible said earth was round and when they couldn't find that verse then they ignored the whole controversy being ignorant of how the bible's trustworthiness depended upon earth being flat with 4 corners. It is because of the knowledge Muslims had from Islam that they were able to do things before they were thought feasible, such as how Muslims first crossed the Atlantic to visit the Americas. Al sharif-al-idrisi who lived from 1099-1161 CE reported Muslims had been to an island in the Atlantic and seen people with red skin, without much hair on their body, who had straight head-hair. In short Christopher Columbus is credited for more than he deserves in the field of discovery and not enough credit for other things that are less flattering. This is a common theme of mythology, in which humans exaggerate some person's achievements in order to develop collective human pride. Although even this historical debate of "who discovered it first" is pointless. The lesson should be that Allah created it and for a long period of time the majority of mankind had no idea it existed or was so close. Similar to how people today don't realize that Paradise and Hell have been created and we are so close to being in one or the other for eternity. Why did Columbus sail to America if not for trade and exploration? Before we can answer that we need to know the historical context of the time in which Columbus lived as well as the mood/attitudes surrounding politics and exploration in his time

    In 1452 CE, as a way to combat Islam in Africa Pope Nicolas V instructed Europeans to enslave all the people who were not Christian. His papal bull Dum Diversas stated: *"We grant you [Kings of Spain and Portugal] by these present documents, with our Apostolic Authority, <u>full and free permission to invade, search out, capture, and subjugate the Saracens and pagans and any other unbelievers</u> and enemies of Christ wherever they may be, as well as their kingdoms, duchies, counties, principalities, and other property and <u>to reduce their persons into perpetual servitude.</u>"* He reiterated his position in 1454 CE and glorified the enslavement of non-Christians as is evident in the following english translation of Romanus Pontifex by Pope Nicolas V: *"The Roman pontiff, successor of the key-bearer of the heavenly kingdom and vicar of Jesus Christ, contemplating <u>with a father's mind</u> all the several climes of the world and the characteristics of all the nations dwelling in them and <u>seeking and desiring the salvation of all</u>, wholesomely ordains and disposes upon <u>careful deliberation</u> those things which <u>he sees will be agreeable to the Divine Majesty</u> and by which he may*

*bring the sheep entrusted to him by God into the single divine fold, and may acquire for them the reward of eternal felicity, and obtain pardon for their souls. This we believe will more certainly come to pass, through the aid of the Lord, <u>if we bestow suitable favors and special graces on those Catholic kings and princes</u>, who, like athletes and intrepid champions of the Christian faith, as we know by the evidence of facts, <u>not only restrain the savage excesses of the Saracens and of other infidels, enemies of the Christian name, but also for the defense and increase of the faith</u> <u>**vanquish them and their kingdoms and habitations, though situated in the remotest parts unknown to us**</u>, <u>and subject them to their own temporal dominion, sparing no labor and expense</u>, in order that those kings and princes, relieved of all obstacles, <u>may be the more animated to the prosecution of so salutary and laudable a work</u>."*
Unfortunately many black people have forgotten their own history despite the historical evidence proving the African slaves in North and South America were Muslims. Some were even huffaz, which are persons who have memorized the entire Quran in Arabic. Surprisingly Muslims have been in the Americas far longer than those of European lineage. George Washington had a slave called "Fatimer", the daughter of Muhammad pbuh was Fatima. The first English translation of the Quran

was produced in 1649 CE. Thomas Jefferson had a copy of George Sale's English translation of the Quran which was originally published in 1734 CE. Even though George Sale included anti-Islamic commentary in the translation, the fact remains Muslims were in America and Islam was being practiced in America before the colonies even united and became known as America. In actuality Muslims were in America before Columbus even set sail. That is important to remember when politicians manipulate anti-Muslim sentiment in order to get elected. If you examine the lineage of most of those politicians you will discover that Muslims were in their country longer than the politician's families have been. Muslims are technically more American than the islamophobes who claim Muslims are ruining America, Muslims have a longer history in America than Europeans and Muslims didn't oppress, exploit or infect the native population with diseases(because Islam teaches strict hygiene and prohibits the type of biological warfare the colonists used when intentionally giving germ ridden blankets to natives). The first map of Florida made in 1564 CE even had Muslim towns depicted which had Arabic names. Muslims also traded with Austrailian

Aborigines long before the Europeans went there. The Vikings of Scandinavia traded with the Abbasid Khilafah during the 8th century CE. Yet while the masses are taught of the Vikings going to America they never get taught that the Muslims were there centuries before the Christians were. So if it is just pro-Christian history why aren't the pagan Vikings excluded too? Europeans did not enslave Africans because they were black, they explicitly enslaved them because they weren't Christian. Christians felt justified enslaving them based on the authority and edict of the Popes. It wasn't just Pope Nicholas V who ordered the enslavement of non-christians either, Pope Eugenius IV said the same in 1436 CE. In 1488 CE Pope Innocent VIII received 100 Muslim Moorish slaves as a gift from Ferdinand of Spain, and rather than free them the Pope distributed them among his cardinals and friends as gratuities. Enslaving the unbaptized was Christian policy for centuries. Christopher Columbus even pompously declared while enslaving Arawak Native Americans, "*Let us in the name of the Holy Trinity, go on sending all the slaves that can be sold.*" This is the side of history that isn't taught in schools because Christians don't like to hear it, particularly Catholics, there is a lot of political pressure to prevent such information from becoming public knowledge. Many children of black Muslim slaves were forced to convert to Christianity. Unfortunately many black Christians like to believe Christianity "saved them" from slavery, instead of the historical fact that it was Christianity that enslaved them. This is why the black slaves were often given different names, because names like Muhammad, Bilal or Ali were undesirable to Christian slave-owners. By changing their Islamic names it gradually made them forget their Islamic roots, making future generations more susceptible to Christian evangelism. Evidence for the Islamic names of slaves is found in the September 7th, 1774 CE issue of the Savannah Georgia Gazette where a notice about a runaway slave "Mahomet" was placed. Some of the Muslim slaves knew how to read and write Arabic, breaking the stereotype of African racial inferiority much to the chagrin of illiterate Christian slave-owners. Abdulrahman Ibrahim ibn Sori was one such literate Muslim slave who wrote a letter in Arabic to Africa and was later freed by President John Quincy Adams due to pressure from the Sultan of Morocco. During the campaign for the next election, Andrew Jackson (the guy on the $20 bill) publicly criticized

Adams for freeing the Muslim. Bilali Muhammad, a slave in Georgia, was the imam of the plantation he worked on and led the Muslim slaves in prayers. Bilali published a thirteen page document on Islamic beliefs and how to perform Islamic rituals in America in 1829 CE. Another prominent Muslim in America was Estevanico, also known as "Black Stephen" or "Stephen the Moor". Estevanico explored South Western America being among the first non-natives to ever explore that area of the world. He went to what is known as the Dominican Republic, Cuba, Texas, Mexico, Arizona and New Mexico. Why do you think historians and textbooks have removed Muslims from American history?

Black vs. White and other types of racism plays into the hands of politicians and make it easy for oppressive governments to pursue a policy of divide and conquer and tax. Governments want their citizens to blame fellow citizens of a different skin color for many of the problems bad government has caused, thereby keeping people disunited unable to be of any political threat. Adam pbuh is mankind's common ancestor who was made from clay, that clay had various shades just as how there are different shades of dirt in the earth today, some light some dark. The DNA of Adam pbuh was passed on so that the genes of the various shades of the human species survived through hereditary traits. Likewise with eye color and hair color, skin color was just one of many traits present within the genetic code of our Father Adam pbuh. Adam pbuh had the genetic makeup of all the races. As his descendants reproduced, the different shades of skin developed among humans. All skin colors were in our ancestor's DNA, which skin color was first is just as irrelevant as his eye color or hair color. The various pros and cons of different skin tones are negligent and in no way make one skin color superior to another. Look at animals, birds alone have so many different types of feathers and beaks, likewise with cats and dogs. These animals are not racist or go to war because one has brown fur while another has white fur; they recognize they all belong to the same species. More differences exist within animal species than among humans and their differences actually have an effect on their abilities and could make some types of animals superior to others, yet they don't make a big deal of it as we do. Animals interbreed with animals of different colors without any stigma. There are no racist animals, what does that say about racist people? Racism is a trap of Satan to disunite humans causing them to oppress one another developing arrogance and hatred. Satan leads racists to justify sins because of their skins. Your skin color is not going to determine whether you go to heaven or hell. The only thing that makes one human superior to another in the sight of Allah is their piety. Nationalism is just an extension of the same racist fallacy. Nationalism is even dumber than racism because if no one told you that you or your parents were born in X country and if another person didn't know their family's history of citizenship, both would just agree they are human without enmity. But if someone is told you're German and the other person is French then Satan exploits this to the misfortune of both. A prime example is America and Canada. I was born in New York State through no choice of my own, yet somehow people would have me believe that a person born in Honolulu, Hawaii has more in common with me than a person born in Toronto, Canada. Realistically I'm more likely to have similarities with a person in Toronto who has experienced the same weather. In fact the only thing I have in common with a person from Hawaii over other humans is that we both have the same government tax us. Basically modern national ties mean that you are all getting robbed by the same thief. That is what binds citizens of a country together, mutual victimization. Other than that, humans are mostly the same in their relations with each other. From a technical viewpoint a German and French man actually live closer together than a New Yorker and Californian. If we don't count the language barrier, people of different European countries are actually closer to each other than Americans. What about the cultural differences? Many cultural traditions have satanic roots and started out as cult practices, but if anything the various foods and recipes only serves to make mankind more interesting. Imagine if everyone had the same color skin, eyes, hair, spoke the same language with the same accent and ate the same food all over the world. This would be a boring place to live in and we wouldn't care to learn about humans living in other places on the planet. Therefore we should be glad Allah has created such diversity among humans because it makes life more interesting, encouraging us to learn and treat each other with respect. Linguistically racism isn't even the right term for thinking skin colors reflect superiority or inferiority, the term for that is colorism. While for those thinking the colors of your nation's flag determine superiority or inferiority isn't racism either, that's called nationalism. Nationalism is colorism based on the colors of national flags. Between the two I don't know which is dumber or more sinful. Colorism causes people to believe in pigmentocracy. Pigmentocracy is governmental authority based on skintones, this can be in the form of a skin color caste system or a skin-color based democratic style of system or some other style of colorism. However regardless of the way one desires or practices pigmentocracy or doesn't, the color of colorism is the color of sin. Don't let Satan use the diversity Allah has created to divide and conquer us. Satan told Christians God was racist and that all humans are born damned because of our ancestors doing one sin. That is the "Original Sin" it is racism, Satan hated our race and he made people think God did by default simply because we were human. While mankind's first sin was in taking Satan as a friend/advisor. If you are going to hate another human being it should be because Allah hates them, not because of their skin or ethnicity. Satan hates humans at large of all shades and sizes, it is he who creates this colorist idea making us think that we are better due to our birth and because of things we can't control, such as skin color. Every colorist, nationalist or racist essentially hates for the sake of Satan instead of for the sake of Allah. Also by hating for the sake of Allah and loving for the sake of Allah those you hate can always change and then become those you love for the sake of Allah, whereas Satanic racists/colorists and nationalists will hate someone their whole life just because they were born looking different than them or in a different country. How foolish we are to forget that we all came from dirt to begin with? Our ancestor Adam pbuh was made from clay! We are not that special. What is the difference between black dirt, brown dirt, yellow dirt and white dirt? At the end of the day dirt is dirt and that's what we are. Would you ever insult or fight your neighbor because their property had different dirt than your property? Don't let Satan make you look stupid and cause you to hate someone because they are made of a different shade of dirt than you. You are dirt just like me, let's not embarrass our species. Racism can be defined as: Dirt vs. Dirt. I wasn't clever enough to come up with this idea on my own, but got it straight from a hadith in which Abu Nadrah reported: *"I heard the farewell sermon of the Messenger of Allah, peace and blessings be upon him, and he said:* **"O people, verily, your Lord is one and your father Adam is one. There is no favoritism of an Arab over a foreigner, nor a foreigner over an Arab, and neither red skin over black skin, nor black skin over red skin, except through righteousness. Have I not conveyed the message?"** <u>Grade: Sahih Source: Musnad Ahmad 22978</u> A grade of Sahih means the hadith is authentic and proven to be 100% true. Keep in mind Muhammad pbuh said this in Mecca during Hajj in the 600s CE publicly in front of approximately 100,000 people; this was not a time when racism was considered even slightly incorrect. When Muhammad pbuh said this people had no qualms about being colorist and would actually use rudimentary science to "prove" their incorrectly assumed superiority of their colors. This shows how genuine prophets and revelation correct science. Another lesson from this hadith is that Islam doesn't teach that everyone is equal and unjudgeable as other philosophies may teach, rather Islam and Muhammad pbuh teaches people to judge everyone but only according to their righteousness/virtue and not factoring in their skin color, nationality or ethnicity. Now that's all well and good, as most people will agree that colorism is satanic. Yet nationalism is similar in satanic origin but it still persists in popularity to a greater extent than colorism, even amongst people claiming to be Muslims. So for such people there are other authentic hadiths from Muhammad pbuh that may lead them to realize nationalism is just as evil as colorism. As related in the hadiths of Abu Dawud and Al-Tirmidhi, Muhammad pbuh said: *"Undoubtedly Allah has removed from you the pride of arrogance of the age of Jahilliyah (ignorance) and the glorification of ancestors. <u>Now people are of two kinds. Either believers who are aware or transgressors who do wrong.</u> You are all the children of Adam and Adam was made of clay. <u>People should give up their pride in nations</u> because that is a coal from the coals of hellfire. If they do not give this up Allah will consider them lower than the lowly worm which pushes itself through Khara (dung)."* In a hasan(good) hadith reported by Abu Dawud, Muhammad pbuh said *"He is not one of us who calls for `Asabiyyah, (nationalism/tribalism) or who fights for `Asabiyyah or who dies for `Asabiyyah."* This is very significant because Muhammad pbuh taught that anyone who believes in nationalism or tribalism is "not one of us" meaning not a Muslim, and this applies whether one dies for it, fights for it or even calls to it. Just preaching nationalism (of any country) can take one outside the fold of Islam making one a disbeliever/non-Muslim. Yet people will say Muslims do that stuff so how could it be wrong and sinful amounting to disbelief in Islam if so many Muslims do it, I reply Muhammad pbuh taught that those who do that are not one of us even if they say they are. But what if they pray and fast? How can one say someone isn't Islamic or Muslim if they pray 5 times a day, pay zakat, do the Hajj and fast during Ramadan? Because as reported by Al-Harith al-Ashary, in a sahih authentic hadith, Muhammad pbuh said what means: ""*whoever adopts the call of Jahilliyyah (nationalism/tribalism/unislamic unity beliefs or practices) will be one of those who crawl on their knees in hell.*" A man said: '"*O Messenger of Allah, even though he observes Salah (Prayer) and Sawm (Fast)?*' He said: '"*Yes, even though he observes Salah and Sawm and claims to be a Muslim. So adopt the call of Allah whereby He called you Muslims and believers and servants of Allah.*" So it is explicitly clear from Muhammad pbuh himself that nationalism and patriotism for one's nation leads to eternal hellfire even if one prays and fasts and claims to be a Muslim. But what about family? Shouldn't one be proud to be a ____(whatever their family name is)? Not really, no. Tribalism is merely another form of nationalism and pre-dated nationalism. Family units were the forerunners of nations and nations were originally just big families, "national diversity" came about when tribes decided to ally/enslave rather than kill each other to the point of extinction. Plus regarding family we all descend from Adam pbuh and are the offspring of sinners. How can you be proud to be the offspring of someone who sins? Even if some are descended from prophets that has nothing to do with who we are and there is no reason to boast or brag or take pride in our ancestral lineage or relatives. I'm not saying don't treat your family members special but family shouldn't be a source of arrogance or pride. Once relatives die then that's it, you shouldn't be praising or glorifying them because you don't really know if God likes them or not and if not then all that praise would be sinful. Besides praising one's relatives is pointless as it cannot benefit them but only poses a spiritual risk to oneself. In Islam to help eradicate this ignorant tribalistic attitude of pride/arrogance Muhammad pbuh taught Muslims what to say to someone who boasts of their ancestors or lineage. It's quite controversial and many Muslims don't know what Muhammad pbuh told Muslims to say in such situations. However before I mention what he taught, I have to stress he was a kind and respectful man who showed the utmost reverence for people and only offended them when absolutely necessary due to utterly filthy religious beliefs. Similar to how Jesus pbuh was a paragon of politeness and manners, unless he was talking to the Pharisees who had such wicked speech and beliefs. So don't take this out of context thinking Muhammad pbuh was uncouth or disrespectful in his character. Harsh speech when/if used was only used to refute such a wicked belief/statement/deed, like boasting about one's familial lineage. Which when you really consider what it means to take pride in one's family, all you are "proud of" in actuality is the fact that the sexual parts of some people interacted instead of the sexual parts of others. That's all family really is, it's people who have a closer connection with a certain penis/vagina than other people have. So pride for family all amounts to pride for private parts. One day the companion of Muhammad pbuh, Ubayy ibn Kaab, overheard a man boasting of his ancestral lineage so he said *"Bite your father's penis!"* and there was social shock and scandal at the statement because he was a companion of Muhammad pbuh known for his fantastic manners and polite respectfulness. For him to say that stunned people and they thought either he lost his temper in a big way or he has a very good reason to have said such a thing in response to such speech which he heard. Ubayy bin Kaab said in response to the shock, "*Do not blame me, for the Prophet of Allah said to us: "Whoever you see boasting in an ignorant manner of his tribal lineage, then tell him to bite that, and do not use a metaphor."* This incident is popularly related by many sources, the hadith is narrated in Musnad Ahmed and the incident of Ubayy ibn Kaab is reported by Utayy ibn Damurah. So in Islam colorism, racism, nationalism, ancestral pride is all condemned and forbidden. Many, including extremely ignorant Muslims, take such things lightly thinking national or familial pride is good or even enjoined by Islam, but it is condemned by Islam and prohibited. With good reason too, for not only does nationalism, colorism, racism and tribal pride lead to arrogance, warfare and disunity amongst believers while causing unity with disbelievers, but such things damage a person's personal relationship with God.

    The motivation for the journey of Christopher Columbus still remains to be identified. It is no coincidence that Ferdinand and Isabella's Spain, now 100% Catholic, with severe anti-Muslim foreign and domestic politics was the nation to sponsor the voyage of Columbus; the crosses on his banners were not for decoration. The distorted history they teach in American public schools lists 3 reasons Spain sent conquistadores to the Americas, the three G's, for **G**od, **G**old and **G**lory. Think about that first G. During the Inquisition, in the very same year they banned Jews and Muslims from their country forcing them to either convert or die, Spain is sending armed men overseas with the number 1 reason being "God". This sounds exactly like militarized missionary work, or a *"Salvation Army"*. Otherwise known as spreading the faith of the cross by the strength of the sword. But what about that second G, Gold? What did they want the gold for, where they just covetous of metallic money? Do you know what happened to the first shipment of gold the Spaniards brought back from America? The first gold shipment was brought back by Christopher Columbus, given to the Spanish rulers Ferdinand and Isabella and given to the Spanish Roman Catholic Pope Alexander VI. Then Pope Alexander VI ordered that the first gold to be brought from America be used to gild the ceiling of the famous Papal basillica Santa Maria Maggiore. So the first gold shipment ever taken from America was used to beautify the ceiling of a Catholic Church in Rome. Thus when historians stress that the early explorers went to America seeking gold, you must remember that gold they found and stole was being used to make churches more extravagent. Money and consumerism was not the primary motivation for getting the gold, they got the gold in order to build fancier churches which were only built to inspire the same placebo faith feelings the holy land tourist traps inspired. The colonization of the Americas was almost entirely done for religious reasons with the resources being sought for the sake of Christianity.

Anyways without dispute the majority of Europe at the time of Columbus was Catholic and trade with the Middle East and Far East was increasing since the fall of the Byzantine empire as trade flourished under the Ottoman Empire. Yet everyone is always taught exploration was done in order to trade with Asia. If that is the case then why were further expeditions launched after Columbus didn't find much gold or spices and the native Americans were far less wealthy than the "Indians" were expected to be? To find the answer we have to look before Columbus to the original European Christian explorers. Spain was not the trailblazer of

European exploration, Portugal was. In the 1420s CE, 70 years before Columbus' voyage, Henrique of Portugal, later known as "Henry the Navigator", launched a program to explore the west coast of Africa, it wasn't for trading reasons. Without going into a history of Portugal, suffice it to say the Kingdom of Portugal was established by the Crusader Alphonso Henriques in 1139 CE and was cemented by the conquests of the 2nd Crusade in 1147 CE. Basically Portugal, the trailblazer of exploration, was an original Crusader state explicitly created by Crusaders; so trading was not their national interest or primary motivation for exploration. In 1412 CE at the age of 17 Henrique requested that his father King John conquer the Muslim island of Ceuta, Africa which his father later did in 1415 CE after 3 years of planning. However the invasion was nearly aborted because prior to departing Portugal experienced plague during which the Queen Philippa died. The expedition was set to be cancelled but as her dying wish the Queen requested they invade and kill the Muslims for the sake of Christ. Queen Philippa had a piece of the alleged "True Cross" she wore on her neck and on her death bed she broke it into 4 pieces and gave a piece to her husband and sons for them to wear in the battle and in future battles against the Muslims. Later the young prince Henrique was so zealous when fighting the Muslims that despite the Battle of Ceuta only lasting less than 1 day, because the Muslims were surprised and surrendered, he got wounded in it. So you really must wonder what kind of warrior Prince Henry the Navigator was to get wounded in a battle where the enemy surrendered and fled on day 1. Henrique was then appointed governor of Ceuta. In 1419 CE Henrique led an expedition to explore the coast of Africa. This exploration was intended to establish ties between Portugal and the fabled Christian ruler called "Prester John" who was thought to be in control of a Christian kingdom inside Africa or India who would be a valuable ally to wage war against Muslims. A popular legend emerged in the 1100s CE that one of the 3 kings/magi who had visited Jesus pbuh when he was born had a modern descendant called "Prestor John" who became King in "the East". Allegedly the 3 Kings/Magi were Hindu and then converted Hindus to Christianity upon their return. It was rumored that Prestor John ruled in the original Garden of Eden or that the Fountain of Youth was in his land and he had become immortal. Others said that the Christian

Kingdom of Prestor John was so rich that the people used golden tiles for thatching their roofs. Prestor John was also said to have a "Magic Mirror" that showed him everything that was happening in the world and told him exactly what God/Christ wanted him to do. He was also thought to be John the Presbyter mentioned by Eusebius who was thought to have written 2 epistles of John that made it into the bible. (Yet today most Christians think the epistles of John were written by the same author who wrote the gospel of John, and think Jesus pbuh only had one disciple named John but that's not what Christians thousands of years ago thought.) Naturally medieval Christians really wanted to meet this epic Prester John character, whoever he was. As long as he was a Christian ruler in Africa or India he seemed like the perfect candidate to ally with to destroy the Muslims. In 1165 CE the Byzantine Emperor Manuel I claimed to have received a letter from Prestor John as did the German Crusader King Frederick Barbarossa but today we don't know what these letters actually said because so many different versions exist it is impossible to determine authenticity. Nontheless Pope Alexander III saw it fit to write a letter to Prestor John himself, but nobody knows if he ever got it or where it got mailed to. In 1221 CE the knights returning from the failed 5th crusade told people that the descendant of Prestor John, King David of India, was planning to fight the Muslims and retake the Holy Land and had already conquered Persia and was about to conquer Baghdad. In the late 1290s CE Marco Polo then regaled Christians with tales that Prestor John was still alive and lived in the Mongolian empire. Others believed Prestor John was a forefather of Genghis Khan or that Genghis Khan was Prestor John, and since the Mongols had Nestorian Christians living amongst them with influence in the Mongol court that practically confirmed it according to medieval media. To some every Khan ruler was Prestor John or at least he served as someone who could play the role they dreamed Prestor John would play, which is why Christians tried to ally with the Mongols to fight the Muslims and destroy Islam. William Shakespeare even wrote about Prester John in one of his plays. Prior to Prestor John most Christians were apocalypticists expecting Jesus pbuh to come back any minute, after the search for Prestor John ended Christians returned to being apocalypticists. Fundamentally Christians are always hoping some leader in their lifetime comes to rule them and convert all of the non-Christians by the sword, most just hope that its Jesus pbuh others are frighteningly more practical. It was to find Prestor John and team up with him that Christians wanted to get to India. Don't let anyone ever tell you differently, if they try then they either don't know about the legend of Prestor John or if they do know they are lying to your face. Finding Prestor John was the reason and hope for most Christians when going on foreign journeys, from peasant, trader, King and Chaplain. Prestor John was like the medieval Santa Claus except to get his gift of Muslim bloodshed some good Christian had to find him. Marco Polo was even looking for Prestor John and that's why he traveled. For 600 years from the 11th to the 17th century Christian Europe searched for Prestor John but never found him, today one finds many of them but they have Muslim names and rule over Muslim lands. Prince Henrique of Portugal, as well as others, made it their life mission to ally with Prestor John in order to destroy Islam and the Muslims. In 1420 CE Prince Henrique was made governor and grand master of the infamous "*Order of the Knights of Christ*". This order was the new name for the Templar Knights in Portugal. As a state founded by

Crusader knights, when the Pope gave orders in 1312 CE for the Templars to be destroyed Portugal refused to comply and instead the Templars reorganized and renamed themselves as the "*Order of the Knights of Christ*" in 1319 CE. Two other militant Christian orders existed in Portugal, known as the "Order of Santiago" and the "Order of Aviz". Henrique's father and king, John I, belonged to the "Order of Aviz". Ever thirsty for Muslim blood in 1432 CE Henrique planned expeditions to conquer Morocco. His father, King John, thought Henrique's plan to conquer Morocco was unrealistic but because he believed Christ was on his side John accepted Henrique's proposal, then John died in 1433 CE. Henrique's older brother Edward became the King and he called off the invasion saying it was impractical and doomed to fail. In 1435 CE Henrique finally got somebody else to agree to his plan, his younger brother Ferdinand. Ferdinand was a member of the "Order of Aviz". Together they told their brother/King Edward that they were going to invade Muslim Morocco whether he liked it or not and he could either help them or watch them. So King Edward relented and supported the planned invasion, despite 3 other royal brothers insisting they be legally recorded as opposing

Henrique and Ferdinand's plan. In September 1436 CE Pope Eugenius IV sanctioned the invasion and said all who participated would be entitled to the same rewards as if it were a Crusade to Jerusalem, he also sent a piece of the "True Cross" which Henrique would use as a symbol by which to lead his army. In 1437 CE Henrique, Ferdinand and their army, famously began the invasion carrying the Pope's piece of the "True Cross" before them and laid siege to Tangiers attacking 5 points of the city simultaneously(the 5 point plan was because Jesus allegedly had 5 wounds on the "true cross"). However the city did not fall and the invaders returned to their camp as the siege continued. On October 3rd, 1437 CE Portugese soldiers reported seeing a large white cross in the sky, which they took to be a sign of divine favor and imminent victory. So after building new siege equipment on the 4th, Henrique and the troops assaulted the walls a second time but they were driven back before they could even reach the walls. Shortly thereafter the Portugese army was roundly defeated by the Muslims and surrounded so they negotiated a peace treaty. As part of the peace treaty, in exchange for the Muslims allowing the Portugese invaders to withdraw unharmed and unarmed

Henrique agreed to return the island of Ceuta to Morocco. As collateral until Ceuta was transferred to Muslim authorities it was agreed that Henrique's younger brother Ferdinand would remain in the company of Muslims as a prisoner to be released after Ceuta was returned while the Muslim leader Salah ibn Salah's son would remain with Henrique until after they evacuated Morocco safely. Another clause of the treaty was that Portugal promised 100 years of peace between Morocco and all the Muslim nations of North Africa. After returning with his troops to Ceuta, then eventually in disgrace to Portugal Henrique decided he was not going to be giving Ceuta back to the Muslims, nor would he be returning Salah ibn Salah's son as he promised and Henrique believed it was better to abandon his and the king's brother Ferdinand than to give the Muslims back their island. However neither Henrique nor Edward told their brother Ferdinand they were abandoning him and Ferdinand would send them letters asking why he hasn't been released yet and why Ceuta was not returned as they had agreed last time he saw Henrique. Thus it was from 1437 CE until 1443 CE, Ferdinand remained in Muslim captivity while the Muslims waited for Henrique to transfer Ceuta as he promised and waited for Salah ibn Salah's son to be returned as he was supposed to have been. Then the depressed Ferdinand's health declined and he died in 1443 CE. Portugal then labeled Ferdinand as a saintly martyr and in the future would use him dying in captivity as an excuse for them to attack Morocco in 1458 CE thereby making that 100 year peace agreement in reality last only 21 years. However Henrique's life mission to find Prestor John and convert Africa to Christianity was not to come true, because since according to his maps Prestor John was in Abyssinia and none of the rivers Henrique explored in West Africa led to Abyssinia. Henrique realized he would have to go under/around Africa to reach Prestor John in order to team up and exterminate the Muslims. This "Good Hope" of Henrique needed better ships to become reality, so he commissioned Portugal to copy the Muslim ship sails and improve the Portugese fleet so future generations may achieve his dream. In 1488 CE, after failing to find this mythical Christian kingdom , Portuguese ships rounded the southern tip of Africa and Europe learned that the Indian Ocean could be reached from the Atlantic. The southern tip of Africa was then named the "Cape of Storms" by Bartolemeu

Dias when it was "discovered" by him in 1488 CE. However King John II of Portugal renamed it as the "Cape of Good Hope". The son of Bartolemeu, Antonio Dias, was a member of the "*Order of the Kinghts of Christ*". Historical records maintain that even after Columbus' voyage Portugal continued sending ships around the cape of Africa, which some historians mistakenly maintain was strictly for trade. Although you might be wondering why if Portugal was so keen on exploring did they refuse to fund the expedition of Columbus? The answer to that is because the famous explorer Pêro da Covilhã said not to. Who was Pêro da Covilhã? He was the Portugese explorer who reached Ethiopia, the land of the legend of Prester John. The Portugese goal was to find Prestor John so they could team up and fight the Muslims to extinction. Since Ethiopia was the Christian state of Africa and Pêro da Covilhã had been there and allied with the Emperor Eskender he told Portugal that the goal had been achieved and while the Ethiopian King fell short of their expectations there was no need to go to India to search for Prestor John until they tried the joint military conquest with Ethiopia first. Funding Columbus would just waste money that could be used on the Portugese military in it's upcoming war against the Muslims. The highlight of Emperor Eskender's reign was when he sacked the Muslim city of Dakkar, of the Adel Sultanate in 1478 CE; long before he ever met the Portugese. Eskender was born in 1471 CE and became Emperor in 1478 CE. Meaning in his first year as ruler, at the age of 6 he massacred the capital of a Muslim nation. So Portugal loved this king and he was who they dreamed of finding as ruler of Ethiopia. However even in Eskender's shining moment he was kind of a loser King, because while returning from his massacre the Muslim army led by Muhammad ibn Azhar ad-Deen attacked and defeated him. Although not expecting the King to be 6 years old, they let him escape assuming he was a innocent kid, but Eskender later said he only escaped the Muslims because angels helped him to do so.

Fortunately other historical records relate events which also prove trading wasn't the reason Columbus went sailing. The famous Vasco Da Gama was one such Portugese explorer, he belonged to the "*Order of Santiago*" and then changed clubs in order to join the "*Order of the Knights of Christ*". In 1497 CE, on his very first crusading/exploring voyage, something very special happened to Vasco Da Gama's crew which changed medical history forever. Upon rounding the "Cape of Good Hope" Vasco Da Gama's crew contracted the 1st ever recorded case of naval scurvy. Prior to reaching India, Da Gama landed at Mozambique in East Africa and was mistaken as a Muslim by the sultan, who was going to provide Da Gama a pilot as a guide to India. When it was discovered they were Christians trying to create alliances for future crusades, the sultan refused to give Da Gama a guide and Da Gama left after bombarding the town, with 2 confirmed casualties as a result of his attack. Next Da Gama went to Mombasa and looted the Muslim trading vessels which were unarmed. After that Da Gama went to Malindi where the people were at war with those of Mombasa, so they treated him with friendliness as he proved himself to be an enemy of their enemy. At Malindi Da Gama got a guide to India but the faith of this guide is unknown and it's unclear whether they knew why Da Gama wanted to get to India. Thus for Da Gama's first voyage to India he ended up going straight to the Malabar Coast. The very same Malabar Coast from where the Hindu King Chakrawati Farmas set out on his journey to meet Muhammad pbuh and then gave orders to establish a masjid there and advised his people to become Muslim. So the Christian Crusader Vasco Da Gama searching for another Christian king to fight Muslims, actually landed on the right place Christians used to be, except they had been Muslims for over 800 years. So he was a little late and at the wrong place if he wanted to find people to fight Muslims. On May 20, 1498 CE Da Gama anchored at Calcutta, a man was sent ashore to investigate and went to a Muslim merchant from Tunisia. Da Gama's man was asked "*What the devil brought you here?*" and he replied "*We came in search of Christians and spices*", notice his first response was they came in search of Christians; spices were a secondary concern. This statement implies the European exploration was done for religious reasons more than economic, as many are taught today. The economic reasons themselves weren't to gain cheaper prices for spices, because <u>the shipping costs would make them more expensive for the consumer than if they bought directly from the Ottomans. Economically it made no sense to have a direct trade route with India or Asia. The reason Europeans wanted to trade directly with Indians, even though it would be more expensive, was because they didn't want to buy spices from Muslims</u>; they were waging economic warfare. You might think this is farfetched, but this is the true history behind the age of exploration, history isn't always pretty. There were many spices in Calcutta, but few Christians. Da Gama mistakenly assumed the Hindus were Christians because their rituals are so similar. Yes Hindus were still there despite Muslims having been there for centuries. Da Gama thought the Hindu temples were churches, thinking that the idols of Hindu goddesses were statues of the virgin Mary and that the other Hindu gods were venerable Christian saints. Plus it had been rumored that Christians had been in India since the time of "Doubting Thomas" but since Europeans didn't know those Christians became Muslims, Da Gama assumed the Hindus were just a different Indian denomination of Christians. Da Gama was surprised when the Hindu King didn't want to form an alliance or trade with the Christian state of Portugal to the exclusion of all Muslim traders, especially since Muslims included a sizable portion of his population. During his stay Vasco Da Gama witnessed vast fleets of Muslim traders coming in and out of port and he noticed they were all unarmed. This was the standard practice in the Indian Ocean at that time because there was no dominant military power. The different ports competed with each other offering low tariffs in order to increase trade. If a particular port mistreated foreign merchants the local merchants would then lose business, since the foreign traders would go to a port that was safe with better business. Therefore unarmed trade was the normal way of doing business. Although Portugal didn't want free trade, they wanted to dominate trade in the Indian Ocean and put the Muslims out of business. To curry favor with the Hindu King Da Gama gave him lavish gifts. Yet the Muslims realizing where Da Gama wanted this relationship to go and hearing of what Da Gama had done to the Muslims on the way to India told the Hindu King that Da Gama was nothing but a pirate and no good-willed peaceful ambassador as he claimed. Shortly after Da Gama returned to Portugal another expedition was sent in 1500 CE led by Pedro Alvarez Cabral, who was also a member of the *"Order of the Knights of Christ"*. Cabral landed in modern day Brazil and claimed it for Portugal, sending one ship back to give news to the king, while the fleet then went to Calicut where he set up a Portugese factory. Cabral then sailed away and captured unarmed Muslim ships taking about 600 people captive. As a result Muslims seized and killed 40 Portuguese merchants in the town. So Cabral captured more Muslim ships and burned them while their crew was still onboard, then bombarded Calicut for two days before sailing to Cochin and Cannanore, whose rulers agreed to trade with Portugal fearing what would happen if they refused. After this Pedro Alvarez Cabral sailed back to Portugal hailed as a hero, since he eliminated Muslim trade in Cochin and Cannanore. Vasco Da Gama, not wanting to be outdone, led an expedition pillaging the eastern coast of Africa. On the way he captured a ship called the "Mir" which was transporting over 400 Muslim pilgrims on their way from Calicut to Mecca, including 50 women and an ambassador from Egypt. The Muslims offered to pay him ransom in gold and jewels so much that he could afford to free all Christian slaves in the Kingdom of Fez and more besides that. Although instead of taking their money or accepting a ransom, Da Gama decided to burn the ship with all the Muslims inside including their jewels and gold. This indicates that his voyages were not about money or getting rich, as modern history books tend to say, they were clearly about war against Muslims. Da Gama just wanted to kill Muslims, he didn't want their money, Muslim blood was his motivation. Logically Da Gama could've at least taken the Muslim's money before burning them but he didn't, because he didn't want to be viewed as a pirate since he was a Christian. Afterwards Da Gama sent a letter to the Hindu King of Calicut informing him of the "good news". In India Da Gama burned and bombarded towns until they promised to only trade with Portugal and not to trade with Muslims, after agreeing the port would be given a "cartaz" or a trading permit. This was the beginning of the extortion tactics later made famous by the mafia. Da Gama then went back to Calicut and rebuked the Hindu ruler for "siding with the Muslims" against Cabral and letting the Muslims harm the Portugese in retaliation for Cabral's attack on the Muslims when Portugal considered the Hindu King to be their ally. To Portugal his behavior was not befitting, especially when they were doing big business with and in his city. Portugal found it to be a serious offense that he didn't side with them against Muslims and they threatened him with economic punishment if he were to maintain such a "hostile uncooperative attitude". Therefore Da Gama offered to renegotiate peace with the Hindu King on condition that he expel all Muslims from Calicut. The Hindu King said he wants peace but he's not going to kick the Muslims out of the city. So Da Gama bombarded Calicut for 2 days and all trade on the entire Malabar coast stopped. Da Gama also sank and looted the Muslim vessels he came across. It is recorded that he once used Muslim prisoners for crossbow practice and would cut off the hands, noses and ears of the "missed targets", their body parts were sent ashore in a boat while the people themselves were burned to death on their own ships. This was Vasco Da Gama's standard policy when it came to Muslims, because they were Muslims and he was a Christian. Violence was used to maintain the "cartaz system" and King Manuel ordered Muslim ships traveling between the Red sea and India to be harassed so that, *"everyone in India would lose the illusion of being able to trade with anyone but us."* King Manuel, like Henry the Navigator was also a "Grand Master" of the *"Order of the Knights of Christ"*. Christian Royalty such as James I and Charles I further attempted to establish an anti-Muslim trade by giving European and American pirates "licenses to steal" from Muslim vessels in the Red sea, Persian gulf and Coromandel coast. Europe let pirates plunder Muslim vessels unhindered as long as they didn't bother European ships. This is similar to the international community today causing uproar in response to genocide in areas of economic value, while ignoring ongoing extermination when Muslims are dying in places of little international economic significance. The pirate James Plaintain got rich off raids in the gulf of Aden and became king of Madagascar, through bloody force. Madagascar became notorious as a pirate kingdom as it was close to the Red sea and the Arabian gulf. In November 1694 CE the pirate Thomas Tew of the Amity received a commission from Governor Fletcher of New York for 300 British pounds specifically to loot middle eastern ships in the Red sea. Fredrick Philips actually ran a piracy business robbing Muslim ships, he became the richest man in colonial New York and owned a 21 mile estate along the Hudson river. This pirate Frederick Phillips, who preyed on Muslims, built the Old Dutch Church of Sleepy Hollow in 1697 CE and had his name engraved on the silver chalice they used for the sacrament of Communion. It was common for pirates to loot pilgrims on their way to and from Mecca. The pirate crew of Henry Every once slaughtered and raped pilgrims returning from Mecca in two ships called the "Fateh Mohammed" and "Gang-i-Sawai". Non-Muslim historians refer to this time period as the "*Golden Age of Piracy*". It overlaps the "*Age of Exploration*". With the timeline being "*The Crusades*"-"*The Inquisition*"-"*The Age of Exploration*"-"*The Golden Age of Piracy*". Guess what came next? Colonization and Imperialsim followed by WWI, WWII, the creation of Israel, the Cold War to determine which new religion would replace Christianity, leading to the "*Global war on terror*". But remember "*The Crusades*" allegedly ended a long long long time ago.

Eventually as Christendom grew in size and strength it was no longer sufficient to simply isolate the Muslim world from the international economy. Thus the colonization of Africa and the middle east began. The geopolitical relations in those regions have been screwed up ever since, somewhat owing to the colonizers drawing national borders mainly for ascetic reasons without regard to actual geography, culture, religion or population. From 1460-1462 CE Pope Pius II ordered a boycott of Turks and "infidels", linguistically an infidel is anyone who believes something differently than you, in order to put economic pressure on the Muslims. Unlike many other Popes, Pius II lived a very frugal lifestyle and his personal expenditure as

Pope was the lowest out of them all. Do you know why? It was not because of piety, he just hated the Muslims so much he wanted every penny to be spent on a Crusade against them so he lived as cheaply as possible to spend more money on a Crusade. A month after he became Pope he called a Council inviting the kings and princes of Europe to coordinate as part of his Crusade. Yet by this time Europe was a little weary of crusades and surprisingly the Pope did not have support from the clergy. This was because Pius II said that cardinals, bishops and priests would also have to pay money out of their salary for the crusade. However due to Papal authority nearly everybody paid financial support and Pope Pius II decreed that every Christian would pay 1/30th (3.33%) of their income for his Crusade and all Jews would pay 1/20th (5%) of their income while all clergy would pay 1/10th (10%). Which might sound like a small % today but these were considered large amounts to pay back then, the clergy were so upset that the Pope said they had to give up 10% of their income they opposed him saying how he was crazy and tyrannical. Makes you wonder what they would say if they saw the average government's tax code today. They'd probably say that only the devil would dare demand that much. Nevertheless Pope Pius II persisted, bought a papal fleet and sailed himself to personally lead the crusade. Yes, this Pope Pius II was personally going to be the General of the Crusader army. When we talk about religious wars, that's almost as religious as you can get without having a prophet or the antichrist involved. In 1461 CE Pius II sent a letter to Muhammad II, the Sultan of Turkey, requesting him to convert Christianity and promising that if he did so then West and East could unite under his rulership and there would be world peace and if he would just convert to Christianity the Pope would declare him Emperor of the world. In response Muhammad II didn't reply. In 1462 CE rich deposits of alum were found in papal soil at Tolfa which made the papal states the richest government in Italy giving Pius II even more money for his crusade. On June 18, 1464 CE, Pope Pius II took the cross of a crusader and sailed to Ancona to await the rest of his army before marching into combat against the Muslims. However the Milanese troops never came, those from Florence had useless equipment, the Venetian fleet got the plague and it caused them to get delayed. Still Pius II believed God was on his side so he waited and on August 14,

1464 CE he saw the Venetian Armada arrive. Suddenly Pope Pius II died on the spot. The very second he saw his long dreamed of Crusader army was ready he died. Then Venice decided that this Crusade against the Muslims was probably not a good idea given the plague they got and the Pope/General dying when they arrived. So the Crusaders dispersed and the crusade collapsed, almost. The super Crusade of Pope Pius II actually involved another infamous character from history known as Vlad III from Wallachia, in Romania; also known most popularly as Dracula. Dracula was a crusader who fought on behalf of Pope Pius II, but that is a whole other story. Shortly summarized the cross or "holy water" are not weapons to use against Dracula, on the contrary Dracula venerated crosses and likely used "holy water" himself. Dracula impaled 33,000 Muslims. He impaled their dead bodies inserting long poles through their butts, through their guts emerging through their mouths. He lined 23,000 dead impaled Muslims along the road to his capital. Eventually when the Muslims defeated Dracula they beheaded his dead body and impaled his severed head just like how he impaled 33,000 Muslims. This way people could see that the evil Dracula was truly dead so no one would mistakenly think Dracula would come back to slaughter Muslims. Today part of the myth of Dracula is that to kill him you must behead him, well that's exactly what the Muslims did. Scientifically speaking, getting beheaded is the least painful way to die. So even when Muslims took revenge upon Dracula, it was done for justice not to take pleasure in causing pain; Allah will cause him pain in the afterlife. God-willing by writing this it will kill the myth of Dracula and replace it with the truth. Dracula was killed by Muslims who were waging jihad. I mention this so you can realize firsthand how distorted our view of history is. When you think of Dracula you don't tend to think of him as a Christian Crusader funded by the Pope fighting Muslims, because the writers of history and the special interests of today for whatever reason do not want people to know the truth about Dracula, who he was, what he did or that the Muslims rid the world of the Christian monster Dracula. When you carefully think about it, the fable and myths about Dracula reveal the truth. Dracula is said to drink human blood in order to live forever, while Christians drink wine which some literally consider to be the blood of the human Jesus pbuh, others think it's symbolic, thinking it gives them eternal life. In one sense the Eucharist ritual is an act of vampirism. Just as we have been lied to about Dracula we have been lied to about many other people and things in history. For instance when you hear the name of Pope Pius II, do you think of a Pope who would starve himself to save money for a Crusade and was the top general of a Crusader army himself? That's the truth. Sometimes the gritty uncensored reality is actually more frightening than the fiction.

History is important because it influences future decisions and is used as propaganda to justify criminal actions. When what the masses believe to be true affects the actual truth, then what will be true in the future becomes entirely uncertain, because we cannot know in the present what beliefs we will eventually have or else we would already have them. It matters what people believe about the past. For instance had Americans thought it was wrong for America to invade Iraq and bomb it to bits in 1991 CE then perhaps America wouldn't have done it again in 2003 CE, but many Americans felt the past was the past and it didn't matter what they believed about it since it already happened. That indifferent view of the past effected their present actions when it was 2003 CE and affected the future. Had Americans never entered WWI or any war after that and followed George Washington's plan of international isolation the world today could be a very different place. That is why it is important to know the truth about what really happened and how things came to be the way they are today, because in the near future the time we are living in now will be seen as history and it will not be seen accurately. As you read this some people are creating a false version of what the world is like today for future generations to be taught to believe. This is happening while the people of today ignore worldwide events and constantly busy themselves with entertainment. Historians in the future will try to distort our history and if we don't care about knowing the truth in our present time, or the truth of what happened in the past, then we place ourselves into danger. Many people are actively burying the truth about our present so thoroughly that even archaeologists won't be able to uncover it. Never forget we have an enemy Satan who wants us to live in hell forever. If we start to believe lies about this or about that, small ones and big ones, then eventually we won't be able to tell what is true and what is false. A person in that condition is guaranteed to be led astray by Satan to hell unless Allah guides them and saves them from such a fate. This is why I'm writing excessively on historical deceptions because they make peoples who have been historic oppressors think they are the good guys and that their actions are pleasing to God. Do you really think the people joining the Nazi political party in Germany during 1919 CE would have considered themselves evil or monstrous? They thought they were good hardworking Germans that shouldn't be forced to pay for the whole cost of WWI since many hadn't even supported the war nor participated in it. Whereas the result with the ancient vote for the "lesser of two evils" gimmick always results in evil, as the Jews found out after voting for Hitler. Today we say those Jews were fools and technically Jews shouldn't complain about Hitler because they voted for him to be in power, so they got who they voted for. Keep in mind Hitler's slogan was "Freedom and prosperity!" and his official goal was *"the union of all Germans"*, all meant and included Jews. Most at the time would not believe Hitler could be evil, even the Jews because almost everything he said sounded perfectly good and right. Truly if Adolf Hitler ran for political office today in any "democratic country" with a different name and face, he would win and become a leader cleanly because of the support of "good people". Ignorant people wonder how Hitler could come to power when he was so bad, but the way he came to power is the same exact way every single politician comes to power in democratic countries. However rather than demonize the game that created this opportunity for evil to occur, they demonize the individual and the symbols rather than the game, because today most countries are playing the same game but they are just playing it a lot better than Hitler did. The bad guys are never deemed to be bad guys until they lose the game. Nazis thought voting for Adolf Hitler was a good thing to do and that he truly was a good guy, millions of smart people believed this wholeheartedly. Although modern history depicts these Nazis as some of the most wicked and stupid humans to have ever existed. Future generations could depict you and I in the same way Nazis are portrayed today. Yet God knows the truth and that is what we will be judged by. Just as some good people can be portrayed as evil, some evil people can be portrayed as good. Therefore when there is a holiday for some historical "good guy", the truth may be that he was evil and damned by God, by celebrating or praising this person you would be praising someone whom God may hate. Someone who loves God does not praise or think well of an enemy of God whether they are living or dead. Going back to Dracula, some Romanians today consider Vlad the Impaler a national hero and are proud of Dracula. If we knew the truth about our ancestors or peers we would be less likely to blindly follow them and would choose to follow who was good not who was wrong. Because our history books tell us that we have always been the "good guys" then we cannot recognize when we are doing evil. Although whether we recognize it in this life or not, we will be brought to account for our deeds and judged accordingly by our Creator. We won't be able to blame our history books, culture or teachers and say to God as a response: *"But I was taught we were the good guys! I had good intentions! I was a good person! Everyone told me I was good! How come I'm getting punished in hell forever?"* Never consider knowing the truth about history to be unimportant because your personal history will determine where you will spend eternity. Don't be deceived about yourself. If you honestly study history you will realize that everything that has happened in this world has something to do with religion, or religious implications and effects on morality. Satan has always been on one side or the other, sometimes even both sides playing humans against each other. This is another reason why it's important to know the truth, because then we can recognize the tricks of Satan and how he influences politics and people causing wars for no reason. A secular attitude towards history disguises our enemy. If you can't recognize Satan in the past then how will you be able to recognize Satan in the present? Afterall most people would vote for Hitler just due to his flyer alone, if it were published today with different dates and names. Today people in general are no better, they are actually worse. So I repeat if you can't recognize Satan in the past then how will you be able to recognize Satan in the present? If you cannot recognize your enemy, Satan, then you are sure to be defeated. Our history is "his story", the story of Satan misleading mankind and tricking us into creating the sinful environments that we live in today. In our present time Satan wants you, me and the rest of humanity to pave the roads to hell for future generations. Satan usually gets the "good guys" to do more evil than the "bad guys" do, because when thinking you are a "good guy" you work harder. Thus Satan doesn't want any "bad guys" working for him. Satan gets most of his evil done by "good guys" with good intentions. The "good guys" are a reason the world is as bad as it is today. Most historical heroes go to hell. Only God can define "good". If you don't use God's definition of good then you will go to hell.

    The previously mentioned crusade of Pope Pius II against the Ottomans is thought to have been motivated by the Venetians. During this crusade the Venetians pressured the Vatican to make it a sin for Christians to do any business or trade with any non-Christians, specifically Muslims. However the embargo was limited to the Ottomans. Drastically in 1464 Pope Paul II made the "sin" of trading in Turkish Alum to be tantamount to excommunication meaning if you bought from the Muslims you were automatically apostate from Christianity. Since the boycotted Ottoman empire was quite vast in the 15th century CE <u>this is the reason why Europe wanted to discover a route to the East to trade directly with Asia</u>. It was because of economic sanctions due to Christian religious prejudice against Muslims. <u>The Pope made it a sin to trade with the Muslim Ottomans</u>. This was because the more Christians in Europe interacted with Muslims and learned about Islam their hate for them vanished and Christians actually started choosing to become Muslims, depriving the Papacy from profits and power. For example when Christian knights saw how Muslims all had access to the Quran as individuals, it revolutionized the European world in their desire to finally break the rules the papacy set limiting biblical readership to clergy and once everyone had access to the bibles then everyone had their own interpretation and made their own denomination. Basically Christians splintered theologically because they saw all Muslims could access their sacred text and they wanted that too, and once they got it they had schism after schism. Thus though most crusaders rejected Islam their exposure to Islam and Muslims led them to reject their own falsehood that they were crusading for in the first place. This is the same reason certain people in Western nations today want Muslims to leave their nation. Medieval Christian Europe was faced with 2 options, either they disobey the Pope and trade with the Ottomans or they find a way to trade with Asia directly even though the shipping costs would make Asian goods more expensive. Some didn't obey the pope and as expiation for the sin of trading with Muslims the "indulgences" scheme was invented. This is something many Christians are ignorant of, in that the main reason renaissance era Christians paid for indulgences was not simply to buy a place in paradise or fund extravagant church construction, it was because they were conditioned to believe trading with Muslims was such a severe crime that they needed to pay expiation for it in order to remain Christians. Protestantism is commonly thought to exist as a primary result of opposition to the indulgence system. The European Christian world was forced to do 1 of 3 things: Trade with Muslims and apostate from Christianity as they knew it, pay the expiatory indulgence fees for trading with Muslims becoming poor or find a way to trade with Asia that didn't involve Muslims. The islamophobic Christian rulers also wanted to pincer the Islamic world so they could attack it from all sides. However when the Christians conquered Spain they found out from maps that Muslims had colonies in America, realizing they could isolate and annihilate those Muslims while the Muslim world would be too distant to prevent them. Afterwhich the Americas could become a Christian colonial territory to develop and increase their numbers until they were strong enough to overwhelm the

Muslims in Africa and the Middle East. This is why the early colonists were Christian extremists like Conquistadores, Pilgrims and Puritans. Queen Isabella even made a law requiring all Spaniards who went to the "New World" to prove their family had been Catholic for at least 4 generations. Although to be fair many Christian extremists stayed in Europe, though silly as it may sound some Christians said that it was sinful to travel to America because America was not mentioned in the bible. However most Christians insisted that to convert the heathens and win the crusades it was necessary to go, it was just a matter of whether they should root out the heretics in Europe first or not. Then when some of those heretics fled to America it made their decision easy. Basically the Crusades and the Inquisition were exported to the Americas. Then the plan became even more diabolic when they realized they could enslave the Muslims from Africa and isolate them in the Americas, thereby weakening the Muslim nations while forcing the Muslim slaves' children to convert.

In the 1490s CE Christopher Columbus actually landed on the same spot which we know of today as Guantanamo Bay. In 1493 CE Columbus wrote in his diary "*The women here dress in the cotton clothing that is similar to what the Muslim women wear in Granada."* and on top of that Columbus even wrote about a masjid he found that existed then in what is modern day Cuba. The reason you haven't learned about the Muslims being in America before Columbus is because after the Christians came the American Muslims were killed and Christian Europe didn't want the world to know that the Muslims were there before they were, so they tried to eliminate all the records, but they failed. Christopher Columbus, while a Genoan, moved to Portugal in the 1470s and enrolled at Henry the Navigator's school of Navigation. In 1479 CE Columbus married a Portugese woman allegedly descended from Queen Philippa. He met her at a monastic convent for Catholic nuns where he would attend church services. Her name was Philipa Moniz Perestrelo and as a member of the "Order of Santiago" her marriage had to be approved by King John II (the great-nephew of Henrique) who at the time was acting as regent King in his father's stead. Following in Henrique's footsteps Columbus also became a member of the "*Order of the Knights of Christ*" even though they had declined in popularity and the "Order of Santiago" was superseding them. The son of Christopher Columbus, Diego, became the Governor of Santo Domingo (which is modern day Dominican Republic) and owned a large sugar plantation staffed by imported Muslim slaves captured from the Woff Empire in West Africa. In 1522 CE the first African/Muslim slave revolt in the Americas took place on Diego Columbus' plantation in Santo Domingo. The Muslims revolted, escaped and established a Muslim state in the mountains and formed a confederacy with other slaves who revolted and escaped who made their own states. This slave confederacy was called "the Maroons" they intermarried with the natives and waged war against the colonizers. In 1501 CE Christopher Columbus claimed to be the Messiah prophesied by the Calabrian Abbot Joachim. Yes you read that correctly, Christopher Columbus proclaimed himself to be the Messiah. He thought he had found a place for missionaries to make into a Crusader continent and ushered in a "new kingdom". Columbus then began to call Christians to participate in a "last crusade" that was to be the climax of history before the end of time, but then he died. However before dying Christopher Columbus wrote a "Book of Prophecies" wherein he explained how all his discoveries perfectly fulfilled biblical prophecy and Columbus told the world what has to happen and what they must do so Jesus Christ pbuh can return. The prime religious prophecies/commands of Columbus were as follows:

1. Christianity must spread to every spot on earth and most of the masses must be converted to Christianity, one way or another.

2. The Garden of Eden still exists, is on earth and must be found.

3. The Holy Land must be taken from the Muslims and all Muslims must be removed from it, until that happens Jesus pbuh can't return to the Holy Land because Muslims are there.

4. An Emperor of the World must rule over everyone, this is necessary for the final Crusade to win the Holy Land and the Emperor will be the first to meet Jesus pbuh when he returns.

Despite Columbus claiming to be a Messiah and having written his "Book of Prophecies" over 500 years ago, many today actually fully agree with the above points numbered 1, 3 and to a lesser degree 4. Some Christians even want Columbus to be declared a saint. Yet oddly enough most people never learn this side of Columbus nor that he was a false a prophet who wrote a "Book of Prophecies". Most just get told he was a jolly genius explorer who discovered America for everyone, and if they are "honest" they'll admit he killed and enslaved a few natives. They don't teach the fun, dark, disturbing and exciting truth in schools. Schools even make it boring to learn about Columbus. Even when schoolteachers say Columbus was bad, they make him seem good because he was so much worse than what they know and they don't even know the half of nearly everything they teach. Its truly criminal the way Columbus gets portrayed even by his detractors who criticize him for his abuse of the natives. Most of those denouncing him are actually improving his image and in truth he was much worse than they think and say. Columbus is a man who is worse than the rumors allege. His oppression of Native Americans by the *"Knights of Columbus"* aside, the ignorance surrounding Christopher Columbus, as well as historical figures in general, and the glorified pedestal the masses put such persons on is shameful. In comparison prophets such as Lot, Moses, David, Solomon, Jesus and Muhammad pbut are slandered out of ignorance. It is evident that Satan has deceived the majority into having the wrong role models and heroes from history. Therefore we must be extra careful regarding celebrity figures whom the world adores today. A little too much enthusiasm plus a little lie from Satan and the next thing you know future generations will be wearing idols of that person around their neck thinking they are some type of protection and one of the greatest persons who ever lived. Just ask a kid *"who do you idolize?"* The answer should be nobody because idolatry is abominable to God, but our children and ourselves have been led astray so far off the path that we can't even recognize idolatry even when we use the word idolize. Look at Christopher Columbus, how is it that a man who oversaw the slaughter, rape and enslavement of previously unknown nonthreatening peoples and claimed to be the Messiah, gets a holiday where kids and teachers take off each year and businesses close out of dedication to this ruthless inhumane crusader who proclaimed himself to be a prophet? People may call Columbus a fool incorrectly thinking he thought he landed in India, but they are even more foolish than they think Columbus was because they are clueless about Columbus. Why do you really think the capital of America is in Washington, D.C. ,

Maryland? (The District of Columbia) Then they dare to say "Columbus day" is a secular holiday? The man was a Catholic religious fanatic, one of the most fanatical in all of history even by the standards of fanatical eras. Columbus was a religious fanatic's fanatic who was employed by tyrannical fanatics and belonged to a fanatical cult and wrote a "Book of Prophecies"! But, "What does Columbus Day mean to you?" The only good thing about "Columbus day" is that kids are released from the brainwashing factory called public school, thereby giving the kids respite from the child abuse they endure in that institute for the academically insane. At the end of the day you really have to wonder who the bigger criminals are, the criminals of history or the ones who teach history ignorantly distorting and neglecting to report the truth about history or historical figures. One type makes history, the other type practically makes it up.

Ferdinand Magellan, the man known to have named the pacific ocean whose crew was the first to circumnavigate the earth, is another example of a Christian Explorer; with just as much ignorance about who he was and what he did. Firstly you should know that Ferdinand Magellan also belonged to the "*Order of the Knights of Christ*". In

1521 CE Magellan landed on a Muslim territory in the region which is called the Philippines today, the name of which comes from the Spanish King Phillip II meaning the islands of Phillip whereas Phillipinos literally means "Phillips people". Immediately upon stepping ashore Magellan placed a cross in the ground and declared it to be a Christian land. However Muslims were there and when Magellan told them to become Christian they told him no. They said it was their land since they were living there and it was not for sale nor was he welcome to stay after the stunt he just pulled. As a result Magellan went to nearby islands making alliances with pagan polytheists to team up against the Muslims. Then prior to the Battle of Machtan Island, Magellan and his men snuck around to the Muslims' homes and set them on fire hoping it would cause the Muslim army to go back to their homes and disperse, thereby dividing them so they could more easily be conquered. Yet the Muslim army stood their ground in unity, not caring their homes were on fire, ready to fight Magellan on the beach with their bamboo weapons in defense of Islam vs. the Christians' guns and steel. As Magellan and his troops charged the Muslims in the shallow water the Muslim fighters identified

Magellan and focused their attention on him. After he was wounded, Magellan fell facedown in the water and the Muslims pounced killing him before he could even step foot on the shore, after which the Christian soldiers retreated having been defeated. That is how the famous Ferdinand Magellan died, he was fighting Muslims trying to impose Christianity upon them by force. But don't expect Magellan's end to be part of the school curriculum even though he is a prominent subject of study. Schools don't want to make it seem as though history revolves around religion or anything, because then they might actually have to teach something about religion and they can't do that without violating the religious doctrines of Secularism and actually learning about religions themselves which would require them to not believe in Secularism in order to study. That's one core problem with the Americanist curriculum in that any who teach it can't actually learn much of anything unless it's technical and for practical application. But let's get back to history, not that we ever left, it's just that when discussing the past you have to tie it to the present because otherwise it's not relevant and there is no point in learning it. Unlike in other regions, the Christians were unable to roundly defeat the Muslims in the Philippines, so for centuries the Northern and Eastern regions which were primarily polytheist became Christian as the polytheists became Christian while the South remained Muslim. The Muslims were labeled "Moros", coming from the Spanish name for the Muslims of Andalus whom they called Moors, and the Muslim land was called BangsaMoro which literally meant "land of the Muslims". Then in 1896 CE when America went to war with Spain, they acquired the Philippine territory. Afterwhich they declared BangsaMoro was just a part of the Phillipines and claimed the whole archipelago as theirs. Which was illegal of course, but when has legality ever mattered when it came to American expansionism or the use of violent force to serve U.S. interests? To top it off and further prove the anti-islamic policy, U.S. General James Rusling publicly reported that the American President William Mckinley told him: "*I walked the floor of the White House night after night until midnight; and I am not ashamed to tell you, gentlemen, that* **I *went down on my knees and prayed Almighty God for light and guidance more than one night. And one night late it came to me this way — I don't know how it was, but it came***: (1) *That we could not give them back to Spain — that would be cowardly and dishonorable;* (2)

*that we could not turn them over to France and Germany – our commercial rivals in the Orient – that would be bad business and discreditable; (3) that <u>we could not leave them to themselves – they were unfit for self-government</u> – and they would soon have anarchy and misrule over there worse than Spain's was; and (4) that **<u>there was nothing left for us to do but to take them all, and to educate the Filipinos, and uplift and civilize and Christianize them</u>**, <u>and by God's grace do the very best we could by them, as our fellow-men for whom Christ also died</u>. And then I went to bed, and went to sleep, and slept soundly, and the next morning I sent for the chief engineer of the War Department (our mapmaker), and I told him to put the Philippines on the map of the United States (pointing to a large map on the wall of his office), and there they are, and there they will stay while I am President!"* Now I don't know about you, but to me that seems very much like what the Popes who launched the Crusades and promoted the enslaving of Africans and Native Americans had said to justify their crimes, and it also sounds similar to what George Bush said when saying that God told him to invade Afghanistan and Iraq. You don't think politicians recycle speeches made by previous historical figures do you? Could it be that history seems to rhyme because politicians plaigarize the past? To be clear the U.S. soldiers who were to enforce Mckinley's plans may not have wanted to "*Christianize them*" yet American policy seems to have been based on Christian Crusaderesque beliefs and goals nevertheless. But at the time the media didn't really promote the war policy in the Phillipines as a Christianization war at all. This religious motive was not expressed publicly but was only revealed by General James Rusling after Mckinley was assassinated. This is important to note because when the Bangsamoro Muslims first fought back against the U.S. the Muslim Khalifah in Turkey was persuaded to mediate peace between the Muslims and the American Government. After talking to the American diplomats he sent a message to the Muslims on the Philippine Islands forbidding them to enter into any hostilities against the Americans, "*in as much as no interference with their religion would be allowed under American rule*". So the Muslims stopped fighting and agreed to have peace, but then it became clear to them that despite what the American government was publicly telling the world, they were severely "interfering" with them practicing Islam. Thus they fought back again and the American government said: "*These people are just extremists because even their own Muslim Khalifah said not to fight us and they agreed not to. So they not only broke their word, but are going against what Islam teaches and what the leader of Muslims told them to do"*. However not even the Americans could beat the Muslims in Bangsamoro and U.S. soldiers would complain that they would shoot a native Muslim warrior 5 times filling him with bullets but they still kept fighting back. Therefore the U.S. government specifically asked U.S. gun manufacturers to create a special type of bullet in order to shoot the Muslims in the Philippines that could kill them with less shots. At the time the .41 caliber round was just a prototype in development, but that wasn't good enough for the U.S. soldiers and as a result the .45 caliber round was invented along with the .45 Colt revolver with the explicit purpose for them to be used by the U.S. military to kill Muslims in the Philippines. The U.S. brutality was so excessive against Muslims that even the famous American author Mark Twain denounced the U.S. military for glorifying the massacre of Muslim men, women and children at what they called the "Battle of Bud Dajo", also known as the Moro Crater Massacre since the U.S. soldiers fired artillery and what were the most advanced guns in the world upon Muslims with primitive weapons who were trapped by the military on top/inside of an unactive volcano crater. Twain expressed disgust that the U.S. troops were honored and that the few who died were touted as heroes when he considered them monsters. Twain condemned the American media for not mentioning anything about it and critically lamblasted U.S. president Theodore Roosevelt for congratulating the general who commanded the slaughter when Roosevelt wrote a letter saying: "*I congratulate you and the officers and men of your command upon the brilliant feat of arms wherein you and they so well upheld the honor of the American flag.*" After which Twain was even more outraged after the media reported the details citing how it was a 4 day "battle" and how the dead Muslims' genders couldn't even be identified since they had been killed so greatly by the "heroic" U.S. troops who had lost 15 brave soldiers when killing the 900 Muslim men, women and children. Twain had condemned the use of artillery and guns against those who couldn't properly defend against such weapons and thereafter the media reported it was "hand to hand fighting". To which Twain found it hard to believe that hand to hand fighting would result in 900 dead on one side with 15 dead on the other, especially if on the side of 900 their women and children were being killed. After which General Wood replied in a dispatch saying *"no wanton destruction of women and children in the fight, though **many of them were killed by force of necessity** because the Moros used them as shields in the hand-to-hand fighting"*. As you can imagine Twain found this explanation even more ridiculous and then asked why the 585 who survived out of the 600 U.S. troops deployed had then decided to kill that final woman or child who was left, because if it truly was *"hand to hand fighting for 4 days"* there had to have come a time when only 1 was left. Also it's hard to imagine any Muslim man using their wife or child as a *"shield in hand to hand fighting"*. How do you use a live human as a shield in hand to hand fighting anyways? Now, does this type of government praise and explanation of genocide sound familiar? It should, because George W. Bush said this "battle" was his model for how the 2003 CE American occupation in Iraq would be conducted. What's sad is that nearly every American know lots of stuff about Mark Twain and Theodore Roosevelt, but not this. Students learn about both and are required to read Mark Twain's novels in school, which were written before his anti-American outburst and coincidentally banned throughout

American libraries shortly thereafter at the behest of "religious organizations", allegedly for containing swear words. Although they also might've been banned because of Mark Twain's view on Christianity in which he wrote: *"There is one notable thing about our Christianity: bad, bloody, merciless, money-grabbing, and predatory as it is – in our country particularly and in all other Christian countries in a somewhat modified degree – it is still a hundred times better than the Christianity of the Bible, with its prodigious crime – the invention of Hell. Measured by our Christianity of to-day, bad as it is, hypocritical as it is, empty and hollow as it is, neither the Deity nor his Son is a Christian, nor qualified for that moderately high place. Ours is a terrible religion. The fleets of the world could swim in spacious comfort in the innocent blood it has spilled."* On the other hand Theodore Roosevelt got his face put on Mount Rushmore, won a Nobel Peace prize(just like Obama) and Teddy bears were named after him. Although most Americans don't know about how Theodore Roosevelt ordered and praised the butchering of Muslims, forced Cuba to allow the U.S. to have Guantanomo Bay to use as a prison in 1903 CE after Marines made camp there in 1898 CE and that Mark Twain expressed enmity for the American president, military and media in defense of the massacred Muslims and also wrote such material on Christianity. Most people in the world, don't even know that the U.S. military was killing Muslims in Muslim lands since the 1800s CE. However George W. Bush did. Although wasn't George W. Bush's continuation of George H.W. Bush's war on Iraq all about oil? No, not at all. The price of oil for Americans has nothing to do with how much oil they have, oil is a global commodity that sells for the same price all over the world. A barrel of oil is sold for the same exact amount whether it's sold to Australians, Americans, Africans or Aliens. Whereas after the invasion people thought U.S. oil companies would get all the contracts but Russia actually got the oil contracts. The U.S. oil companies actually lost money because of the Iraq war and it led to them getting out of the country entirely. The Iraq war was actually bad for U.S. oil interests. So then what was it for? Well along with the U.S. soldiers deployed there were also thousands of Christian Missionaries deployed from America to go to Iraq and evangelize the Iraqi people. These missionaries were not the chaplains of the army, they were strictly missionaries sent to convert Iraq to Christianity, they were even called "Christ's Army". What America did was bomb the nation to bits and take over, and put a Shia stooge regime in charge while alongside them the Christian missionaries would build an infrastructure with hospitals, schools, orphanages etc all while converting the Muslims of Iraq. This is exactly what they tried, it wasn't as successful as they hoped but that is what they did and the real reason the Iraq war took place. Of course George W. Bush couldn't go on TV and tell the world the U.S. was going to invade Iraq so that they can convert them to Shiism and Christianity, because then it would be too obvious as being a crusade and crusades are taboo nowadays. This is the classic American strategy for evangelization and it's not a strategy that gets used solely on Muslims either.

You will notice there is a distinct difference in the Protestant way of converting by force as compared to the Catholic way, the Protestant way is usually done in the name of economics since that's mainly why German and English royalty first embraced Protestantism establishing it, while Catholicism relies more on military since that's how the Roman Empire first established it. Just because they don't openly say "We're fighting for Christianity!" doesn't mean they aren't. They don't have to say it anymore, they just do it. A similar case happened with China. China was invaded in 1898 CE by

Germany on the pretext of 2 missionaries being killed. Unfortunately many wars have begun on such pretexts of nations defending their citizens in foreign countries, but if you do the research when normal citizens get murdered in foreign countries their home countries don't care. War is usually only declared on a nation of another religion when a missionary tends to get killed, then war is declared in the name of national duty even though it's really for the purpose of religious propagation. Now I don't have a problem with this concept, or principle because Islam teaches this principle in that if one Muslim is unjustly harmed in a foreign country then that is a declaration of war on all Muslims. For instance say a crazy lunatic goes killing people and by random chance some foreign tourists get killed, but then the government punishes the murderer. In such cases of crime I don't think a foreign nation would be justified going to war since justice was served. If crimes were to occur and justice was not served or if the crimes were perpetrated/endorsed/overlooked by governments then war would be justified. However I do take issue with nations who go to war because of their citizens getting harmed when they do this pretending their wars aren't being done for the sake of their religious beliefs and attempts at spreading those beliefs. If they want to wage war because a missionary got killed when spreading his faith then that's a religious war. There's nothing wrong with that, what's wrong is them claiming such a war is not a religious war. I just want them to be honest. They're going to fight the war anyways, the least they can do is be honest that it's a religious war. Thus as with many wars, the recent Afghanistan and Iraq war/wars were done in the name of freedom, and that "freedom" was the freedom to accept Christianity/Americanism or suffer without using the Christian/American aid infrastructure. This is why the Shia were put in charge of the puppet Iraqi democratic government instead of the Sunni majority. The Shia have always helped Christians to fight against and convert Muslims to Christianity as they did during the papal crusades and as the Shia invited the Mongols to invade Iraq. Whereas Afghanistan didn't have Shia, but since the Sunni flavored Taliban were a threat to Shia Iran the secularists were used to be the puppets to repress Islam instead. The point is when you look at history in depth, you will see that the crusades really never stopped, they were just renamed different things such as "Exploration",

"Colonialism", "Imperialism", the "War on Terror" and so on and so forth. You see the Christians already publicly fought wars against Islam and labeled them as such. Those were the official Crusades, they lost and acquired a bad reputation, so there will likely never ever be another war officially labeled as a "crusade" because it's a bad name. However perhaps one of the most important things about the official Crusades is that they were never even called Crusades. The word "crusade" was first used around 1570 CE long after the "crusades" officially ended. The english variant derives from the Spanish "crusada" and the French "croisade". Linguistically these words literally mean "cross aide" or "to aid the cross". Always remember the official papal crusades were not called crusades until they were long over, so it is possible for you to live through a crusade and not know it as one. Today they call it *"financial aid"* or more frequently aggressive warmongers say they are *"Creating a Good Investment Climate"*. If all of the non-Muslims waged an official "war against Islam" it would suffer the same stigma as a war "to aid the cross"(crusade), so that's why there will never be a war publicly declared to be a "war against Islam" either. Naturally the labels are meant to help the war effort, it is known if anyone starts a "war against Islam" or "war against Muslims" then 100% of people claiming Islam or Muslimness would feel obligated to fight back. So instead they'll just say "radical islam" or something like that thereby the doubt in the label will not be able to be used as propaganda by the opposing side. Actions speak louder than words, yet unfortunately many people associate words with reality and ignore the actions. So it's not what people call it, the actions determine what it is. For instance Jihad has rules, calling something Jihad doesn't mean it's Jihad and saying something isn't a crusade doesn't mean that it isn't. As big of a problem as this violence is, the bigger problem is that people don't know, think or care to know or think about what is the cause, reason and solution to this ongoing systematic slaughter of human beings. Many people, and I used to be one, even think Muslims haven't been killed enough and that the problem with the world today is that Muslims haven't been exterminated. Sadly some will publicly and confidently express such attitudes, frequently with the most foul language possible, while few blink an eye as a result of such excessive hatred or dare to oppose it. No country even considers such stuff to be a crime, if you say the same stuff about Jews you'll be jailed but with Muslims it's okay to say. Some even agree, thinking that suppressing Islam and killing Muslims is the best, righteous and only solution not realizing that very attitude is the main problem and causes bigger problems. One such plan non-Muslims are promoting to be put into effect to "*solve the problem of Islam*" is the Winslow Plan. Rather than have you just trust what I tell you anti-Muslims say about Islam it's best for you to read it yourself. There are several plans floating around but many seem to be subsidiary to the "Winslow Plan" and are sub-plans of the Winslow Plan. As such some of the proposals and rhetoric put forward in this plan will sound familiar to things you may have heard. This is because such people are training and preparing the world at large to accept the Winslow Plan before it is fully implemented. It's quite a plan as you will see, some of which has already been implemented, so that's why a certain attitude and mentality are being inculcated amongst the non-Muslim masses prior to the Plan's execution. I apologize for the false and foul language contained within the Winslow Plan and I'm sorry if you find it disgusting or repulsive, but this plan is currently being circulated amongst world government leaders. Here are some excerpts of the Winslow Plan:

"the Quran, whose very name means recitation, is also an evil dark mirror into the mind of total hate. It drains the life from the mind, turns it to shit, and makes it hate and obey militaristic commands, with zombie-like devotion and kamikaze-like fanaticism. The so-called moderate Muslims have brains that are part living and part turd, but the infection is virtually incurable, and is threatening complete takeover at any time, it's beyond the reach of modern science, sorry. On the other hand, no Quran, no Islam, so let's get serious, the Quran must go, it really must go for there to be world peace. It's way worse than Mein Kampf, which is one of its many evil children. Speaking of children, it should be a world crime for a child to imbibe a Quran, period, requiring arrest of the child and any and every person who had anything to do with it. We'll get to that later.

But I'm talking about exterminating one of the world's great religions? No, I'm calling for a world war by the three-fourths of the world that isn't Muslim to exterminate an ancient evil world domination ideology that masquerades as a religion. While organizing to make the Winslow Plan happen, DON'T DEBATE WITH MUSLIMS OR MUSLIM SYMPATHIZERS, just organize and do it. Muslims can read this plan, so they will know what you're trying to do, and shouldn't be given any opportunity to slow you down. Action is called for, and speaks for itself.

To gauge our progress in the war against Islam, we need to enact two metrics:

1. The Disarmament Metric (DM): Nobody who accepts Allah as their god and Muhammad as their prophet should be allowed to be armed.

2. The Apostasy Metric (AM): The only Muslim who can be trusted is one who has openly apostasized, as proved by cursing Allah and Muhammad, and desecrating a Quran. This metric necessarily has to be complex, incorporating degrees of apostasy such as renouncing the violent verses in the Quran and the punishment for apostasy, and accepting proselytizing of Muslims by non-Muslims. A world where all Muslims have apostasized will be the best possible world.

Mass apostasy: Let's cut to the chase. There's one other indispensable chore if we want to end the threat of Islam as a world domination ideology forever: nuking Mecca. While my fellow Coloradan Tom Tancredo proposed it once and I made fun of it earlier, seriously I think I've proved that it's the only answer. Mecca is the source of the infection of enemies of mankind, and to stop the infection you first have to sterilize the source, the so-called holy city of Allah where infidels are killed for trying to enter, and from whence the whole cult sprang, and the orders to spread the territory ruled by horrible Sharia emanate. The very existence of this evil city is an affront to the entire world.

Despite all the left can do to make "Islamophobia" the new racism, more and more are waking up and admitting they have common ground with the right when it comes to Islam, their common enemy. Islamophobia is a category mistake, because it's about Muslims not non-Muslims. For the world to survive, Islam must go, it really must go. I think we should do Medina too for good measure, call it a package deal. After their evil idol Allah has been proved to be dead, the hardcore Muslims will lose their mojo and have nothing to face while praying, and nothing to kill infidels for. If there's a New Islam left after this, it will be like a snake that has been defanged. More likely it will fuel the Great Muslim Apostasy (GMA), disintegrating the Muslim World and erasing the ancient battle lines, allowing it to rejoin the human race as proved by mass non-Muslim immigration and the creation of Western-style democratic governments with human rights for infidels of all kinds, plus women, gays etc.

I'm an insane mass murderer? No, quite the contrary. While killing or locking up 1.x billion Muslims is impossible, nuking Mecca is actually easy for a govt. like the U.S. which has thousands of nukes lying around gathering dust, so the question is when will the willpower be found to do it before it's too late and Muslims nuke the U.S. and do us grievous injury in the name of that city? When you got rats, you get a cat, when you got cobras, you get a mongoose, when you got a horrible mental AIDS infection center like Mecca you get nukes. Of course I haven't got any nukes, but several nations do, and did I say there's thousands of good nukes just lying around while madass Muslims engage in jihadist attacks on a daily basis? It will take just one anti-jihadist attack on Mecca to do the world a great favor. Who who who will have the brains and guts? The U.S. govt.? A rogue element inside it? Russia? China? France? Let's hope we hear about Mecca going poof soon, and I hope it was by somebody who read this article and has the kindness to buy me a mansion in Hawaii.

An asteroid wiped out the dinosaurs, the atomic bomb is God's gift to end Islam, join the Mile Hi Club. Ever heard of Shock and Awe? It's time for Shock Allah. The details, such as giving them fair warning so they can evacuate, and what happens if they instead crowd by the millions into it to become martyrs, are for the govt. doing the nuking. Maybe all the hardcore Muslims will want to present themselves for martyrdom at one time. If so, it is their choice, and they deserve the paradise they get. Else we can try to choose a time when the pop. is at an ebb and hit them quick. Either way, once Mecca is a giant radioactive hole in the sand, the spell will be broken, the prayer mats will be pulled out from under Muslims' feet, and they will dance in the streets singing Ding Dong the Witch is Dead, finally admitting that Allah isn't great at all, Allah is dead, and Islam was a horrible evil fraud along with Muhammad, and give up Islam entirely and join the rest of the human race and have no more reason for jihads, whose purpose was to spread the territory ruled by Allah outward from Mecca. What Mecca? Used to be, used to be used to be. But using nukes again after Hiroshima and Nagasaki sets the wrong example, making a nuclear-free world impossible? Yes, a nuclear-free world is a nice dream, but not as long as Allah and his evil idol in Mecca are being worshipped, sorry. No wonder that despite coveting the world, Islam held back science for so long until the West survived its initial thousand-year jihad and passed it up, Allah doesn't know twat about science, because Allah doesn't exist, but humanity must survive Allah, and Allah must go, he really must go. What other god is so tied to his main shrine, other than Jehovah, who if he is real can defend it himself, get it?"

Now at this point I have to interrupt the Winslow Plan and mention the chapter of the Quran which ironically refutes this very claim of the Kaba in Mecca being defenseless. The year Muhammad pbuh was born was known as the year of the elephant to the people of Mecca. It was known as that because a ruler from Yemen named Abraha brought an army of elephants to attack Mecca and destroy the Kaba, so as to gain tourism at a church he built in his land. Or at least that was his official cover story, the other reason was because he was a Christian ruler and was aware a prophet would be sent to Mecca he figured if he destroyed the Kaba then perhaps the next prophet wouldn't be sent to Mecca and possibly disrupt his luxurious lifestyle in Yemen. This campaign is estimated to have occurred during 568, 569 or 570 CE, but the Arab calendar at the time was not well recorded so it's an estimate. On the warpath to Mecca this Christian army met two arab forces from other cities and fought against them defeating both, the third city Taaif didn't bother to fight the army and offered to help guide Abraha to Mecca but their guide died before he could be of much use. Anyways when the army came near Mecca it took the animals of the citizens of Mecca. So the Grandfather of

Muhammad pbuh, Abdul Muttalib, was appointed as the leader to negotiate for peace and hopefully get the livestock back, since the Meccans had no way at all to physically defend themselves against an army of elephants that had already devastated 2 armies on its way. The Christian ruler of Yemen explained that he didn't want to harm any of the Meccan people but he just wanted to destroy the Kaba, so if they stayed clear they wouldn't be harmed. It was a Christian military campaign solely for religious reasons. Abdul Muttalib said that none of the Meccans would interfere as long as he returned their animals to them. The ruler agreed and found this funny that the Meccans cared more about their animals than the "house of Allah". In response Abdul Muttalib replied, "*The Owner of this House is its Defender, and I am sure He will save it from the attack of the adversaries and will not dishonor the servants of His House.*" It turns out that's exactly what happened contrary to the Christian King Abraha explicitly saying that Allah will not protect the Kaba from him. But rather than tell you what happened I'll share the narrative from Allah himself in the Quran. However don't think that because I'm quoting the Quran then it's biased or not historical. It is the accurate and agreed upon historical narrative by the disbelievers. This chapter was revealed over 40 years after the events which took place to remind the elder people of Mecca of the power of Allah, which they themselves had witnessed, as an encouragement to embrace Islam. Also since Muhammad pbuh was born in this year, about 50 days after the event took place, he couldn't have known the details of what actually occurred which was another reason why Allah revealed these verses to prove to the elders that Muhammad pbuh is getting information he could not know unless Allah told him. The Quran says in chapter 105,

أَلَمْ تَرَ كَيْفَ فَعَلَ رَبُّكَ بِأَصْحَابِ ٱلْفِيلِ (١) أَلَمْ يَجْعَلْ كَيْدَهُمْ فِى تَضْلِيلٍ (٢) وَأَرْسَلَ عَلَيْهِمْ طَيْرًا أَبَابِيلَ (٣) تَرْمِيهِم بِحِجَارَةٍ مِّن سِجِّيلٍ (٤) فَجَعَلَهُمْ كَعَصْفٍ مَّأْكُولٍ (٥)

Which in english means:

"Have you not seen how your Lord dealt with the Owners of the Elephant? Did He not make their plot go astray? And He sent against them birds, in flocks, Striking them with stones of baked clay. And He made them like (an empty field of) stalks (of which the corn has been eaten up by cattle)."

Initially when the leading elephant was near Mecca and prodding forward, it sat down and refused to proceed. They couldn't get it to move and even hit it in the head with a pickaxe. So they tried seeing if it could move in other directions and it did, it just refused to go into Mecca. Eventually the elephant walked off on its own and left the army it was a part of. Then Allah sent birds carrying tiny stones the size of chickpeas with one in each foot and one in their beaks. The birds began dropping stones on the army from above. The ruler even got hit with such stones and later died as a result. Those who didn't get hit with the stones later died of disease. When he got back to his city Abraha's fingers were falling off oozing with pus and he died from some disease of biological self-destruction. So that this Winslow Plan challenges Allah to defend a place in Mecca where he is worshipped is very silly. Allah already defended it from an army with an elephant. In fact once in Mecca the elephant refused to destroy the Kaba when commanded to, it just sat and disobeyed orders. A nuke is easy compared to an elephant. The wind or an electrical malfunction could simply protect Mecca from a nuke. At that time elephants were the big weapon of mass destruction, war elephants were the ancient nukes. Furthermore Muhammad pbuh himself described the details of how the Kaba will be destroyed permanently. Muslims know the country the guy will be from, his skin color and all kinds of details, it is actually required for a Muslim to believe the Kaba will be destroyed permanently in the future. Yet the Kaba has already been destroyed in the post-Muhammadean era by non-Muslims. During 930 CE the Shia Ismaili Qarmatian leader Abu Tahir Sulayman al Jannabi, who had been on a rampage killing Muslims in the middle east, attacked Mecca. Abu Tahir not only attacked Mecca, he attacked during the Hajj pilgrimage, slaughtered about 30,000 pilgrims and destroyed the Kaba. While demolishing the Kaba during the days of Hajj he specifically mocked Islam and the Quran shouting out so the Muslims could hear him say *"Where are the birds who throw stones to protect the Kaba?"* repeatedly challenging Allah and then he left without getting physically harmed. He also dumped the bodies of dead Muslims into the well of Zam Zam defiling it. Abu Tahir took the famous corner "black stone" out of Mecca with him too. As a result of this massacre and the dangers posed by the Qarmatians the Hajj was cancelled in Mecca for 8 years, because it was not safe for pilgrims to come. The next year in 931 CE during Ramadan Abu Tahir believed he found the Shia Mahdi, and put this guy who fulfilled their prophecies about their warped version of the Mahdi in charge of his entire country. The guy Abu Tahir said was the mahdi was named Abu Fadhl. Well Abu Fadhl was not the Mahdi he was just crazy and ordered people to start worshipping fire and return to the Zorastrian religion. Then Abu Fadhl decided to kill the rich and noble folk of the Qarmatian state and even killed some of Abu Tahir's own family. So after an 80 day reign, Abu Tahir killed his Shia Mahdi and apologized to his country being entirely embarrassed and regretful. In 944 CE Abu Tahir died in a terrible condition, nobody today really knows what type of disease it was but he was recorded to have died as a result of a gangrene sore combined with being eaten while still alive by infectious worms. So I guess Allah got him in the end as he died by what was apparently decomposition, or we could say he was so filthy he literally rotted to death. After Abu Tahir died the "black stone" was brought back to Mecca by Abu Tahir's successor. Many Muslims don't know this history of Abu Tahir's evil massacre, the Shia dismantling of the Kaba, the stoppage of Hajj for 8 years and the theft of the black stone; but it is very important. This incident was horrific, yet it happened. So what? The point which anti-Muslims make is that *"Islam must be false and Allah must not exist because the Kaba was destroyed and the black stone was removed so therefore how can you still be Muslims? If Allah was real and the Quran story about the Kaba being protected by the birds was true then this wouldn't have happened!"* However these are separate events that are not related. Allah has never promised to permanently protect the Kaba or Mecca. Just recently in 1979 CE some guy claimed to be the Mahdi next to the Kaba and had his friends start shooting people saying he was the new leader of all Muslims and they all have to pledge allegiance to him. After a few days the Saudi Arabian military fought their way into the masjid and killed the extremists. End of story. So people getting killed in Mecca in the Masjid by the Kaba happens. Allah has never said it is a murder proof zone. While Muhammad pbuh has said it will be destroyed near the end of time and never ever get rebuilt. So Muslims believe the Kaba is guaranteed to get destroyed. The anti-Muslims use such past destruction as an argument against Islam for two reasons. 1. They either don't know about Islam and think Muslims worship the black corner stone of the Kaba or the Kaba itself. 2. They have nothing else they can say to dissuade someone from Islam. Whereas there is a great benefit in the Kaba having been destroyed and the black stone being removed from Mecca for decades because it refutes the lie which the enemies of Islam tell about Muslims worshipping the Kaba or the black stone. Throughout the years the black stone was elsewhere, all the Muslims still prayed facing Mecca despite the black stone being on the opposite side of the Arabian peninsula and the Kaba being dismantled. This proves beyond all doubt that Muslims do not worship the black stone and don't face the Kaba because of worshipping it either. The Kaba was destroyed when the corner stone was removed. So there was no Kaba and the black stone was in a completely different direction, yet Muslims still did the same prayers in the same direction. We aren't lying when we say we don't worship the Kaba or it's black corner stone! For years we proved it, we prayed without a Kaba and we prayed facing away from the black stone. What further proof can be presented? The accusation of stone worshipping has absolutely no credibility and has been refuted in every possible manner. Everything Muslims could possibly do to refute the accusation we have done. Yet the lie still continues to be told and believed. Why? Because the enemies of Islam can't argue with the truth of Islam, they either have to lie, become Muslims, be silent or fight us. We only face towards the Kaba in Mecca because Allah said to face that direction in the Quran, that's all and we will pray in that direction whether the black stone is there or not and whether the Kaba is there or not and we will make Hajj and pray facing Mecca even after the Kaba is permanently destroyed near the end of time. If someone steals or destroys the black corner stone of the Kabah, it's just a stone. The reason Allah didn't and won't always protect the Kaba is to prove this to Muslims and mankind. Landmarks and symbols are just that, they are not divine or invincible or indestructible or special talismans or anything of the sort. Plus these instances of destruction provide a lesson for Muslims today in that things have been much worse for us. The Abu Tahir incident happened in 930 CE. Jerusalem fell to the papal crusaders in 1099 CE. This shows us that things can always get worse if Muslims don't get their beliefs, intentions and actions corrected. Because you would've thought after the Abu Tahir incident Muslims would've united and reformed, but they didn't and got more disunited and even less islamic. Such tragedies are supposed to be wake-up calls to Muslims to show that just because one is a Muslim doesn't automatically mean they get special protection from all harm, and just because things are bad does not mean they can't get even worse. There are conditions for protection and other times God doesn't protect people or things for his own reasons. Afterall the prophet John pbuh was beheaded. Does that mean he wasn't a prophet or that God doesn't exist because John pbuh got killed? No. So even if destruction and calamity falls upon Muslims it's not the end of the world and it doesn't reflect on the truth of Islam. Getting beat up doesn't mean your religion is false or that God doesn't love you. Likewise winning a war doesn't mean your religion is true or that God is on your side. That is the other lesson from Allah protecting the Kaba from the Christian army with the elephant. Religiously at the time the Christians had the better religion and Mecca was inhabited by idolaters. So why then did Allah favor the idolaters when they were the worse of the two sides? Because of the long term big picture in that Muhammad pbuh was going to be sent to Mecca and would need a stable environment to grow up in. Also the protection made the people of Mecca aware that something special happened and they should show gratitude to Allah alone which prepared them to accept Islam years later. Even prophets themselves would lose battles occasionally, yet they were prophets commissioned and guided by God. Did God want his prophets to lose battles sometimes? Yes. Because if the good guys always win then nobody would ever be on the good guys side out of sincerity, they would just be siding with the invincible team. Therefore God allows bad guys to get victories because it makes the good guys better and reveals who chooses the right side regardless of the worldly pressures. The Kaba has been destroyed before and it will be destroyed again. The Kaba in Mecca has nothing to do with Allah being real or Islam being true, just like how the temple in Jerusalem being destroyed multiple times has nothing to do with whether the religion of the biblical prophets was true. Yet aside from the Christian Abraha, the Crusaders and the modern Winslow Plan have Christians or Jews ever tried to destroy the Kaba or Islam's holy sites? Yes.

After Muhammad pbuh died Christian spies in Medinah went to inform the Byzantine Emperor Heraclius about how his successor, Abu Bakr, was sending a 2,000 man army to Syria led by Yazid bin Abi Sufyan and Rabiah bin Amir. After Heraclius informed his Imperial Officials of this they unanimously replied: "*Send us against them and they will never fulfill their desires. We will drive them back to their Prophet's city, <u>demolish their Kabah</u>, uproot its foundations <u>and not spare a single one of them</u>.*" Thus Heraclius sent an army of 8,000 with the Chief Byzantine priest saying, "*O God! Help whichever party is on the truth.*" and the Byzantine generals saying to their soldiers "*Encircle those who have come intending to snatch your Empire, dishonor you and slay your kings. Draw help from the Cross so that it may come to your assistance.*" Yet when the dust cleared the Byzantines had 2,200 dead (27.5%) and the Muslims had lost 120 (6%). Afterwhich the Byzantines asked to speak to the Muslims to see what they actually wanted. That's right, despite the Byzantine generals telling their soldiers what the Muslims wanted giving them reasons to fight, in reality the Byzantine generals had no clue what the Muslims actually wanted when telling their people to fight the Muslims. Rabiah then informed the Byzantines of their 3 options and a Christian priest was sent to debate with him about religion. (For brevity I have not included the debate.) Eventually the Christian priest told the Byzantine General Sergius that according to the Christian Scriptures he had studied, "*Truth is with these people.*" but then an advisor told Sergius that Rabiah had killed his brother earlier in the battle. So in revenge Sergius tried to kill Rabiah on the spot but Rabiah killed him in self-defense. Once the Muslims saw Rabiah was in danger they invaded the Byzantine camp killing all the soldiers with this battle of Dathin resulting in 8,000/8,000 Byzantines dead and 120/2,000 Muslims killed. Things escalated as Heraclius sent his general Rubius with 100,000 men, to fight the army Abu Bakr sent an army led by Amr bin al-Aas with 10,000 Muslims. The end result of that battle was 11,000/100,000 Byzantine Christians dead while 130/10,000 Muslims were killed and the Kabah was not destroyed despite plans of the Christian Byzantines. **So the plan to demolish the Kabah, and kill all the Muslims has been the Christian plan ever since the Khilafah of Abu Bakr in 634 CE. According to the definition historians give to what a "crusade against islam" is, the first "crusade" started in 634 CE and they have not stopped to this day.** If you get anything out of this book, that is the lesson. Total elimination of Muslims and any Muslim holy land has always been the crusader plan, the Winslow Plan is ancient. Yet the drafter of the Winslow Plan is an ignoramus because they should know that the Kaba has been destroyed and the black stone removed before and it did not destroy Islam. Thus this Winslow Plan is designed to fail in it's goals, but we must still examine it, for no matter how doomed it is one would be foolish to risk ignoring the fools and their foolish plans. The worst part is that while many might think nuking the Kaba might offend Muslims "too much", Muhammad pbuh taught us that a single drop of Muslim blood is worth more than the Kaba. So Muslims would actually prefer that disbelievers blow up the Kaba millions of times over and over again than shed a single drop of Muslim blood or even verbally insult a Muslim whether they are living or dead, or slander Islam. That is the certain truth. If I heard on the news tomorrow that everyone who was killing Muslims stopped and all Muslims were safe but the Kaba was destroyed, I would be happier than if I heard on the news that 1 Muslim was slapped or insulted while the Kaba remained standing. Another example would be if X country was collecting tax dollars saying it was for nuking the Kaba, I would be more likely to give them money to do that than I would if they were collecting tax dollars to wage wars that resulted in Muslim blood or innocent blood being shed. Thus for Muslims, disbelievers nuking the Kaba would be taking their war a notch down from what it is already at. We'd even trade the Kaba and the black stone for a truce if it would stop the shedding of Muslim blood or even free one Muslim prisoner. Although if the Kaba is less important to Muslims than Muslim blood and Muslim blood is more important to the survival of Islam why do the enemies of Islam target the Kaba when it is known to be a mere building and that it isn't a "moon-god" idol or anything like that? Are they just mistaken that the Kaba is a "moon-god" idol and have good but misplaced intentions to stop people from worshipping the moon? Some might but their leaders don't. The reason enemies of Islam started the lie about the Kaba being a moon-god idol/shrine comes from the bible. The verses of Deuteronomy 17:2-7 declare, "**_If a man or woman living among you_** *in one of the towns the Lord gives you is found doing evil in the eyes of the Lord your God in violation of his covenant,*³ *and contrary to my command* **_has worshiped other gods, bowing down to them_** *or to the sun* **_or the moon_** *or the stars in the sky,*⁴ *and this has been brought to your attention, then you must investigate it thoroughly.* **_If it is true and it has been proved_** *that this detestable thing has been done in Israel,*⁵ **_take the man or woman who has done this evil deed to your city gate and stone that person to death._**⁶ **_On the testimony of two or three witnesses a person is to be put to death_**, *but no one is to be put* to death on the testimony of only one witness.⁷ **<u>The hands of the witnesses must be the first in putting that person to death</u>**, *and then the hands of all the people.* **You must purge the evil** *from among you."* So this bible passage obligates Jews and Christians to kill any and all of the Muslims if Muslims are "accused and proven" to worship the moon. This ruling does not recognize "freedoms" or citizenship but is a biblical loophole for Jews and Christians to kill off an entire religious group if they are "proven by Jews or Christians" to be guilty of worshipping something like the moon or "other gods". The zealous bible thumpers know these verses and when they passionately accuse Muslims of worshipping the moon or say Allah was a pagan moon-deity they are passing a death sentence on all Muslims. Of course currently they don't portray their accusations as a death sentence, but are mere *"witnesses to the 'truth about Islam'"* Yet the majority of non-Muslims still doubt whether it's been "proven" that Muslims worship the moon as they accuse us of doing. However once officially "proven" and accepted by the masses then the bible is clear on what Jews and Christians have to do to all Muslims wherever they are in the world. Hence this bloody Winslow plan is actually taken right out of the bible. It is a Jewish/Christian plan originally but biblically everyone should participate in the bloodshed, it's just that "witnesses" to the alleged moon-worshipping of Muslims have to cast the first stone. There is no Christian concept of "He without sin cast the first stone" regarding this religious genocide, the biblical rule is "those who know the truth about Muslims" should start the slaughter and everyone else should join in later. In case you haven't been paying attention to history, the stoning has already begun by the "witnesses" and now they're asking people to start throwing more stones/bombs at any Muslims they can find "testifying to the truth of the Muslim evil and plots" and "bringing all Muslims to the city gate" to make a smaller easier target. Plain and simple the Winslow plan is fundamentally a modern version of the ancient Biblical plan. Sorry for interrupting your reading of this Winslow Plan, but I had to comment on the stupidity of this plan, the ignorance of it's drafters and it's biblical origin. The Winslow Plan continues:

"After nuking Mecca and its evil idols and worthless antique crap which are the greatest threat to peace the world has ever known, my mind tells me that despite copies of the Quran floating around, and Muslim rats hiding in caves with databases of other rats, Islam will

finally be kaput as a threat to the world after the Great Apostasy, and we can move on after we bring a new generation online that isn't controlled by evil malevolent male supremacist holy nutcases taking orders from a Dead Hitler. Even after the Great Apostasy, it's still necessary for the West allied with the rest of the non-Muslim world to occupy the former Muslim World and supervise its disintegration, reeducation, and reintegration into the human race, and this will call for an unprecedented alliance.

The Winslow Plan for Winning the War Against Islam

1) Begin Muslim Ideological Profiling (MIP) to screen all Muslims worldwide for signs of radicalization, and quit screening all non-Muslims and wasting resources. Ban all radicalized Muslims from international travel.

2) Stop Muslim immigration to non-Muslim countries until Islam as a viable political ideology has been exterminated worldwide, and the Muslim World has disintegrated. End citizenship and deport all Muslims from non-Muslim countries back to where they or their forebears came from until the new apostate reeducated generation can be raised, after which their possible reimmigration will be on the table again. Make Sharia a world crime, and preach the Great Muslim Apostasy (GMA) as a way out for every Muslim.

3) *Call up at least 50 million troops and switch to a wartime economy, with the goal of disarming all Muslims worldwide and keeping Muslims from access to arms. U.S. Winslow Plan allies will include hopefully the EU, Russia, China, and India. Too bad, the sad fact of Islamization of Europe might make them into a target for the Winslow Plan instead.*

4) *Nuke Mecca and Medina with dirty bombs to prove to all Muslims that their Allah and Muhammad were frauds, and demoralize radical Muslims. Create at least a 20-mile and better a 50-mile dead zone that will last ten thousand years, and station a permanent military force encircling it to prevent all entry until Islam is declared dead by the U.N.*

5) *Force the U.N. expel the 57-member Organization of the Islamic Conference (OIC), including Saudi Arabia and Yemen, Pakistan, Iraq, Iran, Afghanistan, Syria, Jordan, Egypt, Malaysia, Indonesia, and North Africa. If they won't, the U.S. should expel the U.N. and set up its own that does. Isolate, quarantine, and contract the Muslim World, and occupy and disarm their countries with the Winslow Plan force for as long as it takes to exterminate Islam as a viable ideology that makes its true believers enemies of the human race. Dissolve the Muslim states of Pakistan and Bangladesh and let India reintegrate them. Help Greater Israel from the Nile to the*

Euphrates solidify control of the ex-Muslim World in order to help lead ex-Muslims back into the human race as citizens of Israel or other new countries carved out of the old Muslim World.

6) End the ability of any Muslim nation to make or keep nukes, dismantling all weapons, nuclear materials, and nuclear facilities, and capturing all nuclear scientists and engineers.

7) Stop Sharia, disarm and dismantle all violent Muslim orgs., and imprison the members for life. Make it a world crime to arm a Muslim, or for a Muslim to be armed.

8) Take the women away from the men and the children away from the parents to break the cycle of indoctrination. Make it a world crime for the Quran to be taught to a child, with immediate arrest of all involved, it's like stopping an infection. Recruit 30 million teachers and engage in long-term occupation until a new generation of children can be raised with a globalist secular mindset that breaks the cycle of indoctrination into the Quran, meaning they should never be allowed to see a Quran or set foot in a mosque or pray to Allah or read anything about Muhammad, and even their names must be secularized to make a clean break with the past, especially any name even remotely related to Muhammad or Allah. The Arabic language should be banned except for scholars for safety. That's right, bring up a generation

of Islam history ignoramuses, this crap should only be studied by the mature. After reaching age 18-21 they will be set free and can choose any religion they want, or none, as well as any political ideology except Islam. If they choose Islam as a religion, repeat this step; at least the mental bacteria of the Quran will be greatly weakened when trying to take over a mature educated mind. The educational curriculum should not only be secular, scientific and technology oriented, but nonpolitical and nonreligious, preparing the children to take their place in a global society. The local culture should be ignored as retro and dangerous, suitable for study only by mature educated adults. Of course in practice the teachers will bend these rules and try to lead their students to their own political and religious viewpoint, but nothing's perfect, and any result that reduces the number of believing practicing Muslims is a positive step.

9) Make occupied countries pay for our police services with their oil and other natural resources as best they can. Only after the new generation matures and proves they are worthy should political power be entrusted to them, in a phased manner, with the goal of having their former Muslim countries rejoin the human race without Islam.

10) Once the back of the Muslim World has been broken, help speed its disintegration by a mass immigration of non-Muslims from the West, India, China et al. They can help green the deserts and turn this giant hellhole into a bustling vital part of the world economy.

Immediate action items for the U.S.:

1. The Winslow Amendment to the U.S. Constitution shall be passed: "Congress shall have the power to make laws restricting the free exercise of religions other than Christianity and Judaism, including but not limited to Islam."

2. The Congress of the United States of America shall declare the U.S. to be at war with the Muslim Nation or Umma(h).

3. Congress needs to make it a federal felony punishable by 20 years in prison to knowingly act in furtherance of, or to support adherence to political Islam and its Muslim Nation or Umma(h), or to allow, permit, or conspire to allow or permit a minor to read the Quran (Koran). Deportation to Muslim World must be an option.

4. The President of the United States of America shall immediately declare that all non-U.S. citizen Muslims are Alien Enemies under Chapter 3 of Title 50 of the U.S. Code, subject to immediate deportation.

5. No Muslim shall be granted an entry visa into the United States of America except under extreme conditions of security, and never permitted to be armed."

This Winslow Plan is no joke either. It's a real policy. That Tom Tancredo, the Winslow Plan mentions as having earlier announced plans to nuke Mecca, is a prominent U.S. Congressman who to date has served 2 terms in the House of Representatives and 5 terms in Congress while playing an active role in creating and passing U.S. laws. The guy ran for President of the United States in 2008 CE on the republican ticket but dropped out to help the bid of the Mormon Mitt Romney, who was superseded by Baptist(formerly Episcopalian) John McCain in 2008 CE who ran with the Pentecostal(formerly Catholic) Sarah Palin as running mate for Vice President. Although later Mitt Romney got the Republican nomination in 2012 CE and had the Catholic Paul Ryan as his running mate for Vice President. Both those elections were "won" by the Protestant Barack Obama and his Catholic running mate Joe Biden, who later became president himself. Meanwhile this Tom Tancredo (formerly Catholic, currently a non-denominational Christian) who advised nuking Mecca, ran in elections for governor of Colorado in 2010 CE and came in 2nd place with 36.7 % of the vote. Which is pretty close to victory considering Abraham Lincoln became president with 39.2% of the vote. Tancredo ran for governor in 2014 CE also but lost the republican primary election. So while this Winslow Plan may seem completely crazy to most people, this is the legitimate plan prominent U.S. government officials are working towards implementing. This plan is the unofficial policy the American federal government and other governments has covertly had and currently has towards Muslims and Islam. Both Democrats and Republicans implement this plan in different ways but Republicans tend to be more public about it. Ironically the Winslow plan is similar to the plan the Christian army of the elephant had which the Quran chapter mentions, the ironic part is that the Republican party mascot is an elephant and they tend to be the "Christian party" as well. But don't judge a party by its mascot, for the democratic donkey is akin to the donkey Christians think Jesus rode on his entry to Jerusalem. Coincidentally lots of influential prominent American politicians are Christian, and charismatic Christians too with deeply religious personal lives which some proudly display while others take great pains to make people overlook. Realistically with so many Christian American politicians can government policies truly be free from Christian prejudices and motives? Or are they simply designed to appear free from Christian influence for political, international and American ideocratic reasons? Many Christians who do interfaith plan genocide and see it as a way to weaken their religious rivals making them less attached to their faith and less likely to be emotionally and mentally prepared when the violence starts. A few interfaith folk are just ignorant not knowing the designs of interfaith actually believing the empty sacreligious slogans that get uttered/promoted. For example in 2016 CE my mother showed me an article in the Catholic Newspaper about some seminarians who I had personally met when I visited the seminary I planned to go to after high school. The article was about how they went to Israel for 12 days on a spiritual pilgrammage and while there spoke to Muslims, thus my non-Muslim mom was trying to imply how interfaith is good and right because Muslims allegedly do it in Bethlehem with the same "evil people" who I used to be co-religionists with. The article subtly implied that they enjoyed speaking with Muslims in the Holy Land and were going to be compassionate holy priests who are not religiously intolerant. However I personally met these seminarians 6-7 years earlier and spoke with them about their religious views. Despite the article implying they were interfaith I knew better and it was disgusting to see them portrayed as interfaith when I personally talked to them about Catholicism and how they believe it is the only acceptable faith and everyone must believe it or else. I used to be their comrade and knew and participated in formulating their gameplans for intolerant world domination, now I can see them publicly progressing toward the ecumenical goal I used to share with them but their plans are unknown to the world at large. Thus when I see "interfaith Christians and Jews", I laugh because I can see right through their facade. But I cry when other Muslims can't see it and fall for the empty slogans not realizing what the Christians and Jews are planning for them. The vast majority of Interfaith stuff is done to further a highly religiously intolerant genocidal goal, the minority of interfaith folk are ignorant as to the purpose behind interfaith. Those who believe in interfaith when they preach it are like a skunk that can't smell it's own stench, of which there are few. Contrary to popular belief skunks actually do smell their own foul smelling spray but it doesn't bother them because it harms their enemy. Not all Christians are bent on global domination, some like the monks just want to be left alone or they are ignorant and don't care about religion, but of the religious Christians and Jews most desire global religious supremacy and see interfaith as a trick or tactic to use to further that aim. Violence is only shunned by interfaith groups in the present because they don't want the enemy to be able to fight back when they finally do attack with violence. I ardently desired the killing of all Muslims, yet in public I would pretend that I wanted peace with them, except when I was amongst fellow Christians. You see the real mass murderers are able to murder the masses because they care about the numbers above all else even at the expense of pride, honesty and recognition. They would rather more people die and live a life of public lies than be honest, get credit for it and kill less. So the safer ones are those who admit a desire for war, because you can actually have fruitful negotiations sometime due to their honesty. But the interfaith negotiating types who prefer to compromise rather than fight or cannot disagree without "agreeing to disagree", those are the most dangerous types. Those who want to be friends with everybody tend to do so simply because they want their enemies to let their guard down, since it is much easier to destroy someone who thinks you are their friend than someone who thinks you are their enemy. Friendly fire is the most fatal. Hence those who want the most of other faiths to die tend to be the most friendly towards those of other faiths, until it's time to pull the trigger. Christians particularly are prone to implement such a doctrine since they believe Judas got Jesus pbuh killed by kissing him. Thus for Christians to utterly destroy members of another faith they now believe that you kill more with kisses than with intolerance. That is why Abraham Lincoln taught that "*If you would win a man to your cause, first convince him that you are his sincere friend.*" and said, "Am I not destroying my enemies when I make friends of them?" Another example of this tactic is found in the phrase "You catch more flies with honey than with vinegar", why would they want to catch a fly? They want to catch it with honey so as to kill it since they can't stand it peacefully buzzing about. Such people view kindness as a way to help them at a later date literally personally kill the one they are kind to, or they might abstain from personally doing the "dirty work" since getting dirty might make it harder for them to do the "clean work" part of killing others. The intolerant ones are typically just too honest to be clandestine until genocide becomes a viable option, so they take risks to achieve their goals. The interfaith Christians care too much about religious dominance and genocide to risk a battle or even a debate. They don't want the glory they want things to get gory, and things can't get gory if the enemy knows you plan them harm. The biggest messes of manslaughter happen because everyone was prepared for cleanliness. The bottom line is not whether politicians admit to following the Winslow plan with their words, it's about what their actions say that will determine whether they are following the anti-Islam plan or not. Perhaps like many others you think this "Winslow Plan" is a recent post 9/11 fringe plan; despite it being taught to the future leaders of the American military. Only the details are post 9/11, this fundamental plan has nearly always been American government's plan for Muslims. In 1987 CE the U.S. President Ronald Reagan actually planned to put all the Muslims into internment camps or deport them out of America. This was before ISIS, before the war in Libya, Syria, Yemen, Iraq, Afghanistan, the "war on terror", 9/11, the U.S. war in Somalia, the gulf war, in Lebanon, etc. In 1986 CE the INS (Immigration and Naturalization Service) had "Group IV" of their

"Alien Border Control Committee" draft a 40 page document. Tom Walters was the man in charge of drafting this "emergency plan" on what to do with Muslims, according to his own confession. Being aware of the American government's stance on Islam and Muslims at that time as well as American history, Walters drafted a plan during June 1986 CE which was then sent to his superiors who had requested it. The plan was to allocate 100 acres of Oakdale, Louisiana to build an internment camp similar to those built for the Japanese who were interred in America during WWII. However unlike with the Japanese this camp was only to be a holding camp for Muslims and middle easterners while they were in the process of being deported. Why did America want to deport Muslims and middle easterners? Well since the Cold War was coming to an end with Americanism becoming the dominate religion, the American government deduced that Islam was the only religion which could pose a threat to global Americanism. As a result it was decided to take the next steps to plan for the war against Islam ahead of time thinking that pre-planning before the Cold war ended would speed up the conclusion of the next one. The goal was to accelerate the war on Islam(then being waged covertly mainly through its colony Israel) and purge America before the official Crusade to impose Americanism in the Muslim lands began. In November 1986 CE the memo Tom Walters drafted, *"Alien Terrorists and Undesireables: A Contingency Plan"*, concerning Muslims and middle easterners was reviewed in a meeting he had with 13 representatives from the "Justice Department", the FBI, the US Marshals and Customs. Tom Walters later reported that during the meeting he was shocked because typically most of all the stuff he ever drafted was ignored and merely clerical fantasies, so he thought when drafting this plan the same ignoring of his plan would happen especially since it was such an immoral plan. However despite the moral objectivity what Walters said surprised him most was that the government was really interested in the technicalities of how to actually put his plan into practice to get Muslims and middle easterners out of America. Walters was also taken aback by the various government agencies acting as though Muslims were all terrorists and enemies of America, which as far as he knew they weren't but he had just drafted a fantasy plan suggesting what could be done in case such a crazy fantastical scenario ever arose. During that meeting in 1986 CE Tom Walters learned that Ronald Reagan was waging a "war on terror" that was apparently directed at Islam and Muslims which he had unwittingly become a part of not knowing this war was ongoing. He was just "doing his job" not knowing he was a soldier in the war against Islam and Muslims. After the review of this plan an official government request was made for the sum of $2 million so that the camp could be built within the next 4 weeks so it would be ready when the plan was to be put into effect. However it was agreed that the plan would be phrased in such a way as to only apply to "immigrants and aliens" rather than American citizens because of legalistic reasons whereby if Americans ever learned that citizens themselves were targeted then it might be popularly rejected. Essentially the government can't say they are taking away the rights of Americans to protect America but it's very easy for the government to say they are taking away the rights of "foreigners" to protect America and Americans (by which they mean Americanism). Thus the phraseology was intentionally left cryptic so as to only apply to the 230,000 middle eastern and african residents, so in case of legal or political backlash the excuse of it being a foreign policy rather than a religious policy could be used. The memo denoted there would be a test case during which a legal precedent could be established and it could be discovered how the world would react to the implementation of such a policy if it were to be implemented at that time. In January 1987 CE such a "test case" took place when 8 Palestinians were going to be deported from America based on classified information, as the memo indicated would be the case. You see that's how the government decided they would be able to get away with mass deportation of people for religious reasons, first they would make a registry and then deport the people on that registry because of "classified information" that would never be made known to the public. Basically classified information was to be the government's way of saying, *"We just want to do it and know the world will let us if we say the reasons we have are classified."* Whenever a government says the information justifying their policies or actions is "classified" that's their cheat code for getting away with crime. Which sounds childish but it's the same way the Inquisition operated and it's actually worked in the past and the present with how the "war on terror" has been waged with innocent people being imprisoned, tortured and killed for "classified reasons". In reality the reason America wanted the 8 Palestinians deported was because they were activists publicly opposing Israeli Zionism. Yet the government insisted it was for legitimate reasons that had nothing to do with religious beliefs opposed to Zionism. What were those legitimate reasons? Well the FBI went undercover for 3 years and couldn't find any legitimate reason to deport them. Thus according to the lawyer of the "L.A. 8", Marc Van Der Hout, the FBI went to immigration and said *"Can you figure out some way to deport these people? Why? Because we don't like their views. We don't like what they're doing, about their supporting the rights to a Palestinian homeland and their organizing efforts in the Los Angeles community."* So the government passed a law saying that furthering terrorist activity in any way is a deportable offense. Thus the 8 Palestinians were accused of supporting terrorists in Palestine by publicly opposing Israeli Zionism and supporting the dream of Palestinian sovereignty. Thus the 8 were to be deported as the first ever to be charged as "supporting terrorists" until the government memo drafted by Tom Walters was leaked to the lawyers of the Palestinians and newsreporters by an unidentified inside source. This document was then read by one

American named Norman Mineta. Mineta, or "Norm" as was his nickname, got interred 45 years earlier by the US government during 1942 CE because he was a Japanese American. As a result of his experience he became a public spokesperson against the document detailing how the plan if funded, implemented or allowed to be potentially accepted, would lead to worse than what happened to him as an 11 year old in 1942 CE. Norman Mineta explained how it's not just about "foreigners" as the document claimed, because he witnessed himself in 1942 CE how quickly the "foreigner" excuse was dropped when the inhumane anti-Japanese plan was implemented against US citizens such as himself. Since Mineta was a member of the US government's "House of Representatives" the proposed plan to inter and deport Muslims from America was officially abandoned. But was it really? I think not, and believe it was just temporarily postponed until it could gain more popular support. Meanwhile the trial of the "L.A. 8" took 20 years. Why? Because the government tried to say that sending money for humanitarian causes to Palestine or distributing pro-Palestinian / anti-Zionism or anti-Israel literature was a furtherance of terrorist activity.

Why is that? Because America is Israel's ally and Israel and America say those who oppose Israel in Palestine are terrorists. So for 20 years the US government tried to get these 8 Palestinians deported claiming that by denouncing Israel they were terrorists because it helped terrorists since terrorists were enemies of Israel and as an ally to Israel automatically any threat to Israel would be a threat to America. The U.S. government lost the case 6 times, but each time they lost they passed a new law to try to get the "L.A. 8" deported. Literally the US government lost and got told what they were trying to do was illegal, so they turned around changed the law and then said that the "L.A. 8" broke the new law they just made before it was made into a law and the Courts again maintained that the "L.A. 8" didn't break the law even under the new laws, so the US government tried again 6 consecutive times. Why? Because the US government really really likes Israel and wants to have a precedent set so as to have the ability to deport or label as a terrorist any who do/say something that they don't like, such as giving money in charity to starving people in Palestine or denouncing Israel/Zionism. The US immigration judge finally ended the matter when he ruled in

2007 the case was "*an embarrassment to the rule of law.*" However now America has many new anti-terrorism laws thinking they are about stopping violence when they were really just made up to try to get 8 Palestinian activists out of America. Seriously many anti-terrorism laws were not made to protect people but to try to convict peaceful people who peacefully opposed the religion of Zionism in America. So these anti-terror laws are really religious laws designed to convict people who have certain religious beliefs. Then in 2012 CE the FBI mailed a criteria of possible clues of a terrorist to look for to every type of commercial enterprise imaginable, this criteria included denouncing/opposing Israel and Zionism. Meaning according to the FBI if you don't support Israel and Zionism then you are a "potential terrorist" who should be reported and observed. Yet they claim one has "*Freedom of Speech*". Anyways the point is that the idea to expel all Muslims from America, is NOT a post 9/11 dream, such stuff has been officially planned by the American government for a long time and they nearly passed a law allocating $2 million in the 1980s to build an internment camp for such a purpose. Although perhaps what's most important is whether people will remember the current war on Islam. I say this because America first waged war against Muslims in 1800 CE, when they sent the U.S. Marines to Tripoli because Thomas Jefferson didn't want to continue paying the Jizya which America had previously been paying to the Berber states. Yet how many people know one of America's first official wars was against Muslims in 1800 CE? The U.S. also fought Algiers in 1815 CE, then the Aceh Sultanate in 1832 CE, and fought the Aceh Sultanate again in 1839 CE. They don't mention this in schools. Then America took a break to fight it's "civil war" to establish the federal union. After which it fully conquered the Native Americans converting them to Americanism while practicing foreign imperialism and interventionism. Next it bulked up for WWI, learned the interest debt game before WWII and after becoming a super power with new atomic bombs went back to war with the Muslims after creating a neo-colony called "Israel". Then while preparing for the "final crusading centuries" America had to win a "Cold religious war" with the USSR who had a rival religion to counter Americanism and in that war they learned the spy, propaganda and surveillance game. They also established the doctrine of the

"Domino Theory" in that if one country believes in X then those next to it will too and those next to that and just like dominoes X will rule the world if we let a single country believe in anything other than Americanism disguised as Democracy. This comes from the popularly influential but rarely explained or credited "Ant-Hill theory". The "Ant-Hill theory" of politics is as follows:

1. In any 2 political systems, differences in procedures, institutions and values will vanish in the long run.

2. The rate at which differentials between political systems vanish is directly proportional to their physical proximity, the size of their respected resource bases, and the amount of communication and interaction between them.

3. Procedures, institutions and values in the 2 systems will stabilize at a point that reflects the needs of the largest and wealthiest urban population included in the 2 areas.

The "Domino Theory" semi-related to this "Ant-Hill Theory" proves that Americanism and Democracy is 100% false if an alternative religious/political belief were to rapidly spread like dominoes toppling it. Basically the Domino theory is like the

Ant-Hill theory except rather than mutual diffusion and dilution creating a hybrid system over time, the Domino theory teaches one political system is 100% going to rapidly supersede and annhilate the other in a zero-sum winner take all game. The Domino Theory is in most cases unrealistic and used as a propaganda piece by extremists or rudimentary idealists who don't understand political, cultural or social change. The only way the Domino Theory could be valid is if the alternative to Americanism or Democracy was truly better 100%, otherwise not every country would accept it nor would they accept it fully as an alternative as the theory goes. However since the Domino Theory was accepted to be true by the allegedly Capitalistic nations pertaining to Communism, (which doesn't even make sense according to the ant-hill theory since the ant-hill theory results in Capitalistic victory) now people use it as a justification to prevent Shariah being established anywhere on the globe, rightly fearing the Domino-esque effect Shariah would have to the neighboring nations and nations worldwide. You see Shariah causes falsehood and oppression to fall like Dominoes, when Shariah loses it gets replaced bit by bit via the ant-hill theory style of change/defeat but God's prophetic system is never 100% replaced/abrogated just as Jews and Christians never abrogated 100% of the Mosaic law. Every non-Jew knows Jews changed and replaced the law of Moses pbuh with rabbinical law and others as time goes by, but everyone also knows that a tiny % of the Mosaic laws still exist amongst Jews, it's minimal but never vanished 100%. It's not enough % to be on good terms with God but nobody ever eliminates 100% of God's prophetic political system/laws because fundamentally they are good and human nature prevents 100% pure evil systems without even a shred of God's good influence in it. <u>No satanic system is possible of being totally 100% anti-prophetic regarding everything God wants/decrees/commands</u>. Any such theoretical satanic system would be extremely vulnerable and easy to peacefully refute/destroy when compared with the prophetic system. A 100% Satanic system would be the 2nd worst type of system Satan could envisage, the only thing worse and counterproductive from Satan's perspective would be a 100% prophetic system but a 100% Satanic system makes the prophetic system an immediate eventuality too easy to establish. Basically if Satan ruled the world 100% and 100% of people did 100% of things wrong, the prophet's job would be easy because not one Satanic thing could be justified in any way and the truth and falsehood would be clear cut in a way which none could deny. Binary systems of black and white without any confusing grey areas makes religion easy, it's because Satan operates in shades of gray that things are so difficult to change/correct. Thus evil people can always say "*I'm not 100% wrong/evil am I?*" then when you admit they aren't Satan convinces them they must not be satanic then thereby trapping them in error since they foolishly think satanic people are 100% wrong in everything and that since they aren't then they must not be satanic. Anyways if one accepts the Ant-Hill theory to be valid, which it seems to be in most cases throughout history, the Domino theory is invalid unless it were to be applied by Satanic systems in opposition to God's system. Basically the Domino theory can only ever be applied to the prophetic system and since we know Communism was not that then it makes one wonder why the Domino theory was applied by America towards it, until one learns what America had done for the sake of the Zionist state before the Cold War occurred and what America had done to Muslims and in opposition to Shariah after the Cold War against Communism ended. Also that the

Cold War was "cold" is another anomaly in history where a "war" was peaceful. Why was it peaceful? Because it was a fake war game in preparation for the real war which was to follow against the prophetic system. Thus during the Cold War America was molding the public opinion and shaping the state to prepare it for war against Islam, even though the doctrines it taught like the "Domino Theory" were not valid if applied to Communism. Basically Americans were coached to fight Muslims/Shariah while they were told they were fighting Communism/Russia. McCarthyism was practice for the police state yet to be completed.

Before the Americans ever waged war against Muslims, from 1785 CE to 1800 CE America paid Jizya(tribute) to Muslims. The British Empire and France also paid Jizya to Muslims at that time. Although few are aware of this fact, most people think America vs. Islam started in 2001 CE when it really started in 1800 CE. George Washington paid Jizya, John Adams paid Jizya, but Thomas Jefferson led a USA crusade and created the U.S. Marines to fight the Muslims. This was for religious reasons as the U.S. Navy Agent to the Berbery States said in his diary dated April 8th, 1805 CE, when Muslims offered a truce. U.S. Captain William Eaton wrote,

"*We find it almost impossible to inspire these wild bigots with confidence in us or to persuade them that, being Christians, we can be otherwise than enemies to Musselmen. We have a difficult undertaking!*" This is a telltale sign of eternal enmity when a American Christian military commander privately complains in his diary about having difficulty convincing Muslims who propose peace that Christians religiously can never not be the enemies of Muslims. The Muslims offered peace to America in 1805 CE and the U.S. Christian-Americanist military said "*These Muslims just don't get it, we are not Muslims and thus will always be their enemies until they stop being Muslims and convert to our religion!*" So how can we have lasting peace when this is the attitude of the American-Christian military for the past 217+ years? Til today the Marines official hymn, yes they call their theme song a hymn, cites their first combat experience when it says, "*From the halls of Montezuma to the shores of Tripoli.*" This verse is a direct reference to the policy of Marines who followed Muslim Berber ships back to their villages and then killed every Muslim man, woman and child. They did it then, they do it now and they plan on doing it tomorrow. In fact in Syria during May 2016 CE an American soldier fighting with the Kurds against the Khawarij group ISIS proclaimed that when they got to Raqqa (which at that time was an ISIS city only about 20 miles away) they planned to kill every man, woman and child leaving not a single human alive. This is the stuff which US soldiers who have loaded guns in their hands, paid for with tax dollars, are saying in public on camera when they are just miles away from cities which they threaten with mass genocide. It's not just lunatics on the internet! (or in political office) The non-Muslim soldiers with the guns and bombs in the middle east have this policy of killing anyone who they think is Muslim, even if they are babies. Except they don't want people to keep track of their bloody rampage so that it can continue, thus this stuff doesn't get reported in Western news outlets. While this kill everybody policy isn't just used with ISIS extremists it has always been the unofficial American middle eastern policy and before that it was the British and French policy and before that the Byzantine policy. The US soldiers who fought in Iraq in 2004 CE have confessed that in April 2004 CE they were given orders and new procedures which stated if fired upon in a crowded area (like any civilian area) the US soldiers were to respond by killing everybody in sight so that the people learn when US soldiers lives are threatened then all bystanders die. Thus the Iraqi people were supposed to learn to help and expose/oppose the "insurgents" resisting the US soldiers if they wanted to live. This was the explicit US military policy and they said that such "civilians" are guilty active combatants because they allowed US soldiers to be attacked in their vicinity. The theory was that if they were innocent they wouldn't be present at the time of the attack and no attack would've happened, thus they not only can be killed under the American rules of engagement but the US military said they should be killed and orders were given for all bystanders to be killed in such situations as they arose. Also this order to massacre need not actually be executed as the result of a legitimate attack, the order was to fire "if there is a threat of an attack" and frequently if an insect buzzed by a soldier's ear then that was used as sufficient reason to shoot people because US soldiers were told it's better to assume it's a bullet than a bug lest you become "soft targets". This is because the number one priority for US soldiers is "Come back home safe". Most all they care about is getting themselves back to America alive and unwounded, if they have to kill civilians to keep their gang safe then they feel that's justifiable and so do many Americans. Many Americans actually think the blood of an American citizen is holy and worth more than the blood of non-Americans. US soldiers themselves have confessed that this practice of killing civilians en masse, because of a fear of possibly getting hurt, happened frequently. A US soldier reported that once because another soldier said they heard something fly by their ear he immediately opened fire and killed dozens of peaceful protesters. He did this because that's how they are trained to react. When checking the dead bodies no weapons were found except for a bunch of rocket launchers neatly lined against the wall 50 meters away, when he saw that the soldier realized that if the protesters wanted to kill them they could've easily done so since they had the weapons safely stored elsewhere. But he concluded they purposely didn't use them out of restraint because it truly was a peaceful protest and the US soldier was shocked that he had murdered innocent peaceful civilians. The very same day while guarding checkpoints, 3 consecutive cars where driving to the checkpoint "too fast" so the soldiers shot everyone inside thinking it was a suicidal car bomber. 3 times in one day they did this and everytime they found it to be regular unarmed people who they killed because they were driving too fast for the soldiers' comfort. Clearly such a day would frazzle any decent human and when his commander asked him if he was alright he replied saying "It's been a bad day." and his commander who knew of all his murders and knew of even more responded to his soldier saying "NO. It's been a good day." At that point the soldier said he just wanted to get out alive and go home because he knew he was on the wrong side. The US policy even rewards soldiers for getting their first "confirmed kill". They all get congratulated by the whole gang when they kill someone for the first time, even if they are innocent civilians. Sadly many soldiers form such deep bonds with their comrades that they become even more and more ruthless thinking they need to be bad in order to save the lives of their comrades and to get their comrades to do the same for them. All the US soldiers want to come home ASAP, except for the nutjobs who really enthusiastically love to kill innocents or Muslims and are thoroughly brainwashed by the patriotic propaganda. Which sadly happens to many because most soldiers join when they are young and dumb because the military is advertised as a way to get cheap college, marketable job experience and economic preference or "valor". The problem as stated by US soldiers is that the non-soldiers have too much respect for the military and give all kinds of benefits to soldiers and veterans not knowing the military has a policy of war crimes. They say those who join the US military should be shunned and not honored or respected, maybe in the past the US military was different but today veterans say the members of the US military should be viewed by Americans as evil criminals. This is why the US military veterans nearly never talk about their experiences with their families, because they were evil. They are not hiding good deeds, they are hiding wicked sins. Good guys talk about their battle experiences to inspire others, bad guys sulk, regret and struggle to continue living with themselves or others. That's why US veterans kill themselves, because they became monsters and since most are disbelievers on top of that life becomes torture for them. As a result of them being disbelieving war criminals Allah makes their life difficult and miserable in the hopes that they repent and believe. Even the US soldiers on the battlefield kill themselves. For example in 2012 CE there were 349 active duty US soldiers who committed suicide when only 176 active duty US soldiers were killed in action that same year. So the

US soldiers who are deployed are killing themselves more than their enemies are. If you are a US soldier deployed to fight, then you are statistically more likely to kill yourself than to be killed by the enemy. That is not normal. When you study military history, you will not find any other armies where their soldiers kill themselves more than their enemies do. So the US military is very special in a very bad way. The rates of suicide are higher among members of the US military than they are for Americans who aren't in the military. Also consider whether the army of good guys kills itself? Does it sound like the actions of soldiers who feel, think or believe that they are good guys fighting for good causes? Whereas their suicides are out of depression too, it's not like an extremist blowing themselves up in a car bomb while hurting others which serves some utilitarian purpose in warfare, US soldiers just kill themselves via suicide and nobody else. Thousands of US veterans kill themselves every year. Statistically speaking every 65 minutes a US veteran commits suicide, averaging 22 veteran suicides per day. Clearly this is not the behavior of heroes or people who served on the right side of a conflict. Do you think the army of Moses, David or Solomon pbut had such rates of suicide among its members? It seems like we'd be more likely to find suicide among the ranks of Pharaoh and Goliath. Thousands and thousands of US soldiers have confessed to the evil US military practices and agendas and went AWOL refusing to serve in the US military as a result of these official policies of "*Kill everybody*". They've even exposed the trickery soldiers do when they kill innocents. US soldiers are given extra guns to carry with them so they can plant them on any civilians they choose to kill. That way no charges can be brought against them since the soldiers can just call their victims terrorists who had weapons, to corroborate their story they take a picture of the dead body with the gun next to them. But in reality they were really civilians who had weapons deliberately planted on them after being murdered, the soldiers just frame their murders so that they become legal. That's also one reason why soldiers confiscate guns in the middle east, since a confiscated gun is a much better one to plant on somebody than a standard issued gun. US soldiers in the middle east do this so much these weapons are called "Drop Weapons". It's a common practice. Majors and Colonels even openly issue orders to carry "Drop Weapons" because "Just in case" it's easier than being legal and nobody in the military wants any US soldiers to get a criminal case for any "accident". It would make the military look bad, so "Drop Weapons" become the standard protocol. Israeli military and police have also been killing Muslims and planting "Drop Weapons" on Palestinians claiming they were going to attack them with knives. Israeli soldiers have even been documented on video placing knives on the bodies of dead Muslims after murdering them. Of course to be fair some attacks are real and legitimate, but many "attacks" are just plain murder. Those who use "Drop Weapons" aren't crazy rogues, they are the majority. US soldiers have publicly confessed that they kill unarmed Muslim civilians for sport. If they are angry or bored they shoot at masjids and minarets, sometimes even using mortars or tank rounds to have fun blowing up masjids, even though it's illegal. Some US soldiers collect fingers or other body parts as souvenirs. This is why even the unislamic secular democratic armies that get trained by the US military, like in Iraq and Afghanistan, turn on the US soldiers and kill them. The Taliban never infiltrated the Afghan military, it's just that the US and Western forces were so immoral and anti-islamic that the native people the West puts in charge to fight the Talban decide to fight against their trainers; because they can see it's the right thing to do even though they still opposed the Taliban. Just consider how bad the Western armies must be when those natives who side with them against the Muslims change their minds and fight the western forces despite still having the same anti-islamic pro-western goals. Whereas one of the biggest lies the media reports, is their claim that insurgents infiltrate the native unislamic militaries and police forces that get trained by western forces. It doesn't happen, as individuals they just see with their own eyes that the anti-islamic Western forces are clear oppressors and wrongdoers until they decide to fight against them of their own initiative despite previously siding with them. Those who work and collaborate with western militaries against proper Muslims nearly always decide to fight their bosses because they learn their bosses are just that bad and that the system cannot be reformed or changed from the inside. Then the West complains why the new unislamic democratic governments they set up are so corrupt, because only the scum of earth is willing to cooperate. The good people don't want anything to do with the Western puppet unislamic governments. Thus the Western bad guys install the middle eastern bad guys, because nobody else was willing to work with/for them. The US Marines motto may be "The best of the best" but in reality they are working for the worst of the worst and when the west sets up puppet governments they get staffed with the worst of the worst in kind. The only defense the US military makes for the war crimes they commit is to prevent the American public from knowing. They don't deny the crimes because they can't, they just ignore them and stop the news about them from being circulated. They can do this because they claim it "threatens the national security" of America by letting Americans know their soldiers are evil war criminals. The US government tells the media that if the truth were known it would be tantamount to "aiding the enemies of the US military" and any media outlet who reports on war crimes done by the US military will then be treated as "terrorists". Meaning they threaten to basically kill you if you expose them intentionally killing innocent people. Thus most Americans never learn about the war crimes their tax dollars pay for which are the deliberate policy of the US military. If some crimes ever do become widely known because of international uproar the US media is instructed to just frame the guilty soldiers as drug users or say they are crazy and extremely isolated incidents not indicative of the majority. It's eerily similar to how the Nazi's kept Germans ignorant about the concentration camps. Most German civilians did not know about the camps until after they lost WWII, they just thought it was all anti-patriotic lies just like how Western Europe lied about them in WWI. Yet people in the middle east know, see and record the modern crimes on video to try to inform the world as to what is really going on attempting to explain why they aren't as bad as they are made out to be. Some US soldiers or veterans also confess because they morally can't keep the crimes a secret. But most in the West just don't care and refuse to believe the truth because it contradicts the news and they religiously need to think they are the good guys. Well now you know better, America has waged war against Islam and Muslims even when it was still just a nation of 13 states. Regardless of what ISIS or other extremists have done, they don't have a policy of killing babies. Yet Western soldiers fighting ISIS and other extremists do have that policy. So who are the badder bad guys? I'm not a supporter of ISIS or their evil actions but Islamically speaking while executing prisoners is generally wrong, in rare situations where the enemy takes no prisoners or kills the prisoners they take, then Muslims are instructed to kill their prisoners until the disbelievers change their policies and stop killing Muslim prisoners. So there are the nice rules of Jihad for fighting humane civil disbelievers and then there are the harsher rules for Jihad when fighting bloodthirsty inhumane enemies of Islam. I have not focused on Jihad or counter crusading campaigns in this book because I have done so already in my book "Proper Jihad" which I suggest to any wanting to know about Jihad as Muhammad pbuh taught. Yet if people don't know the rules of Jihad and don't know the people fighting for one side have bloodthirsty inhumane policies, then of course it's going to make anyone who fights back look bad or extreme if the full story isn't known or reported. For instance do you think the Crusaders were advertised in Europe as cannibalistic rapists who killed and robbed without mercy? No, they were depicted as saints and angels in the flesh for hundreds of years and some were even canonized and are prayed to by Catholics to this day. Therefore because the U.S. forces are so wrong to do what they are doing, they are making extremists actions right, permissible and sometimes even

Islamically justified. The real issue is that many only get the patriotic USA version of what is going on which doesn't tell you about the US soldiers raping, robbing torturing and murdering explicitly for anti-Islamic reasons with total impunity while under direct supervision by their commanders. Or they get the unpatriotic USA version of events, which tells a tiny bit of the bad stuff that's happening but the little they allow to leak through is just a tip of a tip of the iceberg so that people think they are getting an uncensored story. Just like Pharaoh did, you don't think Pharaoh actually let his nation know just how many babies he butchered do you? He didn't share the full number with them, but he didn't pretend the number was zero either. War crimes are the policy of US soldiers and others like NATO and the U.N. "peacekeepers", but they just don't report on them much, if at all, in the Western mainstream media. I'm just focusing on America not because it is the only or worst war criminal nation fighting Muslims, but because I'm American myself and feel shame to be one. This is because they act differently when reporters are with them, they put on a show for TV that is nothing at all like the reality. They won't tell you that the drone strikes which have civilian casualties reported as "Collateral Damage" in the newsroom, get called a "perfect shot" in the war room. Plus they don't even consider many war crimes to be war crimes, because they are doing them and they think they are immune from committing war crimes. The first step in resolving this and any long violent conflict is to admit it exists, for people to deny the violent religious conflict exists means those people don't want it to stop. And yes we have to admit it is about religion, we might not want it to be about religion but it is and if we want a solution we must admit it. Admitting the conflict exists means letting all of the truth be known without either side lying or distorting the facts in their favor. If people continue to lie painting themselves as the good guys there will never be a peaceful solution to the conflict. As bad as the pagans who fought the prophet Muhammad pbuh were, they were honest and didn't lie about their warfare. When they mutilated and ate some of the corpses of Muslims at the battle of Uhud their leader Abu Sufyan admitted what happened, he said he didn't order it but wasn't sad over it, yet he admitted what happened. Whereas Pharaoh was the type who lied in warfare. Nobody can ever win a war if they lie about what they've done in it. Liars will not achieve victory in either this world or the next. Satan is the one who wants us to lie, that's how Satan gets us to lose the test of life. God does not aid liars. Those who fight for God do not need to lie. Wars involve lies, while Jihad does not. Thus for the sake of God we must tell the truth if we ever want peace. Let's just publicly admit it, not all wars need be violent but this one against Islam has some violence in it. The war is ongoing. Pick your side. Or don't and try to be neutral, even though taxation and the necessity of believing something and sharing/supporting your beliefs makes that extremely difficult. Which side will win? Telling the truth whether it's in your favor or not is the first step on the road to victory, yet it's not about gaining victory in this world but gaining victory in the next. The road to paradise is the road to victory, will you travel it? Til death? When truth is a casualtie in wars then the whole world loses. An honest enemy is always better than a dishonest friend. To lie in and of itself is a war crime against all of humanity. Liars are a type of war criminals and war criminals get judged and punished by God. Lies may sometimes be permissible religiously in extreme circumstances, even in Islam, but permissible does not mean it's the right thing to do. There is what is right and what is wrong and what is permissible. God loves those who do what is right and hates those who do wrong. Believers don't lie about theological wars. When peacefully fighting disbelief, prophets allowed deception as a military tactic but forbid it as a theological tactic. The real eternal war is between truth and falsehood, the side of the truth can never win by using falsehood as a tactic or weapon. The permanent eternal victory comes from God alone. Whatever you do in your life/war, never lie in this world to win a battle when doing so will make you lose the eternal war known as the test of life, and be doomed as a prisoner of war in the dungeons of hell for having fought for falsehood or sided with falsehood on behalf of the truth. If you or your side is lying, then you are losing automatically. For you to compromise, conceal or deny the truth is to destroy yourself. While if you aren't on the side of truth then you aren't on the side of truth. I don't think there really is a safe middle between falsehood and truth because the prophets were on the side of the truth and so is our Creator. If you are not with God's team on the prophetic side in this life then whatever team you are on is not one that goes to paradise. So maybe one could be neutral but certainly "team neutral" goes to hell. Thus before you die you must choose a road or a warpath. Which warpath will you die on?

Don't mistake the killing of Muslims by the masses of unified non-Muslims as some post-9/11 phenomenon, that's just the most recent excuse used by enemies of Islam to justify their modern crusades. I guarantee that 100 years from now, 500 years from now and 1,000 years from now, if the world hasn't ended by then, the non-Muslim governments will still come up with reasons as to why they are waging war against Muslims. Governments always play the victim when they are doing wrong so that they don't get in trouble for violence since they are perpetual victims. Don't think that this modern day extermination is a temporary measure that's only against extremists. The Europeans said the same thing about their wars against the native Americans, it was always *"just one or two extremist Native American tribes who terrorize colonists"*. Or actually I don't think they called them "Native Americans" back then, but the term was "savages"; although the Christians called them "gentiles", since at the time "gentile" in Christian languages meant "non-Christian and non-Jew". The Europeans and Christians persistantly made it crystal clear to everyone that they never had any public plans to kill all the native Americans and take their lands, they "never ever had such motives" it just sort of "happened by accident, not by design". The violent Muslimish extremists arose as a response to Muslims being killed. For centuries non-Muslims have been viciously attacking Muslims before the violent extremists arose and should they defeat the extremists they will continue attacking Muslims anyways. They will never voluntarily say that there are no extremists left, because then they would need to come up with another excuse to attack Muslims. They will just label any Muslim they want to kill as an extremist. If you actually study the "terrorism laws" everyone on the planet can be legally defined as a terrorist even if they are a baby in the womb. Although currently the majority of people who are poor and/or Muslims are having the label applied to them. According to most States though whenever a victim refuses to be a victim they are terrorists and get treated like one. They get treated as terrorists because criminals have lots of legal rights which terrorists are not given, soon there may not even be criminals and terrorist may become the new label in order to cut costs and make it easier for States to punish whoever they want to punish. It is a historical fact that the non-Muslims have waged war against Islam and Muslims throughout history. For example during the Japanese occupation of Singapore during WWII the head of the Japanese government, named Tojo, intended to use the Muslim holiday eid prayer to proclaim himself a powerful reformer of Islam to update and modernize it, which according to him meant that Muslims were no longer to face Mecca when praying but were to pray facing Tokyo instead. Muslims rejected this Japanese corruption of Islam, so Japan cancelled and forbid Muslims from performing the eid prayer in Singapore. Therefore Allah used the Americans to wreak havoc on Japan in a manner that had never been witnessed before, because they oppressed Muslims. <u>The prime problem is most non-Muslim historians cover up their anti-Islamic history in order to trick their population into thinking it's only temporary and that they really aren't prejudiced.</u> <u>Afterall in all you ever learned about WWII did anyone ever tell you before that the Japanese tried to force Muslims to pray towards Tokyo instead of Mecca?</u> Isn't that something noteworthy? I mean don't they teach and preach about Jews being persecuted in WWII?

Why not add the Muslims to the WWII victims mix and then give them Palestine as recompense for their suffering? Or wait they already had Palestine, but it was given to the Jews who now kill the Muslims in the state of Israel. So the Muslims don't even get a mention for being persecuted by the Japanese but the Jews are given the Muslims' Holy land, oh but we can't say it has anything to do with religion. This historical cover-up and neglect is done because by hiding the fact that Islam has been constantly assaulted it dissuades people from researching Islam. If people were told the truth, that people have been fighting Islam and Muslims constantly for thousands of years, then the masses would ask what Islam actually is and what do Muslims actually believe. Since this leads people to embrace Islam and change sides, as I did, the anti-Muslims don't want people to ask these questions. They will and have manipulated history to make it seem like Muslims have been on the offensive against the non-Muslims eternally for no reason by ignoring most, if not all, of the vicarious attacks that the non-Muslim world has made and continues to make on Islam and Muslims. Enemies of Islam will claim Muslims have been on a rampage forever, but as a Muslim I'll tell you honestly that there hasn't been any offensive military jihad in hundreds of years. Muslims have been on the defense for so long that some ignorant Muslims mistakenly think jihad is only defensive. And now the foolish amongst them are retreating to make the theological war defensive as well. The flow has gone both ways through the centuries, sometimes Muslims have the military victories sometimes not. However <u>if one side's losses go to paradise and the other side's losses go to hell, there is really only one side winning every battle regardless of the score</u>. But the important thing is to look at history objectively, most people will only see history through one perspective so they don't get the full picture. The non-Muslims must look at history from the Islamic as well as the unislamic viewpoint. It is because they only look at history through their own side of the story that people end up aligning with the Evil side against the Good. It is actually outrageous how frequently Western historians entirely ignore Islam and the Khilafahs, as well as Muslim Civilizations, practically pretending they never existed. Especially when they are at a level where it is professionally irresponsible and blameworthy to be ignorant of such things. The reason they ignore Islam and Muslims in history is because of the historically scientific way Islam has been preserved it proves that in comparison most history is not reliably verified, thereby damaging the credibility of the entire history industry and the undeservedly high reputation of the historian profession. Also because if Islam and the Khilafahs were studied, everyone would see that all of history's social problems of the past were solved by Islam and that all the present problems would likewise be solved if people adopted the same system. Yet since in most countries that would mean a change of religion and government, the governments strongly prohibit historians from teaching people about this. Therefore the historians don't even get taught about Islam or Muslims themselves, except for basic vocabulary. The non-Muslim historians who do learn about Islam tend to have anti-islamic dispositions because the religious books of Islam are historically more authentic than the historian's history books are, yet instead of attack Islam, which they can't do honestly, they simply ignore Islam so people remain ignorant of it. They choose their bubble of historical fantasy which they've invested so heavily in rather than let Islam burst it with reality. Politically historians are valued for manipulating history in favor of their benefactors, whereas Muslims expose these lies of history simply by having historically and scientifically preserved transmissions of the Quran and Hadith. Thus many non-Muslim historians tend to ignore Islam because it proves that it's religious books are more trustworthy than their history books. I've found most historians preach a religion of Social Darwinism mixed with hedonism and humanism, misleading people to think that our modern society is the most advanced and "civil" despite archaeology having proven that past generations of humans were bigger, better, stronger, smarter, lived longer and were more advanced technologically. The problem is that many of them were destroyed by "unexplainable natural disasters" such as windstorms, earthquakes, supervolcanoes, floods, the ice age and solar flares; which was a result of their sinfulness. Some of these societies the Quran relates the destruction of so we don't repeat their mistakes and some of which archaeology informs us of, with the archaeology not only confirming things the Quran says about prior generations but also humbling our species making us realize that we aren't the most materially advanced of our species, thus destroying all national pride, arrogance and the evolution myth.

Although since according to Western law "freedom of religion" means that history and archaeology can't be used to support or prove a religion, especially when it's Islam, such archaeology gets forbidden and the past which is rediscovered is intentionally hidden and censored. Therefore due to politics and Satanic religious dispositions, academically history is distorted and disfigured to be prejudiced against Islam, and Muslims too, because the religion of Islam proves that history isn't 100% true. The reason history in school is boring to many and exciting to others is because they are being taught fiction. Why else do you think the bible is such a boring book? According to current standards, nearly every historical figure was an extremist so learning about history in the modern times should be exciting. If learning about history is boring to people then what's being taught might not be true. France's Napolean Bonaparte said, "*History is a set of lies agreed upon.*" and "*History is written by the winners.*" While the infamous vilified Adolf Hitler said: "*The man who has no sense of history, is like a man who has no ears or eyes.*" Whereas if you have sense of Hitler's statement you will understand that he wasn't talking about knowing historical information but having a "sense of history". Because he had a "sense of history", Hitler knew what history was and that having a sense of what history is in reality is much more important and advantageous than knowing what history says. Thus Hitler made more history than he learned because he had a "sense of history". Having a sense of history allows one to be able to see and hear what is going on around them in their present time. Simply knowing historical factoids doesn't give you that sense of present history in the making. Basically if you don't know what history is then you are almost clueless as to your present political and religious surroundings. Hitler's statement doesn't mean the person can't see or hear what is going on but that they have no ability to perceive in the present moment what is actually taking place when it is taking place. Hitler actually didn't know much historical information at all, since he made many military mistakes that any average historian could see coming well in advance due to foreknowledge of the mistakes made by past nations. In fact if Hitler did know a little more about historical information he may well have won WWII. Hitler even failed to learn from the mistakes Germany made in WWI which he personally fought in, but still despite being historically ignorant he had a "sense of history" and due to that "sense of history" he influenced history. But how many history textbooks, volumes or historical movies do you think share these lessons about history? However to paraphrase Napoleon we can religiously say, "*A false religion is a set of lies agreed upon.*" and thereby conclude that history is actually a religious dogma. Most people understand that their religious beliefs influence their beliefs about history, but few are aware that historical beliefs are religious beliefs too. You can't look at history without painting somebody as good/right and others as evil/wrong and to do that is to make a religious judgement. Yet governments say they don't teach kids to believe in certain religions in school? To claim beliefs about history are not religious beliefs is perhaps the biggest lie historians teach about "history". There is no such thing as "historical objectivity", even the information that gets recorded about events is recorded based on subjective religious biases. <u>It is impossible for history to be impartial and unbiased</u>. Nobody can merely observe or learn about history, instead they "believe in history". Many historians are religious preachers teaching from their own book which they frequently expect and tell people to believe in as if it were divine revelation. History books are seen and marketed as if they were sacrosanct holy scriptures written by prophets. Once history is known as a subsidiary of religion and source of religious beliefs then one can scrutinize what kind of history they are being taught in schools, in songs, in the news, in movies, on TV, on the internet, from co-workers, from family, from friends and deduce which type of religious beliefs those history teachers are espousing based on their historical beliefs. You can actually learn someone's religious beliefs simply by learning what their historical beliefs are. Most history lessons today are religious sermons teaching Darwinism/Hedonism/Nationalism/Humanism etc. That way people are proud to be hard-working oppressed atheist taxpayers who die off quickly, before they get old enough to witness and expose the false historical lies and social myths the governments and media will teach the younger generations. Afterall the Tanakh(Hebrew Bible) is simply the Jewish history book while the New Testament is the Christian history book. Now not every religious book is a history book, but every history book is a religious book and if many people believe in it then it can eventually become a religious "Scripture" just as the Jewish and Christian history books evolved into their sacred scriptures. That's actually exactly what Joseph Smith tried to do when he wrote the Book of Mormon, but he made a mistake because his history book contradicted true history and science and contradicted itself as well as the bible he claimed it correlated with. Yet still millions of mormons think the history book that Joseph Smith wrote is an english translation of some golden tablets which a reincarnated dead guy turned angel showed him, afterwhich the "angel" called Moroni took the original source documents leaving Joseph Smith with a english history book that contradicts everything else known about American and Religious history. Hence Joseph Smith became a false prophet, but in reality he did the job historians do. The only difference was that he claimed he was copying a religious historical document that explicitly taught a religion while other historians just claim to be teaching historical lessons without religious connotations or claiming to have spiritual authority. So while most historians may not claim to be prophets, all prophets both real and false are part-historians and history is a part of religion that shapes one's religious beliefs influencing one's behavior. Therefore the teachers of history, whoever they are in whatever format they teach conventual or otherwise, can exert influence and control over present and future human beliefs and behavior. Thus the people who teach about history are very powerful people. While because most don't have a "sense of history" to realize the powerful influence and motivations such historians may have when teaching various things about history it gives the historians and history teachers even more power over other people. Especially if people think history is boring. No math, grammar or science teachers I know of ever changed religions, nations and entire continents, but historians have been continuously doing that for millenniums. Why else do you think a historian/history teacher is one of the oldest professions in the world? Religions teach history and historians teach religions. Adam pbuh was the first history teacher and the main message he taught in his prophethood was a history lesson we still forget. Sadly due to the internet everyone can now act as a historian and be treated as such by future generations due to long-term data preservation. Hence to be safe in the afterlife teach responsibly. Whether you like it or not you are a historian teaching religion. Teaching is a type of Jihad which everyone does every single day, though whether we do it correctly or for the right reasons is another matter. However always remember that teaching, however you do it or fail to do it, is a type of warfare more dangerous than violence. Teachers and preachers are those who truly make history, the rest just watch, record it or play a role in the plan of preachers. Every "leader" simply follows their teacher, though commonly the teacher/preacher of most people is Satan. Every person is always teaching/preaching to everyone around them every second of the day but few of us follow the legitimate teachers known as prophets, nor do we teach their message as our Maker has told us to do. We are bad students and bad teachers. This is why things are messed up because we failed to learn from the prophets and fail to practice/teach/preach what the prophets did. Yet fortunately the prophetic curriculum is there for us, if we would only focus, prioritize and do what God our singular unique Creator wants us to do.

The false religions which oppose Islam wouldn't be able to keep changing over and over again as easily if people lived longer and could tell the young people how what the unislamic religions teach today is not what they taught last century.

Thus unhealthy lifestyles, toxic foods, "medicines" with harmful side effects which require further such "medicines" to cure the cure, "old folks homes"(or human zoos for historical prisoners as I call them, since their "crime" is aging) and euthanasia are supported by unislamic governments so that they can more quickly and thoroughly change history from one generation to the next. Especially in regards to pharmaceuticals and allopathic medicine (the popular mainstream kind) the drugs legally prescribed to people as medicine today will likely be illegal drugs tomorrow. Take the history of Cocaine as an example. In 1860 CE Alfred Niemann produced cocaine from a coca leaf to increase muscular action, remove hunger and fatique as well as increase speech abilities. It was largely ignored until 1883 CE when the German Army used it with troops to increase their stamina and reduce their need for food and sleep. In 1884 CE the psychiatric "genius" Sigmund Freud began using it and called it a "gift" from nature and even recommended and gave cocaine to his friends to use. In the 1890s cocaine was mass marketed in pills, lozenges, tablets, toothache drops, energy drinks and it was even the main ingredient in the "nervine tonic" called "Coca-Cola" which cured hysteria, headaches and melancholy. Marijuana was also popular and used to aid childbirth, cure insomania and stomach cramps with Queen Victoria herself even using it based on her royal physician John Russel Robert's advice who said marijuana was *"one of the most valueable medicines we possess"*. While Queen Elizabeth I, following her doctor's advice, would eat a pound of bacon and drink a tankard of ale everyday for breakfast and became a heavy smoker. Morphine was named after the Roman god of sleep Morpheus and invented to help Alcohol addicts rehabilitate, but then people found out Morphine was even more addictive and dangerous than alcohol. But don't worry because the pharmaceutical company Bayer came out with a cure for morphine addiction in 1898 CE, called diacetylmorphine which is also a cough suppressant too. I'm certain you've heard of this drug heroically made and proscribed by pharmaceuticals and doctors as a cough suppressant, it's called Heroin. Yes, Heroin was advertised by doctors to be a cough suppressant and sold as such to the masses for years. So the next time you have a cough, remember in the past doctors would give you heroin for that. Another brilliant medicine prescribed in 1837 CE and sold as a cure for diarrhea, cholera, baldness, athlete's foot, jaundice, indigestion and the common cold was ketchup. Although maybe you doubt the efficacy of ketchup as medicine, in that case should you contract malaria or syphillis during the 1950s doctors would prescribe arsenic for that. Today people use arsenic to kill rats. Maybe you are fat and want to lose weight? Well in the 1950s the popular medically sound way to lose weight was to eat a tape worm, that way the tape worm in your body would get fat off of the food you eat and you could stay skinny due to the deadly parasitical worm inside your body. That's good civilized medicine right? Well it passed the clincial trials and was proven to work, the people actually did lose weight when they took tape worms as medicine. Opium was another popular legal medicine which was mass marketed in most of the Western world until the 1930s CE. Then during WWII amphetamines were invented as the new over the counter medicine to help people live life. Yet those were criminalized along with many of the previously mentioned "medicines" because the pharmaceutical companies invented new and improved barbituates, sedatives and narcotic "medicines". If you actually research the history of the evil illegal drugs today, most of them were invented and proscribed as medicine by pharmaceutical companies and doctors. (not counting ketchup and tapeworms) After the patents expired the products became cheaper so more could use them, but then the masses were told these "medicines" were destroying people. So new "medicines" had to be made and the old "medicines" were called drugs even though they aren't chemically much different than the current modern legal medicines. The main difference is the patents on modern medicines haven't expired yet, once they do and the medicines become cheap then they may admit the stuff is dangerous, but by that time they'll have a new expensive patented medicine for people to buy instead. An example of this is smoking. Originally in the 1600s CE the masses were told that smoking was healthy and tobacco was medicine which everyone should take because smoking was a cure for many diseases and prevented many diseases as well. That medical racket lasted over 400 years and is still going to a lesser extent. But why was tobacco thought to be so good? It was because the Native American "Indians" said so thinking it would drive away ghosts, expel witches, heal the sick, bring rain, ensure good weather before a journey and even force someone who is smoking to tell the truth making it impossible for a smoker to lie. An alliance signed with a peace pipe was even thought to be an accord eternally guaranteed. Yet what Christian European would be dumb enough to believe this stuff? His name was John Rolfe and he married a famous native American woman formerly called Pocahantas in 1614 CE. Before the wedding she had converted to Christianity while a 19 year old prisoner in 1614 CE and changed her name to Rebecca, after having been held hostage for about 1-3 years. However Rebecca/Pocahantas' 1614 CE marriage to John Rolfe was not her first, she had married a native called Kocoum in 1610 CE when she was about 15 and had a son with him. But perhaps what's most surprising is that her name was never really Pocahantas at all but Matoaka, Pocahantas was a nickname given to her prior to her conversion to Christianity. Pocahantas means *"playful one, sportive, frolicsome, mischievous and frisky"* so make of her nickname what you will but know that she died in 1616 CE at the age of 21. The english considered her to be a young frisky, mischievous girl who was famous for doing cartwheels with children, and because of how native American women dressed this means when doing these cartwheels her male colonial captors would've seen all her private parts. So that they called her Pocahantas might mean she's not someone who is a role model for kids. Although considering that the english had killed her husband Kocoum prior to kidnapping her (her son was at another village at the time) she might have just been *"mischieviously frisky"* in order to survive enslavement. She also reportedly had a nervous breakdown while hostage because the English repeatedly told her none of her family loved her and they even staged false prisoner exchanges designed to make her think she wasn't wanted by her people. John Rolfe fell in love with her while she was a captive, maybe after seeing her famous nude cartwheels. Then she became Christian, changed her name and got married. Her English husband's last name was Rolfe, it was not Smith. John Smith was the founder of Jamestown, Virginia. John Smith did not marry Pocahantas, Rolfe did. In fact Rebecca Rolfe later went to England and met John Smith and it was only after she died as a British celebrity that John Smith wrote in his memoirs stories about how she romantically saved his life. Yet this famous Smith myth didn't exist until after Rebecca Rolfe had died, and he never claimed this while she was alive in England so it's probably a false fable. John Smith even told the Queen that Pocahantas was too overwhelmed with emotion to talk to him much when in person so that's why they didn't seem as close as Smith later claimed they were after Rebecca died. The Rolfes' only had one child but that child had kids making Pochanatas, or Rebecca Rolfe, the ancestor of many famous American families like the Lees, Masons, and Jeffersons. Famous descendants of Rebecca Rolfe include Edith Wilson (wife of Woodrow Wilson), Nancy Reagan (wife of Ronald Reagan) and Pauline de Rothschild. Although whether this child of Pocahantas and John Rolfe was born out of wedlock, or as a result of rape and was born prior to her conversion to Christianity, depends on which historian you ask. Whereas since Pocahantas/Rebecca Rolfe had endorsed tobacco as a medicine when she went to England, her later influential descendants were deeply inclined to think she was right about tobacco being medicine solely due to ancestral devotion. Basically Pocahantas/Rebecca Rolfe was tobacco's first international advertiser or postergirl for smoking. Tobacco isn't the only product globally portrayed as medicine once the American colonization began, in the 16th and 17th centuries chocolate was considered medicinal. Sugar was marketed as medicine too, for hundreds of years. Tea was also promoted as a medicine and the English loved that "medicine" especially when it was made twice as healthy when mixed with the other "medicine" called sugar. As the saying goes "*A spoon full of medicinal sugar helps the medicinal tea go down.*" Thus the American colonies made their cash crops of tobacco and sugar on huge plantations growing medicine for Europe. But then when those Americans decided to stop selling "medicine" like tobacco and sugar to England because of taxes, it was a threat to national security by those colonial terrorists. In the 1760s CE Americans banned all tobacco and sugar exports to England and at the time it was considered medicine. So when Britain then sent their soldiers to America they were fighting for medicine in their opinion, but the US school textbooks never mention the detail of the global medicine ransoming done by the Americans. Thus since Americans were fighting for money the world would not look too kindly on a nation fighting for money against a nation fighting for medicine, thus the religion of Americanism and it's subset religions had to be invented to justify the revolutionaries as "good guys". Yet many colonists remained loyalists because they thought the Americans were just greedy and that Britain was right to invade to secure medicine for the British nation. Although what was the revolution's trigger point? Remember the "Boston Tea Party"? Well tea was considered to be medicine, so when Americans dressed up as Indians to dump tea into the ocean rather than pay taxes they had to dress as Indians because they were dumping what was globally considered medicine into the ocean and no "sane civilized white man" could do such a thing. Many would call that barbaric, terrorism, crazy or evil, but it was taxed tea and they really did not want to pay taxes even if it was for medicine. But they didn't want to be called crazy or evil for dumping taxed medicine into the ocean either. Thus Native Americans got the global public scorn while privately the British government was informed of the real political reasons behind the "Boston Tea Party". Although they didn't really need to be informed because the colonists could've stopped such an attack if they wanted to and that's why the British called them out on it and didn't let the Native American costumes get used as a scapegoat. Although remember that Tea, Tobacco and Sugar aren't really medicines at all. So those Americans refusing "medicine" to their own British Mother Nation and dumping British "medicine" into the ocean weren't really barbaric terrorists as they were portrayed. Yet the medical industry exacerbated the whole issue and Britain nearly won as a result. If Britain did win the war they would've been heralded as good guys for centuries to come for having saved the world from the American terrorists, who if they got independence would've surely held the entire world hostage by threatenting any nation they wanted with a medical embargo and medical sanctions until they complied with the American demands. Britain used the medical industry to say the Americans would create a global menace to medicine and were trying to found a terrorist nation based on heretical religious/political notions even though the vast majority of colonists were loyal to Britain and didn't believe in the faith of Americanism. Unfortunately the medical industry also caused other wars. Like the Opium wars Britain fought with China. As a nation Britain was addicted to Chinese tea but China didn't want anything Britain had to trade with except for silver, but Britain couldn't afford to pay China for all the tea they wanted in silver.

From 1800 CE to 1810 CE Britain had already paid nearly 1,000 tons of silver to China for tea since the American trade had sharply declined, Britain simply could not keep paying for tea with silver. Thus a new medicine called Opium was imported to China, sold by the British Empire via the East India Company, and thus the "Chinese Health Crisis" was "solved" coincidentally in a way that solved the British economic crisis so they no longer had to pay for tea with silver but paid with Opium instead. But wait, why did China need to import Opium? They didn't, Britain just didn't want to keep paying for tea with silver so the British medical industry created a market for Opium in China. Think of it like a parent's child using candy they got from the kid's doctor in order to pay the pharmacy for the medicine their doctor says the kid needs. Since they don't want to use money to pay the pharmacist, the parent of the child tells the pharmacist that they will pay them with the doctor's medicinal candy that will cure the health problems the pharmacist has but didn't know that they had. Oh and the parent gets a doctor's note from the pharmacist's doctor explaining how the doctor's candy will heal them from their illness. This was done to China in the name of Free-Market

Capitalism. Then people wonder why China later embraced Communism. Under Capitalism China went from selling tea leaves for silver to selling tea leaves for opium, that's called "free-trade". However the Chinese Emperor, who did not study medicine at Oxford, decided that Opium was not a medicine but a poison and he banned all Opium from entering China. Thus interfering with Free-Market Capitalism. I mean what kind of tyrannical Emperor would ban the medicine of opium in all of China? Surely those oppressed Chinese had to be liberated by the British so they were no longer deprived of medicinal opium. Britain had "pure intentions" of freeing the Chinese from their evil anti-capitalist tyrant. Many Chinese were even reportedly dying because they couldn't get access to their much needed medicinal opium. Yet how could the British government convince their nation to invade China so the Chinese would sell them tea for opium? Especially when some "unpatriotic conspiratorial nutjobs" were starting to say opium is poisonous just like the Chinese Emperor said. The solution was illegally smuggling opium into China for tea. This happened for awhile but it was too difficult because it was illegal and the Chinese navy would prevent it and punish smugglers. But alas the firm of Jardine and Matheson, who were smugglers with a fleet of the fastest ships in the Sea, got an idea to solve the smuggling debacle. They were also Christian missionaries and they would distribute thousands of bibles on the Chinese mainland, while secretly trading opium for tea on the side. But there was nothing morally wrong with that, they were simply "good Christians" selling medicinal Opium to needy Chinese Christians who had converted because they said they really believed in Christianity, the Opium had nothing to do with it but even if it did opium was medicine. So if Opium had anything to do with the Chinese becoming Christians then it was probably just because of their humanitarian Christian manners in giving out free medicinal opium to needy peoples whether they were Christian or not, isn't that what Jesus pbuh would do? This was an entirely moral Christian enterprise based on the teachings of the bible and Jesus pbuh, or so they said, it was lucrative too. These missionaries would bring back special Chinese tea made by Christian converts which sold for extra because Christian Brits simply had to pay extra to help out their needy Chinese brethren in faith who were prohibited from getting the opium they needed because of the cruel evil non-Christian Chinese Emperor. Rumor had it this whole ban on the medicine of opium was just an excuse to have the Chinese Christians die off by preventing them from getting the opium they needed to live. This missionary business continued for awhile, during which time the British went from paying nearly 1,000 tons of silver for tea from 1800-1810 CE to having China in 1830-1840 CE pay Britain 366 tons of silver for opium. By 1840 CE the Christian missionaries Jardine and Matheson were selling 6,000 chests of opium a year, but remember it was medicine for the "Christians". Well the Emperor realized what was going on and appointed a new high commissioner to make sure opium was not entering China "by any means" even if it were by Christian missionaries. Well it turned out the new Chinese commissioner caught the Christians with Opium, which was an illegal poisonous drug according to China and not a medicine like Christian Europe was saying. So the Commissioner imprisoned the opium traders in his office until they gave up all their stock. They ended up handing over 2,613,879 pounds of opium (note that's millions of pounds). It was suggested to burn all the contraband but it was thought the residue might still be smokable, so it was dumped in the ocean and churned with salt. A letter was then sent from the Chinese to Queen Victoria in 1839 CE informing her what happened and telling her she should destroy all the opium in her territories. What did Queen Victoria do? Courageously for the sake of religious freedom/Christianity and the very health of the Chinese people she and the British Parliament declared war on China. British fury was unleashed and China had to sue for peace in 1842 CE giving the island of Hong Kong to Great Britain. Yet for some reason the Chinese Emperor didn't learn his lesson and still insisted opium was not medicine but poison and hindered the opium trade/Christian missionary activity. So in 1856-1860 CE Britain attacked the mainland sending troops as far as Bejiing and destroyed the Emperor's palace along with his regime, thereby freeing China and making it a semi-colony of Britain. Finally the Empereor conceded and opium became lawful. Oddly enough though once China was under British authority most of the Chiristians seemed to have disappeared because opium was legal and could be gotten from non-Christians. Opium then became China's cash crop and Chinese industry developed to service and facilitate everything to do with opium from poppy seed to overdose. The

Chinese opium industry was primarily the result of the actions taken by a banking organization called *"The Hongkong and Shanghai Banking Corporation"* that was established in British Hong Kong in 1865 CE, today this company still exists under a different but similar name of "HSBC holdings plc". However HSBC, which today has trillions of dollars in assets, got their start via the Chinese opium trade so they were drug dealing banksters; and not much has changed since then with them or the banking industry at large. By 1887 CE according to official statistics nearly a third of the arable land in the province of Yunnan was growing the opium poppy and two-thirds of the male population in Szechuan were regular opium smokers. Chinese opium began to dominate the world opium markets but as a result of Chinese love for opium, China became a pretty poor country to live in since they were the main consumers of their national produce and opium was the product , but since they couldn't make as much opium as they consumed they sold their silver to Britain, France, Portugal and Persia in exchange for more opium. China was literally smoking more opium than they could grow and using their silver to cover the difference. Famines and economic turmoil led Chinese people to move to Europe and America, bringing opium dens with them. Around this time, oddly enough, Europe found out that opium is not a medicine but a vice because the good Christians informed the world it was and clearly it was the reason why the Chinese heathen were so "uncivilized". It was no wonder there were so few Christians in China, with all that opium how could the message of Christianity get through? This is actually what the Christians said, they blamed opium and the opium pandemic as the reason Chinese people weren't responding to the Christian missionaries in China. The Christians said if only the opium were removed from China then the Chinese would become Christian. It sounds crazy but you must remember this was decades after the opium wars, people had short attention spans; probably because they were using opium as medicine. Yet the record stands that first Christians claimed importing opium illegally to China promoted Christianity, then they went to war to promote those 2 exports, then they claimed opium then legalized due to the Christian war efforts was preventing Christianity from spreading in China. You may notice a theme of desire for Christianity to spread, but that was never the official reason for the actions of the British

Government. Fortunately being the good Christian nation that it always had been, Great Britain appointed a royal commission in 1895 CE to "examine the opium question". This commission concluded that as bad as opium is, yes they did conclude opium is bad, it would be "unjust" for a foreign power to impose a ban on opium in China even though every decent Christian and Englishman dearly wishes for it to be done so as to save the poor Chinese from that devilish tool of Satan known as opium. Great Britain declared that China had sovereign rights and no foreign nation could dictate it's policy on opium. As expected the world applauded Great Britain's noble humane stance defending and promoting freedom and independence throughout the world, despite having the military capacity to do what it wanted and ban opium in China they choose not to because they held such lofty principles. Then Germany entered the picture in 1898 CE by invading and annexing portions of China because 2 German Christian missionaries had been killed. You see the Chinese finally figured out all their trouble was coming from the Christian missionaries trying anything they could to convert people and create unstable conditions leading to conversions to Christianity.

For example Christian missionaries had not only introduced and imported opium to China against the will and desire of the Chinese people and government, but Christians also introduced tobbaco to China even before that. For the Jesuit missionary Matteo Ricci brought tobacco to China in 1581 CE in the form of snuff that caused smoking to become widespread by 1630 CE. So it's no surprise China eventually had 2 Christian missionaries killed after centuries of intentional destabilization and corruption done in the name of Christianity. But what China didn't anticipate was Germany invading them just because they killed two criminal Christian missionaries. Russia joined the party and took a piece of China too, which caused Britain to get some more of Chinese territory as well lest the Germans and Russians get too much. Thus the Boxer Rebellion occurred in China during 1898-1901 CE, specifically as an attempt to expel the christian missionaries, afterwhich opium became unpopular as a sign of foreign colonialism. The Boxers however didn't win the war and as a result China was forced to pay the European powers 450 million taels of silver. Which in effect meant practically all the silver China had earned after centuries of selling tea to Europe for silver was back in European hands, resulting in what in essence amounted to Europe getting centuries worth of free Chinese tea after which the Chinese were made to trade their tea to feed their opium addiction. Economically it is hard to think of bigger international screwjobs than what Christian Europe did to China, except maybe the Christian slave trade in Africa or the Christians "trading" with the Native Americans. In 1909 CE an International Commission in Shanghai decreed opiates to be a "grave danger" and China demanded international regulation. This embarassed Britain because China diplomatically said *"We don't want this opium! We never wanted it, you illegally forced it upon us and now you are saying nobody can help us to get it out. We never chose it and can't get rid of it and beg people to get this opium we never wanted out of China!"* So in response to the pleas of the Chinese, at the Haque in 1911 CE the first International Opium Commission met, which was chaired by the famous Bishop Brent who obliged the signatories to enact regulation in their own lands to pave the way for an international treaty. In 1912 CE the Imperial Qing Dynasty of China was overthrown, since paying 450 million taels of silver to Europe to pay for the Boxer Rebellion led to a bankrupt budget and some quite unpopular taxation, and China returned to chaotic warlord feudalism and semicolonial status. Christian missionaries then began to attack the opium problem in China by running detox clinics and asylums for recovering opium addicts. How did they help the Chinese kick opium? Well with Christianity of course, AND with hypodermic injections of morphine, heroin, strychnine, quinine and another type of innovative drug called "caffeine". Yet the problem with the Chinese and opium was that the smoke was thought to be spiritual like ancient incense, so it was widely adopted. Whereas with the needles, unlike the West, Chinese people did not have aversions to needles because of a long history of acupuncture. Needles were seen as naturally medicinal in China. Thus China easily became addicted to the needle drugs given to them as medicine by Christian missionaries to get them off the opium which was given to them by Christian missionaries as medicine to get them off the tobacco which was given to them by Christian missionaries as medicine in the 1500s CE. Perhaps you've noticed a pattern with Christian missionaries and their "work"? Sadly that pattern continues today. In the Western lands the Christians serve wine to people every week in church from a young age and simultaneously help alcoholics recover via Christianity. In church they make you an alcoholic then they use alcoholism to turn you to Christianity. Christian social systems consistently turn people into addicts to give them Christianity as a cure, just as Santa Claus in the long-run promotes Christianity. The proliferation of sin leads wicked sinners to see the cross/christ as their only life-raft and chance to get to paradise. This is because if society wasn't so sinful and so immoral then Christians would have no target audience desperate for a saviour because they'd realize God can just forgive them. Sinful societies promote Christianity. Moral societies are athema to Christian proselytization. If people weren't "hopeless sinners" they wouldn't think they need to be "saved" with a fatal sacrifice paid with the blood of God and/or his son. Only if everyone is really wicked can Christianity make a case for the bloody atonement via Christ. If people "aren't that bad" we don't need God to bleed and die for us, so this is why Christians inherently promote sin even if it's unintentional because their theology requires evil societies or nobody would ever accept Christianity as plausible in any way. Politicians and Clergy know this and that's why clergy rarely/barely complains when politicians create sinful societies because the clergy knows sinful societies help them preach and get people involved with Christianity. The clergy also likes war because then they can pray for peace. During war lots of people go to church to pray, and while in church they tend to make monetary donations as well. So while today clergy stresses the "need to turn the other cheek" they'd be out of business if the politicians ever established world peace. If the world is not a sinful evil immoral place filled with evildoers then Christians have no salespitch they can make. This is why governments historically have been very friendly with clergy. It's a symbiotic relationship. States profit from the sin as do the Christian preachers. The Christian preachers ensure the population doesn't get "too sinful" so that it's uneconomical, while the politicians ensure there is enough sinfulness to create a crowd and outlet/opportunity for zealous Christians who hate sin and want people to stop sinning. Meanwhile the clergy inspires people to fight for the state, so the state wages war to spread Christianity and as a bonus the clergy preaches "Pay to Caesar what is Caesar's" and "Turn the other cheek" so as to quell sedition and revolt due to oppressive governments or obscene unjust taxation. The Churches cannot survive without the States unofficially promoting sin. The "Separation" was so people didn't wise up to the game they've been playing on us. This has always been the Christian habit, they invent the sin so they can take it away. For example Original Sin was made up by Saul/Paul so that Baptism could be made, it's a political profiteering puzzle. With Christianity the "Law of Moses" was abolished, because governments didn't really want to follow the moral code of Moses pbuh. Pharaoh didn't want the Law of Moses or God, and that was even before the law was revealed. Saul/Paul abolished the Law of God to please Caesar, and Constantine saw the opportunity. With the "Law of Moses" abolished, governments can legally do anything just like Pharaoh always wanted. Hence this is why the Roman Empire actually became more degenerate AFTER Christianity spread throughout it, because even the pagans had a moral code of conduct but Pauline Christianity gave states a blank check to cultivate sin as unofficial policy. Do the research, <u>the Roman Empire and morality declined as the citizenry converted from Paganism to Christianity</u>. Thus proving Christians were and are more immoral than polytheistic Pagan Idolaters. Christianity was and is a religion where governments of Christian peoples never actually have to morally reform and improve their citizens because Christian clerics need and subconsciously desire the opposite. Except for the rare clerical minority who actually believe and try to practice what they preach. Governments + Christianity = the economics of sin + a theological necessity for an economy/nation based upon sinfulness. The culprit behind China's problems is easy to identify, IF you pay attention to history. But few do because most get told historical fiction instead factual narratives. Of course lying historians will give you facts and vocabulary, but the narratives they give you are fictional fantasy. For example why did America enter WWII? Most Americans will say it was because of Hitler or Britain or Freedom or because of Japan attacking American warships at the Pearl Harbor prostitute base(which they probably don't know was a prostitute outpost), but all of those answers are wrong. The American president John F. Kennedy, who actually fought in WWII, explained the real reason why America fought in WWII, "*It was clearly enunciated that the independance of China...was the fundamental object of our Far Eastern policy...that this and other statements led directly to the attack on Pearl Harbor is well known. And it might be said that we knowingly entered into combat with Japan to preserve the independence of*

China." In 1937 CE Japan entered and began annexing mainland China due to territorial gains in the 2nd Sino-Japanese War. Why did America care? Because the influential American missionary Reverand Arthur Henderson Schmidt who had lived/preached in China for 54 years from 1872 CE to 1926 CE said *"China can never be reformed from within. The manifold needs of China, will be met permanently, completely, only by Christian civilization."* Americans were led to believe that Christinaity was what China "needed" and what China wanted, but with Japan's national religion being Shintoism the world of Christendom opposed Japanese expansion in China. It was with the goal/promise of a New Christianized China that the China Lobby encouraged a US military intervention in the 1930s and 1940s to drive the non-Christian Japanese out of China. A Christian China could become the Prestor John type nation crusaders always dreamed of. At that time America supplied Japan with 80% of it's oil, so America simply cut off the Japanese oil supply forcing Japan to either withdraw from China or violently break the oil embargo. Japan warned in advance they would attack the US ships if the oil embargo continued and they eventually fulfilled their promise which brought America into WWII with most of it's citizens thinking they were victims not being informed that America blockaded Japan first depriving them of 80% of the oil they had been receiving. After Japan capitulated and Mao Zedong rose to rule China in 1949 CE, America thinking the Chinese people wanted Christianity sided with his opponent Chiang Kai-shek who was a Methodist Christian. However Mao Zedong had the support of the Chinese people and won the Chinese civil war, after which it was presumed Capitalism would reign in China since in 1944 CE Mao Zedong had tried to ally with America in the name of Capitalism. Although America didn't want a Capitalist China as Mao Zedong originally proffered, because America believed in a "New China" where Christianity was the official state-sponsored religion. Neither Mao nor his supporters wanted to make China into a Christian state though, so since the USSR didn't require a Christianization clause in exchange for aid Mao turned Communist. In response to American Christians "Losing China" the Catholic Senator Joseph McCarthy suspected it was due to anti-Christian influences in the American government, so a famous "witch hunt" of McCarthyism stratified US politics all in the name of anti-communism because officially they couldn't say they were seeking out anti-Christians, but since Communists tended to be atheist, to be a Communist was synonymous with not being a Christian. Unfortunately America's Christian dream for China also extended to the rest of Asia and this Christianized Asia plan later led to America waging war in Korea and Vietnam, of which both were allegedly done in the name of Capitalism but Christianity was the unofficial policy motivator. Over time the Americanists gained more influence in the American government than the Christians, so now both groups cooperate more smoothly than they had done before as their tactics evolve and they've found that the goals of the Christians and the Americanists are often found to be similar. With many US politicians today it even becomes difficult to determine whether they are a Christian at heart promoting Americanist politics or an Americanist at heart promoting Christian politics. One needs political astuteness to be able to tell the difference but sometimes one still can't distinguish because both faiths overlap in this modern era as Christianity blends with Americanism. Even the Catholic Joseph McCarthy couldn't tell which was which during his "witch hunt" as he said

"McCarthyism is Americanism with its sleeves rolled." while also teaching/preaching that, *"Today we are engaged in a final, all-out battle between communistic atheism and Christianity."* The 20th century American international policy started out as Christian but eventually became more Americanistic until today where both the American and Christian sides are nearly symbiotic, within American politics. Both sides practice Americanism to different degrees, one is the denomination of Secular Americanism while the other practices a denomination of Christian Americanism. Currently China still has a needle drug epidemic and the Christians keep on preaching there passing out their bibles saying Christianity will save China from pollution, materialism and even overpopulation. Which is actually true, I firmly believe if China were converted to Christianity then it would solve the "problem" of Chinese prosperity, and reduce the Chinese population which would reduce the pollution. Whether it'd be good is a different question, but it would end the materialism and population largesse for sure because China would be poor and have many Chinese who died in the conversion process. Every nation would do well to keep Christian missionaries out, because history

repeatedly shows what happens to countries when Christian missionaries infiltrate it. Although now there are also business missionaries promoting the religion of Americanism. Missionaries also delve into education and infrastructure as well using them as covers for their religious missions. John Chapman is a famous example of a Christian missionary famous for worldly reasons.

John Chapman is more popularly known as "Johnny Appleseed" who allegedly roamed America during the colonial era planting apple trees everywhere he went. In reality "Johnny Appleseed" was a Christian missionary of the "New Church" religion also known as Swedenborgianism. It was a Christian faith founded by Emanuel Swedenborg who taught that Jesus pbuh was not the "son of God" but just plain old God 100% with no trinity at all. This "New Church" taught/teaches that their founder Swedenborg was a prophet of God/Jesus who received divine revelation. The Swedenborgians most famous missionary, John Chapman or "Johnny Appleseed", became famous for planting apple nurseries as part of his business. Yet why did this apple tree businessman become so famous? Well the apples that grew on his trees are not the types we can buy in grocery stores today, they were explicitly apples grown to create alcoholic hard apple cider. Hence a Christian missionary following a false prophet with a disgusting faith planted alcoholic crops to produce alcohol and got famous, so he is considered a folk hero with most people not knowing the truth behind the missionary myth. Another less famous member/missionary of Swedenborgianism is the American biblical scholar George Bush. By which I'm referring to the 19th century George Bush who was the ancestor of his more famous descendants, George H.W. Bush and George W. Bush; both of whom served as American presidents the former from 1989-1993 CE and the latter from 2001-2009 CE. Another interesting thing about the biblical scholar George Bush, forefather of the American presidents and other influential members of the Bush family, is that he wrote a lengthy book about Muhammad pbuh in 1831 CE. Yes indeed, the 19th century George Bush, ancestor of American presidents named George Bush, wrote a book about Muhammad pbuh where he degraded Muhammad pbuh denouncing him as a fraudster and hoax saying many nasty things that are untrue. The 19th century George Bush declared himself to be an enemy to Muhammad pbuh, Islam and Muslims.

So it's rather characteristic that George Bush's modern descendants of the same name acted as they did when presidents. In retrospect we should've saw them coming since 1831 CE. Oh and I almost forgot, this George Bush born in 1796 CE who died in 1859 CE was a public promoter of returning the Jews to the Holy Land taking it from the Muslims to give it all to the Jews, and even wrote a book about it in 1844 CE called "*The Dry Bones of Israel Revived*". Yet people say history ain't got nothing to do with the present problems the world faces today? History is the present, we are living history at this very moment. What you just did last minute is history and what you are doing now will be history. History is made by you and me. We change history by changing the present. As a related sidenote the modern history of opium in Afghanistan is very pertinent and puzzling as regards the relationship between drugs, religions and missions. After the Muslims forced the Soviet Russians out in 1989 CE, Afghanistan fell into tribal infighting and warlords developed opium plantations selling to druglords throughout the world. Crime was rampant until a group of Muslim students (known as "Taliban" which is the plural of the word "Talib" which means "student") took up arms to defend women who had been raped. They liberated one town and whenever injustice was done they would go to that town to stop the criminals and set up a system somewhat based on Shariah law. I say "somewhat" because they were "students", so sadly it was not a perfect 100% islamic system, but compared to the chaos Afghanistan was in after the Communists were driven out the Taliban system brought peace, stability and some justice to the nation. By all accounts it was better than communism. From 1994- 2001 CE the Taliban went town to town consolidating territory making it a united country again, ending the civil war between tribal warlords. By 2000 CE the Taliban controlled 95% of Afghanistan. Since intoxicants are forbidden in Islam, in November, before the opium poppy planting season, the Taliban made opium farming illegal and a punishable offense by death or imprisonment depending on the severity of the crime. The Taliban's top drug official Muhammad Haqqani made it clear saying *"It is our decree that there will be no poppy cultivation. It is banned forever in this country"*, *"Whether we get assistance or not, poppy growing will never be allowed again in our country."* This was a big deal because 75% of the world's opium was grown in Afghanistan, and in 1999 CE

4,600 metric tons of opium had been exported from the country. Much of this opium was eventually consumed as heroin by drug addicts throughout the world, as 80% of the world's heroin came from Afghan opium. The British Prime Minister in 1999 CE even suggested invading Afghanistan to destroy the opium fields because 90% of the heroin used in Britain came from Afghanistan. Keep that in mind, in 1999 CE Britain suggested invaded Afghanistan to eliminate the opium trade. Apparently their views on nation's rights which they used as their reason not to invade China to eliminate opium in 1895 CE were no longer the same. Thus the Taliban ban effectively destroyed the entire heroin industry, even though it would cause temporary economic distress since so many in Afghanistan were getting rich off of the opium trade. So ironically Britain did not have to invade because the Taliban got rid of the opium all by themself, and that was the reason Britain suggested invading wasn't it? The U.N. was overjoyed and applauded the Taliban, offering to help them eradicate opium in their nation glad that peace had found a way and nations were doing the "right thing" after so many years of nations invading each other to change policies and alter people's beliefs or behaviors. So in February 2001

CE the Taliban leader Muhammad Omar had the U.N. surveyors visit to inspect the country to see if any opium was being grown just in case the Taliban had missed any fields. Since it was before harvesting season and too late to plant, any more fields they found would be destroyed and no poppies could/would be replanted. The U.N. had been in Afghanistan the year before so they knew where to look and they were surprised to find that out of about 175,000 acres that grew opium before, they only found 17 acres in the whole country that had opium, and when they told the Taliban those farmers got imprisoned until they agreed to destroy their opium crops, which they then agreed to do and did. After the U.N. survey was reported across the globe most people were happy and the emotions can best be expressed in the statement of a narcotics official when he said *"We do not think by any stretch of the imagination that poppy cultivation in Afghanistan has been eliminated. But we, like the rest of the world, welcome positive news."* The U.N. drug control liason in Jalabad, Karim Rahimi, said ""*It is amazing, really, when you see the fields that last year were filled with poppies and this year there is wheat*". As a result of the Taliban crushing the opium trade the price of opium soared because there was so little supply. In 2000 CE a gram of opium cost $44, in

2001 CE a gram of opium cost $746. So the drug dealers and drug users who relied on opiates were going bankrupt throughout the world. However opiates aren't just used in heroin but other drugs like morphine, oxycotin, painkillers and lots of the dangerous "medicines" made by Western pharmaceutical companies and prescribed by doctors in America and other Western nations who believe in, preach and profit from the religion of allopathic medicine. Opioids are also a type of opiates commonly prescribed as painkillers in America that were originally only used for people who had pain from cancer but in the 1990s CE they started getting prescribed for general pain and chronic pain. Opioids are also highly addictive and cause thousands of deaths per year due to overdoses which have tripled in America since 2001 CE. Opioids are the "happy pills" or "pain pills" people take when they feel pain. Out of all ingestable substances known to man opioids are the most addictive. On top of that they are the gateway to other deadly drugs and it's proven that 80% of people who take illegal heroin had previously used medically prescribed opioids before trying heroin. Meaning this legal opioid "medicine" leads many to take illegal opiate "drugs", frequently because they are cheaper and produce similar effects. But aren't opioids safe painkillers? No. Usually they are prescribed to the elderly to deal with pain but health wise the elderly are at higher risk of being harmed by opioids than any other category. When old people take opioids it causes them to suffer mental sedation, nausea, vomiting, constipation, drowsiness, urinary retention, itching, difficulty breathing, depression, hormone imbalances, confusion, hallucinations, delirium, headaches, memory loss, dizziness and taking opioids causes old people to fall. But of course it's extremely rare for any old person who falls or suffers these side effects to have a doctor say "Well you fell because you take this pill." instead old people just get told that they're old and what they are going through is called "a side effect of old age". Ironically many of the problems which old people experience are actually side effects of their medicines, which they take to deal with the pain of problems which they got from taking allopathic medicines. It's truly sad because when you meet an old person in America taking medications if you examine the side effects of the pills then you will see that everything they complain about and suffer from is a side effect of the medicines. When you ask them why they take the medicines when all of the health problems they have are explicitly known to be caused by the medicines they take they just reply they need the medicines to solve their health problems. Of which stupidity is an unlisted side effect of the medicines. Basically they take pill B to heal them from pill A and take pill C to heal them from pill B and take pill D to heal them from pill C and take pill A to heal them from pill D and they tell you if they didn't take pills A-D then the experts who sell them the pills say they'd be even worse and have more problems if they took less pills. Did I mention these pills are highly addictive? So even when doctors conclude and are willing to admit the pills are damaging someone's health they frequently say that the person can't just stop because once you start taking XYZ you can't quit but must gradually reduce dosages or transition to a less powerful pill. Yet the worst part about these opioid painkillers is that taking them causes paradoxical hyperalgesia, which is increased sensitivity to pain. Meaning that taking the popular opioid painkillers makes pain in the future feel more painful, therefore to solve the problem of painkillers reducing your threshold for pain the solution is to take more and stronger dosages which then make pain even more painful and add extra painful side effects. However there are always more pills one can take to deal with such pain as long as one has the money or the ability to buy them on credit. In short with most painkillers once people start taking them they can't stop because the painkillers create their own demand. Of course selling all these painkilling pills that increase pain sensitivity is a lucrative Western business which was effected by the Taliban eliminating opiate production. The Taliban ban on opiates made the pharmaceutical companies lose billions if not trillions because the cost to make their "medicines", which they were making for pennies and selling for thousands, had increased. The consumer price didn't increase, any more than it typically rises each year, but instead of making an opiate pill for less than a penny it cost pharmaceuticals more money so instead of making a million% profit per pill they made a little bit less. However Afghanistan became poor because the population had relied so much on selling opium that many families were not ready to switch to regular farming. For example when growing opium a farmer could make $5,200 per acre per year, but if they grew wheat they would make $121 per acre per year. To put that in a macroeconomic perspective in 1999 CE about 225,000 acres were used to produce opium in Afghanistan which would mean a national revenue of $1,170,000,000 per year due to selling opium. When those acres grew wheat the national revenue became about $27,225,000 meaning in 2001 CE Afghanistan as a nation had to deal with about $1,142,775,000 less revenue. Whereas for Afghanistan who has a much smaller economy than other countries this was extra significant. To put it in perspective in 1998 CE the total worth of all imports to Afghanistan was reported to be $500 million. So when a nation imports a total of about $500 million of goods then has to adjust for having about $1 billion less revenue, that's a huge economic change. Although numbers don't really do it justice. For perspective because of the currency exchange in 1998 CE in Afghanistan one could buy 21 loaves of bread for $0.63 (63 cents) for a bread unit price of about 3 pennies a loaf. Now an American during that same year was paying about 99 cents a loaf, or $21 for 21 loaves in comparison to the Afghan paying $0.63 for 21 loaves. But again don't get the wrong idea, the hourly wage in America was $6.72 in 1998 CE and the average daily wage in Afghanistan was $1.14 in 1998 CE. Notice the American was making $6.72 <u>an</u>

hour, and the Afghan made $1.14 a day. The average American was making more money in 1 hour than the average Afghan made in 6 days, and the average Afghan's work was a lot harder than the average American's. So it's difficult to fully appreciate the difference in prices in bread between the 2 countries, when in reality the Afghan would be paying more of their daily income for bread even though it's for a cheaper price. As a sidenote, people in the West tend to think it's so bad in poorer countries just because they live on less per day, but they don't know what things actually cost. If western people actually went to "poor countries" they'd be rich there and wouldn't even have to work because the cost of everything they are used to would be so cheap. I even know of people who were broke in America and living below the poverty line and they moved to another country and buy a mansion and have butlers because the currency exchange turned them from broke in America to rich outside of America. This is why the fiat money system is so oppressive because it creates such inaccurate wealth distribution. Many times whether you are rich or poor has nothing to do with how much money you have but is determined by invisible borders drawn by governments and which company printed the paper money you use to buy stuff. In the future they will condemn us as idiots for thinking green paper printed in America was worth more than blue paper printed elsewhere or that a green note with $100 written on it was worth 100 times more than an identical green note with $1 written on it. Regardless of how stupid and unjust fiat money is, it's a fact that many if not all Americans could retire 20-30 years earlier if they chose to retire in a different country, and if they did they'd have a higher quality of life because they'd be rich in another country due to the currency exchange but because they love America so much they choose to work 30+ extra years and then if they retire they live below the US poverty line likely never realizing how fiat money and geo-economics is screwing them over. That paper in their pocket be causing all the pain in their buttocks for their entire life and they don't even know it and foolishly love that paper more than anything else. Of course this rule doesn't always apply and economic conditions always change. By the time you read this the exact opposite may be the case, in that foreigners would be rich if they came to the poor land of America because of the currency exchange. While some countries frequently get doubly screwed by the fiat money scheme where they have high prices and low incomes. Yet these economic statistics of Afghanistan do partially demonstrate how big of an impact a loss of $1.1 billion in revenue in a single year would have on a nation of 19 million people where the average daily wage was $1.14 and the nation's total value of imports was about $500 million. Obviously in 2001 CE many former opium farmers had a difficult first year because their budgets had to be completely redesigned since they were making $5,079 less per acre. It was tough for many and some were even starving because it was such a rapid transition which they hadn't fully been prepared to make. In food terms if we take the 1998 CE stat of a loaf of bread being $.03 in Afghanistan and even say triple that price just to be on the safe side for any possible inflation and assume it cost $.10 a loaf during 2001 CE, which again I'm just making that 10 cent number up since the real market price at that time is unknown. Then the $1,142,775,000 less revenue in Afghanistan meant in food terms over 11 billion less loaves of bread for 19 million people or say each person would have 579 less loaves of bread to eat that year because they stopped growing and selling opium. Just imagine if you told any other nation that everyone had to eat 579 loaves worth of bread less this year than they did last year, many people would get hungry. Especially if say you were poor and were only eating 2 loaves of bread per day to begin with, such a person would go from over 700 loaves a year to less than 200 loaves of bread worth of food to eat for an entire year. Clearly that's an economic nightmare but this was the price the Muslims were willing to pay to eliminate the global drug trade of opium. To be fair the Taliban had told them for the 1999 season to reduce their opium planting by 1/3rd and for the 2000 season to have it reduced by 1/2 of what they reduced it the year before, but not everyone had been reducing their opium production in the seasons before the total ban was decreed. To alleviate the economic shock, the Taliban informed the U.N. that millions of Afghans were starving because the farmers had lost the knowledge of farming food so their crops weren't as successful as projected and on top of a weak food harvest the families were poor since they weren't profiting from opium anymore. The Taliban asked for money for temporary food aid, non-interest, and promised to pay it back when possible. Instead of helping, the U.N. viewed this as an opportunity to exploit as political leverage, so as to control/change Taliban policies. What policies of the opium trade ending Taliban did the U.N. not like? In September 2000 CE the Taliban announced all foreigners can invest in Afghanistan tax-free and no customs duties would be levied on any trade goods traveling to or fro between Afghanistan and Pakistan. Now that's something they won't tell you on TV or put in the history books. From September 2000 CE until they were invaded by the US and NATO over a year later, under the Taliban there were no taxes in Afghanistan. So if people say *"How can a country exist in this modern world without taxing people?"* the Taliban did it until the West invaded them and brought taxation back to Afghanistan calling it "freedom", which you can imagine why governments who tax didn't like a country abolishing all taxes and letting the world see it can be done. This is why all the governments who oppressively tax their citizens really don't like Muslim Fundamentalists, because we tell them taxing people is a major sin and we have a just government system that can work effectively without any taxation. Now I'm not saying the Taliban was 100% right in everything they did, they had some issues but at least they did not have taxes.

It is an economic fact that you don't need taxes to have a powerful government that provides many services for it's citizens and residents. If you or anyone thinks taxes are needed for public services that is a religious belief, not an economic reality, the economic reality is taxes are not needed and it's proven that taxation actually hurts economic growth and progress. Some governments and their slaves religiously proclaim, "*No taxation without representation!*", as if representation justifies the crime of taxation, but Muslim Fundamentalists simply say, "*No taxation.*" because Allah says so. People generally agree that nobody likes taxes, but Islam is a religion which states that God has forbidden man-made invented taxation. So when people say Islam is at war with Western ideas, it's true; Islam is at war with the Western ideas that fallible humans can make-up laws and tax people. Taxes need not exist! Full Islamic Shariah means no taxes and most Muslim countries that implement Shariah have no income taxes or other taxes on their citizens, they just nationalize other industries like oil and mineral resources. So when the Western governments who tax people say they have no problem with Islam they must be lying, or just not realize that Islam has a problem with them. Aside from no-taxation for its citizens or residents there was another issue the UN had with the Taliban. On February 26, 2001 CE the Taliban leader of Afghanistan Muhammad Omar issued a decree boldly stating *"Based on the verdict of the clergymen and the decision of the supreme court of the Islamic Emirate (Taliban) all the statues around Afghanistan must be destroyed."* This decree was in complete conformity with Islam and it was approved unanimously by 400 religious scholars in Afghanistan, but the U.N. does not agree with Islam. But the U.N. did not control Afghanistan, the Taliban did, so in accordance with Islam the statues in Afghanistan started getting destroyed. The U.N. complained and condemned the destruction of statues, in response the Taliban leader confidently said *"all we are breaking are stones"*. Nobody was getting hurt or anything, it was just that rocks which had been made into graven images were being made into tinier rocks that God would like better than the sinful statues. However there were some gigantic Buddha statues, one being 50 meters tall (165 feet) with another being 34.5 meters tall (114 feet). These were thousands of years old built in the 500s CE and used to be worshipped as idols by Buddhists when Buddhism was one of the religions practiced in Afghanistan. In the 7th century Islam came to the region and the Buddhists started becoming Muslims. By the 11th century Buddhism was no longer around in Afghanistan because after hundreds of years of Islamic exposure and invitations to Islam the Buddhists had become Muslims. The statues while idolatrous weren't destroyed then because they were so huge, the technology did not exist to safely destroy a 165 foot tall statue and the statues had been carved out of mountains. It's a similar story with the Pyramids and the Sphinx, nobody had the capability to destroy these; although with the Egyptian idolatrous architecture the sands had covered up those things for a long time and it is said the Muslims didn't even see them when they conquered Egypt since they were buried at the time. Anyways since one couldn't topple a mountain nobody knew how to destroy such ancient Afghani Buddhist idols. Although people did try throughout history. In the 18th century the King Nader Ashfar shot cannons at them, to little effect. In the 19th century the idols' faces were destroyed. Although by 2001 CE explosives could finish the job that had been delayed for so long. Yet there was the U.N.'s claim that the statues are special because they are so old and belong to the world heritage of art, almost as if being old meant they were holy or something. I mean when did something being old, make it good? If you have a 5,000 year old pornographic magazine, does it become a sacred relic or is it still sinful filth? Really who cares how old something is? At the end of the day no matter how old ancient dinosaur poop is, the ancient dino droppings are still poop. Now of course poop is different than an idol, some may say it's even better than an idol but age or sentimental value in itself does not give something immunity from destruction. If you really want to get sentimental about old stuff then don't use oil because oil is a liquid antique. Why else did you think oil was so expensive? It's because oil is a liquid antique, yet despite it's age everyone agrees it shouldn't be so expensive. Yet the U.N. told the Taliban that the old statues cannot be destroyed because to do so would be a violation of international/U.N. law. To which the Taliban's leader of Afghanistan Muhammad Omar confidently replied: *"According to Islam, I don't worry about anything. My job is the implementation of Islamic order. The breaking of statues is an Islamic order and I have given this decision in the light of a fatwa of the ulema (clerics) and the supreme court of Afghanistan. Islamic law is the only law acceptable to me."* But if you remember the Taliban had asked for genuine economic charity in food so that the Afghan people could survive the economic transition from an opium economy to a drug-free economy. Hence the U.N. used this need for food as leverage and threatened the Taliban saying that they will not give any money unless the money goes to restore the Buddhist statues and make them better than the state they are in so that they look as good as they did thousands of years ago when they were first made. Such a request was completely against Islam and the Taliban's position, the Taliban was getting the statues prepared to be safely blown up and the U.N. says they are going to give them money that can only be used to make these very same statues get polished and improved. So it wasn't even a blackmail offer of "We'll give you food if you don't blow up the statues." It was, *"We won't give you food even though you begged us and people are starving. But we will pay for the Buddha statues to be upgraded, on condition that you pay us back for the renovation costs with interest."* Needless to say the Taliban was appalled by the U.N.'s refusal to give them food during a famine and disgusted by the U.N. wanting them to upgrade idolatrous statues and then sinfully and stupidly pay interest for the cost of doing such sinful stuff. Thus after asking again for food aid and having the U.N. refuse to give food aid and insist that they agree to pay interest on the cost to upgrade the Buddha statues, on March 9th, 2001 CE the Taliban safely blew up the Buddha statues. Then the U.N. was again asked for food aid, since it was known they had the money for the statues that could no longer be used, the Taliban offered to use that money for food since it could no longer be used on the statues since they didn't exist. The U.N. said no and kept their money raised for the upgrading of statues that no longer existed. In comparison to the praiseworthy world reaction of the Taliban ending the opium trade and crippling the drug industy, the reaction to them blowing up the Buddha statues was hostile. After this the international media starting circulating stories about how they are extremists and "medieval" and how "someone should do something about them" and of course the famine of 2001 did not make the Taliban look good on TV since it was such a tough year due to the economic restructuring and the Taliban's avoidance of resorting to criminal taxation. In the summer of 2001 CE the U.S. government asked the Taliban to give them Osama bin Laden. The Taliban agreed he had extremist doctrines but said they needed proof he was guilty of the crimes the U.S. government said he had committed before they hand him over. This was standard international protocol, in that you don't just give someone who is in your country to a government of another country who wants to punish said person unless they have evidence justifying the person as guilty. It is a basic law of international extradition. A example of this is how China and Russia refused to give Edward Snowden to the U.S. government when they were asked, even though it is proven that he revealed classified NSA documents revealing America is illegally spying on everyone in the world. So even with Snowden confessing his guilt, China and Russia still declined to give him to America when asked. Did America invade China and Russia for harboring Edward Snowden? No, and Russia even gave Snowden citizenship. Then on September 11th, 2001 CE some planes flew into buildings, which later fell down and a bomb went off at the Pentagon and America blamed Osama bin Laden though he denied the accusations. Once again the Taliban said Osama has extreme doctrines they don't agree with but they need evidence before they give him to a foreign government. This was also due to the deeply imbedded tribal history of Afghanistan in that tribes would rarely give up a guest who had sought asylum with them. Yet the Taliban simply asked for evidence that he was guilty, if evidence was given then they would hand him over to America but they didn't want to start a policy of just handing people over to foreign governments simply because they were asked to do so. But America tends to think they have special privileges over the sovereignty of smaller nations. On top of that the Taliban had reported Osama bin Laden missing on February 13th, 1999 CE so they did not know where he was in their country anyways if he was even there. They knew he was likely to be there but didn't know where, since he was reportedly hiding in the mountains and with millions of people starving in their nation, searching for Osama in the mountains simply because America wanted him was not the Taliban's number one priority; especially when no evidence was provided to indicate he was guilty of the charges brought against him. Still the Taliban issued a decree that Osama bin Laden was to be deported, once found, but he was nowhere to be found in Afghanistan. The Taliban simply had bigger priorities with millions of people suffering from economic shock and sanctions that had been placed on them from the U.N. because they blew up an ancient Buddha statue. To the Taliban international news and popular opinion was not evidence of criminal activity and it was unprecedented to be given 25 days before being invaded. What justification did America have? Politically the Taliban did need solid evidence because many Afghans considered Osama a hero for having fought the Soviet invaders and giving so much money to help people in Afghanistan before the U.S. froze his funds, despite his extremist ideas. Otherwise islamically Osama would've been forced to repent from his Khariji ways or be executed. It was because to the average Afghan Osama was a rich guy who came from another country to fight the Russians until they left and then donated money to help rebuild after the war, if the Taliban government just handed him to unislamic America to be killed then the Taliban would look like bad guys or American puppets to their own people. The Taliban needed 100% solid irrefutable evidence that would hold up in court proving that Osama was guilty and they didn't know where he was yet to be able to do anything either. But alas as the world found out, America did not have evidence that Osama bin Laden was solely or even partially responsible for the tragic criminal events of 9/11/01 and they still don't. To this day, over 20 years later, not a single individual has been charged with plotting the 9/11 attacks in any way. In fact the evidence would prove that the U.S. government played more of a role than Osama bin Laden did and any role Osama played could have been easily thwarted if America wanted to stop it. Unfortunately Americans are often the last to know and are a few years or decades behind when it comes to international news about the world and their own government, since they tend to get their information and beliefs from hollywood movies or mass USA-based media. Logistically military experts say that its not logistically feasible for America to have even executed its invasion of Afghanistan on October 7th, 2001 without having made some preparations for it before the 9/11 attacks took place. Typically it takes 3-4 months of training troops for the climate of the region they are to wage war in before they can adequately wage war there, plus to determine and setup logistical support to transport food and equipment for a overseas invasion takes even longer. Meaning America logistically must have been training to invade Afghanistan before 9/11 took place in order to have done so by October 7th 2001, only 25 days later. Militarily its just not possible no matter how motivated America was after 9/11 to have physically invaded and had as much tactical strategic success in Afghanistan in just 25 days time. America had to have privately prepared to invade Afghanistan before 9/11, unknown to the American people. This was admitted by Tony Blair, the former Prime Minister of England, when he publicly stated his own country was finding it hard to justify their military preparations to invade Afghanistan until 9/11 took place. So England has confessed they were planning to invade Afghanistan before 9/11 happened, so why won't America? Or perhaps the bigger question is why was England going to invade Afghanistan before 9/11 took place and how would they have done so if it didn't occur? Anyways what did the American government do to punish the alleged 9/11 mastermind? Did they bomb Osama's house in Afghanistan? As the adulterous President Bill Clinton had done in Sudan when Osama wasn't home on August 20th, 1998 CE which is why he had gone into hiding. Did the USA send in a swat team to kidnap/extract him? You would think that would be the logical, even though illegal, action. Because by all accounts true and false the Taliban had nothing at all to do with the criminal events of

9/11 AND in the 20 year war between the American government and the Taliban not a single attack was made on American soil by a single Taliban member. So it begs the question if the Taliban were responsible for 9/11 why wasn't there even a single Taliban individual able to attack a single American on American soil, nor was there even a single alleged Taliban attack on American soil or any other of its allies when other groups were able to do so? It must be that the Taliban simply didn't want to kill American citizens even when America was killing its citizens and that is why it wasn't done for over 20 years, because such attacks were unislamic even when in a state of war with the US military and other nations. However if you recall the Taliban did have something to do with the Western pharmaceutical industry and drug industy losing billions if not trillions because they crushed the opium trade and where setting an example of a modern state that had a 0% taxation rate. They also blew up a few statues too, but who would go to war over spilt rock? I mean a war is not going to bring back a blown up Buddha idol. However a war would and did bring back the opium fields and taxation. Coincidentally America and NATO invaded Afghanistan in October 2001 CE, just before it was time to plant opium and the fighting was nearly done by December so that most all of the opium fields returned in 2001 CE for a large harvest in 2002 CE. The opium production in Afghanistan continuously increased ever since the invasion. Now I'm not going to imply the invasion of Afghanistan was solely due to the Taliban banning opium because Afghanistan was not just the world's leading exporter of opium before the Taliban banned it. Afghanistan was also the leading exporter of "Cannabis"; in America and South America they call it Marijuanna. Of course the Taliban banned Cannabis as well and crushed the global Cannabis industry in early 2001 CE too. Few know that Afghanistan produced most of the world's Cannabis and Opium before the Taliban banned both and ended those trades. So it really is remarkable that the Taliban brought down the two towers of Opium and Cannabis, of which America was and is the number one consumer of Opium and Cannabis, then months later two towers in Amercia fall down of which one extremist Khariji guy allegedly living in Taliban Afghanistan gets blamed for but it results in a global invasion of a international coalition to cause a regime change even though that guy was not even a member of the

Taliban government. The democratic Afghanistan government set up by the U.N. and America allowed both opium and cannabis to be grown in Afghanistan and even unofficially taxed it. It's ironic that before this America was known for it's "War on Drugs" since the 1930s CE (as well as it's "War on Poverty" which they seem to have won with debt) but then it's "War on Terror" which is fought using terrorizing tactics and weapons like "hellfire missiles" has revived the allegedly endangered drug world. The Taliban won and nearly ended the war on drugs in a single year, but the American war on terror brought the drugs back and has since legalized the very drugs they fought the "war on drugs" for. Yet some will say it was all about Osama and not drugs. Okay, well the U.S. says Osama was killed in 2011 CE, which is rather pathetic that it took the U.S. nearly 15 years to kill one guy. They were officially trying since 1996 CE weren't they? Yet they say they killed him in Pakistan, so if they invaded Afghanistan to get him then why didn't they also invade Pakistan once they found him there? Why not invade democratic Pakistan for allowing bin Laden to live there for years when they invaded Afghanistan for that very same alleged reason? Also why didn't America withdraw from Afghanistan in 2011 once Osama was killed in Pakistan, why stay 10 more years? Its unprecedented in that a country simply cannot invade another country due to a alleged criminal non-state resident simply allegedly residing in that country and not being turned over by that state upon immediate demand. Legally the invasion of Afghanistan in 2001 was a violation of international standards, but so were the papal crusades too. Initially America also said they invaded Iraq in 2003 to get bin Laden because an Al-Qaeda member Ibn al Sheikh al Libi tortured by the CIA in Egypt told them Al-Qaeda was in Iraq with chemical weapons, even though they weren't and he lied to the CIA to get the U.S. to invade Iraq so Al-Qaeda could create their own state there as they had planned to do since the 1990s CE, which a splinter group of theirs later did do in 2014 in the form of the ultra-khariji state ISIS. America bought Al-Libi's lie and sold it to the world, then claimed Saddam had weapons of mass destruction and/or was linked somehow to 9/11. However these weapons were never found and just like how the Taliban had nothing to do with 9/11, Saddam Hussein had nothing to do with 9/11, and neither did Saudi Arabia (who is America's next 9/11 scapegoat so they can justify invading and occupying them too.) Imagine if Osama allegedly went to every country in the world or had followers in every country, would that mean America would have to invade every country in the world and launch a global inquisition to stop extremism from spreading? Another point regarding the alleged WMDs which Iraq never had is that if Iraq did have them they would've used them. The whole reason there was a "Cold War" was because the US and USSR both had WMDs and if a country with WMDs gets invaded then the invader fears those getting used against them since the occupied nation has nothing to lose by using them. Thus if Saddam had em, he would've used em to defend his regime, but he didn't and America knew this before they attacked because if they actually thought he had them they wouldn't have attacked because he would've used them to bomb Israel like he used scuds to bomb Israel during the Desert Storm war. Wheras Israel is the main reason that motivates America's middle eastern interventions. This is because no matter what any nation in the middle east gets in military hardware, the middle east is too far away from America to use any weapons against it. No warplanes can fly from the middle east to America because they'd run out of fuel, and no Muslim owned missiles can be fired that far. So America is geographically completely safe from the middle east, but Israel, who America wants to protect, is not. So the U.S. scares their citizens into thinking they are somehow threatened when they aren't, even if people try to threaten them. The American government knows this and admits the biggest threat mainland America faces from foreign nations is cyberwarfare, the American mainland is just too far away from it's enemies to be threatened with violence. This is why for international legality America never claimed they invaded Afghanistan for defensive reasons, that's what many Americans thought but defense was not the official reason the US government gave for the invasion. Because afterall Alabama had no interests to defend in Afghanistan to justify bombings or sending Alabamians to Afghanistan, yet somehow because the US says US interests instead of listing the states themselves people think what is called "US interests" are real things that match the interests of Americans or American states, though not a single state in the US had a genuine interest in warfare in the middle east. Why then did the US government invade Afghanistan if not for defense or for interests of the states? On October 7th, 2001

CE the US government listed 4 offensive reasons and goals for the war in Afghanistan.

1. *To make Afghanistan self-sufficient.*

2. *To end the narcotic production/trade in Afghanistan.*

3. *To form a government according to the will of the Afghan people.*

4. *To establish peace, stability and security in Afghanistan.*

In reality not a single one of these American goals were achieved after 20 years of fighting. Notice that regarding America's 4 official reasons for war in Afghanistan not a single one had anything to do with America or Americans. Regarding point 1, they were already self-sufficient before the invasion, just struggling. Regarding point 2 the narcotic industry was dead in Afghanistan because the Taliban killed it as was verified and applauded by the UN itself, but it returned for the entire reign of the democratic puppet USA approved Afghan state. Regarding point 3 the overwhelming majority of the Afghan people wanted Shariah law, but America implemented democracy. So basically Afghan people are told they have to do what they want or they get punished but they can't do what they want because what they "really want" is what America tells them they want which is democracy, freedom etcetera. Regarding point 4 statistically after the American withdrawal violence dramatically decreased, due to Americans no longer killing Afghans. Crime even decreased despite the Taliban releasing all the "terrorists" who were unjustly sentenced by other than Shariah law. After returning to power in 2021 the Taliban let all the prisoners throughout the nation go free due to the unjust American imprisonment system that wasn't based on Shariah law and crime actually decreased despite all the "criminals" being freed. So either America makes the problems it tries to fix bigger, is extremely incompetent, or they lie about the reasons they invade and occupy other countries. Whereas the real reason for the American invasion of Afghanistan is clear. On February 22nd 2012 CE American troops in Afghanistan were caught burning copies of the Quran. Not just 1 or 2 copies, but about 2,000 books because according to the American government about "75% of the books contained extremist content". Yes according to US soldiers and US government officials who are stationed in Muslim countries, 75% of the Quran is extremist content and rather than keep the 25% that isn't extreme they just burn 100% of the Quran, just to be safe. Which I remind you, according to some US politicians, and the Winslow plan, any Muslim "suspected of intending to view extremist material" should be imprisoned and according to members of the US military 75% of the Quran is "extremist material" and some US politicians say the US military should be in charge of "fighting/defeating Islamic extremism". Which means that if "in theory" the US military were to ever control/influence the US government either explicitly or implicitly then it would be an imprisonable crime for Muslims to be "suspected of intending to view/read/teach the Quran" even though Muhammad pbuh taught us to do that every time we pray. Thus it would be a crime for Muslims to be "suspected of praying" any of their 5 daily prayers. Fundamentally Americanists believe that reading the Quran is a felony and act of treason, they just haven't publicly told this to the world yet (if they even realize this is where their beliefs lead) and the sheeple have yet to be sold on their plans to legally make reading the Quran or performing an Islamic prayer a punishable crime. The people of Afghanistan rioted as a result of the Quran burnings demanding the US soldiers who burned the Qurans be punished, and some US soldiers and contractors got killed in riots. The very next day the Afgani Minister of Defense Abdul Rahim Wardak called the US government to apologize for "the wrongful deaths" of US personnel and offered his personal condolences to their families. The Afghan Minister of the Interior Bismillah Khan Mohammadi also apologized for the deaths of the US soldiers and offered condolences to their families. In regards to the Quran burning Aziz Raf'ie from the Afghanistan Civil Society publicly said "*The political consequences are much worse than the crime itself.*" You see Democratic Afghanistan apologized for killing foreign US soldiers who occupy their country and burn the word of Allah. However to be fair to the Democratic Afghani government, they didn't all grovel to the Americans and apologize. One Afghani MP Abdul Sattar Khawasi, who represented the Parwan province, said "*Americans are invaders and jihad against Americans is an obligation.*" Khawasi along with 20 other members of the democratically elected parliament even called on the religious leaders, "*to urge the people from the pulpit to wage jihad against Americans.*" While Ahmad Shah Ahmadzai, the chairman of the Afghanistan National Front political party, said: "*It's not for the first time that foreigners had desecrated the Quran... As long as foreign troops remain in Afghanistan, peace will elude the country."* The Muslims and Afghan people demanded that the US soldiers responsible be turned over to Afghan authorities so they could be punished for burning the Quran. Although rather than let US soldiers be punished under Democratic Afghan law America extracted them and ruled that what those soldiers did was "not a crime" but as a show of international goodwill the soldiers would receive "non-judicial administrative punishment". What that was has never been made publicly known but can include, *"a letter of reprimand, reductions in rank, forfeiting pay, extra duties or being restricted to a military base".* Which for all intents and purposes isn't even a slap on the wrist but is more like getting a firm honorary handshake that hurts. For the record Obama did technically "apologize" and expressed regret to Hamid Kharzai, the Afghan president, for the *"inadvertent mishandling of the Quran"* although most Muslims don't consider his apology very apologetic but just a international political requirement. Otherwise had Obama been 100% as unapologetic as America is about killing Muslims throughout the world then it would be crystal clear to any sane person that there is a war being waged on Islam by America and the Muslims would fight back collectively in large numbers. That's why white house correspondent Jay Carney explained Obama's response by saying, "*It is wholly appropriate, given the sensitivities to this issue, the understandable sensitivities. His primary concern as commander in chief is the safety of the American men and women in Afghanistan, of our military and civilian personnel there.*" Although for some Obama's "apology" was too much to tolerate. Many Americans have the same view as George H.W. Bush expressed when on July 3rd, 1988 CE the USS Vincennes shot down an Iranian passenger airliner, accidentally, killing 290 civilians. As acting President George H.W. Bush was asked to comment, he firmly said, "*I will never apologize for the United States. I don't care what the facts are.*" Some would call that extremism but many call that Patriotism and loyalty to America. On Obama's reaction to the Quran burnings, Newt Gingrich, who was running against Obama for president, commented, "*There seems to be nothing that radical Islamists can do to get Barack Obama's attention in a negative way and he is consistently apologizing to people who do not deserve the apology of the President of the United States period. It is Hamid Karzai who owes the American people an apology, not the other way around. This destructive double standard whereby the United*

States and its democratic allies refuse to hold accountable leaders who tolerate systematic violence and oppression in their borders must come to an end." In summary American soldiers in a Muslim country which they had invaded 11 years earlier and had occupied for 11 years were finally caught burning thousands of copies of the Quran and Muslims were outraged at the American lack of justice or remorse, while the Americans were outraged that the US President expressed any political regret over the Quran burnings at all. On top of that the commander in chief George Bush labeled the "War on Terror" as a crusade himself and said God told him to invade Afghanistan and Iraq and to support the Jewish state of Israel. Everyone with insight on either side knows that America invaded Afghanistan to replace Shariah law with democracy and burned the Islamic scriptures trying to brand Islam as a radical terrorist ideology due to hatred for Islam and Muslims. Otherwise America would have kept Shariah law with whatever Puppet regime it established. You don't need to be a genius to know such basic facts. Even if America decided to eliminate the Taliban they did not invent Shariah law, so whoever was put in charge of Muslim Afghanistan should've ruled according to Shariah unless Shariah was deemed the problem due to religious hatred of it and thoughts that the religion of democracy was superior. Now is it fair to say that there is a religious war being waged and the Americanists might have a few more extremists on their side than the Muslims have on their side?

    Naturally anyone who has a different belief system or lifestyle than you is extreme in your opinion of that person, based on the simple fact that you are different than them. However they may not be extreme according to their belief system. A Hindu sitting in cow feces pouring cow urine on his head might be regarded as extreme for someone who doesn't believe that cow feces and urine is holy with curative properties. Someone with a code of conduct might be considered extreme or restricted by someone who follows no rules in life. A citizen of one country may consider the laws of another to be extremely repressive, while the inhabitants of that "extreme" country think other countries without such laws are extremely chaotic, immoral and unstable. Extremism is just a matter of opinion and perspective. When it comes to religion and extremism one has to know the religion of that person before labeling them extreme, otherwise it's just an ignorant person giving an ignorant opinion on something they are not qualified to make a decision on. When it comes to Islam and extremism, the only people qualified to say whether something is extreme from a Muslim perspective are those who know Islam in depth; this would be the scholars. A person who doesn't practice Islam, doesn't believe in Islam and doesn't know about Islam has no right to say whether someone is a Muslim extremist, because they don't know what they're talking about. Something may be extreme in their eyes whereas it's actually exactly what the religion teaches and not extreme at all. There are nudists("naturalists") who wear no clothes, thinking that people who wear clothes are extreme for putting on so many different pieces to cover themselves. Likewise some people who wear clothes will think a Muslim woman who covers her entire body in public, so no one sees her physical features except for family, is extreme. There are people who think brushing one's teeth more than once a day is extreme and unnecessary. Some people only bath once a week and consider those who bath everyday extreme and vice versa. Oftentimes those who think others are extreme are just unaware of the reasons behind the other's beliefs or actions.

When non-Muslims or Muslims who are not Islamic scholars label people as a Muslim extremist, because in their opinion that person is extreme, it only serves to create the conditions in which extremism will flourish. The way prejudices are being used to combat Muslim extremism today actually increases the extremism in the world. The more Muslim extremism there is, the worse Islam appears to be. This has led me to believe that there are forces claiming to combat Muslim extremism while intentionally doing it in a way that increases the number of Muslim extremists. It is a plot to deliberately tarnish the reputation of Islam. The way to make Muslim extremists disappear and to have murder that's done in the name of Islam stop, is to let the Muslim scholars take care of it. Simply put a non-Muslim doesn't know enough about Islam to tell whether someone is extreme or not, most Muslims don't even know enough to be able to tell. If Muslim scholars were the only ones labeling there would be far fewer mistakes in accusations and the conditions in which extremism thrives would cease to exist. Muslim extremists physically hurt Muslims more than they do non-Muslims, and they destroy our religion. Muslim extremists are used as a scapegoat to justify Muslims being killed, while these same extremists are killing Muslims as well. Extremists then use the deaths of innocent Muslims by the forces claiming to combat extremism as a justification for their own violence. Then they are seen as the just opposition to the aggressive oppression, which they themselves caused. Thus Muslims have the greatest motivation to see Islamic extremism vanish, so please let us handle it. The Non-Muslims are not helping the situation, even if they are sincerely trying to. The surveillance which the non-Muslim governments have done in masjids and their entrapment of Muslims makes some afraid to talk to each other in the masjid and elsewhere, for fear of being labeled an extremist and targeted. If Muslims weren't afraid to be mistaken for an extremist then when extremist ideas spread amongst us they would be easily identified. Then they could be corrected as they arise so incorrect extremist ideas wouldn't gain traction. By having the non-Muslims arrest and suppress these distortions of doctrine it doesn't solve the problem, rather it gives the ideas more credibility and discourages discussions that would reveal the flaws in the extremist views. For example if there is an annoying sound in your house that's disturbing your sleep, you don't start making loud noises trying to drown it out so the annoying sound can't be heard over your own noise. Doing that will just make it harder for you to get back to sleep, which was the original goal. Having spies and surveillance target Muslims is like using gasoline to put out a fire, the more you try the bigger the problem gets. While I understand it might seem that action must be taken to stop the problem, sometimes the best way to get rid of a fire is to let it die down on its own without interfering. Especially if you don't know much about fire, by meddling with it you're likely to get burned and spread it further, unintentionally giving it more fuel. I'm sure many would like to have fewer extremists in the world. The best way for you to help that cause is to not label anyone as an extremist, or to suspect them due to a lack of understanding. Let those who are qualified handle it, extremism can never be defeated by the ignorant or arrogant. The more "crackdowns" there are the harder it is to identify an extremist attitude, which is often just harmless intellectual confusion that could be rectified with a simple conversation. When people feel victimized and fear being labeled as extreme, they are scared to ask questions when they get confused, fearing they might be reported or ostracized. I can personally attest to being too scared to ask important questions in the masjid, fearing someone might overhear me mistaking my ignorance and confusion for extremism, then report me causing serious trouble. If governments are serious about stopping the spread of dangerous extremist views, then they should stop the spying and surveillance because it prevents the discussions that would refute such views from taking place. Cloak and dagger tactics do not defeat extremism, anyone who employs them claiming to combat extremism is only serving the very extremist cause they wish to defeat. Violent retaliation breeds extremism, so does ignorance, arrogance and hypocrisy. May God protect us from such diseases.

Should Muslims apologize for acts of criminality done by extremists in the name of Islam? For example if somebody claiming they are a Muslim doing jihad kidnaps children, kills babies, or bombs a hospital, some people think Muslims should condemn it and apologize for every unjust violent extremist act that occurs. Personally I have nothing to do with such acts and am not affiliated with any group that does such a thing, nor do I subscribe to that type of ideology. So why would I apologize for something I didn't do? As a Muslim I know that Islam doesn't encourage or permit violent criminal actions. Anyone who researches Islam will also know that such unjust violence is not Islamic. To apologize for what extremists do it implies a feeling of guilt. When neither Muslims nor Islam has anything to do with atrocities there is no reason for them to apologize for extremist actions. Islam and Muslims are innocent of what violent extremist criminals do. Consider a violent gangster who robs, rapes and murders a person while wearing the jersey of a professional sports team. Would that sports franchise apologize? No, because everyone knows the sports team had nothing to do with it and that the gangster is not a member of that sports team, even though he is wearing the jersey. The gangster could have gotten that jersey anywhere, just because he is wearing the jersey doesn't mean he is connected to the sports team in any way. If someone blamed the sports team for the crime it would be foolish and unfair. Yet this is exactly what happens to Islam and Muslims. When someone who dresses like a Muslim, has a Muslim sounding name, or even claims to be Muslim does something evil, connections to Islam and Muslims are made unfairly. Even if the gangster in the jersey claimed to play for that team, everyone would realize the gangster is not on the team and it is easily verifiable. Even if the gangster was on the team people would recognize that the crime was done by an individual and that the sports team never sanctioned anything the gangster did. Likewise extremists claim to be on the Muslim team, but to anyone who researches a little about Islam it is obvious they are not. Therefore Muslims don't need to apologize because the Muslims of the world are not responsible for the acts of one individual. If Muslims had to apologize every time some Muslim, or someone who claims to be Muslim, or looks like a Muslim, did something wrong there would be daily apologies. The same would go for every other group who had to apologize for wrongs done by those who appear to be members. Isolated individual deeds done by people do not represent the collective group's beliefs, attitudes or morals. If Muslims apologized for every act of criminality that an extremist does in the name of Islam, despite their act being against the tenants of Islam, it would actually encourage criminality. Muslims would apologize and it would incorrectly imply Islam was guilty for the deed, then someone who wants to deliberately tarnish the reputation of Islam would speedily dress up like a Muslim and commit a criminal act in the name of Islam. Enemies of Islam would commit acts of crime framing Muslims hoping it would cause another apology that would make Islam seem responsible and provide an excuse to kill Muslims. The unislamic governments don't want people to second guess and scrutinize all the other plots Muslims were blamed for, so it is against their interest to publicize their success when they actually do stop a legitimate criminal who tried to frame Muslims. Muslims trying to clarify that jihad isn't criminal violence and denounce extremists not only wastes time which could be better spent, but it encourages hate-filled enemies of Islam to frame Muslims in order to cause Muslims to react in such a manner. Rather than tell people what Islam isn't and say jihad isn't criminal violence, Muslims should tell people what Islam is and the details of jihad without making it seem less confrontational than it actually is. If Muslims really want to prove to disbelievers that they have nothing to hide then they should stop saying they have nothing to hide. The apologetic cycle is a waste of time that simply promotes ignorance and confirms stereotypes. Muslims would be better off coming forward and saying something like, "*It's true, Islam does encourage*

Muslims to kill certain types of people. Do you want to know who? And how to get on the safe list?" Now that would be a useful conversation. As would a public lecture on *"The Islamic rules for Muslim warriors when waging Jihad against non-Muslims"*. This is the stuff disbelievers want to know and it will benefit society. So that when the next extremist group comes out Muslims won't even have to say anything about them because non-Muslims would have an Islamic Jihad checklist and be able to identify for themselves why group X is not waging Jihad correctly and their Jihad is not truly Jihad and the same for group Y and for group Z. That's also an important distinction that's rarely even thought of, let alone made. The Taliban, Al-Qaeda and ISIS violate the rules of Jihad in different ways. The reason the Taliban's Jihad was not 100% Islamic is different than the reason Al-Qaeda's Jihad was not Islamic which is different than the reason why ISIS's Jihad was not Islamic. When Muslims say Islam doesn't teach X so we aren't like group A, B or C they are lying because Groups A, B and C teach A, B and C. While A, B and C may be considered by some to be types of X they cannot be equated with each other when C is not A or B. On top of that these groups are human and change through time, for instance the Taliban is a very different much improved organization today than they were 20 years ago and some of their errors have been rectified. So that's where people change, even if they're violent extremists or non-violent extremists. To condemn groups today for beliefs they used to have and abandoned years ago, is extremism, stupid and sinful slander. Yet that will take a lot of time to explain to a non-Muslim, so just teaching them what Islam and Jihad is covers the whole alphabet and gives people knowledge about Islam so they understand something which will be useful to them if they remember it in the future. Saying what you aren't doesn't let anybody know anything about what you are or what you believe. People want answers they don't want to be told why all the other options are not the correct answer. Teachers tell their students what the correct answer is and by doing so they simultaneously convey why all the other answers are not valid or correct. It seems that it's only when it comes to terrorism that people don't teach in an offensive manner. Defensive teaching will never get you points. If you are a Muslim then never ever explain why X group is unislamic until AFTER you explain Islam, and never ever tell someone what Jihad isn't until you explain what Jihad is. While if you are non-Muslim never let a Muslim try to say why X group isn't Islamic or why Jihad isn't X until they tell you what Islam is and what Jihad is. This method of teaching isn't my method but the prophet Muhammad's pbuh. When Muhammad pbuh was in Mecca the pagans called him insane, demonic and accused him of being a magician. Do you know what he did? He didn't do damage control to the masses saying: *"Please don't worry I'm not a magician, I'm not insane, I'm not demonic."* He simply told people he was a prophet, what he believed and what he was teaching people <u>AND that they should become Muslims</u>. He never defended himself from such outrageous slanders because he was too busy practicing Islam and inviting people to Islam. As a result the lies became self-evident and ceased to be told because they weren't given any attention by the Muslims and such preposterous notions were refuted indirectly by living examples instead of defensive apologetics. As a matter of fact Dimaad Al-Azdee was the expert specialist at the time for treating insanity and when he heard the disbelievers say that Muhammad pbuh is an insane man he personally took it upon himself to cure this guy who the leaders of Mecca said was insane.

When Dimaad came to Muhammad pbuh he offered to cure him of his insanity, thinking he was genuinely crazy. Did Muhammad pbuh tell him he wasn't crazy? No. Instead he ignored the crazy claim about him being crazy and said the beginning part of the Khutbah al-hajjah. Upon hearing it, Dimaad asked him to repeat what he said several times and then Dimaad said how that speech is not like anything else and is not the speech of an insane person, soothsayer, magician or poet and thus he accepted Islam right then on the spot proclaiming Muhammad pbuh to be a prophet. Yet the whole time Muhammad pbuh never even addressed the claim that he was crazy because acting Islamically and teaching Islam was proof enough to refute any slander. Whereas if Muhammad pbuh had done all he could to convince Dimaad he's not crazy then a different result may have occured. Similarily after Muhammad pbuh was pelted with stones when expelled from Taif a Christian named Addas saw him all bloodied up and taking pity on him went to give him some water. Muhammad pbuh said "Bismillah"(In the name of God) before drinking and the Christian realized he was not like the polytheists. So they had a short chat during which Muhammad pbuh displayed knowledge that Addas was from the same town that Jonah pbuh had been sent to and after saying only a prophet could've known such an obscure detail Addas became a Muslim, without Muhammad pbuh ever refuting the slanders Addas had heard about him from the people of Taif. Thus I say if Muslims don't want people to think they are terrorists then they should just stop thinking people think they are, stop telling people they aren't and just be a Muslim and live Islam. God did not create Muslims so they could tell people what Islam isn't, on the contrary God tells Muslims to practice it and tell people what Islam is. So true Muslims are neither terrorists nor apologists. The problem is the apologists keep on saying Muslims aren't terrorists and by repeating that over and over they make people suspect it might be true because why else would Muslims be so ardent in refuting it if it weren't? The reason is because those people are apologists. Truly people do not think Muslims are terrorists because of people committing acts of violence, they think that because the Muslim apologists keep on saying we aren't terrorists. An apology is to say you're sorry for something you are guilty of. If I have nothing to do with terrorism then why would I apologize to anyone who gets harmed by it? I wouldn't and don't. The non-Muslim liars will always be liars and always tell lies til they die. The cure for the Muslim public image would be for the Muslim apologists to just not apologize. I've even been in a masjid where disbelievers come to meetings to hear speeches on what Muslims believe and the whole time the Muslims just tell them how "We're peaceful, We're peaceful, We're not terrorists etc." And they never even suggest the people become Muslims or warn them that they are on the road to hell and this goes on for hours at a time, repeatedly month after month. During such "anti-terrorism" speeches which stress people distort Islam, the speakers themselves say false things about Islam and incorrectly explain verses of the Quran out of context while they accuse violent extremists of doing the same. They treat Islam like it's a chameleon in that whatever the crowd likes and believes in they say that's also what Islam is and teaches. Whereas it's just frustrating because that's not how the prophets were. It is a fact that any prophet of God who were to publicly preach today would be considered controversial and fanatical. But the worst part is how the whole program doesn't even make sense. If those non-Muslims actually believed Muslims were terrorists and Islam taught terrorism they wouldn't be anywhere near a masjid or Muslims to begin with, and they wouldn't regularly be visiting for such *"inter-faith solidarity conferences"*. Those who think Muslims are terrorists are not coming to these meetings to hear such speeches nor are they willing to believe what Muslims say anyways. The big *"Islam is peace, tolerance and love. True Muslims aren't terrorists."* campaign is not only giving the wrong message but they are telling it to the wrong people too. So the cure for violent extremism and the idea of Muslims being terrorists could be solved if non-Muslim governments and Muslim apologists would just shutup and keep their hands to themselves. Activism is the root cause of most problems. The solution is as simple as "Just Shutup." but the problem is that many people believe they have "freedom of speech" and the right and duty to make themselves get heard loud and stupid. Unfortunately I'm no exception, but I will attest that most of my problems get resolved when I keep quiet to the people and complain only to the Creator of the Universe.

Most go to extremes in condemning extremist criminal violence. Thus I turn around and condemn their condemnation because their condemnation is a lie as well as an extremist misrepresentation of the Islamic faith, even though they are intending to defend Islam and Muslims. Whereas personally I don't condemn the criminal violence because I've never been in a position to do so. In order for a condemnation to be of any value, you have to be part of the group that's responsible. For example if a spouse condemns their spouse, that means something. If an employer or employee condemns a co-worker that means something. For a stranger to condemn somebody they don't know and never met and have no personal or professional relationship with, means absolutely nothing. Such as me condemning the Catholic Church and Christianity means something because I have a history with it, for me to condemn say the "Black Panthers" or "Girl Scouts" means nothing because I'm not a member and have never been a part of those groups. Therefore if you've never been affiliated with a terrorist organization for you to publicly condemn it or their actions means nothing. The whole point of a condemnation is for the party being condemned to change their beliefs, attitudes or policies. Events themselves cannot be condemned, only people or groups can. If the guilty party has no connection with you then you can't condemn them. Thus for most Muslims in non-Muslim lands technically the only violent organizations they can condemn are non-Muslim governments, yet those tend to be the only ones such Muslims don't condemn, instead the foreign "extremists" get most all of the condemnations from Western Muslims. Thereby these condemnations make Muslims seem guilty/foreign and that's why people expect Muslims to make them because they already believe Muslims are responsible and want an apology. If Muslims would just stop apologizing then people would get the message that we don't feel guilt and are not responsible. I am not sorry that I'm not sorry for evil I have nothing to do with. If someone expects such an apology from me or a condemnation then I get insulted. The prophets only condemned something if people who were their companions did something wrong. The prophets didn't condemn tragic criminal actions which they had nothing to do with and no connection to. Jesus pbuh is a prime example, there is not a single known record of him condemning any of the terrorist acts of the Zealots who killed Romans and Jews in the name of his God and Judaism while he was on earth. So if there were a benefit in condemning extremist attacks then why didn't Jesus pbuh denounce and condemn the attacks the Zealots made on innocent Romans and Jews? If Jesus pbuh didn't denounce criminal violence done by extremists in the name of his religion then why should I? Jesus pbuh knew much better than me. If there is no connection to link you to it, then you can't condemn it. If I'm to apologize for and condemn something evil, then I'd apologize for contributing to the US government's budget, condemn it and expect all Americans to do the same. We all have enough sins of our own to repent and ask forgiveness for, so we should apologize to God for our sins rather than apologize or condemn the sins of extremists. That is what God wants us to do, Satan wants us to cry about crime and constantly condemn criminals because it wastes our time, leads to sins and sometimes leads to disbelief. Honestly I feel more sorrow when I see the Muslim apologists issue statements of kufr than I do about the things they condemn. The true tragedy of extremist criminal violence is the reactions to the tragedies. It would be better if some lunatic killed Muslims as revenge for extremist attacks than for Muslims to react to extremist violence in the typical unislamic and anti-islamic ways they have been doing. It would actually do less damage to Islam and the Muslims than the damage the condemnations do to Islam and Muslims.

So how do we reduce the occurrence of violent crimes against civilians and make the world a safer place? Most don't realize terrorism can only work if it gets attention, to ignore acts of terrorism is to stop the goal behind that action from being achieved. Yet because of the phenomenon of mass media terrorism is effective. Without the mass media, made possible by technology and our desire for constant real-time news, terrorism would not be effective and was not used as much when media played a negligible role in world affairs or daily life. You can actually trace the evolution of terrorism to have risen as media availability and popularity has. Satan and our access to current events are the 2 main factors that have aided terrorism and made it a tool for change that people use today and will only increasingly use as our ability to access up to date sensational information increases. Basically the spread of news created terrorists since it made terrorism a viable tool to influence the world. Think of terrorists like bullies, if nobody paid attention to or reacted to the bully, including the bullied, then their motivation and ability to bully would drastically decrease. Admit that you cannot stop someone from being a bully or bullying people, as much as you might want to you can't stop them. Bullies do what they do to get a certain reaction, it is not just to vent or make money or get popular, there are many other ways they could achieve such goals. A bully only commits an action of physical or verbal abuse in order to get a certain reaction which they desire because of the ultimate effects it will have on themself, the bullied and those who witness or learn of the bullying. The difference with terrorists is that they have a goal behind their violence and it is never just for personal emotional or psychological reasons. Bullies can be bullies for purely personal reasons to gain personal satisfaction but terrorists cannot. Terrorism is never done without a desired reaction to it aside from the immediate cause of violence. Assassinations are separate from terrorism. The motivation of an assassin or a murderer is different than that of a terrorist. For thousands of years people have assassinated figures and nobody ever said "*That assassination was an act of terrorism!*" Just consider Julius Caesar getting assassinated, was that terrorism? Nobody ever said this, so assassinations can not be labeled as terrorism today regardless of how they are done or by whom. Many times innocents were killed during assassinations or attempted assassinations but it was never called terrorism. Assassinations are just murders, but because the targets are deemed to be much more important than regular folk its called an assassination. Terrorism is far more complex in motive than simple murder. Assassination is based on the objective while terrorism is about the effect caused by the plot, in assassinations the murder is the goal but with terrorism causing a chain-reaction is the goal. Giving terrorists attention makes them popular and gives them motivation to do more sinful crimes to use that public outcry to achieve their desired objectives. Terrorists can only win if you pay attention to their act of terror and react to their violent actions. They don't care about the numbers, they are willing to harm less in order to get the reaction they want or kill more to get the reaction they want. The goal of terrorism is the reaction to terrorism. Terrorists want X effects to happen in the world and they calculate that if they perform a particular act of violence against civilians in a certain area at a certain time in a certain way then that will result in the desired effects. They believe that terrorism is a cause to obtain certain results, and frequently they correctly calculate the results their actions have. It doesn't matter whether you agree with their methods or desires, currently terrorism works and gets results. That's where terrorists are smart, no matter how people react to them they win based on the attention and ability to trigger a reaction. Even if they miscalculate the reaction to their terrorism they have been a cause of a reaction that influenced the course of events and that was their goal for doing terrorism to begin with. Their goal was not to harm, but to directly or indirectly obtain influence as a result of harming others. Even when they fail to harm, the reaction to attempted terrorism can have the effects they wanted. Thus terrorists don't need to be willing to actually harm people in order to use terrorism. Just to plan terrorism without even intending to ever go through with it can achieve the goals the terrorist desires depending on the reaction to their "failure". Sometimes getting caught in the act and stopped is much more effective than and desirable than doing the terrorism itself. Thus to catch a terrorist is still a victory for them because of the influence they gained due to the reaction of attempted terrorism. To ignore is to take away their power to control or influence via reactions. Now I'm not saying ignore

100%, sometimes justice must be done, and sometimes justice can only be done with public awareness. Also lack of attention gives some people a seemingly justified reason to use terrorism to get attention, an example being the anti-Zionist movement. It's because the Western world ignores the crime of Zionism that many commit terrorism in the hopes that people pay attention to it and solve the problem, ending Zionism. So when I say ignore terrorism, I don't mean ignore the positions terrorists view as important, the positions must be addressed and terrorists should be civilly engaged in dialogue so a solution can be reached so those positions can no longer be used to justify terrorism. When I say to ignore terrorism what I mean is that the media must stop reporting it and making it popularly known to the masses, which they do because terrorism helps them sell the news and increase their own public attention and influence. A violent crime should be reported so justice can be pursued, however the average person is not going to be able to productively pursue justice. So for the masses, it truly does not matter whether we learn of a violent crime or not because we aren't going to bring about justice. Acts of violent crime, like terrorism, should only be reported to those with the responsibility and ability to bring the perpetrators to justice, such as law enforcement and perhaps the family of victims who should not go public with news of the act unless the government advises them to do so if it helps their work in pursuing justice. It's not healthy or useful for the masses to know about all the violent acts of crime being perpetrated in the world. What will the masses do? React, think about it, talk about it, devote time, energy and money doing so and then beliefs will change, society will change, economic reactions will take place, political change will occur and then that means the terrorism worked. By people paying attention to the violent crimes against innocents and reacting as we do then we are unwittingly encouraging more terrorism because we are reacting on a largescale. As long as the masses are informed and react to terrorist attacks then terrorism will occur, because there is no easier way to influence the masses to create massive changes to the world. Publicity makes terrorism effective and popular as a force of influence and change, few things can motivate the masses as much as or as quickly as terrorism. Crowds are the easiest to influence because the democratic "Group-think" is to not think, people are most susceptible to be controlled when they are united and there is nothing that unites people quicker than victimization; especially if it is in response to random senseless terrible violence because then shock value increases emotions making them more pliable. I'm not saying mental/spiritual/political crowd control methods are inherently sinful or wrong, I'm just saying it's easy to do and sometimes evil people do it; so it can be dangerous. Sometimes good people do it too like Moses pbuh or Noah pbuh and it results in good. I'm just saying unity due to terrorism is a powerful method of control that can be used to cause tremendous changes to people's beliefs, environment and behavior. Therefore to publicize specific terrorist attacks is to encourage terrorism because it sends the message that future acts of terrorism will get attention and cause reactions that facilitate quick drastic changes. So to talk about acts of terrorism gives future terrorists incentives to commit more terrorism. When you realize terrorists do what they do solely to trigger certain reactions that will cause certain effects and conditions, then you will be better able to understand why things happen and what the terrorists want the result of their actions to be. Then you may be able to understand how to react correctly, or not react as the circumstances dictate. Similarly Satan has the same plan and wants us to react to things he does in certain ways. Therefore the true solution to this whole mess is to be aware of God watching you and how you react, then earnestly devoting oneself to act/react how your Creator wants you to in every situation for every second of your existence. One should only react to God and do so the way God wants you to, simply ignore everyone's attempts to influence you except for your Creator's instructions and you will stop extremism. At its core extremism is to go to extremes and there is nothing more extreme than letting something other than your Creator influence or effect your beliefs, intentions and actions. Even to let your desires influence your thoughts, speech and actions is to be an extremist and sometimes can be a form of disbelief, as the Quran mentions those who take their desires to be their God by letting them have more authority over them than their Creator. To be God's slave is the only way to not be an extremist. Therefore religion is the only solution to extremism and that is why so many people react in different ways to extremism, because of their various religious beliefs. Fundamentally the reason why people who claim to believe in the same religion can have such different reactions to extremism is because so many people today actually believe in multiple religions and don't know it. This is also why despite my suggestion that people ignore violent extremist acts of terrorism, they will not be able to because their different religious beliefs cause them all to react so differently. Yet perhaps if we begin to realize our religious beliefs and character determines all our various reactions to life then we can start to focus on uniting upon the true religion's solutions so as a society we can react correctly the way our Creator wants us to. But first we must admit that everyone is reacting to extremism in the way that their individual religious beliefs and character dictate. Does violent and peaceful extremism have something to do with religions? Yes, as do the reactions to violent and peaceful extremism. The problem is most religions today are not considered religions by the masses of people. Most don't think they have beliefs belonging to multiple and contradicting religions. As a result many religions get blamed for acts of extremism or reactions to extremism when those religions that get blamed/credited are not the real or primary influences behind the acts of, nor the reactions to, extremism. In short the first step to solving extremism is religious awareness of all the different religious beliefs that people act upon. Then we can see which religious beliefs are the true culprit, and which fuel the problems promoting extremism of many shades and flavors, and which will not solve the problems. To end violent extremism you must simultaneously end peaceful extremism, they feed each other. To have a solution we need to identify all the causes of all the problems and all the effects all the possible solutions will have. Although only Allah is able to sort out how many problems our universe has and know all the causes of them and the effects of every possible/proposed solution. Thus we must trust God's solution takes every factor into account and do what God wants and it will solve the problem, eventually. And at the very least if it doesn't, it's the way to get to paradise. So the road to paradise is the same road to take to defeat extremism. Religions are the problems, while the true religion has the solution. To think the true religion is not the solution is a doctrine of some of the religions that are causing the problems. So the true religion is the solution and if you think it is not or needs something else to help it then you are part of the problem.

Since every act of extremist violence is caused by many different religious beliefs held by many different people, and has the primary motivation of causing those many different people set off a chain-reaction that works towards fulfilling the extremists long term goals, it is unfair, unjust, unwise and unacceptable to blame Islam or Muslims for isolated acts of crime done by particular individuals. Every religious belief held by people today plays a role in every single act of extremism. Blaming a religion and/or all its adherents for the acts of a minority who have no authority to represent that religion or its adherents, is extremism. Any person who blames and/or expects all the Muslims in the world to apologize for something which Islam does not sanction and the Muslims of the world are not responsible for, is an extremist. If you expect Muslims to condemn suicidal attacks and explain how it's not related to Islam and jihad, then you should also expect Christians to condemn water-boarding and explain how that's not related to Christianity and baptism. Which is a legitimate question many Muslims would be entirely justified in asking concerning the relationship of water-boarding and baptism. This is because Christian politician Sarah Palin (who ran for vice president on

John McCain's ticket in 2008 CE) publicly stated at a NRA rally on 4/27/2014 CE, "*Now, I do have to apologize for that, I AM sorry. Not ALL intolerant anti-freedom leftist liberals are hypocrites. I'm kidding! Yes they are! And they are NOT right, policies that poke our allies in the eye and coddle adversaries instead of putting the FEAR OF GOD, in our enemies. C'mon! ENEMIES, who would utterly annihilate America. THEY would OBVIOUSLY have information on plots, they'd carry out jihad. Oh, but cha can't offend them. Can't make them feel "uncomfortable". "NOT EVEN A "SMIDGEN"". Well, If I were in charge...*(crowd applauds, hoots, hollers and whistles) *They would KNOW that water-boarding, is how we BAPTIZE terrorists.*" The crowd celebrated. Now many Muslims don't know the specifics regarding baptism except that it's a Christian ritual that initiates people into Christianity. Maybe they never met Christians or Americans either and all they know is what they heard on TV. So shouldn't Christians and Americans "clarify" that Christianity and Americanism doesn't really condone water-boarding and it isn't really baptism? George Bush said the "*war on terror*" was a crusade, that God told him to invade Iraq, and in his State of the Union address on January 28, 2003 CE he said, "*The liberty we prize is not America's gift to the world, it is God's gift to humanity."* Sarah Palin basically said all terrorists are Muslims who do jihad and the U.S. government doesn't torture terrorists but converts them to Christianity, coincidentally using the same water-boarding methods used by the Spanish Inquisitors as well as other torture methods invented during the Catholic Inquisition. Sarah plainly said the solution for America's *"enemies"* is to *"put the FEAR OF GOD"* in them. So does the *"war on terror"* the U.S. started really have nothing to do with religion? Is it possible to have a war policy that says *"we don't negotiate with the enemy"* unless it is a religious war? Why is it they used to call it the *"war on terror"* but now its the *"war on radical Islam"*? If we went back 900 years do you think the crusaders would say they were waging a *"war on radical Islam"*? In fact that's exactly what they said they were doing, because to them Islam was radical by definition. In 2016 CE President Barack Obama said directly to Christian clergymen while celebrating at an Easter breakfast party that *"the intent of the terrorists, is to weaken our faith."* Now keeping Obama's stated goals of "terrorists" in mind, which he says is to "weaken" the faith of Christian clergymen and Christians, what do you think the U.S. government would say about me who publicly states Christians and non-Christians should abandon their faith, revile and denounce Christianity and become Muslims changing their faith to Islam? Do you think words would even be used? Or would a decisive executive action for the "good of the nation" be the outcome? If the American government says the goal and intent of a terrorist is to "weaken a Christian's faith", then what am I when my intention goes considerably further than just "weakening their faith"? Whereas keep in mind that Islam commands Muslims to propagate Islam and refute all falsehood, even if that falsehood is a religious faith such as Christianity or Americanism. So since Islam teaches all Muslims to do more than just "weaken a Christian's faith" then if a terrorist as defined by the American government is one who "weakens a Christian's faith" what in the world would they consider a "moderate Muslim"? And what is this "Islam" the U.S. government talks about when they say they have no problem with Islam, when the Quran says that Allah has sent Muhammad pbuh with the Quran to make Islam prevail and dominate over all other religions? The Quran also says the disbelievers are going to hate that Islam is made superior to their false religions and yes it specifically says Christians are disbelievers as are all non-Muslims. Now if you don't like it you don't like it, but that's what Islam teaches. Every religion teaches that those who aren't members are disbelievers and should change their religious beliefs accordingly. Every religion instructs it's members to "weaken the faith" of those who have other faiths. Is that a crime? Anyways you have Allah in the Quran and Muhammad pbuh calling the Christians disbelievers and you have the president of the United States telling Christian clerics during an Easter celebration that terrorists intend to *"weaken our faith"*. It's funny because that's the same thing my parents say I'm trying to do to them. Based on that definition does the Quran teach terrorism and would all practicing Muslims be considered terrorists? Does it make a difference or change your answer if I use the word "radical" or "extremist"? But hold on just one minute, weren't we always repeatedly told the "war on terror" had absolutely nothing to do with religion? I guess nobody ever told that to President Obama of the United States during his nearly 8 years as president. However nobody had to because he was the one telling everyone in his televised speeches that he has no qualms with Islam and the war is entirel free from religious motivations. Yet when Obama is with the Christian religious celebrating Christian holidays he tells them a religious war is being waged against them, in which he is fighting back to protect their faith from those seeking to weaken it. Does that count as radicalizing someone? Is President Obama one of those radical Christians practicing "*radical Christianity*"? Wait, is there even such a thing as "radical Christianity" I don't know, I've never heard the phrase used before. Maybe I invented that term and it doesn't exist, but nevertheless would you like to join me in waging Jihad against "radical Christianity"? I've never heard the term "radical Judaism", "radical Hinduism", "radical Buddhism", "radical Atheism" or "radical Democracy" either. But why not wage Jihad against those things too? Or is Jihad itself something only radicals ever do? (As Sarah Palin says) What about a war on radical Americanism? Or how about we just eradicate radical vocabulary? Anyways Obama had no reason at all to say what he said to those Christian ministers at Easter time about terrorists intending to "weaken our faith" unless it was what he really believed. Most Christian ministers already support the war against "radical Islam" and any other version of Islam because Christianity teaches that everyone should be Christian, so Obama didn't need to curry Christian favor or let them know he was serving their interests. If it were a secular war the Christians wouldn't care because if it hurts Islam then they see it as a victory. On the other hand since Obama declares it to be a secular war to the secular public when on tv, this means he is lying to somebody. Since no Christian soldiers have an issue fighting a "secular war against Muslim extremists" they don't need to be lied to in order to sign up and fight. On the other hand Secular Americans might not be so supportive if the truth were told that the "war on terror" is really a religious war. Thus the secularists get duped into fighting a war to defend the Christian and American faiths and they don't even know it. While anyone who claims the American "war on terror" isn't a religious war has absolutely no idea what a religious war is. They don't even know what war is, or else they don't know that religion is the only force strong enough to lead nations into war. The problem is most religions aren't recognized as religions. Yet every single person who has ever fought in any war or ever will can only do so for religious reasons. This is why in Islam if someone fights for something other than the sake of Allah and dies then they go to hell, because to fight for something besides God is to worship that thing instead of God since fighting is a severe act only to be done with the permission of, for the sake of and according to the rules of God. Every act of violence is by default a religious act of violence, even though it may not be acknowledged to be one it still is. Thus if you are perpetrating an act of violence then that is a religious act, unless it is accidental and unintentional then it's simply a mistake. May God protect us all from committing such a grievous mistake. Yet even when Moses pbuh made such a violent mistake he labeled it as a religious deed that was the plot of Satan. So according to Moses pbuh even accidentally killing is a religious action. Religions don't inherently cause wars, it's just that wars can only ever be religious because any war is by definition a religious activity. Just the same way prayer is a religious activity even if you aren't doing it according to the way any religion teaches and even if you don't label it as having any religious connotations. It's because God created our life that everything in life becomes a religious activity that has a religious spiritual effect, if there were exceptions then we wouldn't be held accountable for all we do.

Recently during his 2016 presidential campaign Donald Trump said that all Muslims in America would have to register in a government database and carry special Muslim ID cards. Trump, like many others, also said the U.S. needs a solid impenetrable walled border with Mexico, which he says is to keep illegals out. Although to keep people out also means trapping people in as well. Trump declared that no Muslims from outside of America would be allowed to enter the U.S. either. Another famous multi-time Presidential candidate Newt Gingrich publicly said: "<u>Sharia is incompatible</u> with western civilisation. Modern <u>Muslims who have given up Sharia</u>, glad to have them as citizens. Perfectly <u>happy to have them</u> next door,". As a caveat to his policy towards "Modern Muslims who have given up Sharia"(who in islam would be considered disbelievers since it is obligatory to believe/practice Sharia) Gingrich stated, " *Western civilisation is in a war.<u> We should frankly test every person here</u> who is of a Muslim background and <u>if they believe in Sharia they should be deported</u>,*" Isn't that the Winslow Plan? Can anybody honestly claim there is no "war on Islam"? Shariah law is part of Islam, it's an obligatory doctrine all Muslims must believe. Is it incompatible with American values? Yes it is. I'll admit it, it truly is incompatible but we can just debate our differences and choose which political system is best can't we? Especially if one is a religious belief and one is a "non-religious belief" technically Americans should be more ready to change their system since their ideas of freedom, equality and democracy are "not religious beliefs" or so they say. If we have to discard one, which text is more important the Quran or the U.S. Constitution? Muslims say the Quran is the literal word of God, with no human influence or input and hasn't changed in thousands of years while the U.S. Constitution was written by racist misogynist men a few hundred years ago and keeps on getting perpetually changed with new amendments to fix its corruptness to this day. If freedom is an option and opinion then why do so few today believe it is a theory? Why do people in "free" countries have such intolerance toward people who disbelieve/refute "freedom"? Is it just a political philosophy or something more? If freedom is not a religion then why do those who oppose Shariah because it is incompatible with the Western ideas of freedom say *"freedom is more sacred than any religion"*.

How can something be more sacred than a religion if it is not a religion? Wouldn't that make it more religious than religion or denote a type of super-religiosity? If we theorize that freedom were a faith and that some countries believed in freedom and others didn't, then how many heretics or disbelievers in freedom exist in those "free countries" where the majority of the population believes in freedom? In "tolerant free countries" how many people disbelieve in, reject and are publicly free to denounce the concept of freedom? And if they do what happens to them? Do they not get treated as if they had disbelieved and rejected a religious doctrine? Are they not treated as a treasonous apostate teaching blasphemy? How can freedom be an obligatory belief which everyone in the world or the West is expected to believe in, without anyone labeling freedom as a religion? Because for freedom to be classified as a religion would mean it is a contradictory false faith, in that freedom is ideologically forcing people to believe in it through pressure rather than merit. If there is any type of penalty or stigma associated with opposing freedom, disbelieving in it, or denouncing it and offering an alternative belief, then that means freedom is an intolerant religious belief that is intolerant of all other religions. The problem with freedom is that it doesn't allow people the right to disbelieve in it or try to eliminate the belief in freedom. It is a tolerance of everything except for intolerance of anything, such as tolerance for everything. Freedom is intolerant of the opposing religious views that say the religion of freedom is wrong and false and should not be believed in, practiced nor applied in any legal system. Some staunch anti-Muslim authors have even written that *"We need to unambiguously say to Muslim living in the West: "If you want to live in our societies, to share in their material benefits, then you need to accept that our freedoms are not optional. They are the foundation of our way of life; of our civilization-a civilization that learned, slowly and painfully, not to burn heretics, but to honor them."* Now tell me if this statement is not the statement of a "religious fanatic". The statement is *"You need to accept that our freedoms are not optional."* What does "need to accept" mean? Does that mean we have a choice or not? The "not optional" part leaves no doubt. So basically Muslims "need to accept" X and Muslims don't have an option about it. Is this the speech of a peaceful non-religious person? Or is freedom a very intolerant faith of which the believers in freedom think everyone "needs to accept our freedoms" or else and there is no option if you want to be alive or live amongst us. Their unspoken doctrine is "Convert to freedom, move or die". While Islam says "Convert to Islam, Pay Jizya under Shariah, or move to a non-Muslim land, or die". So you see Islamic Fundamentalists are actually more tolerant than freedom lovers are. Fighting someone for religious supremacy is different than fighting them to make them believe. Muslims fight to eradicate oppression that is caused by unislamic law. You don't have to believe in Islam but we will ensure Shariah is established so that people don't suffer injustice. Crime must be stopped and unislamic laws encourage crime of many kinds and don't prevent it nor justly punish it. So Muslims do indeed fight for religious reasons but those who lose don't have to become Muslims. They are free to disbelieve and pay Jizya while living under Shariah (Muslims pay zakat which is more expensive than jizya, so it's actually more expensive to be a Muslim living under Shariah than it is to be a non-Muslim) or if the non-Muslim doesn't want to become Muslim or pay Jizya to live under Shariah(if they can afford it, if they are poor they don't pay) then they are free to move to another non-Muslim land. To force Islam upon someone is disbelief in Islam. There is no contradiction between 2:256 and Quran verses promoting Jihad. Yes there was abrogation of total passivity, for example in Egypt Moses pbuh was peaceful but then violence was ordained. Violence is not for every time or place. Sometimes demand peaceful interactions, sometimes demand violent interactions. Muslims fight not to convert but to eliminate the oppression that occurs on earth which disbelievers are guilty of because they make up their own laws to oppress people with instead of using the laws God has given to mankind. So yes we fight democracy and freedom, but you can still believe in the false religions of democracy and/or freedom if you want while living under Shariah. It's just that if you practice them then that will result in people getting oppressed and Muslims don't allow that so we try to protect all people whether Muslim or not from oppression. Sometimes that requires fighting and sometimes it doesn't. However advocates of the freedom faith, democracy or Americanism don't allow people to disbelieve in their faith. Muslim rulers will say *"You can believe in kufr but there is a limit as to how much you can practice it."* Freedom rulers say *"You can't believe in anything that contradicts/opposes freedom and you are limited in how much you can practice any other religion, of which you can only partially believe in since belief in freedom is 'not optional'."* Muslims leave the hearts and minds of non-Muslims alone and when in power just restrict the external capabilities of evil, but Americanists or Freedom promoters feel and believe they must control the hearts and minds of Muslims and get them to agree/believe in their faith while also restricting the external capabilities of practicing Islam. Freedom is a contradictory bigoted faith that feigns tolerance but is actually more intolerant of other religions than the intolerant religions are. To further test this theory of freedom being an intolerant religious faith of crazy fanatics, we can simply look at the prophets of freedom and see whether they allow people to disbelieve in it. Do they? No. As their prophet Francois Voltaire, who was a freemason, famously stated, *"I disapprove of what you say, but I will defend to the death your right to say it."* Which means that they don't give you the choice of having freedoms. If you say *"God said don't take his name in vain, swear, gossip, backbite, lie, or slander so I don't have the right to do that."* They will say you do have the right to do that and God can't tell you that you can't say what you want and they are willing to fight in order to force freedom upon you, whether you like it or not and whether God likes it or not. Meaning they will fight God for telling you that you don't have the freedom to say or believe or do as you please. If you tell them that God said freedom is forbidden then they say they got to kill that terrorist who is oppressing you and telling you what to believe, say and do threatening you with eternal and worldly punishment if you disagree or disobey them. The lovers of freedom believe people have the right to disagree with and disobey God without any consequences in this life. They fight so people can disagree with and disobey their Creator and think they are heroes for doing so and expect gratitude as if they were holy warriors since according to them *"freedom is more sacred than any religion"*. All freedom fighters are fighting against God. The prophets like Moses, David, Solomon and Jesus pbut would fight against them. Whereas the mainstream man-made faiths incorporated this heresy of freedom into their own since it made it okay for them to lie and lies are how they can spread their faith, but Islam has not. This is because the religion of Islam does not spread through lies and lies don't benefit Islam. Therefore since lies are incompatible with Islam, freedom is also incompatible with Islam and hence we have the war. Except because those who believe in freedom believe it's okay to lie then many of them lie and pretend there is no war because they are cowards and don't want to confront Islam head on intellectually or spiritually on religious grounds, or political grounds. Thus to survive, they will eventually be forced to resort to force to fight for freedom so they don't feel bad or stupid or sinful for not believing in Islam. Whereas don't misunderstand that to mean one cannot choose to disbelieve in Islam, one can choose that, but if one learns about Islam and chooses that then they'll be socially humiliated for making such an illogical decision and in an Islamic nation many would have to pay Jizyah for their right to disbelieve. Hence to avoid the disgrace of recognizing that they intentionally choose to believe in a false religion and will go to hell when they die, the kuffar concocted the Winslow Plan wherein those who believe in Islam will be sent as far away as possible from those upon the faiths of falsehood and killed, while those who stay will have to convert to Americanism or whatever other false faith they concoct and agree to force upon people. Meanwhile their dream is that Americanism will win the war with Islam and abolish it leaving no faith but freedom or hedonism. This way Americans can live enslaved under their ideocracy and feel good about being slaves to people and being on the road to eternal hellfire. Yet Americanist politicians and Americanist prophets aren't the only ones preaching the "Winslow Plan", the US military teaches it to new recruits. In 2012 CE Lieutenant Colonel Matthew Dooley was the instructor at the US Defense Department's Joint Forces Staff College in Norfolk, Virginia wherein he taught future army officers the American plan for the war with the Muslim world. Dooley taught that just as Hiroshima and Nagasaki were bombed to win WWII then Mecca and Medinah would need to be bombed for the US to win it's "total war" against Islam. There were 4 different war plans for combatting and defeating the Muslim world and the religion of Islam, some included having an international boycott of Muslims or labeling Islam as an illegal cult. Dooley explicitly taught that, "*We have now come to understand that there is no such thing as "moderate Islam". It is therefore time for the United States to make our true intentions clear. This barbaric ideology will no longer be tolerated. Islam must change or we will facilitate it's self-destruction.*" Such are the doctrines and war plans the US military teaches it's officers who are training to be the future leaders of the military. God knows best how long they've taught this but officially they've publicly admitted to teaching it since 2012 CE, which was the same year they were caught burning thousands of Qurans in Afghanistan, even though documentary evidence proves this has been taught since 1800 CE. So for any who think the "American war on Islam" is going to simmer down, the evidence points to the contrary. The US military taught total war publicly in 2012 CE, to its officers, then during the next election we start hearing the "war on Islam" rhetoric from charismatic personalities like Donald Trump. Is that a coincidence? Could alleged democracies, like the American ideocracy, be controlled by the military with elections being mere theater? That's how it's always been, ever since General George Washington got "elected". George Washington's election was no cleaner than George W. Bush's. I was even personally informed by an ex-CIA agent on November 2nd, 2016 CE that Donald Trump would be declared the "winner" of the election 6 days before the election took place on the 8th when the "surprise victory" was publicized. Yet Americans still believe the elections are real and they should vote despite me being accurately told who the "surprise winner" would be 6 days in advance by a former government employee. So when the sheeple mention "clean elections" the very idea of an election is filthy. A government must be corrupt to allow voting, being a democracy just means they are so corrupt they try to hide it. The votes are purely political theater done for religious reasons to make the faithful "feel good" about doing something under the illusion that their voice is heard and can influence the one that has a gun to their head requiring them to pay taxes, but in reality they are doing less than nothing to change things. Many Americans actually think the ones with the guns telling them where to vote, when to vote, who to vote for, how much their votes are worth and who "counts the votes" will actually let them tell the government what to do and the government will do it because of voting. The government controls every aspect of the election but the citizens think voting is some type of loophole that will cause them to control and change the government, because the government told them it was. The government lies to the citizens every day of the week and they know this, but then when a ballot can be used they think *"Well the government promised they'd do what we want if we pick who they allow us to pick."* They foolishly religiously believe that the government who they know lies to them about nearly everything, even the weather, is telling the truth when it says *"Your votes control us, we promise."* Honest people know that in general the politicians are liars and lie about most things they say, yet the one thing all politicians unanimously agree upon is that *"Voters control the government."* Isn't it suspicious that the 1 thing professional liars agree upon is their unproven claim that voting can influence the government? They lie about almost everything but when they all agree we are supposed to believe them? Are they more likely to unanimously lie to us or to unanimously tell the truth? It's not even political, it's politrickal. Voting is simply a big joke the governments play on their citizens to prevent ideas of a revolutionary uprising or peaceful movements for real change. Governments give them ballots to play with so they don't think about changing the government via bullets. Ballots don't hurt governments so they let citizens play with them while bullets do hurt governments so they try to stop citizens from playing with them. The problem is that Americanism is a cult so it's members don't realize they've been brainwashed and are manipulated into thinking, saying and doing what their false prophets and mascots desire. Don't worry though, Islam has come to destroy all the oppressive exploitative religious cults and Muslims will one day liberate the Americans, and by Americans I mean everyone who believes in the false man-made faith of Americanism. I suppose rather to avoid confusion I should use the term "Americanists" and clarify that you don't need to be in America or be an American citizen to be an Americanist. Yet the end of Americanism is what Americanists fear and when cult leaders fear for their cult they get ferocious and use force in many ways, whether it's social, financial or physical. Thus the 2016 CE presidential candidate Jeb Bush said the U.S. should let the military and not politicians determine how to stop "radical Islam" by force, because only a military solution will work. Yes the same US military who was taught by Matthew Dooley in 2012 CE that regarding Islam *"This barbaric ideology will no longer be tolerated."* Apparently "extreme radical religious ideas" can only be defeated by "extreme military offensive action" which of course they tell us this war is simply secular and has nothing at all to do with religion. Even though both democracy and secularism are religions. Also remember when they say they are fighting for "American values" that is a reference to the religious doctrines of Americanism, it's just part of the religion of Americanism for its members to not let people know it's a religion or a cult. Whereas to be suspected of viewing extremist material is too easy for a practicing Muslim to be guilty of doing especially when the Quran allegedly contains 75% extremist material according to the US military. But even if they don't view such material they need not actually do it, just to be suspected can be enough, or to be suspected of intending to do it can be enough. Basically speaking it is legal for any Muslim to get charged with being a felonious criminal fit to be imprisoned under the modern terrorism laws. Yes every Muslim can be charged at any time and imprisoned, so that's where I don't care to "watch my mouth" because it doesn't matter if you are guilty or not, if they want to put you in jail then they'll do it if Allah allows them to. Basically the violent muslimish extremsists belief is that the world governments are ruled by Pharaohs, which I agree, but did Moses pbuh ever suggest doing what they suggest doing? Moses pbuh lived under the tyranny of Pharaoh amongst disbelievers but still he didn't teach his followers to go on a bloody rampage. Moses pbuh never told people to poison the water supply or put bombs(start fires) in public places! If that was what God wanted then Moses pbuh would've done it, but he didn't do it nor preach it. You truly don't need to have any exposure at all to extremists to have similar beliefs and say word for word the same exact things as they say minutes before they advocate sinful unislamic violence against civilians. Such an attitude as advocated by the "war against radical islam" group is similar to the one of those who wanted to kill Jesus pbuh, in case some of his teaching led people to join the Zealots. But would we say they were right to try to stop Jesus pbuh from preaching and take legal actions to censor him and silence him just because some people might get radicalized by listening to him? Whereas it's well known what they do to Muslims because they say they preach dangerous Jihadi ideas, but what they never tell people is that not everything an extremist preaches is bad or wrong or incorrect or extreme. It's too easy for non-Muslims to suspect a regular strict practicing Muslim to be a dangerous radical violent extremist because they simply don't know what Islam teaches and it teaches people a different way of life and thinking than all other religions. Afterall the FBI and other "counter-terrorism groups" define homegrown Islamic extremists" as "*U.S. persons who appeared to have assimilated, but reject the cultural values, beliefs, and environment of the*

United States. They identify themselves as Muslims and on some level become radicalized in the United States." Note the FBI says a Islamic extremist *"rejects the cultural values, beliefs and environment of the United States"*. This is serious stuff, legalisticly the FBI is implying that it is a crime and a threat to the nation if one "rejects the cultural values, beliefs and environment of the United States". Yet if those "cultural values, beliefs and environment" are different than or contrary to "Islamic values, beliefs and environments" then by definition every single Muslim would be an extremist and every Islamic book/video/audio educational tool would be "extremist material". However Americanist prophets and the "Experts on Terrorism and Combatting Extremism" say it should be a felony to be suspected of viewing extremist stuff which Muslims should be arrested and imprisoned for. Though as I know you don't even need to be exposed to the true radical extremist ideas to believe in some of their ideas because some of their ideas come from Islam itself. Hence at the fundamental level Islam is a cause for the label of "extremist" by non-Muslims claiming to "combat extremism". Meaning according to non-Muslims their definition of a extremist is a practicing Muslim because to them Islam itself is extreme, since it teaches something diametrically different and opposed to that which they believe in and their laws are based on their religious beliefs and they don't know it. Thus they may think something is illegal, radical or extreme, because of their law and not realize it's a religious law, so they think any Muslim violating that law must be radical/extreme even though it's just a Muslim believing in or practicing their religion. Examples would be telling people democracy is evil and that things like freedom and total equality are conventions invented by Satan and forbidden by God which should not be allowed in any country on earth. Or say a woman covering her face with a veil, or Muslims refusing to listen to music, or work with pig, alcohol, gambling, drugs, holiday junk etcetera. Or saying "Bite your father's penis" when someone praises their lineage, as Muhammad pbuh told Muslims to do. There is a conflict with Shariah and Islam with the West and it's laws/values/culture, but that conflict is due to a difference of religious beliefs. One group must change their beliefs to resolve the issue since Islam teaches Muslims to condemn the unislamic religions and the religions of freedom and equality, but the ideocracies who preach such faiths as part of their composite faiths make that illegal. Or one group must leave and live in another land. Or else one group will simply die off without changing their beliefs but their beliefs will die with them. Those are the only three realistic options. Non-Muslims must change their religion, or Muslims change their religion, or both groups move to different countries and leave each other alone in peace. However that last option is not acceptable to either group in the long-term. This is because Islam teaches Jihad, including offensive Jihad to establish Shariah throughout the world. While Americanism, Democracy, Freedom and Equality also teach that such beliefs should be spread throughout the world and accepted by everyone whether peacefully or violently. In regards to democracy it has never been implemented yet, what most people believe to be democracy is actually "national democracy" I use the term "national democracy" because in theory the faith of democracy is the "rule of the masses" which means it's a global system and to restrict the majority vote to members of your own nation is not true democracy. If the majority vote is always right then the majority of people in the world should vote on everything, because to only have your nation vote would not constitute a majority and thus such voters will, according to democratic beliefs, be wrong every single time. That's the hypocrisy of those preaching national democracy, in reality they are promoting anti-democracy where a majority vote of a minority decides things. Most don't promote global/true democracy because they are nationalists who don't really believe in democratic principles but just think their national majority should be able to decide things for their nation, because their nationalism dictates all other nationalities are inferior or unqualified or untrustworthy. Yet if people of other nations are untrustworthy, then who is to say people of other states or cities aren't? What about the government? Are they trustworthy? If not then why do politicians get a vote? Seriously people are afraid of foreign non-citizen voters but they aren't afraid of their own blatantly corrupt politicians voting? With most governments today a foreigner desires better things for your nation than the native politician. Democracy can only be a global faith/system while national democracy is the hypocritical political exigency, which most think is "democracy" because they are really ideocractic nationalists playing games. No democratic nation in the world today wants a global democracy due to their nationalism, even though if democracy were fundamentally a correct system then a global democracy would be best. Ultimately if the religion of democracy is believed in, preached and practiced, it leads to a global system/faith that has everyone in the world ruled by 1 government in which everyone allegedly has their vote count. However if there is only 1 government that rules the whole world, do you really think they are going to count the votes? Yet that's what democracy leads to, a global government where everyone in the world can influence everyone in the world via votes, in theory. Even in theory if it weren't corrupt, such a global democracy is crazy. National democracy is no less crazy in theory nor practice but people believe it because it's a religion and not just a legal system. Those who do actually believe in democracy believe everyone should believe in and practice it, without realizing the reason they believe that is because to believe in democracy means one must believe in a global democracy, at least subconsciously. Democracy is all or nothing, either everybody votes as a world or nobody is really practicing it. Hence democracy is spread by military violence or money if propaganda doesn't work. Therefore the religious war between Democracy and Islam will continue until one is eradicated, because both teach their legal system is fit to govern the world; which since these systems contradict each other means one is wrong and seen to be an evil oppressive opponent by the other. Plus there is only one world/universe available for us, so we can't have 2 global systems of government. Only 1 global system can ever be implemented. Eventually one of these systems will be extinct. At this time though few are calling for global democracy and in practice "national democracy" is just a myth preached by ideocracies. The main ideocratic political religion/system today taught as an alternative to Islam is Americanism, which has many branches. Neither Islam nor Americanism tolerate the other faith being publicly preached in it's domain since they contradict each other. So neither religion peacefully allows the other to spread in its domain or be taught in its domain and both religions teach that everyone should believe in them and it is a crime to prevent the spreading of the other religion. Thus it's not extreme to say there is a religious war going on. It is going on and it will continue until one of the warring faiths no longer exists. Muslims must realize this and non-Muslims must realize this as well. The sooner we all agree about this religious war existing the more likely we can have it be a peaceful religious war instead of violent. Muslims don't want to fight, but we will if we have to and Allah teaches us that the non-Muslims will not settle for a peaceful religious war because they never ever have throughout all time since they lose those because their faith is false. Likewise regarding the repression of Muslims at the hand of non-Muslims there is a reason this always occurs and increases. Firstly confusion, fear, uncertainty, desperation, habit and perception make brutality likely in any conflict. When a disbeliever knows the believers are right, as deep down every disbeliever subconsciously knows, but can't bear the burden of this knowledge then they repress it and they strike at those believers who irritate their conscience. Or they may think/believe/feel disbelief is correct and may feel bad at the oppression they commit therefore doubting whether the way they are waging war against Islam and Muslims is correct even if their disbelief is. Regardless of whether a disbeliever belongs to the former or the latter category, when disbelievers doubt the defensibility of their war/faith do you know what they do? They either convert to Islam, or abandon their faith and/or it's war efforts, or they intensify the severity of their war effort trying to convince themselves they are right and/or to avoid guilt for their past war crimes. So kafirs oppress in order to make themselves numb to past oppression which they feel guilty about. In short they feel sorry for killing Muslims so they kill more of them more severely to desensitize themselves so they don't feel so bad about it. This is how most sinners operate. We feel sad for doing 1 sin so what do we do? We should repent but typically many do more sins to feel better and stifle the guilt they have for doing the 1 sin, thereby they commit many until eventually they no longer feel guilt for doing sins but enjoy it. Soon non-Muslims will once again reach the stage where they enjoy killing Muslims, many are already at that stage and others want to get there faster. Finally it is well established that maximum violent persecution occurs when a party is fighting for a belief as well as its material interests, and Islam is a threat to the material interests of the West, especially the interests of those who make money via interest(usury). So at the end of the day a violent war is coming, it cannot be avoided. We don't want it, but it is simply a fact of life; unless the non-Muslims decide to embrace Islam or the Muslims decide to apostate from Islam. However we can possibly delay this war or minimize the casualties if we live in separate places or if we publicly admit there is a religious conflict and we all agree to settle it peacefully by deciding to embrace whichever religion is true. Which again may be impossible for our species to do. Thus war will happen, sooner or later. Yet as a ground rule we should try to let those who are living in "enemy territory" leave. This is because it will be a bloodier conflict if everyone is intermixed since it will lead to many accidental casualties due to friendly fire as the line between combatant and civilian gets blurred. This is the problem extremists have, they have blurred the lines and as a result innocents get killed on both sides, because they started the violent war already without giving peace every chance it deserved to be given before fighting broke out. So the war will come, the two types of dangerous extremists whose ideologies and actions will lead to more deaths and the deaths of innocents are those who are already waging the military war and those who insist no war will ever occur. Those who insist "we can all get along and live in peace" are causing more civilian casualties than there need be for the war to finish. So these advocates for peace and tolerance and interfaith nonsense are unintentionally causing more bloodshed by being in denial and fear that the global religious war will be violent. The only thing to really debate now is how the military war will be waged when it is to be waged. Where will the battlefield be and where will the safe zones be, if there are safe zones? Muslims have rules for Jihad, so the only true question is how will the non-Muslims fight us?

  Donald Trump completely agreed with the ideas about proposed solutions to the ongoing religious war expressed by his fellow Americanist non-Muslims and I respect him for at least picking a side because it shows he is semi-honest and wants a solution, albeit his "happy ending" is the opposite of mine. Trump said that because of all the international rules and regulations "*American soldiers are afraid to fight* " since currently the Americanists fighting tactics are internationally labeled as "war crimes". So instead of changing the way American soldiers fight Trump says the world should change the international laws to let US soldiers "*fight*" the "*menace of radical Islam*". Thus we have a very unique case never before seen in the history of the world where the USA "good guys" are saying they legally can't "fight evil" because global laws clearly say that only "evil guys" fight the way

Americans do. Call me skeptical but it seems that's something only the "bad guys" would say, but we're told they're the "good guys" and if you don't think so then you might be an "extremist". And you know what the "good guys" do to "extremists" don't you? Probably not because it's illegal to report all the details of what happens when any "extremists" get interrogated by the "good guys". Regarding interrogation techniques used on Muslims, Donald Trump solemnly promised that as president he'd *"bring back a hell of a lot worse than waterboarding"*. Which sounds like what George W. Bush said on September 11th, 2001CE, off camera: *"I don't care what the international lawyers say, we are going to kick some ass."* And to be tortured you only have to be "suspected of intending to view radical Islamic material". What is the difference between "Counter Terrorism" and the Catholic Inquisition in Spain? The Catholics admitted Islam was their enemy and that they were promoting a rival religion, Americanists don't. But don't think Democrats are any different, some even call Hillary Clinton *"Killary"* and Barack Obama *"O'bomber"*.(not me though, because Muhammad pbuh taught Muslims that it's a sin to call people nicknames they may not like, but both do advocate the killing and bombing of Muslims) Although to demonstrate how Barack Obama and Hillary Clinton are merciless enemies of the Muslims one incident will suffice, even though there are many examples such as what they did in Libya, Syria, Iraq, Afghanistan, Yemen, Somalia and Palestine. The "smoking gun" that proves Barack Obama and Hillary Clinton are merciless enemies of Muslims is what they did in Pakistan in 2011 CE. When Hillary Clinton was Secretary of State American led NATO forces "accidentally" bombed two Pakistani military outposts thinking they were Taliban on November 26th, 2011 CE. This was 2 days after the American holiday "Thanksgiving" and 1 day after their infamous Black Friday holiday, so very few Americans heard the news or would've cared if they did. Two separate outposts of the Pakistani military were bombed resulting in 28 dead soldiers and 12 wounded. Did the US apologize to their Muslim ally? Of course not, it's America. America didn't even apologize when they dropped atomic bombs on Japan, twice. Which considering Japan being bombed by America with Atomic bombs, really I fail to see how Americans think that is in any way legitimate. What did Japan ever do to America to deserve any violent actions whatsoever? The attack on Pearl Harbor? Well that wasn't like a "declaration of war" or anything, really it wasn't. That was just a "tactical limited airstrike, with no boots on the ground". Practically identical to the "tactical limited airstrikes" the USA does in Muslim countries today, and for as long as I've been alive, except Japan's tactical limited airstrikes were in non-US waters and only military personnel were harmed without any civilian casualties and Hawaii was not even a US state at the time, so it wasn't even near US soil. So I guess Japan's airstrikes on Pearl Harbor were less warlike than the US airstrikes in Muslim nations. Nevertheless for some reason, many Americans couldn't understand why, the people of Pakistan were outraged that America, who is officially their ally and stations US troops at US military bases in their country, can bomb their Pakistani soldiers in Pakistan without even apologizing. To compare this, imagine if America's ally Canada dropped some bombs on US soil killing American soldiers and then refused to apologize for it saying, "*It was an accidental bombing, we meant to kill other people when we were dropping bombs on US soil, without asking permission or warning you, but even though it was accidental we aren't sorry for killing them.*" America would consider that a declaration of war, but America's Muslim ally Pakistan isn't allowed to consider having it's soldiers bombed on it's soil a declaration of war. That's just how unislamic America treats it's Muslim friends, or at least the Muslim friends America likes; since not every Muslim friend/ally gets such magnanimous "kind treatment" (especially without even having such kindness reciprocated with elaborate gratitude). America is like a school bully who in order to avoid getting in trouble for bullying tells the teacher they are best friends with their victims and socially pressures their victim to tell the teacher how much they are good friends with each other. Bullies have their muscles and America has it's military. As a result of America's and Clinton's refusal to apologize, Pakistan cut off America's supply route to US soldiers in Afghanistan and forced America to evacuate the Shamsi airfield which they had been using. Even with the blockade of US troops America and Clinton insisted they were not going to apologize for bombing Muslim Pakistani soldiers. Pakistan refused to accept America's refusal to apologize for bombing their soldiers and said they were not going to allow American soldiers in Afghanistan to get supplies via Pakistani routes until America apologized for killing Pakistani Muslim soldiers "by accident". Still Obama, Clinton and America refused to apologize even though they admitted it was an accidental error on America's part and the Pakistani Muslim soldiers were entirely innocent of any wrongdoing. Therefore due to the will of the people of Pakistan, despite the democratic Pakistani government trying to thwart them, from November 2011 CE Pakistan blockaded the US troops in Afghanistan demanding an apology, which if given would end the blockade. It's important to remember that 2012 CE was an election year for the incumbent president Obama. Conveniently blaming the blockade, America said it had to "extend it's stay in Afghanistan" longer than anticipated and delay troop withdrawal once again. Then while Pakistan was still waiting for America to apologize for illegally killing and wounding their Muslim soldiers for no reason, on February 22nd 2012 CE US troops in Afghanistan were caught burning copies of the Quran. Finally 4 months after the Quran burnings and over 8 months after the incident of America bombing the Muslim soldiers in Pakistan, on July 3rd, 2012 CE Hillary Clinton apologized for bombing the Muslim Pakistani soldiers via a phone call to a Pakistani minister. Yes, after holding out for 8 months with the whole country demanding a public apology forcing a blockade, Clinton gave a feeble "*sorry for the accident"* over the phone, President Obama didn't bother because that wasn't his job. Every Tuesday Obama would just look at the kill list saying which Muslims to bomb via drone, but he doesn't have to apologize because his job was to be President not apologetic. Hillary Clinton's long delayed apology took place on July 3rd, 2012 CE so most Americans never heard of it on the news since July 4th is America's national patriotic holiday ritual. Exactly one year after the 2012 July 3rd "apology", in 2013 CE on July 3rd the 13 month old Muslimish democratic government of Egypt was overthrown and replaced by a secular military dictatorship with American support. More Americans heard about that but didn't see the cyclical pattern of how big newsworthy events always seem to happen when Americans are busy/distracted celebrating holidays. It perfectly sums up what George Orwell said after WWII, *"The nationalist not only does not disapprove of atrocities committed by his own side, but he has a remarkable capacity for not even hearing about them."* After the apology, if you can call Clinton's phone call an apology, like a good puppet the Pakistani government lifted the blockade allowing US troops to be supplied in Afghanistan so they could kill Muslims there more easily. Yet in 2016

CE, 4 years after Hillary Clinton held out for 8 months refusing to apologize for "accidentally killing Muslim allies on Muslim soil", some "Muslims" in America dared to say American Muslims should vote for Hillary Clinton to be the President. Clinton literally had foreign Muslim blood on her hands from multiple countries including but not limited to Palestine, Afghanistan, Libya, Somalia, Yemen, Syria and Iraq, as well as ashes from the Quran on her hands, which she was proud of and refused to cover with makeup, but Muslims in America thought she was the "lesser evil" because Trump said he wanted to deport American Muslims and send them back to Muslim countries. Then those pro-vote "Muslims" claim the ones who say don't vote for Hillary Clinton or Donald Trump or any American politician are crazy. In reality who is the bigger enemy of Muslims, the one who kills them in foreign countries and refuses to apologize even when apologizing can help her kill more Muslims or the one who says Muslims should leave America and go live in Muslim countries if they believe in Shariah? In 2016 CE, Trump didn't have any more Muslim blood on his hands than the average taxpayer but Clinton did, so why did "Muslims" think she was the "lesser evil" and think they should vote for her? Because those "Muslims" who vote care about their own interests and not about Allah or Muslims. That's the justification they themselves gave, in that they had to vote for "their interests while living in America", not the interest of Allah or the global Muslim population but their personal interests while living in a non-Muslim country. Hence Muslims who vote in America, vote for allies of Israel and the enemies of Muslims thinking they are their allies as "fellow Americans".

That's why when Donald Trump was announced as the "winner" of the 2016 election I was glad and I'd tell Muslims it was "great news" and would explain to them how good it is for Islam that Trump got "elected" for the purposes of him being bad for America, good for Shariah in America in the long-term, good for the war between Truth and Falsehood, and good in that now Muslims will be better able to identify who the hypocrites are even though the events leading up to the election itself did a pretty thorough job revealing that already. I told them this was the promise of Allah being fulfilled and that they should rejoice when the animosity and persecution from the Kuffar increases. Sadly though the Muslims in the masjid did not share my enthusiasm for Trump being announced as the winner and they were surprised as well, which I found surprising even if they thought it was a real election. This is because the foolish think the sly sweet talking liberal enemies of Islam like Obama and Clinton are helping Muslims, but they are actually worse than the Bushes because the way they attack us motivates other enemies to rachet up their harm because they think and get told we're getting helped instead of harmed. For instance while Trump's campaign platform was to ban Muslims and ostracize them from American society, Clinton's platform was about how Muslims serve in the US military and gave their lives fighting against Muslims in Afghanistan, Iraq and elsewhere. So you see in reality Muslims are being given two options in America, either convert to Americanism and fight for it, or leave. Trump says kick em out then kill them and Clinton says put the Muslims in the US military to fight the Muslims overseas. Which plan is actually worse when you think about it? Yet the Clinton Clan says Trump's team hates Muslims while Trump's team says the Clinton Clan loves Muslims. In reality though when it comes to Muslims the Trump Team and Clinton Clan are teaching the same exact thing and have the same exact goals with only different plans on how to convert Muslims to Americanism and kill those who don't. Honestly not a single politician is saying Muslims are allowed to not believe in or support Americanism. Most non-Muslim politicians are Crusaders where one type fights silently and the other says: *"Because you're not shouting you're their enemy and hate them while fighting, then I gotta scream even louder and do even more damage than you do."* So that's where all the politicians in the West are harming Muslims, yet they trick people into thinking one of them is helping us so that way they always have a reason to motivate further hatred and ramp up the persecution. It'd be like Pharaoh blaming his advisors for being too lenient on Muslims thereby using this alleged leniancy to radicalize the whole nation allowing him to consistently replace his minions with more and more radical people who he always claims are too lenient in order to continuously persecute more severely. The difference is that the people of Moses pbuh didn't fall for it whereas some Muslims today do and support enemies of Islam seeing them as the "lesser of two evils". This despite Muslims not being allowed to vote in American elections or even run for political office in a kafir democracy. And that is actually the legal ruling Muslim Imams in America have given, American Imams have said it's forbidden to vote in the elections every single year for the same reasons; as have Muslim Scholars throughout history. Muslims have officially been recognized and recorded as being in America as a potential "swing vote" since 1965 CE. Yet for 31 years the Muslims in America didn't vote because they recognized it was sinful and the scholars were mostly obeyed when they gave legal verdicts saying Muslims in America cannot vote in elections. In 1996 CE that changed for 2 reasons. In Afghanistan and Bosnia the Muslims waged defensive Jihad during the 1990s and had success without help from non-Muslim nations. Of course the UN and non-Muslim world betrayed the Muslims in Bosnia but in Afghanistan the Taliban was uniting the country and establishing Shariah. This scared the West because they feared Muslims would realize just how powerful they can be if they united, migrated and waged Jihad to defend themselves instead of just making dua asking for kafirs to protect them. The success of the Jihadis led politicians to scramble for some alternative action to give the Muslims so the status quo of Muslim subjugation could be maintained. So what could America give the Muslims as an illusionary action to distract and deter them from Jihad so as to make them think by doing nothing to change things and failing to defend themselves that somehow they were influencing the world and didn't need to wage Jihad? The illusion of voting. But there was a problem, Islam said it was forbidden to vote and Muslims hadn't done so in over 31 years since they "officially existed" in America. Thus in 1994 CE Bill Clinton's team, which betrayed the Muslims in Bosnia, began to "reach out" to the American Muslim community holding Eid dinners at the White house and trying to get them politically involved so they would vote. Money soon flowed to those Imams, Masjids and organizations willing to promote voting despite its sinfulness. Prior to that Salafis were the most influential Muslim group in America and lots of Americans were becoming Muslims at an exponential rate. In the 1996 CE election most Muslims didn't vote, since it was kufr but for the first time the idea that Muslims could vote was popularly being expressed in some communities. The majority of the minority who voted, voted for Bill Clinton. Clinton then negotiated a Palestine peace treaty with Israel ceding land to Israel called the "Dayton Accords" then he was widely exposed as an adulterer even though he had been accused of such long beforehand. In 2000 CE more Muslims had been tricked into thinking voting wasn't disbelief or a sin, but who to vote for George Bush or Al Gore? Well Gore's running mate was Jewish and Muslims were told that Gore/Lieberman would serve Israel more than Bush/Cheney would and that George Bush wasn't as pro-Israel as Gore and that Bush would be a friend of the Muslims if he was elected. It might sound ridiculous today, but Muslims were actually told this in masjids during the 1990s that George W. Bush if elected would greatly help the Muslim community in the USA and abroad. Muslims were told by other "Muslims" that they "must vote for Bush" because if Al Gore were president of America it would be very bad for the Muslims. George W. Bush was marketed as "the lesser of two evils" and *"not even that much of an evil, but almost a friend of Muslims"* afterall he was Christian so he had "good Christian morals" that would make him see "eye to eye" on issues Muslims cared about. So believe it or not about 80% of the Muslims who voted in America during the 2000 CE presidential elections voted for George W. Bush. But more importantly

55,000 "Muslims" in Florida voted and 88% of them voted for George W. Bush. Florida happened to be the key state in the election and if you believe the elections were legitimate it practically decided the election. George Bush won Florida by 537 votes, of which about 48,400 were from "Muslims". Thus if you believe the elections were legitimate the Muslims in America are the reason George W. Bush became President. They rejoiced at the news and cited the results as *"proof that voting works and helps Muslims despite what those Salafis say"*. CAIR's executive director, Nihad Awad, said in regards to the Muslim vote going to Bush that, "*Muslims based their vote on the best choice . . . It happened to be George Bush, but in four years it may be different.*" Newt Gingrich, whose anti-islamic statements I mentioned earlier, is another person who was publicly supported by "Muslim" organizations as a hopeful ally of Muslims in America and they voted for him in his elections. Muslim hopes were high, sure Bush wasn't perfect, but he "owed Muslims" since the data says he only got elected because they voted for him, if you believe the elections are real. But how did George W. Bush work out for the Muslims? On record the "Muslim" groups in America that promote voting in elections like

MPAC, ISNA, CAIR, AMC, AMA, AMT, MSA, AMPCC and ICNA (of which these are only a few of the groups) said Islamically George Bush was the "best choice" for president and publicly endorsed him, which of course such an endorsement was financially reciprocated and these groups have only increased in their popularity and influence over the Muslim communities since then. Of course they endorsed Kerry, Obama and Clinton in the subsequent elections but the record shows what happens when Muslims vote for the "best choice" or "lesser evil" in elections as they get told to do by the "moderates" and "win". When they "lose" because of block voting, such as when 93% of Muslims voted for John Kerry in 2004 CE, who butchered the Muslims as Secretary of State from 2013-2017 CE, the Muslims only expose themselves to more animosity from the establishment. The persecution under the 05-09 Bush administration increased because the Muslim voters voted for his opponent. Basically Muslims are damned if they vote for the winner and doubly damned if they vote for the loser. So for Muslims to vote, is to lose politically speaking as the record shows. Muslims are damned if they vote no matter who it is they vote for, and not voting is the safest both politically and religiously. Muslims not voting for anybody is proven to work better for them than voting for the loser or the winner. The sad thing is that these same fake Muslimish groups who supported Bush in 2000 CE now cite him as the result of what happens if Muslims listen to Salafis or Fundamentalists and don't vote. The exact same groups that endorsed Bush in 2000 CE and told Muslims to vote for him, even falsely claim that *"If Muslims voted in 2000 CE, Bush wouldn't have been elected and we wouldn't be persecuted today. All our troubles today in America are because Muslims didn't vote enough in the past to be able to influence the elections in our favor."* The truth of the matter is the exact opposite, George W. Bush is what happens when Muslims "vote for the lesser evil" and "win". Firstly the elections are fake but regardless even if real, as the naive allege, voting only results in evil every time. If the Muslim votes count, then Muslims singelhandedly got Bush elected. So either the votes don't count, as experts say, and Muslims shouldn't vote or they do and Muslims really shouldn't vote. Allah punishes voters in this life and the next and that is what Islam teaches regarding voting in non-Muslim countries for the non-Muslims, religiously speaking Muslims have no vote. It's not about whether any government say they legally can or can't, Islamic Shariah says while living in non-Muslim lands they can't and it doesn't matter how many "Muslims" say otherwise. The Shariah is clear on this matter and for decades Muslims in America unanimously purposely did not vote because of it being forbidden and Islam was spreading rapidly and Muslims weren't persecuted despite having zero participation in politics. That for decades Muslims unanimously didn't vote in the past proves it is the correct position because Muhammad pbuh said that the Muslims will never unanimously agree upon error. So that there is a "difference of opinion" regarding voting today indicates at least one opinion is an error and since unanimity indicates truth that means since Muslims unanimously didn't vote in the past because they said it was unislamic and forbidden then that was the correct Islamic position. Ironically ever since Muslims started voting in America in 1996 CE, the American government has increased it's global persecution of Muslims and the Muslims have faced more persecution within America as well, and them voting in larger numbers each election is even cited as a reason by persecutors to justify more persecution. The Islamaphobes, believing democracy is real, actually say that the Muslims have to be prevented from voting and that to stop them from voting the persecution of Muslims within America should increase. Thus voting is a primary reason Muslims in America get persecuted, because Americanists believe voting works. So if Muslims didn't vote many non-Muslims would have little to no fear of Muslims being in their countries. Yet the pro-vote voice ignorantly says "*If we don't vote Muslim persecution will only increase.*" despite the statistics proving voting increases persecution. When a Muslim in a non-Muslim democratically themed country votes they are fueling anti-Muslim persecution, even if they don't intend to do that. That's how democracy works. Minorities who vote get persecuted, those minorities who don't vote when they are allowed to vote get left alone because the majorities fear oppressing them since they know oppression will not result in political game playing since that minority group doesn't play politics. Throughout the world Muslims were better off when the Muslims in America didn't vote. I think the increase in global persecution is Allah's way of punishing the Muslims for disobeying his prohibition on voting. Fundamentally it always comes down to religion, if Muslims disobey Allah then Allah will punish them even if they disobey him with the intention of attempting to relieve the suffering they are experiencing from the attacks of their enemies. Votes don't stop the plots of Shaitan, the Shaitan's plot is to get Muslims everywhere to vote. For a Muslim to vote for any kafir is almost like voting for Satan, since it is Satan's campaign to get Muslims to vote for any non-Muslim he can. Satan doesn't care who Muslims vote for, he just wants them to vote. The knowledgeable Muslims inside and outside of America have always said it's sinful to vote but foolish Muslims always ask about voting for every election and some other ignorant Muslims make exceptions for "this election". It's truly pathetic, I've even read what was written about past elections by Muslims who promoted voting to see what they said before and after and it's always the same nonsense. They always say the same things to motivate voters and make them feel/think a new chapter of Islam in America is opened and that things will change and that because of their efforts in organizing to vote then regardless of the outcome things improved because their voice got louder and is heard. With my own ears I've heard a speaker in a masjid say word for word the same things after Trump was "elected" that were said when Bush was "elected" in 2004 CE, and the speaker doesn't even know that he was saying word for word the same post-election rally speech to Muslims as had been said 12 years earlier. He actually believed his material was new and I was stunned because he literally said the same stuff word for word in some instances thinking it reflected the progress Muslims had made. He said how if they do what he suggested they do to move forward the situation of Muslims would improve when the very things he suggested were recommended in 2004 CE, got done, and failed miserably. The ignorant Muslims are a broken record of unislamic failure but they always think they are improving and repeat the same solutions that cause the same problems with the only effect being that the Muslims in America become less Islamic overall. Of course their buildings get more numerous and masjids expand, but they install more prayer spaces and have even less people praying there than they used to have. Financially the communities grow but concerning faith it's a famine that they try to cure with finances and interfaith political activism. Quantitatively they increase in numbers and wealth but qualitatively they get worse and worse because the majority stopped following the way of the salaf. Since many are immigrants they repeat this disaster in earnest, never knowing their "Islamic solution" has caused Muslims in America to become less Islamic over the decades since these Americanist doctrines in the name of Islam have been more widely disseminated. It's a proven fact that the less strict and intolerant and more assimilated and democratically active Muslims have become in America, the slower Islam has spread there and the less Islam has been practiced amongst Muslims. Much of the time, money and energy that Muslims used to spend on learning, practicing and preaching Islam now goes toward "*Muslim rights*" and "*Muslim activism*" and "*Combatting Terrorism*". Many replaced "practicing Islam" with "practicing politics" or practicing Americanism but call it practicing Islam. Beginning to vote was partially the beginning of the downfall of Muslims in America and the more they vote and promote Americanism the farther they'll fall and neither Allah nor the angels will catch them. This problem of voting comes about because of ignorant Muslims adopting the kafir slogan of "choose the lesser of two evils", and they justify this by saying the Muslims rejoiced when the Romans defeated the Persians in a battle.

Thus they say Muslims can vote, but this reasoning is wrong. The incident of the Muslims being pleased the Romans defeated the Persians has nothing to do with democracy. First of all the Persians were the superpower and had recently trounced and destroyed the Romans, when Allah said in the Quran that soon the Romans would defeat the Persians. The Meccan disbelievers cited Allah's statement as a joke and impossible, so when the Romans pulled off a surprise victory against the Persians it proved Allah was right and the Quran was true. On top of that the Persians were polytheists and the Romans were Christians, so the polytheist Arabs would say that just as the Persians are victorious over the Christians they would be victorious over the Muslims; both predictions proved false. Also at that time the Persians were at war with the Muslims and the Romans were not. So in that case it wasn't "choosing the lesser of 2 evils". It was joy that Allah was true when the Quran made a spectacular double prophecy, and it was joy over a neutral party of disbelievers conquering a party of disbelievers who were at war with Muslims. There is no such thing as a pro-Islamic American political party nor can any party in any country be pro-Islamic or a Muslim party if it believes and promotes belief in democracy or voting. On top of that the Muslims did not participate in the Roman-Persian conflict. So that event cannot be used to justify political participation, least of all participation in a kafir religious ritual known as voting in elections. The exceptions arose when <u>**some**</u> scholars in Muslim countries <u>said it **could** be permissible to vote</u> in democratic elections <u>for Muslims to rule a Muslim country,</u> **if** there were a proven benefit and no alternative; yet thus far all such rare electoral incidences have backfired. Voting in American elections, if they were legitimate instead of theater, is like a gun called the American military laying in the middle of a field. One candidate comes running for the gun from the north and the other candidate comes from the south with both intending to pick up the gun and use it to kill the Muslims in the east, meanwhile there is a Muslim in the west watching this take place but they cannot stop either candidate from getting the gun and shooting the Muslims. Now what should the Muslim do? Voting for one candidate is the equivalent of pushing the gun closer to one candidate, if votes actually counted which they don't but the vote shows the intention to help one party get the power to kill Muslims and thus implicates one in the crime. Which if the Muslim chooses that option and votes then that is tantamount to accessory to murder even if the candidate they intend to push the gun closer towards has worse aim and kills less than the other would have. To vote on a ballot is to have the blood of the innocent on one's hand almost as if they fired the bullet. Fundamentally voting is legally being an accessory to murder. The only peaceful passive thing worse than voting would be paying taxes. Voting makes one politically guilty and paying taxes makes one economically guilty, however voting is truly optional and nobody gets coerced to vote so that's why voting can sometimes be worse than paying taxes to the butchers. Even "write-in" candidates are sinful because such "write-ins" legitimize the system and secondly the "write-in" actually gets counted as a free vote for whoever the vote counter, if there was one, decides. The vote counter can just say *"To me that handwriting looks like it says X candidate."* and nobody ever bothers to check to see if who they intended to vote for was actually who the government said they voted for. Honestly voters are so stupid they actually think the government is not corrupt enough to say they voted for X when in reality they voted for Y.

Seriously the citizen voters never check to see if their vote was counted accurately because they just have blind faith in democracy. Also people think that a "write-in" candidate means you can write in a vote for whoever you want, but that's not how it works. A voter can only vote for a registered government approved candidate. A write-in vote only counts if it's for a registered candidate the government approved of but just didn't put on the ballot because they weren't one of the government's top choices for mascot. You see that's the other thing about elections, in that you have to register as a candidate with the government and if the government doesn't want someone to be the leader they just reject their application because they can, because they are the government which makes the rules. So literally all this talk about "the government doesn't want X to get elected, because they'll fix it all and end the corruption" is pure lies. If the government really didn't want somebody to get elected they would just reject their application to participate in an election and nobody would ever be told they were a "possible option". Only people the government wants to be their mascot can ever participate as a candidate in the election. The government chooses who is eligible for office, those who aren't with the government's program never get approved as an eligible candidate. To be a candidate means to believe and agree with what the government bureaucracy wants. No politician can even get on the ballot to get a vote unless they are approved by the government and the government wants them on the ballot to get a vote. Thus you can only ever vote for who the government wants you to vote for because those are the only ones who can be voted for. Basically elections are a way for citizens to pick a mascot who is just a public face for the government without any true power. Citizens if their votes even count for anything, it would only be a matter of whether they wanted a mascot who was male or female, black or white, blue, brown or green eyes, hair color, young or old, fat or skinny, rich or less rich, dumb or dumb, dishonest or dishonest, immoral or immoral and finally evil or evil. Yet at the end of the election the government's choice gets the job no matter what and the policies the government planned to implement get implemented and if people don't like what their government does they just blow off their steam on the mascot thinking it's the mascot's fault for what the government is doing; because the mascot, media and government said it was. Truly elections are the biggest type of fraud by which a institution can control it's people while making their subjects think they aren't really in total control. Democracy is slavery with the illusion of choice/freedom/equality so that the slaves are happy to be slaves and love to be oppressed/exploited. The stupidity of voters is proof enough that voting should never be used as a method to decide anything important. If you want something done right, don't put it to a vote. Another reason this "we must vote" doctrine is wrong is because the Jews of Germany voted for Adolf Hitler under the influence of this very slogan of "choosing the lesser of 2 evils". Hitler was democratically elected by the Jews in Germany, they actually voted for him thinking he was the best available candidate for their interests. So when people today claim Muslims should "vote for the lesser of 2 evils", that is exactly the rationale that led to Hitler getting elected by Jews. In the 1932 CE presidential election in Germany the top 3 candidates were Paul Von Hindenberg, Adolf Hitler and Ernst Thalmann. Hindenberg won 53% of the vote garnering over 19 million votes, while Hitler won 36.8% of the vote garnering over 13 million votes while Thalmann won 10.2% of the vote garnering over 3.5 million votes. In that 1932 election about 2/3rd of Germany's 400,000 Jews are believed to have voted for Adolf Hitler. Most are likely more surprised to learn that Germany only had 400,000 Jews in 1932 CE yet years later Nazis allegedly killed 6 million. More surprising is the fact there were 3,000 Muslim citizens in Germany during 1932 CE as well, 10% of which were native Germans. Muslims lived in Germany before Hitler came to power. Germany even had a Muslim-only cemetery built in Berlin in 1798 CE and 1,000 Muslims were enlisted in Frederick I's German Army during 1760 CE. Today Germans say "Muslims are ruining Germany" but Muslims have served in the German military since 1760 CE. I guess it's taking them a long time to "ruin Germany", how many cite the 1700s CE as the time "Muslims started ruining Germany"? If so they'd be wrong because Muslims were in Germany even before the 1700s CE. Before America was even a country Muslims were citizens in Germany and served in it's military. Thousands if not millions of Muslims have lived in Europe for hundreds of years. Doesn't everyone know that? In 1614 CE France alone had 50,000 Muslims, note that's 1614. Likewise France had 100,000 Muslim soldiers fight and die for them during WWI. Tens of thousands of Russian Muslim soldiers fought the Nazis in Stalingrad and Leningrad. Why don't Muslims get included in European history when they have played such major roles in Europe for centuries? I wonder what happened to the Muslims of Europe during WWII? They never mention in school or the media what the Nazis did to Europe's Muslims. In fact most people don't even think there were any Muslims in Europe until AFTER WWII. Albania was the only Muslim-majority nation in Europe and it was also the only European country to have more Jews after WWII than it did before. Albania's Muslims are documented to have saved the lives of 2,000 Jews helping them escape Nazis so clearly European Muslims were not on the Nazi friend list. Could it be possible that maybe some of those allegedly Jewish circumcised corpses from the "Jewish Holocaust" might have been Muslims? Nevertheless the political analysis states that about 264,000 Jews voted for Adolf Hitler to become the president of Germany in 1932 CE. Mein Kempf came out in 1925 CE so any readers would have known about Hitler's Aryan anti-semitism. Yet to Jews they truly believed and were told by their Rabbies that Hitler was the "lesser evil" and they *"have to vote for their interests while living in Germany"*. Always remember that German Jews are responsible for putting Hitler in power. Jews are not 100% responsible but they are responsible to some extent for all that Hitler did when in office because they voted for him. That's how voting works. You don't vote for a "lesser evil" and not become responsible for that evil. If you vote then that makes you partially responsible for everything that person does or would've done. Spiritually <u>Voting is a pledge of allegiance</u> and it is disbelief for Muslims to ally with the enemies of Islam. Meaning fundamentally if a politician is a known enemy of Islam (aka disbeliever), or even worse an enemy of Muslims, (ex. supports Israel or armies that kill Muslims or supports having Muslims imprisoned/tortured) then for a Muslim to vote for them is to ally with them. A Muslim can't play games saying they don't like them or their policies and then vote for them, a vote means you ally with them and support them in their campaign for leadership. There is no distinction between a vote cast by one who supports 100% of a politician's plans and a vote cast by one who supports 0% but just doesn't want someone else to win. The intentions behind the votes don't matter, all are

equal. Whereas the Quran commands Muslims to not help/support one another in evil and wrongdoing. Islam doesn't teach Muslims to support the lesser evil, it sternly clearly commands us DO NOT SUPPORT EVIL! That means Muslims don't vote for disbelievers or in democratic elections in non-Muslim lands because it's an evil system and by voting one is contributing to wrongdoing and evil. Voting for anybody in a democracy is active support of the democratic system and allegiance to those politicians and Islam forbids such support and allegiance. It's simple if you don't believe in democracy then you don't vote in the elections. To vote means that you believe in the system and are trying to use it. You cannot vote for a leader you hate, it's impossible to do. When people vote for a "lesser evil" they are simply choosing which rope to hang themselves with. They are voting for their oppressor and as such become directly responsible for their own oppression because of voting. Not voting frees you from responsibility, voting to prevent another oppressor from "winning" still makes one responsible for oppression and the desire for oppression. Meaning even if the person one votes for doesn't win and the "greater evil" wins, the voter would still be responsible and guilty for all the evil stuff the other one would've done had they been elected. Thus by voting the voter loses spiritually in the afterlife even if the one they voted for "loses", unless they repent from the great sin of voting.

Why is it that you are only allowed to vote for the politicians of a nation and not the policies it has or abandons? The reason democracies postulate voting for leaders is because if the people are left to govern themselves it's known they would make the wrong decisions. With that being the case then automatically that means the voters will also make the wrong decision when voting for their leaders. If the reason people vote is due to the tendency of the masses to make the wrong choice then it's also wrong to let them vote for a leader because they will make the wrong choice in that regard too. Thus democracy is a contradictory system where for voting to be right it has to simultaneously be wrong to vote. If the people can't be trusted to vote for the right decision on every policy then they can't be trusted to vote for the right politician in an election. Democracy refutes itself. Yet not only are voters not allowed to pick policies to vote for, nor the candidates but the government itself tells the people what the issues the candidates are to differ over are.

People living under democracies or pseudo-democracies can't even get an honest debate between candidates because most government policies aren't up for discussion, like the issue of military alliances or taxation. Furthermore because being a leader is a such a large responsibility which most people will fail to do without sinning or committing injustice, then it follows that good religious people don't want the risk of leadership due to the dangers they'll face in the afterlife for being a bad leader. Due to this any person who desires leadership is disqualified from it because the only ones who desire to take the spiritual risk of the responsibility leadership entails must be either crazy or corrupt and both possibilities indicate a bad leader. Therefore in Islam anyone who wants to become the leader is automatically rejected as a possible candidate to be the leader, since any who want the job are guaranteed to do a bad job because they don't fear doing a bad job, if they did they wouldn't want the job. Any person campaigning to be elected as a leader is automatically not qualified to be the leader and will certainly do a bad job of it. Just the fact that they spend money promoting themselves instead of in charity is proof of incompetence and evil. So democratic elections are schematically designed to give a nation the worst most power-hungry possible candidates. The worst way to get a leader is to ask "Who wants to be the leader?" and then select one of those. Hence democracy always results in bad evil leaders. In Islam the people force an individual to be the leader of their nation because they are the best person and the people won't let them not be the leader. While in democracy people are forced to pick a leader out of those who are eager for the position, the good ones who don't want leadership never become the leaders. It's truly amazing every election because you have politicians who none of the people would want to marry, nor raise their kids, nor have as a business partner yet they vote for them to govern them. Why? Because those politicians said they wanted the job AND the government agreed to let them apply. Yet years earlier none of the voters would have picked those politicians for the job. It is the politician who preaches they are the best for the job first, then the government agrees to let them participate in the election as a candidate and then people agree they should/could be the leader, mainly due to the poor quality of every other applicant which the government agreed could participate as a candidate. The voters never truly choose to vote for X, instead X chooses them to vote for X and the government's candidates A-Z just gave the voters a less persuasive salespitch. What voters should do is not vote and tell these politicians: "*None of you are qualified to be the type of good leader we truly need and deserve. None of you get the job. We will search for someone else because all of you politicians suck. None of us are voting so all of you lose and do not get elected because the election is cancelled, due to inferior candidates who do not fit minimum criteria to be a good leader. We'd rather keep the position vacant than fill it with anyone of you con-artist tyrants. Perhaps the government will be closed until we find quality leaders. It's better to shut down the government or be leaderless than have any of you be our leader. If we can't find any good citizens then maybe we will appoint a foreigner if our country is that corrupt as it appears thus far. As sad as it is, we might actually need to import a good leader for us because honestly our country might not have any good leaders among us and we want a good leader rather than a native leader. We want the best leader in the world. We don't want the best of us. To get the best you have to be the best and we might not be the best, and if not then we are going to get the best even if it's a foreigner. Sometimes the best leader for your country isn't born in your country, doesn't live there and doesn't currently have citizenship. The best country gets the best leader regardless of their location. Being the leader of our great country is too important to vote on. We cannot risk our nation by putting leadership to a popular vote."* In Islam the leader is forced by the people to lead against his will because of the will of the people, while under democracy the people are forced to pick a leader they don't want to lead according to the leader's will. Under Islam the people choose their leader, under democracy the leaders make the people choose them. Linguistically it may sound similar, but under Islam God made the law already and says which few good people get to pick the leader who is just supposed to do as God says leaders are supposed to do. Under democracy the leaders make the law and do what they say they are supposed to do contrary to what God says they should do. Under Islamic Shariah nobody wants to be the leader because the leader is a servant and slave of God and the people, but under unislamic systems the people are the slaves of the leader who usurps the authority of God. The reason democracy is from the devil is because it is literally the people picking their own leader who make their own laws, in opposition to the leaders God desires them to have and the legal code God has ordained. Since we are always repeating that God is the one to judge and the opinion of people doesn't matter why then do we judge who our leaders are and allow the opinion of people to determine both our leaders and our laws? For God to be the only judge means that people have no right to pick their own leader via popular opinion or elections. Why doesn't God allow democracy? Because we are sinners. How can people who routinely elect to sin possibly ever elect a decent leader? Before the masses can be qualified to pick a good leader they have to be able to live a good lifestyle. If they choose to be evil sinners then they will always choose evil leaders. Which since the masses are always evil sinners then whenever the masses get to pick their leader they will select one that is evil because for the masses choosing evil is habitual. Hence it has always been the case for every democratic election that people have said *"vote for the lesser of 2 evils"* and what does it get them? It results in evil. Maybe if people decided not to vote for a "lesser evil" we might actually get a result that is not evil. It's worth a try, because if everybody doesn't vote then nobody wins the election and the system peacefully ceases to exist as a legitimate political ritual to initiate a ceremonial changing of government mascots. The sad thing is that nobody in democratic countries who hears the slogan "*vote for the lesser of 2 evils*" seems to make the correct decision. When you are living in a country where everyone agrees that the next leader will be evil no matter who it is and they only disagree on which potential leader is less evil, then the correct decision for you is to get out of that country which you know is going to have an evil leader. Do I have to say it? Why don't people just add evil + evil = It's time to leave. Vote with your feet. Don't wait for the results when you already know the end result is evil. You wouldn't pick your poison would you? That's satanic. So then why do people pick their politicians? What happened to people that they decided instead of fighting the forces of evil, they choose to vote for the lesser evil? The problem is they got patriotic and are too attached to a certain section of dirt which they live on. They fell in love with dirt and decided they love that dirt patch so much they are sticking to it for as long as they live because their evil leaders tricked them into thinking every other country is ruled by even greater evil, or they are afraid of losing money or the companionship of other humans who live on the same pile of dirt as they do. Thus they decide to live under evil together rather than fight the evil or move elsewhere. They'd rather be slaves working the soil than fight to improve their lives on the soil, if it means risking death and burial under the soil. They'd rather be trampled and disgraced above the soil than buried with honor under it. When you have such stupid satanic materialism, it's no wonder they have evil satanic leaders. Evil people don't rule good people. God has never told mankind to vote for evil and God does not want people to vote for evil. Just ask a pro-voting for evil person if God told them to vote for evil or if it was Satan? Imagine Satan's #1 devil and his #2 devil were pitted against each other in an election. Would you vote for one of Satan's devils? Would you vote for Satan's #2 devil to be your leader? Do you think a prophet would? Actually we know the answer to this. In Mecca the Muslims were horribly persecuted and when the leader Abu Talib died, Muhammad pbuh being a member of the Quraysh tribe had the right to vote for who would be the next leader of Mecca. All the electable candidates were disbelievers and hostile to Islam. Know that whenever Muhammad pbuh was faced with 2 options he always chose the easier option as long as it didn't involve sin. As a member of the tribe Muhammad pbuh could've been elected leader of the city. So did Muhammad pbuh vote for himself?

No, because he didn't believe in democracy and voting is sinful. So an enemy of Islam was elected to be leader of Mecca and the Muslims were persecuted even worse than before, yet still Muhammad pbuh never voted nor did he tell Muslims to vote despite knowing persecution would increase in different levels based on who got elected. He had a chance to vote for the "lesser evil" or himself in an election that impacted all Muslims and he choose not to. So from this one can know the correct prophetic example for Muslims to follow during elections in a non-Muslim country is to not vote, but practice Islam trying to implement it there while also looking for alternative places to preach Islam where the people are more likely to embrace or implement Islam. But perhaps the worst thing about Muslims being tricked into voting is that most don't know that democracy is a religion and it is disbelief to think it a valid system of government. All the Muslim scholars are unanimous on this. Now voting doesn't automatically make one a disbeliever, one could just be ignorant and there is a difference of opinion anyways even if they aren't ignorant. However when you have masses of Muslims in the West see a sign on a masjid door or hear someone in a masjid say to go vote, they never get told "*Just remember democracy is a false religion and thinking it's a valid way to rule is a type of disbelief*". The danger in this, aside from wasting time and sinfully voting for clear disbelieving public enemies of Islam and people who advocate stealing(taxation), is that unlearned Muslims who are bombarded with electoral campaigns may incorrectly start to think democracy is valid anywhere on earth. That's a problem, a big problem. It can make them a disbeliever without them even knowing it. And that's not extreme to say, the extreme thing would be to say any who rule by or live under democracy are disbelievers; since with those things there are circumstances to consider. However to believe democracy is an acceptable system or legitimate or compatible with Islam is disbelief. One could say that X country is ruled by that, but you have to ardently believe that it's forbidden and wrong. Because Shariah is not just for the Muslims, it's for the planet, so there is no concept in Islam of democracy being valid for America but not the middle east. The Quran ardently teaches people to reject all falsehood, it doesn't say "disagree", or just to "go with the flow". It teaches all people to reject it. Rejecting democracy includes not voting in elections.

Because you can't really reject something if you are participating in it seeking protection or benefit from it. Every alleged democracy in the world today is a sinking ship, economically, politically, morally and spiritually, and all genuine democracies if there ever were any are sinking ships of a false religion anyways. Yet people ask *"Who do you want to win the election?"* when I get asked I explain America is bankrupt economically and morally so it doesn't matter who "wins" and it's not even a legit voting process. I say, *"When you are in a sinking ship full of holes that cannot be repaired then who cares who wins the election to be the next Captain? The boat is sinking! It's not time to choose a new leader, if you want to solve the problem you gotta get a whole new boat. If you take part in the vote for a new leader then you are part of the problem."* Muslims are not supposed to be in the non-Muslim lands to influence the system, we are suppose to share the guidance of Islam and implement the Islamic system while rejecting the unislamic beliefs and systems. Muslims can't be voting year after year and then say, *"Ok now that we are a majority, we vote that there are no more elections, time for Shariah"*. That's dishonest hypocrisy and not how Islam works, Shariah doesn't come via surprise or majority vote. Muslims live to campaign for Allah, not for kafirs. You cannot use any system to abolish itself. The Muslims in Muslim countries can't even get Shariah by voting and their nations' constitutions say Islam is the official state religion, so for Muslims to think they will vote Shariah into place in kafir countries where the constitutions and state religions promote freedom is completely delusional. Good deeds result in good, evil deeds result in evil. If voting results in evil then such a vote would be evil. Regardless of whether the results are good or evil, the results themselves do not determine good deeds. The results do identify evil deeds but not good deeds. Bad deeds can have good results but good deeds never result in evil. There are black, white and gray deeds, the gray deeds are not good deeds so don't do them. Voting is something that makes Satan happy, and since people die every second, you don't want to be one who dies voting; especially voting for evil. Likewise voting results in more than 1 type of sin because on the way to the polls and at the polling place one is likely going to see and hear sinful things due to people being dressed improperly or speaking sinful speech. So one's eyes can gets sins due to the voting process. Thus even if voting wasn't sinful it becomes sinful due to the sins that are involved in the process. Another example of this is Voter Registration. When I was pressured to register to vote in high school and told to fill out the forms by my teacher, who was also an elected politician, I registered as "Unaffiliated". That means I'm not affiliated with any political party, not even the "Independent" party. This is important because due to it being forbidden for Muslims to ally with enemies of Islam that means it's forbidden for Muslims to register with any unislamic political party. It's actually forbidden and potentially kufr for any Muslim in America to be a "Registered Democrat" or "Registered Republican", of course if they registered before embracing Islam then that's different. This means regarding party primary elections it's completely forbidden for a Muslim to vote in them under all circumstances because it's forbidden for them to even belong to such unislamic political parties. Furthermore in America on election days you have more self-proclaimed Muslims voting than there are praying in the masjid for their 5 daily prayers. (Keep in mind Allah commands Muslim men to pray in the masjids and he forbids voting in multiple ways.) Sadly there are "Muslims" who don't take off work to worship God in God's house but they will take off work to vote.

Who do those voters really worship if they are away from the masjid voting for non-Muslim enemies of Islam? If they were Muslims they'd pray in the masjid, not in the voting booth. Whereas those who do pray in the masjids don't vote and tell people it's sinful and potentially disbelief to do so. What does that tell you? The prophet of Muslims tells them to pray in the masjid and the politician tells Muslims to vote at a polling station. What would the true Muslim do? Which choice do you think leads to paradise and which choice leads to hell? Those "Muslims" who vote are doing exactly what Satan wants, they abandon the masjid to vote for devils pledging allegiance to kafirs and the kafir system wasting their life to do so. Over a lifetime the amount of total time spent by voters on elections(and I'm including all the pre-election drama, thinking, debating, research etc) adds up to days/weeks worth of life. People literally spend days/weeks/months of their life voting for evil. That's not what God wants people to do with their time, hence voting is also sinful because it's a terrible waste of your life. Then when you multiply that time spent per each voter this is trillions of hours wasted by voters which they could've used to do something useful and good. Good people are too busy doing good deeds to vote. Seriously even if voting weren't sinful, I don't have time to vote anyways. Change doesn't happen via voting, that's not the way Allah changes things. Allah tells Muslims he never changes the condition of people until they change their inner selves. Voting is the problem, not a solution or a way to prevent problems. If people did something God likes instead of focusing on voting the world would be fixed. Following the prophets is the solution for us, not voting for politicians. The politicians are false prophets, I'd rather stone them than vote for them. Truly the politicians are prophets whom people think are the means of their salvation, voting is a religious ritual where you end up picking a devil dressed in human clothing thinking that will prevent another devil from ruling. But after the votes are counted the end result is people voted for a devil to govern them, and God does not reward voting. Isn't it extreme to say that elected politicians are devils? That depends. They'd be devils if they believe that human changes to laws will fix things. Are there any elected politicians who don't believe that? I don't think so, but maybe; on another planet. Any leader who accepts being appointed by the result of an election is unfit to lead. The reason elections always involve voting for a "lesser evil" is because voting itself is evil and only allows evil options. At the end of this dispute of voting, it's either forbidden or not. If it is forbidden what are the potential consequences a voter faces in the afterlife? If it's not then what rewards would they get for voting, in the afterlife? Now if someone doesn't vote will God punish them? After answering these three questions it becomes clear that the risk of voting and it being sinful far outweighs any potential benefit voting could bring. So the risk/reward ratio says don't vote, especially since it's not obligatory to vote and it's not a sin to abstain. The fact that people ask about whether they should vote is proof enough that it is sinful, because their heart is telling them it is and at the very least it's a doubtful matter. Whereas Muhammad pbuh taught that the lawful is clear and the sinful is clear while inbetween that there are doubtful matters, of which the successful one in the afterlife avoids the doubtful matters. Since at the minimum it's doubtful as to whether voting is permissible or sinful or disbelief and it's known 100% that it's not sinful to not vote, then it becomes clear that not voting is lawful while voting is sinful or doubtful. Hence the successful person who goes to paradise according to Muhammad pbuh does not vote in democratic elections. You have literally nothing to lose by not voting and so so much to lose by voting, just don't do it. Don't risk a place in paradise by casting a vote which can put you in eternal hell. Not even 1 prophet ever voted in a democratic election, especially for a disbeliever, so just do what the prophets did and don't vote. The footsteps of the prophets do not lead to voting stations. Dua is more effective and that's something God actually loves and rewards us for. From day 1 Muslims must be open about our intentions, just as Muhammad pbuh was and all the prophets were. Jesus pbuh could have ran for political office and become a Senator in Rome and maybe even Emperor, but he didn't. While Moses pbuh could have chosen to work for the Egyptian government and become the next Pharaoh, which was entirely realistic since he was the adopted son of the Pharaoh. Moses pbuh had a legitimate chance at legally ruling all of Egypt through peaceful succession if he just kept quiet and worked the system for a few years; but he didn't. While another example of Jesus pbuh is how he dealt with the Jewish political/religious structure. For example what about democratic "Islamic Societies" that are in control of masjids, are those exceptions which Muslims can participate in and "work the system, changing it from the inside" if it's an unislamic or democratic system but run by Muslims? Well Jesus pbuh lived in such a time where the religious temples and rabbis in the holy land were based on unislamic systems in religious guises with religious names for them, but Jesus pbuh never ever joined the hypocritical Jewish political systems; rather he openly opposed them. The Jews used to vote for the Rabbis who would manage the Temple but Jesus pbuh didn't participate nor vote. Jesus pbuh didn't preach Jewish unity against the Romans, he preached that you side with the truth against all falsehood regardless of the odds stacked against you, even if it makes the enemies of your enemies ally with each other against you. With his miracles and wisdom Jesus pbuh could have easily climbed the Jewish political and clerical ladder and became the head Rabbi of the Temple of Jerusalem in a few years time, but doing so would mean compromising the truth and accepting unislamic political systems and working with hypocrites so he didn't. Muslims don't "work unislamic political systems" we come with the truth and divine system to abolish the falsehood of all man-made systems. Muslims come to abolish not to polish. If the Western people would just talk with us and after learning Islam and Shariah they decide collectively they don't want to be Muslims or implement Shariah, then the Muslims will leave them and go to the Muslim countries. The problem is the disbelievers don't want to actually learn about Islam or Shariah and many Muslims in the West don't want to move, thus this conversation doesn't happen on a national scale as it should. Peacefully we should be able to come to a reasonable conclusion. Muslims will not assimilate, the Islamic system is superior according to our beliefs and critical analysis so we are trying to upgrade the West with Islam. An easy pitch for Muslims to prove that Democracy is evil is to simply say: *"Why is it that whenever there is a democratic election people always say to "vote for the lesser of two evils"? If Democracy were truly good then shouldn't people be asking every single election how people will vote between "the best of many goods"? Wouldn't the best form of government mean the spot of leadership always goes to the "best of the best people"? If the system continuously makes your leader be the "lesser evil of evil people" then that is a very evil system of government that must be replaced as soon as possible. Muslims believe Shariah is God's solution to democracy and all evil forms of government. We think everyone is unique and not equal and that the best people should have more authority in making decisions. In particular those who believe in God correctly and follow the religion taught by all of God's prophets. We don't think people who are immoral and don't believe in God should have an equal say in government as someone who is moral and correctly believes in and obeys God. So no Islam does not promote equality or democracy, but rejects those political notions because we believe the best people should be in charge and get selected by the best people according to God's criteria of good and bad, and that wealth, race, nationality, or popularity have nothing to do with qualifications for leadership. The majority of people are not qualified to choose the best candidate to lead a country or the best decision that God would want, so we don't believe in majority vote decisions when it comes to political leaders or political decisions. Muslims believe that a government based upon a majority votes by the majority of people will make terrible decisions and get terrible leaders the majority of the time."* Now religiously the West doesn't think they need an upgrade and thinks the Muslims are the ones needing an upgraded ideology, values and legal system. However if the West lets us preach to them then we'll preach, if they don't allow us to preach in their lands then we will leave and if we ever come back we will diplomatically offer the West 3 options. If any government doesn't like Islamic preaching then they should know that we prefer death over life under democracy or man-made legal systems of disbelief. The core problem is that the non-Muslims don't really want Shariah anywhere at all. So they don't want Muslims in the West to preach Islam, nor do they want us to leave, they just want us to change our beliefs. That's okay, but sooner or later something and some people will have to change, the modern situation can not go on as it is forever. For instance when Moses pbuh came to Pharaoh in Egypt, immediately he asked him to change his religion and implement Allah's legal system, if Pharaoh choose not to then he was told he should let the believers leave. Moses pbuh was clear from day 1, yet in the end Pharaoh neither believed nor let the believers leave. The situation today is much the same except not all the Muslims in the West know Islam and are sending mixed messages and some don't even practice Islam. The Muslims today aren't as they were when with Moses pbuh, but then again the Pharaohs aren't the same either. The Muslims didn't want to rule pagan Egypt, yet that's what Pharaoh feared and told people. The enemies of Islam play the same game today, trying to make people afraid of some subversive Muslim takeover. Any such alleged plots themselves are anti-Islamic. Shariah doesn't happen via secrecy or surprise. Islamically there can never be a practicing Muslim president in any democratic non-Muslim land, unless such a person were to become a Muslim after becoming president but that's very rare. In all probability if any "Muslim" were ever elected as president in the West they would probably be the worst oppressor of all towards Muslims, because they'd have to prove they aren't "biased" or "too lenient". Realistically the next "official" crusade will likely be launched by some "Muslim" leader in the West against sincere practicing Muslims throughout the world. Such a leader would be the ideal scapegoat for enemies of Islam to hide behind and justify their war on Islam, they already do this in the middle east. In fact George W. Bush quoted the Quran on September 17th, 2001 CE as justification for his plans to retaliate for 9/11 alluding to his plans to invade Afghanistan. George Bush said, "*The English translation is not as eloquent as the original Arabic, but let me quote from the Koran, itself:* "**In the long run, evil in the extreme will be the end of those who do evil. For that they rejected the signs of Allah and held them up to ridicule.**" The face of terror is not the *true faith of Islam. That's not what Islam is all about. <u>Islam is peace</u>. These terrorists don't represent peace."* I found it odd that he didn't say which verse he was quoting. Later I learned it was 30:10, which in context 30:7-16 in English says, *"They know only the outside appearance of the life of the world, and they are heedless of the Hereafter. Do they not think deeply (in their ownselves) about themselves (how Allâh created them from nothing, and similarly He will resurrect them)? Allâh has created not the heavens and the earth, and all that is between them, except with truth and for an appointed term. And indeed many of mankind deny the Meeting with their Lord. Do they not travel in the land, and see what was the end of those before them? They were superior to them in strength, and they tilled the earth and populated it in greater numbers than these (pagans) have done, and there came to them their Messengers with clear proofs. Surely, Allâh wronged them not, but they used to wrong themselves.* <u>**Then evil was the end of those who did evil, because they belied the Ayât (proofs, evidences, verses, lessons, signs, revelations, Messengers, etc.) of Allâh and made mockery of them.**</u> *Allâh (Alone) originates the creation, then He will repeat it, then to Him you will be returned. And on the Day when the Hour will be established, the Mujrimûn (disbelievers, sinners, criminals, polytheists) will be plunged into destruction* *with (deep regrets, sorrows, and) despair. No intercessors will they have from those whom they made equal with Allâh (partners i.e. their so¬called associate gods), and they will (themselves) reject and deny their partners. And on the Day when the Hour will be established, that Day shall (all men) be separated (i.e the believers will be separated from the disbelievers). Then as for those who believed (in the Oneness of Allâh - Islâmic Monotheism) and did righteous good deeds, such shall be honoured and made to enjoy luxurious life (forever) in a Garden of Delight (Paradise). And as for those who disbelieved and belied Our Ayât (proofs, evidences, verses, lessons, signs, revelations, Allâh's Messengers, Resurrection, etc.), and the Meeting of the Hereafter, such shall be brought forth to the torment (in the Hell-fire)."* So in context George Bush quoted Quran verses specifically addressing the Christian Byzantines and Persian Zoroastrians (as well as all disbelievers) on how the evil powerful disbelievers who rejected Allah's signs and "mocked his verses" were destroyed and will burn in hell forever. The ayat/verse Bush quoted applies to him and all non-Muslims, but he applied it to "terrorists" even though the "evil" mentioned in the verse is the "evil" of not believing in Islam and mocking the ayat of Allah. Yet "Muslims" dressed Islamically were next to him smiling and applauding while he made this public mockery of the Quranic ayat/verse. It was also ironic that when Bush said "Islam is peace" and "terrorists don't represent peace" he didn't say they didn't represent Islam. That 2nd phrase is significant because it labeled violence as unislamic and peace as Islamic even though Islam teaches violent Jihad for certain situations. By Bush saying "Islam is peace" and "terrorists don't represent peace" he made it seem that to be violent is inherently unislamic when it's not. Violence is sometimes islamically ordained, as is peace, but coincidentally violence was Islamically correct as a response in the defensive Jihad against the American invasion which Bush later conducted. Yet unlike when the Russians invaded, the Muslims by and large didn't oppose the US invasion because Bush said "Islam is peace." and that meant to be unpeaceful (fight America/NATO/UN) was to be unislamic. Many incorrectly think this same thing today not realizing that it was a pure propaganda ploy first preached by George W. Bush prior to his invasion of Afghanistan and Iraq. Unfortunately some Muslims even preach this "Islam is peace." to the masses and call it Islamic dawah. To such Muslims you can tell them if telling kafirs "Islam is peace" amounts to teaching people the true message of

Islam then I guess George W. Bush as president was trying to convert the non-Muslim masses to Islam. The way Bush preached Islam was by saying "Islam is peace." so if any Muslims preach this slogan/platform you should know they didn't get that from the Quran nor Muhammad pbuh, they got it from George W. Bush. Sadly many "Muslims" today preach Islam in the way that George Bush taught them to. Surely it is a disgrace upon a disgrace that not only do some "Muslims" believe in and imitate the ways of non-Muslims but they even preach Islam the way the enemies of Islam preach it, using the same exact phrases word for word. But then they say they are Ahlus Sunnah wa Jamah and following the prophets.

When I say that the religion of Americanism is at war with Islam and that it doesn't matter which Americanist is the mascot, that's not just theory or rhetoric. When it comes to Islam all the political parties in America have the same intolerant position, they just publicly appear to disagree over the tactics because their crimes against Islam and Muslims are publicized differently. It's like Muslims are in the Roman Colosseum and the crowd is arguing over who should kill them and how, before they vote on the gladiator to do the job as they promised. While some "Muslims" in the stands watching the show justify voting for the gladiator the Muslims are to face saying, *"It's a religious obligation to vote for the gladiatorial opponent of the Muslims when you are in this situation especially when you are in the non-Muslim crowd after having paid a fee via taxes to watch the show of which the money you paid directly goes to equip the elected gladiator. If you don't vote for the gladiator then you are crazy! Surely Muhammad pbuh would've voted, don't you know Shura(Muslims consulting each other when making decisions) is part of Islam? When you are a member of this non-Muslim colosseum crowd you have a duty to participate and vote in order to get your rights as a ticketpayer of the show. Afterall if you don't vote for the gladiator now then when it's your turn in the colosseum next week you might not be facing the gladiator you want. Can't you see that by voting for who the gladiator is for the next 4 years you help the Muslims and Islam? Can't you see how dangerous and stupid it is for you to not vote?! Do you want us to get killed? Because if you don't vote, Muslims, especially Muslims like us, might get hurt because you not voting for one of the gladiators! And if you tell Muslims it's wrong to vote or stop us from promoting voting (or using Muslim wealth given to us in charity to do so) we're going to say you're dangerous and should be put into the Colosseum yourself for spreading disunity and radical unislamic ideologies! And if you say Muslims should leave the colosseum and go elsewhere we will denounce you as radical unislamic and extreme/crazy. Can't you understand that by us voting in this election for gladiator at the colosseum we are spreading Islam to the non-Muslims, because if no Muslims were here and we didn't take part in the voting process then things would be so much worse for all Muslims. Voting in this gladiatorial election is not only a good/smart thing to do, it is our religious obligation and we'd be sinful/insane not to."* Muslims voting in American Democracy would be like voting for an execution method of the Muslims at the colosseum. While just as democracy is a "method for peaceful change" the famous Roman Colosseum was called "Templum Pacis" which means "Temple of Peace". Yet just because it was called the "Temple of Peace" doesn't make it so and just because politicians claim they aren't at war with Islam/Muslims and claim that voting will make a difference doesn't make it so. The reason militaries have different branches is to get as many members as possible who help the war effort in different ways. It's the same with religious wars. The various political parties are just different branches of the same anti-Islamic Americanist theological army. What happens when all electable politicians on U.S. ballots always unanimously agree that Muslims should be killed? Whoever is elected it never matters, the trend towards Muslim genocide constantly progresses and it has everything to do with religion. Keep in mind the stuff I quoted is only what Americanist politicians said publicly while trying to get people to vote for them. If that's what they say publicly what do they really think that they aren't willing to say? What if one of these types of politicians decides not to say this stuff until AFTER they get "elected" and acquire the power to actually do some damage? Personally before I became Muslim my Crusader plan was to be silent until performing genocide. Those who claim a Muslim genocide is not planned are clueless as to how genocides occur. I myself planned for a Muslim genocide in the past and spent years of my life trying to trigger it, so I have a little experience with deliberately trying to cause genocide and can recognize the steps as they are taken. Basically I know the playbook of the mass murderers and I know some of the plays but those who never planned mass murder don't know the signs or the plays because they don't have the insider information, unless they got it from an insider or God gave the details to them. For example the governments don't label the attacks allegedly done by violent Muslim extremist as "Lone-wolf attacks" for no reason. The "Lone-wolf" label has deep psychological undertones and subliminal meanings. Its known all real wolves hunt in packs but there is 1 type of wolf that hunts alone, so the governments aren't foolish when using the phrase "*lone-wolf*". What is the 1 wolf type that commits "*lone-wolf attacks of terror*"? The notorious infamous monster known as the "Were-wolf"! It is the Were-wolf who is the "lone-wolf". Of course the Were-wolf is mythical, constructed from religious and superstitious beliefs but historically do you know what happened when Were-wolf attacks were reported? No Were-wolves actually existed even though things got killed, some humans though did confess to being Were-wolves responsible for the attacks of terror but it's now known that these were fraudulent confessions and those who confessed weren't actually guilty of the crimes nor were they Were-wolves if they actually did the crimes. However who were the ultimate targets/victims of the "lone-wolf" attacks? Publicly many assumed the victims were the livestock of the European Christian sheeple. Since the sheeple felt so threatened by the "lone-wolf attacks of terror" they eventually were motivated to kill all the wolves in the area. All the Christian sheeple knew that all wolves were not responsible for the attacks, but they still killed most all of them just because it was the only way to protect themselves from the lone Were-wolf who seemed so similar to the regular wolves; since both were so "wolfy" and some were "suspected of being a potential were-wolf" or possibly intending to turn into a Were-wolf at some future date like when the moon was full. Hence the wolves were the real victims of the "lone-wolf" attacks blamed on the mythical Were-wolves. Were-wolves were "the problem" not wolves, but killing regular wolves ended up being "the solution". The lesson being if you want to kill masses of X then just blame it on Extreme X and eventually all the masses of X will vanish. Essentially Christian European rulers wanted to expand their kingdoms into the forests and cut them down, especially since many pagan religions considered forests sacred. The existence of majestic/foreboding forests hindered the spread of Christianity, particularly when pagans could always take the forests as a place of refuge from Christian evangelization. However out of all the various forest dwellers the wolf packs were the only ones who posed a real threat to loggers and could stop them from destroying the forest and Christianizing it. Thus the Were-wolf attacks were staged so that Christians would be motivated to kill all the wolves which the governments couldn't handle all by themselves. Some people said there were no Were-wolves and that if some wolves were really responsible for the attacks on livestock it was a natural result of the deforestation and farmers settling on what was traditional wolf territory. Also wolves, despite any losses from attacks, were overall beneficial to society and the economy because they limited the pest population and hunted the creatures who would steal/eat crops, such as racoons, deer, rabbits, rodents and other animals that damaged the agricultural economy but left the livestock economy unmolested. Others postulated that all wolves were Were-wolves just waiting to wreak terror and turn everyone else into Were-wolves too, thus it was proposed that all wolves should be treated as guilty convicted Were-wolves. The churches split over the myths because the clergy knew deforestation would aid Christianity and destroy the non-Christian refuges but most also knew there was no justifiable reason to kill all the wolves and that the Were-wolves if they existed were a separate species of wolf that shouldn't be used as an excuse to kill wolves when the were-wolf is in essence a man most of the time and not a wolf at all. Yet eventually wolves ended up being slaughtered in Europe so that Christianity could spread into the former forest lands. Thus the label of "lone-wolf" when describing crimes allegedly done by Muslims is purposely done for similar reasons. The Americanists and Christians want the same result that happened to the wolves to happen to the Muslims, but for now it's just advertised to the sheeple as a few "lone-wolf extremists" just as initially it was "just 1 Were-wolf" even though ultimately the government and clerical plan was to kill all the wolves. In fact it was the sheeple who told the rulers that "all the wolves are the problem it's not just the Were-wolf", not realizing the rulers just invented the Were-wolf so their sheeple would help them kill all the regular wolves as was originally intended but opposed by the people when first suggested. So that's where the governments aren't as incompetent or foolish as they'd like you to think they are. But the Muslims who use the label "lone-wolf" when describing criminal attacks on non-combatants might be a "little ignorant". The Muslims denouncing "lone-wolfs" and radical extremists saying they united with the non-Muslims against radical Islamists and Fundamentalists are similar to the wolves who joined the townsfolk in denouncing Were-wolves saying "*Us wolves are on your side in this fight against radical Were-wolves. We hate the Were-wolves and want them dead even more than non-wolves do. They give all wolves a bad name and misrepresent us! We must come together and unite in order to defeat the plan of the Werewolves! The Were-wolves want to split our communities apart and have us hate each other. If us wolves are just nicer to you humans then we can prove ourselves to you and you will never ever think of harming us. We might not be humans or ever be humans and you might not be wolves or ever become wolves but that don't mean wolves and humans can't live together with love, tolerance, equality friendship and peace forever*". Or maybe wolves were too smart to publicly give fuel to the vehicle of their own demise. The Christian rulers' "War on Wolves" was never advertised as such, it was a "War on the Were-wolf terrorist", even though all the normal wolves were the ones that got killed. Although not all the wolves died, the normal ones did but the non-normal ones survived. The intelligent wolves migrated to defendable territories and successfully defended their wolf-land. Other wolves neither migrated, nor fought, nor were killed. How did they survive? They became domesticated pet dogs, some of whom would actually protect the sheeple from wolves and assist the Christians in their wolf hunts. Such inbred unnatural beasts are now referred to by many non-Muslim's as "man's best friend". They are glad to have a leash put on them and publicly displayed as subservient. They are grateful for any scraps their masters toss them or allow them to scavenge for in their owner's backyard and dream of a better doghouse for themselves and/or their pups. They belong neither to the wolf species nor to the satanic sheeple species but are hypocritical. If you haven't guessed, the modernist, peace preaching, interfaith freedom loving Americanist democratic pro-equality secularist "Muslims" are the humanoid version of such dogs. Except unlike the domesticated dog servants the non-Muslims keep as pets, these "moderate Muslims" don't even have the dignity to bark or growl; let alone bite. So the domesticated dogs are actually better than many self-proclaimed "Muslims". They change God's religion of Islam to be friends/friendly with disbelievers not realizing they've chosen an iron dog collar and Satan's leash so they can be walked down the road to the hellfire. They only bark, growl and bite the wolves who try to liberate them from their human masters, under the mistaken impression that they were the same species. Sadly though unlike the dog, the hypocrites claim to be wolves(Muslims) and portray the true Muslims as the Were-wolves. The speech of such hypocrites is more filthy than a dog's saliva. Some are so crazy that they even think "*If there were no terrorists then non-Muslims wouldn't kill us or hate us and they'd all become Muslims just how Muhammad pbuh was. The Non-Muslims only hate and hurt us because of these evil extremists.*" Little do such hypocrites realize that the non-Muslims hate them simply because they belong to a different religion than them, so as long as there are Muslims the kafirs will always hate and hurt. Which is why the hypocrites preach a different religion than Islam which matches the religion of those they preach to, usually today it's Americanism or Pluralism, and thus only feel liked once they are no longer Muslims according to Islamic standards. Eventually the sheeple had enough "Were-wolf attacks" so they waged a wolf genocide. Soon the satanic sheeple will commit a Muslim genocide too. Hence the main problem with the " war on terror" is that its name is a spelling error. Similar to how the "*will of the people*" the "*power of the people*", the "*rights of the people*" or "*vote of the people*" is misunderstood by the sheeple who refer to them. The honest historians in the future will joke that us common folk mislabeled the wars we waged, leading most to completely misunderstand what they were actually about; even after they ended. Since "civilized" people didn't see it fit to use vulgar words when doing vulgar deeds but romantically thought that what you called it was what it was. Today tyranny is called liberty because oppression has become a profession where brutal torture is seen as the way to a safe future to "spread equality" since the public vocabulary doesn't like the word colony. Much of this is promoted by politicians in the name of freedom, this is because everyone else gets stuck paying for it. That's what freedom always was. Freedom means to freely dominate others and to freely accept being dominated by Satan and your own desires. It's pronounced Free-dumb because those who advocate it are unaware that it is really Free-dom. The main issue that obfuscates the reality of what's going on is that the 2 primary religious ideologies are misunderstood and misrepresented. Islam and Freedom are mislabeled and mistaught by extremists so as to make Satan victorious since in a clear unbiased peaceful match he would lose. All the other religions are simply freedom from Islam.

The real situation is that there is Islam practiced by Muslims vs. Freedom practiced by Freedummys, of which some of these freedummys claim to be Muslims practicing Islam. Thus our era may go down and be known through history as the "Age of the Dictionary" because people believed the definition it gave for a word made the actions, labels and claims automatically true by default. While the fault may have been all ours for not accurately labeling the dictionary as an extremist. If you think this book is radical, fanatical or extreme then the dictionary is too because that's the place I got most of these words from. Thus is words, they mean everything and nothing, the only reason they have value is because the Creator gave them value and will reward us or punish us for which words we use, how we use them and why. Therefore never be a linguistic extremist because the less you say or write the less chance there is you will say or write something sinful. Yet there are words that God will reward us for if we say them for the right reasons. Thus we should use Allah the Creator as our source instead of the dictionary for what we should say, when we should say it and how.

    Recently many of the non-Muslim nations have been using a new strategy of covert theological warfare which is truly a form of total war more all-encompassing than the "total war" of the past; it is fought on political, social, ideological and economic theatres to coincide with and complement the military warfare. In the past the wars of religion were about changing internal beliefs without too much care for what the people practiced externally, but today the wars of religion are focused on what people practice more than what they believe. For example in the distant past Christians primarily fought against Islamic beliefs, they didn't really have animosity towards Islamic law and didn't fight Shariah. Today non-Muslims fight Shariah more than Islam, even though Shariah is a core part of Islamic belief they claim it's not. By claiming Shariah isn't theological they are able to eliminate a core part of Islamic practices and beliefs without the resistance that would come from attacking/eliminating a core abstract internal belief of Islam. Because the war isn't spiritual but focused on tangible externalities then Muslims don't react the same as they would if a spiritual aspect of Islam were under assault. If you imagine religion as though it were a castle, before the enemies would fire projectiles over the castle walls into the heart of the city attempting to destroy everything and cause an unconditional surrender while leaving the walls of the city intact and unscathed. Today the enemies claim they have no problem with the people inside the city and mean no harm but they will not tolerate the castle walls of the city to stand. So instead of attacking the heart of the city and the core of what they hold dear, the enemies say they don't want to hurt anybody but are just destroying the walls because they are oppressive, unsafe and it's better to have no walls. Meanwhile those intelligent people realize what will happen once the enemy destroys the walls so they fight back and get called extremists by both the enemy and the city inhabitants because the enemy says they mean no harm and the majority of the inhabitants of the city believe the enemy. Hence the soldiers who valiantly fight on top of the walls defending the internal and external foundations of the faith/city get stabbed in the back by their own kind and thrown off the walls to the enemy. Whilst true extremists then take to the walls and kill their fellow inhabitants of the city along with the enemy as well as attacking the foreign farmers who are just minding their own business trying to live life getting oppressively taxed by the enemy king. Extremists also change the infrastructure of the city, causing confusion, structural imbalance, loss of morale/legitimacy and inciting enmity from the enemy inspiring them to take more destructive measures. Of which some of the civilian enemy incite those working on the walls to fight like they did before, some of the enemy at the walls agrees to use the old tactics, while some try to go with the new devious plan to eliminate the walls first and some of the enemy actually believe their plan to destroy the walls is actually peaceful and humanitarian. Whereas the practicing Muslim is in the city of Islam looking at the non-Muslims outside who are actively chipping away at the external walls (or shooting at them with a cannon on the far end where only some of the inhabitants from the city can see/hear/feel the violence), then sees the violent extremists killing everybody, then sees the loud-mouthed peaceful Muslim extremists saying to side with the civilized foreigners on the outside and open up the gates so they can come live among us and fix the architecture of our city, serve us new foods and teach us how to be civilized like it is in their city. The peaceful extremists are the type of fool who goes outside the city to help destroy the city walls saying it will be beneficial since more sun will shine on the city, and the foreign enemy will like us more and it's what the city's founder would've done and did do in the past when dealing with enemies. And believe it or not they will cite some crazy out of context information from the blueprint of the city to actually make people believe that the founder of the city had a practice of destroying the city's walls that have never been destroyed once in all of history. The peaceful extremist even goes so far as to say the walls are not even a part of the city but were built by the extremists and before the extremists there were no walls to the city at all. Or they claim the city walls were only meant for a certain type of climate and since the weather is different then the walls should not exist anymore. Peaceful Extremists will use the blueprint of the city to say the city isn't supposed to have walls and that the walls aren't a part of the city and if you think the city has walls or try to protect the walls, even if you do so peacefully, they say you are a violent extremist and try locking you in the dungeon. These Peaceful and Violent Extremists are BOTH groups described by Muhammad pbuh where in part of a sahih hadith recorded by Al-Bukhari it is reported from Abu Idrees al-Khawlaani that he heard Hudhayfah ibn al-Yamaan say: *"The people used to ask the Messenger of Allaah (peace and blessings of Allaah be upon him) about good things, but I used to ask him about bad things, fearing that I would live to see such things. I said, 'O Messenger of Allaah, we were in a state of ignorance (jaahiliyyah) and evil, then Allaah sent us this good (i.e., Islam). Will there be any evil after this good?' He said, 'Yes.' I said, 'Will there by any good after that evil?' He said, 'Yes, but it will be tainted.' I said, 'How will it be tainted?' He said, '(There will be) some people who will guide others in a way that is not according to my guidance. You will approve of some of their deeds and disapprove of others.' I said, 'Will there be any evil after that good?' He said, 'Yes, there will be people calling at the gates of Hell, and whoever responds to their call, they will throw them into it (the Fire).' I said, 'O Messenger of Allaah, describe them to us.' He said, 'They will be from among our people, speaking our language."* As the wise true Muslim looks at all this they try to stop the enemy chipping or firing at the walls, stop the violent extremists killing innocents, stop the peaceful extremists trying to surrender/destroy the city in the name of the city, meanwhile trying to encourage the foreigners(non-Muslims) to come live in the city because it's the best and only one whose inhabitants end up going to paradise. That's a basic synopsis about the modern war on Islam if the religion of Islam were a fortified medieval city.

Current religious wars are more of a threat to religions than they were before because previously battles were waged over religious theory/doctrine, but now they are waged mainly over religious practices/implementation. Today the religious wars are waged against entire religious systems while the doctrines are frequently ignored. This is a more severe type of warfare because it doesn't matter what you believe in if you aren't practicing it. To believe is to practice, thus by stopping those of another religion from practicing they are effectively crippling the belief without having to win the battle theologically. Essentially the way the religious wars are fought today any religion can win, truth has little to do with the outcome. Presently there is no such thing as peace when it comes to religious warfare as there was in the past. Previously when the militaries were at peace the war was paused, but today peace does little to affect the theological combat and frequently the military peace treaties amount to pivotal theological battles. One thing about modern religious warfare is certain, most of the battlefields are no longer places of violence and the peaceful soldiers need to be more committed to the cause than the violent soldiers. Also the theological war is ongoing in every location every second. As important as the physical military battles are, now it's the peaceful battles that determine the outcome of religious wars. The believing soldier of truth never sells-out, yields, relents, conforms or flees from the theological battlefield. Because the Muslim soldier of truth has already surrendered, to the Creator.

If someone believes it's permissible to rule by other than God's law then they are disbelievers, if they believe that God's law is the only legitimate law yet they don't rule by it then they are sinful and we don't know what a ruler/judge(since we are all technically rulers/judges to some extent) believes unless they tell us themselves. It is sinful to rebel against a sinful government yet it is required for Muslims to rebel and remove a disbelieving ruler who rules Muslims in Muslim lands. The problem the takfiris have is that even though most leaders in Muslim countries today are disbelievers, they declare sinful leaders disbelievers too and advocate violent revolution regardless of the consequences. In Islam leaders should only be publicly corrected if they do sins publicly and the harm of correcting them in public will not be greater than the benefit, while Muslims should only rebel against disbelieving rulers if they have the ability to succeed. It is an obligation to remove disbelieving rulers who rule Muslims in Muslim lands BUT there is a time for it, just as Hajj can only be done at a certain time even though to do Hajj is an obligation. For instance during the events of the "Arab Spring" Muslim Scholars condemned the protesting that led to the revolutions in Libya, Egypt and Syria for numerous reasons because the protests were unislamic and they weren't calling for Islam, involved sinful music and the sinful mixing between men and women who weren't related. The Muslim Scholars said not to revolt against Gaddafi in Libya or Assad in Syria even though they were disbelievers because the harm that would result in protesting and revolting would outweigh any benefit. Instead of intelligently listening to the Muslim Scholars, the world condemned them as strict extremists who were out of touch and decided to act according to the emotions of the moment and charge into protests and revolutions. As a result of disobeying the tenants of Islam by protesting in sinful manners acting on emotions and ignoring the advice of Muslim scholars, today Libya, Egypt and Syria are far worse off than they were before the "Arab Spring". The so-called "Islamic democracy" is a satanic scam, as is evident beyond doubt in

Bangladesh and Pakistan. Those who claim Islam was democratic before democracy was popular are ignorant of Islam, democracy and history. The same types claimed Islam was communism friendly too, then capitalism friendly and for whatever the kafir world desires they'll lie about Islam to suit the current political climate. Such human windmills would even say Islam is atheistic. Democracy is NOT Shariah compliant, but the West won't even tolerate a Muslimish themed democracy as evidenced by what happened in Algeria(December 26, 1991), Gaza(2006) and Egypt(July 3, 2013) when so-called "strict Muslims" won the elections. Yet the genuinely "strict Muslims" didn't even vote or run in the democratic elections in those countries and 74% of Egyptian Muslims who were polled in 2013 CE said we don't want democracy but want Shariah. Yet despite not wanting democracy they tried it but even then they couldn't get plan D since it was undesired by the unislamic world. So even when the Muslims compromise their religion and sinfully implement democracy, because it has results the West fears, like war with Zionists, or doesn't like they violate their own democratic principles to overthrow and wage war against the very democracies they pushed down the Muslims throats. The West politically forcefeeds Muslims then decides to cut open our stomachs and extract the food inserting feces into our stomach in order to stop us from getting any type of nutrition from the toxic food we were forcefed while giving us the feces so we stay weak. The West only wants democracy in the middle east if it harms Islam and the Muslims, if democracy in the middle east results in a tiny benefit to Muslims or Islam(despite it's systematic harm) they rush to crush it. The West literally kills Muslims until they force them to implement democracy, then when they do the West still isn't satisfied and kills the Muslims in that same country again because their democracy was too Muslimish, then if the dictatorships get too Muslimish the West pushes and shoves those same Muslims back into democracy in a never ending cycle. Then Western people wonder why some go crazy and blow themselves up. Of course rather than the West blaming themselves they blame Islam thus justifying more of the same. When will people, specifically Muslims, learn that Islam is the only true solution and it can only solve the problems when it's practiced fully and fundamentally? Islam without the fundamentals is not Islam and will not solve the fundamental problems of the world. I used to think revolutions could be beneficial, although now I know why it is impossible for a revolution to result in improvement. The word "revolution" itself reveals it is nothing but destructive. For example if you put a sticker on a wheel and then the wheel goes through one revolution, the sticker will end up at the same spot it was at before the revolution began except both the sticker and wheel will be worn and in a worse condition. If you had an old tire on a car that was in a bad state, a revolution would not improve the wheel; it would only damage it further making it less useful and more unstable. If you want to get a better wheel, you get a different wheel entirely, putting the wheel through revolutions only continues the problem by wearing out the rubber. Political revolutions are the same as wheel revolutions, some bad politicians are rubbed out just as the tire of a car wheel is rubbed off in the rotation, but the bad politicians were only a part of the wheel. Removing them doesn't fix the wheel, the wheel must be changed. This is why if you look at the recent revolutions that have taken place, those countries are worse off today than they were before the revolutions. Likewise the vast overwhelming majority of revolutionary groups fail because they are incapable of predicting/preventing/combatting the inter-revolutionary warfare amongst rival revolutionary groups since they start with the delusion that a revolution is binary with only two parties, oblivious to the fact that every revolution has had many many parties jockeying for total victory over all the rest. As a result typically due to their inability to defeat both the ruling class and the other revolutionary parties the revolutionary populace ends up with the incumbent suppressing all the revolutionaries together or one at a time contrary to their hopes/dreams/achievements. Every single revolution, even the peaceful type, has been a multi-faceted civil war. Truly there is no such thing as singular binary revolutions between 2 parties, there are always a plethora of people/ideas/faiths/groups always trying to achieve dominance commonly within the same groups making it extremely confusing and difficult for any particular sect to achieve it's goals in full. Hence most revolutions just lead to greater disunity, especially if they aren't done prophetically. Seeing as the wheel symbolizes government, even if instead of a revolution a different wheel were tried in the form of a different political system, a different wheel won't necessarily solve the problem. A rubber wheel will wear out sooner or later and cause problems regardless of what brand it is, or what mixture of rubber it is. Therefore the vehicle of humanity needs perfect tires that will last forever. No human can make such a tire, humans didn't make the species or environment either. Since every other part that drives humanity forward has been made by the Creator, the only tires that will propel the human species are those made by the Creator. The wheels being a symbol of political and government systems means that only a divinely ordained political or government system will work. Every man-made tire will expire and wreck the car if it's not continuously replaced. God has made a form of government for mankind and that's the only solution. No revolution will bring any long-term benefit to mankind. Humans are prone to error, therefore a man-made government system will be prone to error. If you want a good government you have to go to the Creator of goodness. The only good government is one where the laws of God are the laws the people are governed by. Any other government is invalid and will cause nothing but misery for those living under it. It is the Jews who believe "*The law of the land is the law.*" which they preach with their phrase "*Dina demal khuta dian*" Muslims do not believe that whatever laws the land is ruled by are legitimate laws just because they are used. The existence of a legal code does not amount to legal legitimacy. Although just because a government is invalid doesn't mean a Muslim can disobey its laws. When a Muslim is in a certain country they are bound to uphold their promise to abide by the laws of that country which don't conflict with Islam. For instance most traffic laws don't conflict with Islam so those types of laws can and should be followed. Yet just because a Muslim follows the laws that don't conflict with Islam doesn't mean they recognize the government, its legislation or judiciary to be valid for even a millisecond. Following the law doesn't mean respecting the lawmakers, or acknowledging them as legitimate authority figures. Just as following the laws of God doesn't mean a person loves God or believes in God. On the other hand someone cannot respect the lawmakers if they don't obey the law. Likewise a person cannot love God if they don't obey the divine laws. To sin is to prove you don't really love God while you are sinning, to obey and believe in God is to prove your love via living it.

Love for God shows itself through your actions as does lack of love for God. People didn't make the earth or any of the elements in it for themselves. The world is basically rented to mankind for a short amount of time. Part of the rental agreement contains certain clauses for the rules concerning governing of the world. God has appointed humans to be custodians of the earth. Custodians have rules to follow in order to do their job. If the custodians aren't following the rules of their employer then they won't be doing their job correctly and the object they are custodian over will suffer, making their job harder and joyless, leading to eventual termination by the employer for not doing the job they were appointed to do. The earth is the property of God. In order for mankind to act as custodian over God's property they have to follow the rules God has made for the earth. If the owner of a building says no fires are allowed on the property and they hire a custodian to take care of the building, the custodian has no right to change the rules and say fires are allowed on the property. Even though the custodian has authority to do their job, that authority is limited and conditional to them following the rules of the property owner. This means any government who exercises authority and rules over God's land must rule by the laws God has legislated, as should we in ruling ourself and our families. If a government were to prohibit something God has commanded, or to legalize something God has forbidden then that government is unacceptable, invalid and blameworthy. Man-made laws are like grass, too many to count and they get chopped up by people in seconds. If people don't like the grass then they just cover it up to ignore it or take it out and plant different grass instead, then when the political seasons change all the laws die and the cold grip of a police state covers the land like the snow, until the seasons change again and new grass grows repeating the cycle of oppressive unjust instability. With many thinking the grass will always be greener if they just added another blade or removed another blade thinking that if they just have a good system to select a good gardener then winter will never come and they won't be oppressed. Yet God is the gardener we should have and the one who controls the weather and political seasons causing snow as well as oppressive governments so people learn that choosing to live by man-made laws results in fruitless and dangerous winters. God has perfected his garden for us with the final prophet to add the final flowers to the landscape of legislation for humanity. Where if we choose to tend the worldly garden God has given us according to God's instructions, then when we leave this temporary garden we will live forever in heavenly gardens that we don't have to tend. Otherwise we will be burning forever for having slashed and burned in order to customize the worldly garden God entrusted to us and specifically told us how to maintain. It's simple, God gave us life and laws, if we don't follow the laws that God gave us to live our lives by we won't have a good life or afterlife. Many laws made by governments today are illegal in the sight of God. Such a simple statement of pure noble truth would be considered a *"threat to national security"* by many criminal governments across the world. To such a government "security" means the taxation status quo. *"National Security"* is typically defined as government authority, it has nothing to do with protecting the economic interests of a country, the personal safety of its citizens, or the environment; unless threats to those things would threaten the taxation system and government authority. The government is not your "big brother" or your "Uncle Sam". Most governments in the world don't care about your security in the afterlife. Most governments don't care whether you spend eternity in hell. The man-made laws are not designed to protect you from hell. If the laws of your country are not the laws of God then you can be a law-abiding citizen in the sight of your government, yet a criminal in the sight of God. This is why religious government is necessary. Throughout history secular governments created environments of sin and immorality. Today we have countries where a "model citizen" can be a disbelieving sinner who possesses all the attributes of a person who will spend eternity in hell, but the secular government portrays them as a good person or role model. If you look at secular countries like America, sin is legalized. In America a person will get in more trouble for a traffic violation than they will for breaking the laws ordained by the Creator of the universe! The priorities of American politicians are wrong. The goal of a government should be to protect its citizens from disbelief and sin. Of course a government can't force belief upon a person and that is against the religion of Islam, but a government can and should prevent sin from becoming rampant in its domain. Instead most secular governments tell their subjects they have "freedom", and view "the pursuit of happiness" as a value essentially giving them a license to sin. That is what "freedom" is, it's a license to sin. Sin is sin, God has given governments temporary authority over others so they can protect people from sin, not so they could legalize it. Unfortunately secular governments do the opposite of what governments are supposed to do and they profit from sin. If it weren't for the revenue from taxes on pornography, prostitution, alcohol, drugs, gambling and all other vices and evils of society, secular governments would be broke. In every secular country you will find the same, sin has become industrialized and ties into the interests of the secular governments. Such governments actively promote a sinful culture because if people were moral it would mean lower tax revenue and smaller government budgets. For secular governments it is actually in their interest for you to sin. A secular government essentially wants you to disobey God and burn in hell. Satan has deployed secularism as a tool to mislead mankind from the true religion. As much as Satan invests in false religions, because they are religions it still makes people think religion and worship are important, even though they are doing it all wrong. For Satan even having humans care about religion is too risky, because one who cares about religion can still be guided to the true religion if they grow up upon a false religion. The satanic idea of secularism was promoted under the guise of interfaith coexistence and peace, but the real reason and effects of this have been to dilute religion and eliminate morality from humanity altogether. Of course Satan will fail to eliminate the true religion, but by diluting religions Satan hopes to cause deviance, negligence and laziness among the believers. So even if a person finds the true religion, because the secular world sees religion as unimportant and extreme, they may not fully practice the true religion. That is Satan's goal, to stop people from fully practicing the true religion, he knows he will never stop people from believing in it, but technically if you believe in the true religion you would practice it fully. Unfortunately this secular trend has led many to end up believing in one religion but in reality not practicing any religion. This is where the other type of extremism shows its face. Satan wants disbelief and extremism. Just as Satan makes more than 1 false religion, Satan makes more than 1 extremism to offer more roads to hell to mislead more people.

Typically whenever people think of a Muslim extremist they think of criminal violence. That is because Satan has given up trying to make people disbelieve in Islam and instead has attempted to change what being a Muslim means and how it is seen. The most common type of Muslim extremist is typically non-violent, but is more dangerous than a suicide-bomber. These people actually contribute to criminal violence unknowingly. They are an over-reaction to the violent extremists in the opposite direction. While the Khawarrij/Takfiris take Islam to the over-board extreme, these others dilute Islam to the extreme. They think it is only what is in the heart that counts and that actions or speech cannot make one a disbeliever and every believer has the same amount of faith. Whereas Muslims believe faith increases with good deeds and decreases with bad beeds. These extremely diluting deviants believe things are lawful which Allah and his prophets have prohibited and abstained from. They are interfaith to the point where they are no longer a member of their faith in their attempt to mix and get along with members of other religions. In Islam they are classified as the Murjiah, but some identify themselves as *"modernists"*, *"moderates"* or *"progressives"*. This name they've chosen is dangerous and deceptive. Initially when one hears it they think it means "modernism" and associate it with improving technology or social progress. Although these "modernists" are trying to "modernize" religion, in reality they are secularists. The religion of Islam is for all time. Someone who believes the religion of God is out of date and needs to be adjusted is claiming to be a prophet. Only a prophet has the authority to amend the religion of God. God knows everything that will happen for all time, to claim the religion of God is not fit for our current and future time is to claim that God doesn't know everything. The truth is never out of date. Modernists and secularists tend to be lax in practicing their religion and stress that it is more about what you believe than in how you live. In secular countries these are the most common types of Muslim extremists you will find. Like the violent extremists these secularists are also funded by secular governments and supported by them. While it might not surprise you to read that secularists are funded by secular governments it might surprise you to find out that secular governments fund Islamic extremist groups who commit criminal violence. U.S. Officials publicly admit funding jihadis in the 1980s CE who later joined Al-Qaeda. Take ISI/ISIL/ISIS/IS/Dawlah for instance, created in 2006 CE as an offshoot of Al-Qaeda in Iraq. Who has ISIS/ISIS killed? Non-combatants, heretics, hypocrites and Muslims. How can non-Muslims think people who are killing Muslims could possibly be practicing Islam right? Do they really think it's part of our religion to kill the members of our own religion? Actions speak louder than words. The way ISIS fights to establish Sharia law violates Sharia law. When discussing ISIS the situation is extremely complicated. I have heard many different things about them, from Muslims, disbelievers, ex-ISIS members and by examining ISIS propaganda itself. Before any opinion regarding them can be formed we have to be honest, if there were a genuine Islamic State in the world today that established Islamic Shariah 100% and correctly practiced Islam, non-Muslims would call it an extremist state and attack it whether it actually was or not, because disbelievers view Islam as extreme. So just because it's condemned as a criminal state of extremists by the non-Muslims doesn't make it true, but that doesn't mean it's not a criminal extremist state either. Do you think that the bad guys will one day tell all of their citizens, "*We didn't tell you this before, but just so you know we've been the bad guys for a long time"*. If you think not then you're wrong, because the bad guys will say, *"You know we've made lots of bad mistakes with good intentions, but we've changed and will never do bad stuff again."* Then by saying that they will be able to continue being bad guys with the full support of their people who will think that only good guys would say such a thing. Yet this is exactly what nearly every convict says to get released, both the reformed and the hardened criminal. After all I've learned about ISIS, my information is limited about them because I'm not there to witness it for myself. When it comes to Muslim extremism don't listen to anything that a non-Muslim or layman has to say about it, they just don't know Islam; and that includes employees of the FBI, CSIS, MI5, KGB, U.N. and all the rest. You ask the Muslim scholars and that's it, nobody else is qualified to give their opinion on a group or person. It's the same thing with doctors or mechanics, you don't ask someone who's not an elite specialist in that field. There is an overabundance of conspiracies indicating ISIS could've been created, funded, trained and supplied by the U.S. government and/or Syria/Iran, but I can't verify the authenticity of the evidence used to support this theory. Yet such a thing happened in Algeria. After the "strict Muslims" won the democratic elections, the West's puppet government decided to nullify the elections and the military took over the country to "protect it from radical Islamic fundamentalism" and the Muslims fought back. In response the Algerian government infiltrated the rebellion with the GIA, posing as hardline Muslims yet in reality the GIA went around killing and terrorizing the Muslims leaving the Algerian military relatively unharmed. GIA soldiers even wore fake beards and would break into homes rape women and children, then kill innocents in brutal fashions saying " *I'm a true Muslim! This is Jihad!*" with people then believing such filthy lies because of their trauma. The oppressive Algerian military defeated the Muslims during their civil war by pretending to be Muslim Jihadis and then killing the Muslims to make Muslims afraid of the true Jihadis and Islam. This is a reason why authenticity of information is the most important fundamental thing to consider before making a decision. In Algeria the government terrorized it's own people pretending the terror came from Muslims waging Jihad when the real Muslims waging Jihad were trying to stop the government from harming and oppressing the people. But what was the world to believe when they saw the Algierian government's reports on TV showing the GIA deceptively defaming Muslims and Islam as part of their war propaganda? Islamically speaking for a hadith to be useable and relied upon, everyone in the chain of transmission must be known to be 100% honest. If one link in the chain of information transmission is known to have told one lie in their life or reported something false intentionally or unintentionally then it corrupts the whole chain and makes the information transmitted through them unreliable. What this means is that nearly every single news outlet today is unreliable according to the islamic science of authenticity. So regarding ISIS they've been accused of so much stuff that they haven't actually done that if I didn't have exposure to their own propaganda itself to verify their extreme aberrations from Islam, I wouldn't believe anything the Western media says about them. Plus the West is known to lie about Muslims when they are good Muslims, just take the Crusades as an example. If you were living in England during 1102 CE you'd be completely wrong if you believed what the media said about the Muslims in the Middle East. Yet 100% of the English media was saying it was true. So this means if your information about ISIS is coming from unreliable sources, such as the Western media, according to Islam fundamentally whatever verdict you were to make based on that information will be incorrect because it's not 100% authentic information from trustworthy sources. While even if you made the right decision the methodology would be wrong. Know that democracy doesn't make information authentic, meaning if the majority reports something that doesn't mean it actually happened or that it happened the way they said it happened or by who they blame. Thus the reason why I occasionally observe international news is not to actually learn what's going on, but it's to learn what everyone around me thinks is going on so that way I can know what they think is happening in the world and why they think and feel the way they do. Today the news is not a place to learn the truth, it's a place to learn the lies the masses believe. Regardless even though they aren't as unislamic as they are made out to be, there are still things which ISIS does and says that match extremist Khawarij doctrines which are unislamic and go against the very teachings of Muhammad pbuh. Particularly their views on jihad, the tactics they deploy, their treatment of prisoners and takfir. For instance in one of their own publications I was stunned to read them say the following regarding battlefield tactics, *"Commanders will announce a Jihad and the Maqars (bases) whose day is for battle will be called to get their weapons ready and come forward. The fighters do not always know exactly where they are going, or who they are fighting. Their goal is to simply 'hear and obey.'"* ISIS has said in their own recruitment publication that their fighters don't know where they are fighting or who they are fighting. I do not consider it proper Jihad if you don't know who you are fighting. Now of course you don't need to know the specific name and bio of every indidual enemy on the battlefield, but to not even know what army they are or what their religious beliefs are can not be considered a valid Jihad in my opinion. These are things non-Muslims and Muslims should know about these groups. Many of their soldiers don't know who they are actually fighting while they are fighting them. If most of them knew they wouldn't do what they do, so keep that in mind. I'm not saying such ignorance excuses them from being guilty but it does make a difference in regards to how ISIS fighters should be viewed. You could say that's stupid and how could ISIS fighters not know who they are fighting when they are fighting, but the same applies to NATO, the U.N. and many Western nations dropping bombs on Muslims. They don't know who they're dropping bombs on they just get told that they're bad guys and attack. Furthermore ISIS has no qualms about suicide attacks and even specifically calls them suicide attacks. One such former ISIS member, Abu Ata al-San'aani was slated for such a suicide bombing attack and asked his commander where it would take place. His ISIS commander told him that he was the first one to ever ask where the operation would be and that all the rest don't ask but are just ready to blow themselves up anywhere they are told. The guy replied it was his right to know so that way he could be 100% sure that no Muslims or innocents would be harmed. It turned out the operation was supposed to take place in a Sunni masjid! Now if I told you that some Christian organization sends people to churches to blow themselves up during church killing people in the church, would you say that's a Christian organization? No! Both ISIS, Al-Qaeda and those who share their ideologies do this. Of course there is actual justification for doing this, it's not crazy because Muhammad pbuh himself actually burned Masjid Diraar to the ground and killed people inside it who claimed to be Muslims, though they were really Munafiqs. However the Quran verse 48:25 is the proof that refutes the Khariji reasoning that legitimizes attacking masjids. First of all Masjid Diraar was in Dar al-Islam and only Munafiqs prayed in Masjid Diraar, there was 0% chance of Muslim casulties and even then the Munafiq casulties in the destruction of Masjid Diraar were minimized because the goal was to destroy the building not kill people, whereas the goal of the Khariji is to kill people rather than destroy the building. Yet to know of Masjid Dirar being burned by Muhammad pbuh could and does lead sincere Muslimish people to kill Muslims in masjids today due to ignorance, whereas other Muslims are so ignorant of Muhammad pbuh they likely don't even know that he himself burnt a masjid down inside Medinah. Those people would just say "How could a Muslim ever destroy a masjid or kill people inside it?" Whereas Muhamad pbuh did that and Christians also know Jesus pbuh performed violence in the temple against "co-religionists" too as did Moses pbuh. But of course contextual knowledge is critical because otherwise one will either condemn something in a sinful manner or sympathize with something sinful due to incomplete knowledge. This incident is truly a great example of how on the surface people would think a Muslim blowing themself up inside a masjid is clearly unislamic insanity yet the semi-intelligent Muslim or Jihadist crowd is aware of how it could persuasively be justified, the problem is the general "easy way to say something's wrong" is wrong and doesn't dissuade those who would be interested in doing crimes from doing them. Only the truth can protect someone from error, if the methodology for teaching that truth is incorrect then it's unlikely the error will be prevented from recurring and even if it is then one will be stuck with a methodological error that may lead to greater error in the future. Basically ISIS was wrong to plan on having one of their own blow themselves up in a Sunni masjid, but not for the reasons most people would think and say and to think and say that "ISIS was unislamic/wrong for obvious reasons everyone knows" is utterly wrong and perpetuating the problem of popular confidently preached ignorance that triggers radicalization fueling violent extremism. On the other hand there are some things which ISIS says and does that are correct, such as not believing in Muslim borders, nationalism or democracy, not taxing people, collecting and paying zakat and jizya, giving civilians free services and using gold, silver and copper coins as money instead of paper. ISIS appeared sincere in trying to operate a government based on Islamic law and principles yet ignorant too. Yet they did not fulfill the conditions for a Khilafah to be declared and neither had their leader fulfilled the conditions to be called Leader of all Muslims. Historically the only ones to have ever declared a Khilafah without fulfilling the conditions have been the Khawarij and/or deviant extremists. Without a doubt their leader when they held territory was a legitimate leader with a legitimate state, albeit made by force. However Islamically it was not the Khilafah. In the end there are some serious issues with their methodology, tactics and opinions. The knowledgable salafi Muslim scholars have labeled ISIS as Khawarij based on authentic information and according to Islamic criteria, however the problem is that deviant people have also labeled them as Khawarij for the wrong reasons condemning ISIS for things they haven't done and/or for doing Islamic things. I have read fatwas by Imams and "scholars" in the West who in their denunciation of ISIS actually denounce Islam itself. Such fatwas made to please disbelievers only gives ISIS justification in their claims that their opponents are enemies of Islam and heretics; because a lot of them are. It's like bad guys fighting bad guys, both can be right in saying the other side is wrong and evil. Basically ISIS acts more islamic than most Muslims think and they act less islamic than most disbelievers think. Maybe Allah will guide them to repentance and their errors will be rectified, if not then Allah will destroy them just as he will destroy all oppressors regardless of who they are or where they are. Muslims let their enemies know that forgiveness is an option. To sum it up ISIS is not 100% wrong in everything they are doing, but they are not 100% right either. So what is the solution? Gaining proper knowledge about Islam to correct their errors and establishing a true Islamic Khilafah ruled by Islamic Shariah 100%. ISIS and other extremist groups get support because Muslims are being butchered by disbelievers throughout the world, Muslims are fed up with oppression and want a Khilafah to practice Islam 100%. Violence from unislamic Muslimish nations and non-Muslim nations will only make ISIS and groups like them seem vindicated and give them justification for their unislamic violence as revenge for being attacked. Therefore some of the

Sunni Muslims in Syria and from abroad simply joined ISIS out of desperation because they didn't want Assad or Secular Kurds oppressing Muslims or ruling by other than Islamic Shariah. In light of such events we must consider governments' pretext of *"national security"*. If there were no terrorists in the world, there would be no *"war on terror"* and counter-terrorism people would be out of a job. Without a "threat" to frighten civilians, taxpayers would be more reluctant to hand over their hard earned money to pay for a huge government. Assad was getting his butt kicked and was condemned by the world for butchering Muslims and his only defense was to accuse Muslims of being terrorists. Then suddenly ISIS appears and they have actually helped Assad more than anyone could've imagined was possible. The world thought Assad wouldn't even be alive by 2016 CE yet today it's plausible to imagine him ruling Syria another 40 years. I truly don't think ISIS is solely the work of conspiracy but their rise to power was extremely coincidental and beneficial to nearly every unislamic and/or non-Muslim government in the world (excluding South America). Originally Western powers instigated the people of Syria to push for the religion of democracy but then it became a war on Islam, then a war on Extremism, and then a war on Islam in the name of fighting Extremism. Anyone who claims otherwise doesn't know the situation. Without a doubt the war in Syria is a war against Islam waged in many different ways by many different groups, each of which have different intentions all leading to the same ultimate fundamental goals. It's officially a war against Islam too, because the Russian Orthodox Christian Patriarch Kirill publicly said in 2015 CE that Russia is in Syria fighting a "*Holy War*". The telling detail confirming this is a "Holy War" is the American response to Russia. Any student of global history knows that ever since WWII whenever Russia has tried to exert itself militarily in another country, America exerted itself against the Russian allies in order to combat and prevent Russian influence; except for 3 specific conflicts. The 3 conflicts America has not overtly physically combatted Russian encroachments in foreign lands is during the war in Afghanistan when Russia tried to impose Communism and eradicte Islam, in Checnnya where Russia has been trying to eradicate Islam and in Syria where Russia's trying to eliminate Islam. If you ask me these 3 American exceptions to opposing Russia have something to do with religion. When Russia fights Islam or Muslims, America says it's okay, but when they fight Capitalism or Democracy America goes to war. Always remember that in 2015 CE the Russian Orthodox Christian Church declared that Russia is fighting a "Holy War" in Syria. Even when UN proposals were passed to stop the bloodshed in Syria they were never implemented because Russia vetoed the resolutions in October 2011, October 2012, July 2012, May 2014 and October 2016 CE and that's how the UN works. The democratic vote they claim is sacred can be rejected if a superpower says no, as America frequently vetoes any anti-Israel propositions. So based on the international reaction, I guess this means Christians are legally allowed to wage "Holy War" against Muslims? But is it still a "Holy War" if Russia says they are only fighting Muslim "extremists" or terrorists? The answer is yes, according to the Orthodox Christians. Although if Russia's "War on terror" is a "Holy War" then doesn't that mean America's and the U.N.'s "War on terror" is a "Holy War" too? Or does it not count because secular countries don't have the word "Holy" in their extensive vocabulary? Should we call it a "Holy War on Holy Terror"? Would the UN ever tolerate a holy war? Yes that's what it was designed for, the UN was made so that Christian Europe never fought each other again and they could legally work together to establish their religious dominance throughout the world. Of course the UN's religion isn't Christianity, but that's besides the point, all that matters from the Muslim perspective is that the religion the UN promotes is not Islam. The UN is diametrically opposed to Islamic Shariah. Anyways I'm certain that in 5-10 years most of the history books and pundits will present a different picture than the present reality. Most today don't even know what the reality was 2 years ago in Syria. This phenomenon relates to *"Fourth Generation warfare"*.

Today when countries go to war they rarely send physical troops and invade. Instead they perform ideological warfare to change the mentality and culture of the nation they wish to conquer. Then the rival country sends agents, such as EHMs (Economic Hit men) and propaganda into that country to start political change, whether through revolution, civil war or whatever way possible. Afterwards the natives who have been ideologically brainwashed into believing what the rival country wants, will serve the brainwashing nation's interest not realizing their country has just been conquered without having been invaded. It's a way of turning enemies into vassals without them realizing they have become subservient, thereby eliminating the cost of maintaining colonies and ensuring long term control with a low chance of political backlash. Why control a country by force against its will when it's better for public relations and easier to control those who govern a country and/or its economy? In 1996 CE American advisers to Benjamin Netanyahu, who became the Prime Minister of Israel, wrote a "Clean Break" paper which outlined a new approach America and Israel would take towards the middle east to achieve their goals for the region in a more subtle manner. The plan was to cause a Sunni/Shia middle eastern warzone to last over 100 years which would disunite the Muslim middle east thereby securing the continued existence of Israel. The way they planned to go about this was by backing violent Muslim extremists in the middle east to polarize the region and create instability. This is to split up the larger more powerful middle eastern states into tiny, weak states that wouldn't pose a threat to Israel. This would strain the resources of middle eastern powerhouses Sunni Saudi Arabia and Shia Iran, causing both to fight proxy wars in the various middle eastern states with each hoping to have influence in the tiny states when the dust clears. Although since the extremists are supported by secular nations, they won't be easily influenced by Saudi Arabia or Iran. They will be puppets of their secular backers unwittingly. The extremists might be allowed to rule however they want, but the secularist goal is to distort Islam and chop up the middle east while exhausting the resources of the states who could threaten Israel. The secularist western nations will betray and crush the extremists after they served their purpose of damaging the reputation of Islam. Then the native and global populace will be brainwashed into hating Islam and ask western states to "liberate" them with secularism. At that point a dramatic criminal attack done by one of the extremists backed by the secular west will occur, or a false flag attack covertly done by a western state blamed on the extremists will be committed, in order to exploit the citizens emotions and fear so the secular west can gain more control over its citizens to raise taxes and nationalism, while justifying military intervention in the middle east. After the Western secular nations then invade and remove the extremist regimes, the extremists' states will be further split up into ever smaller weaker states, while Western weapons manufacturers would profit by selling weapons to the middle east, creating jobs by making those weapons in the west and of course paying taxes on that income to those Western governments. Any other resources that could be obtained is a bonus, but the interventions supercharge the weapons industry and Western government's taxes on that industry. Thus the gun industry won't care about gun ownership being exclusively restricted to Western governments in the West, thus preventing revolutions and tax resistance, because they'll have more guns to sell elsewhere if they play along with Western governments. This is referred to by politicians as the "new middle east", whenever you hear politicians use that phrase it refers to their plan to redraw the map. Surrounded by weak states constantly warring with each other, Iran and Saudi Arabia will be dragged into a war that will pit Sunnis vs. Shia in a massive all-out regional war, turning the entire Muslim middle east into a battlefield. This war would mutually weaken them both as well as all the middle east, leaving Israel as the strongest nation in the region left relatively unscathed. After all of the middle east was weakened and divided, Israel would conquer the region and rule over a large Zionist empire.

By this time the world would have such a distorted view of Islam the Israeli extermination of Muslims would take place without condemnation, similar to how it happens without condemnation in Palestine today. When Israel exterminates the Christian middle eastern population they will just blame it on the Muslims using it as a justification for their extermination of Muslims. This is public information that was previously proposed inside Israel in 1982 CE, agreed to by America and Israel in 1996 CE and progressed before our very eyes. Average Christians who follow events in Palestine delusionally think this Zionist empire is Jewish and that it's necessary for the return of Jesus pbuh, while other Christians just want the Muslims wiped out because it's easier for them to convert Jews to Christianity than to convert Muslims. Sadly such Christians hate Muslims so much that they don't care if the Jews kill Christians in Palestine so long as it means the Muslims get wiped out. But why do Christians want Muslims out of Palestine? It is because of the Christian tourism industry. You see Christianity is based on emotionalism and there is nothing that makes a Christian more Christianized than being in the holy land getting indoctrinated with Christian propaganda. The problem is when Christians go to the holy land and interact with Muslims the Muslims introduce Christians to Islam and expose the falsehood of Christianity, so many choose to become Muslim as a result. The dilemma Christian Churches have is they need the holy land environment to keep Christians brainwashed and to make them more zealous to give money to Church yet at the same time must prevent Christians from encountering Muslims and Islam at all costs. Thus they need their holy land to be Muslim-free. Pope Urban II's solution to this dilemma of Christian tourists meeting Muslims and converting was the first Crusade. The recent Christian solution is the Zionist state of Israel. The goal has always been the same, to force Muslims out of the holy land so it can be a place to send Christians to in order to keep them brainwashed. It is important to remember God has planned for this evil plan to kill Muslims and the plan of God never fails no matter what. Perhaps the way Muslim countries joined a coalition to fight ISIS they will form a coalition to wage jihad against the blasphemous shia state of Iran, and then Israel. However historically during the medieval crusades the Khawarij and Muslims fought together against the crusaders, until the Khawarij betrayed the Muslims. Yet now we have "Muslims" and crusaders fighting against the Khawarij which is a historical anomaly and enigma. The main reason why Khawarij have such allure today is because of "Muslims" collaborating and allying with the enemies of Islam. The problem began because of this collaboration and now these groups say that more collaboration is the solution. Osama bin Laden's primary reason for creating Al-Qaeda was because America established military bases in the Arabian peninsula and never left after the Gulf War. Once Islam was the religion of Arabia, Muhammad pbuh had prohibited any other religion aside from Islam from being practiced in the Arabian peninsula. Outside Arabia other religions can exist but the Arabian peninsula was specifically set up to be free from other religions as an Islamic base territory. During the Khilafah of Abu Bakr there were rebellions so the Jews of Khaybar and the Christians of Najran were allowed to remain since they had a treaty with Muhammad pbuh. Then during the reign of Umar the Jews broke their treaty by refusing to pay half of their produce as they promised and hurt the arm of Umar's son Abdullah who was sent to collect from them. Thus the Jews were told to leave Arabia so they migrated to Muslim Syria and took their movable property with them. The Christians treaty was different in that it said they would not engage in hostilities against Islam or indulge in usurious transactions. Well the Christians did both and when Umar found out he confronted them and they agreed that because of their violations of their pact with the prophet pbuh they could be expelled, so the Christians were then settled in Muslim Iraq taking their movable property with them and being financially recompensed by the State for their immovable property while being allotted a 2 year exemption on Jizya. What happened later was that Saudi Arabia asked for help against Saddam when he invaded Kuwait in the 1990s and the Muslim scholars were asked if the armies of disbelievers were allowed in and the scholars told the government "NO". Then the Saudi government said *"Well they already landed, so we can't say no now and we thought you'd say yes. So how about if we make sure they leave after the war? Then is it okay?"* The scholars then said while disliked it would be okay <u>only if the Western armies left</u> after the gulf war. Well 25+ years later the West has only entrenched itself and built military bases there to kill Muslims throughout the middle east. Thus the khawarrij label such Muslim regimes as apostates and those who work for them as apostates and their citizens as apostates, which is wrong to do but the bases in Arabia are also wrong. So if the West really wants to stop the extremists, then get out of the Arabian peninsula, but they say they can't do that because there are all these Muslim extremists they have to kill and to support Israel of course. Whereas the extremists only came about in response to the bases, so the bases were never designed to "fight extremist terrorists" because there weren't any when the bases were built. So why were they ever really built? And why were they built with taxpayer dollars? All the recent problems of violent Islamic extremism can be traced to these bases in Arabia and sadly the non-Muslims have no clue that's the catalyst that triggered it. So it is partially because Muslims were "aided" by disbelievers to fight what was at that time a secular Saddam Hussein that has led to violent Islamic extremism today. Thus if having disbelievers in the past help Muslims against the enemies of Islam caused bigger problems, why would the same tactic have different results when it's employed today? It's simple an enemy of Islam is not going to help Muslims fight another enemy of Islam, if we let them try it will hurt us and that's why they keep claiming they want to help. In reality true Muslims don't need help nor do we want help from the kafirs, we disavow kufr and express enmity for the kafirs so our needs and desires get provided by our Creator. This whole mess in the middle east began because of the Ottomans allying themselves with France who then under Napolean's reign invaded Egypt "to help Ottomans establish order". Which led to Britiain and France chopping up the non-Ottomon territories between themselves. Later Ottomons allied with Germany to defend themselves against Russian aggression in the 1800s CE. Afterwhich the Ottomans foolishly sided with Germany in WWI against the British, French and Russians and lost the middle east, the titular Khilafah and became Turkey. Next Saudi Arabia finds oil and allies itself with America to protect it's oil from becoming an attractive target for others to seize. So all the trouble started because of Muslims choosing to befriend and ally themselves with disbelievers instead of Allah alone. This is why when American soldiers entered Syria with Turkish soldiers in 2016 CE to "fight ISIS" the Muslims kicked them out and told Turkey that they will accept Turkey helping them fight ISIS with their artillery, planes and tanks but they will not fight alongside Americans under any circumstances. As a result the Americans had to leave the town of Al-Rai and return to Turkey because the Muslims didn't want the help of the American soldiers who illegally crossed the border to "fight ISIS with them". Do you know what happened the next day? The same Muslims who told the Americans *"We only fight ISIS with Allah's help and not with American disbelievers."* got "accidentally" bombed by American planes the very next day. Truly the American government said it was an untimely "accident", no apologies they just said they were trying to "help them fight ISIS" then ISIS ended up recapturing some towns after the Muslims got bombed by America. The next week America bombed an Assad/Russian convoy in ISIS territory which helped ISIS take over Mt. Thaur. America apologized again, said they thought it was ISIS and offered millions of dollars to the families of the slain Russian and Assad soldiers. So you see the difference? I'm not saying America was helping ISIS intentionally, some would, but they do have a different policy when it comes to "accidentally" bombing Muslims and genuinely accidentally bombing the enemies of Muslims. It also shows how America really doesn't have a clue as to who they are bombing but Americans think otherwise because they watch fictional hollywood movies that paint the West as having technologies and policies they don't have and making "tuff decisions" in scenarios that never existed. The rules for war America has are nothing at all like what is portrayed in hollywood movies. More innocents get killed in the bombings than do suspects, and most of the suspects aren't dangerous either. Statistics actually show that if all the planned "terrorist attacks" succeeded in a given year and all the drone strikes did not occur, there would actually be less death, particularly less civilian death. Hence less people would die if non-Muslims stopped trying to "fight violent extremists" in Muslim lands via violence. Thus by non-Muslims militarily helping in the "war on extremism" more Muslims die than if we had no help from them. So that's where the loss of the Muslims doesn't always come by facing the disbelievers in battle, it can come from joining the disbelievers using them as allies or allowing them to steal the peace that is paid for with Muslim blood. If Allah helps us we don't need anyone else, whereas if for any reason Allah doesn't help us then we got a big problem which nothing but pure Islam as taught by Muhammad pbuh can solve. Muslims allying with disbelievers or taking them as friends is actually prohibited in the Quran. It can actually be a reason why Allah might not help Muslims if they are buddy buddy with those whom Allah labels in his book as his enemies; such as Satan and the friends and followers of Satan. Don't misunderstand this to think it is always forbidden for Muslims to fight alongside non-Muslims, it's not Muhammad pbuh himself allowed non-Muslims to occasionally fight in cooperation with the Muslim army but on other occasions non-Muslim soldiers offered to help and Muhammad pbuh forbid it. A military matter of Muslim and non-Muslim cooperation is based on 2 things 1. Islamic Conditions. 2. The discretion of the Commander, regarding the pros and cons. Two basic Islamic conditions must be met if any disbeliever is to fight alongside Muslims in battle. 1. The Muslims must be few in number so that there is a genuine military necessity. 2. The kuffar must be trustworthy, reliable and subservient to the Muslims without having the ability to betray the Muslims or later dominate the Muslims as a result of such "aid". Muslims can have non-Muslim mercenaries fight alongside them against an enemy but not as co-equal kafir allies. Essentially they can fight "for us", not as partners. Muslims don't need help from kafirs, but sometimes it can be beneficial and wise to allow kafirs to fight other kafirs alongside Muslims. Yet unfortunately today the situation is reversed where the Kafirs are fighting the Muslims using other Muslims as subservient mercenaries. Hence the way America uses it's "Muslim allies" to kill Muslims, is similar to the way a Muslim State could also use Kafirs to assist them in warfare, but it's still just a matter of discretion of which generally its disliked to have non-Muslims aid in militarily permissible manners because indulging in the permissible can always eventually lead to the prohibited. Whereas a true alliance built upon notions of equality, respect and friendship is forbidden between Muslims and non-Muslims, as is a situation where Muslims are subservient vassals of disbelievers as both the political, military and economic "alliances" today make them. Allah explicitly says in the Quran that Muslims don't take Jews or Christians as protectors or allies but the non-Muslim hypocrites do and rush to ally and befriend them citing that they fear they will be met with hardship and catastrophes if they don't ally with disbelievers. Which coincidentally is exactly the justification "Muslims" give for voting for the "lesser evil". The hypocrites' reason for allying, is the voters reason for allying politically by voting. Voting for X is an allegiance to X. One benefit of elections and anti-Muslim rhetoric is that they reveal who the true Muslims are and who are the hypocrites or the ignorant who appear to be hypocrites due to ignorance. The hypocrites and the ignorant will cite Muslims in Mecca using clan ties for safe passage or protection as their proof for modern alliances and voting, when such things were prohibited by later verses of the Quran. That's one tactic of hypocrites in that they frequently quote something from the Quran and pretend the rest of the verses which teach the opposite of what they are trying to extrapolate were never revealed. They abrogate the abrogations. Did Muhammad pbuh accept protection from non-Muslims? Rarely, in extreme situations where if he didn't Islam would have vanished in totality, and when he did it was always on his terms without compromising an iota of Islam or Islamic intolerance; but he and the Muslims stopped doing this once Allah forbid it in the Quran. So those who ally with disbelievers, or promote voting for kafirs which is equivalent to allegiance, pick obscure data out of context to justify it and their conclusions are invalid because the Quran abrogated and forbid such future practices. Not everything Muhammad pbuh did is something Muslims can do today, for example Muhammad pbuh didn't always pray 5 times a day before he became a prophet and was told to do so by Allah. Likewise Muslims didn't use to fast the month of Ramadan until Allah told them to do so in the Quran. Some Muslims drank alcohol too before Allah forbid it, but nobody would cite such historical examples as proof to justify Muslims doing or neglecting to do things today the way they do when justifying allying/befriending disbelievers, voting for them in elections, or seeking asylum or residency in kafir nations when Muslim nations exist. That's another point about Muslims citing the emigration to Christian Abyssinia as proof they can live in dar al-kufr (most of which are dar al-harb) in that the Muslims did that when there was no such thing as a Muslim city in the world, let alone a Muslim nation. Thus the evidence used to justify Muslims living in a non-Muslim land is extremely flimsy because when Muslims did that in the past there literally was no Muslim lands they could go to, but today that's just not the case. If Muslim lands existed during the time of the Muslim emigration to Christian Abyssinia Muhammad pbuh would have ordered the Muslims to move there, but there weren't any Muslim lands so that is why some Muslims went to Abyssinia. When Muslim lands exist, no matter how poor or corrupt they are, the ruling for living in non-Muslim lands is different than it was during the time when there were no Muslim lands at all. So just because someone can confidently and eloquently cite Muhammad pbuh or Muslims as having done something or not done something in the past, doesn't mean that's the Islamic thing to do in similar situations today. The idea of "keep your friends close but your enemies closer", is not Islamic it's anti-Islamic. Our enemy's enemy is not our friend, he's just our enemy's enemy and that's all. Our true enemy is Satan and only Muslims are his enemy, so that's where Muslims can't ally with the allies of Satan just because those Satanic allies are enemies of other allies of Satan. An ally of Satan is an ally of Satan and will always be an enemy of Allah and Muslims unless Allah guides them to Islam. Muslims only ally with Allah, the prophets and the believers, to ally with anyone else only weakens us. So that's why the whole Saudi-American alliance was/is unislamic and toxic and decades later it resulted in tragedy via "military aid" and decades later blossomed into violent Islamic extremists proliferating and Allah will show the end result of that alliance. However I must be just and clarify that the USA-Saudi alliance doomed the American economy due to the hyperinflation that it guarantees America will experience when Saudi Arabia stops selling its oil in US dollars which must happen eventually no matter what because there is only a limited supply of Saudi oil even if they wanted to maintain the petrodollar forever. So truly it wasn't all bad for Muslims when the Saudi government allied with the USA because ever since the invention of the Petrodollar alliance that caused the dollar to be a global currency, it has caused the American economy to inflate and someday that bubble will pop destroying the value of the US dollar causing mass havoc on their economy. Economically Saudi Arabia has guaranteed the destruction of the US economy, it just hasn't fully been realized yet but once Americans do realize then they will blame the Muslims yet again and probably put the Winslow plan into effect with more force than ever before, if they can manage to. Yet that's a future war for future generations to write about. Fundamentally Allah will never ever reward Muslims for disobedience, so to get Allah's help you have to do what Allah wants and globally Muslims haven't been. While it might be easy to point the fingers at Muslimish leaders and blame them, these leaders are the leaders for a reason. To both believers and disbelievers Allah gives righteous people righteous leaders, while sinful people get sinful leaders. If you change yourself for the better then God will change your government for the better. The problem is we tend to want everyone else to change except ourselves, whereas all the problems in the world can exist simply because of your sins. Your sins can negatively affect the way the world spins. Instead of blaming a leader, blame who you see in the mirror.

Since we know that it is in the interest of secular governments for people to sin, it is also in the interest of secular governments to distort the image of Islam which discourages people from sinning. Therefore the secular governments make a two-pronged attack, on the one hand they fund and create violent religious extremists to make religions seem violent and bad which leads people to secularism and sin. However not everyone will be fooled by this tactic and some will still realize religion is important. These types of people are targeted by the "modernists" and secularists who identify as "moderate". The Murjiah or moderates/secularists are funded to mislead the people who still want to practice religion. The secularists go to the underboard extreme, they don't practice the religion and try to make it seem as though anyone who does is an extremist. This has the effect of pushing people into the extremes of religion. An extremist is someone who is extremely deviant in their religion, meaning they are practically outside of their religion and can barely identify as a member. Satan wants extremism because it is a form of disobedience to God and leads to disbelief. This is why secular governments satanically fund both extremes. Publicly secular governments will fund the secularists saying they are combating violent extremism. Yet at the same time they are creating the conditions for violent extremism to flourish, while also funding and training the very same violent extremists they claim to be combating. They do this in an attempt to eliminate Islam. You will never defeat violent extremists with peaceful extremists or vice versa. Only true Muslims and the establishment of the true unaltered Islam as taught and practiced by Muhammad pbuh and his companions will end

Islamic extremism. That means all forms of extremism, both the violent criminal extremists and the pacifist secular extremists. The secular governments don't want the secular extremists to go because they promote sin. In reality their war is against Islam, since they support both peaceful and violent Muslim extremists. Therefore to maintain the extremist status quo we see a continuous cycle. Secular governments covertly aid Islamic extremists in one country to defeat a secular regime, later they invade the extremist state and install a secular government before supporting extremists once more to overthrow the secular regime they created. Then the process is repeated with each state in the middle eastern region, supporting both extremists and secularists so the region is in constant upheaval and instability. As a result each day Muslims are dying and Islam gets misrepresented causing everyone to have extreme ideas about it, both Muslim and non-Muslim alike. While the constant wars reduce middle eastern Muslim populations and wealth making the states smaller and weaker, less of a threat to Israel. Also exhausting international Muslim resources from all the aid sent to the refugees. It's a destructive cycle meant to hide Islam from the world and reduce the numbers and strength of practicing Muslims. Satan inspired this two pronged extremist plan hoping it would discourage people from embracing Islam or practicing Islam. Unfortunately some people have been tricked by this plan of Satan to prevent the implementation of Islam. However many more people have been guided by God to Islam as a result of the extra publicity Satan has given Islam in his attempt to distort it. We must always put things in a religious context, because the goal of life is to please God. The politics of today are all related to religion, most news has some affect on religious attitudes even if it is just a secular distraction. The goal of Satan is to have humans disbelieve and sin. Isn't that all that is on the news? Either negativity, lies or distractions, all of which can lead to sin. Everything in life is either helping us to worship God or preventing us. The Khawarij/ Takfiris label the practicing Muslim as a modernist or disbeliever for not being strict enough; in their opinion. While the non-Muslims, Murjiah, secularists and less practicing Muslims label the practicing Muslim as a Khawarij/Takriri for being too strict; in their opinion. Yet most of the time secularists don't even know the words "*Khawarij*" or "*Takfiri*" because they don't know the difference between Muslims and

Kharijis/Takfiris and neither do most Muslims know. In reality these two extremist groups despite being completely opposite in their lifestyles are unwittingly serving the same satanic purpose of misrepresenting and tarnishing the true Islam. Islam doesn't tolerate extremism in any way, shape or form, Muslims view violent extremists the same as peaceful extremists. Both have good intentions and say some truthful beautiful words but they are both dangerous, upon falsehood and misguidance. The Muslim who correctly follows the way of the salaf, which is Islam as taught by Muhammad pbuh and practiced by the first 3 generations of Muslims, gets labeled as extreme by nearly everyone with disbelievers and modernists even calling Khawarij groups Salafi because they can't tell the difference and there are people who claim they are Salafi when they aren't. This is why both actions and words must be examined according to the Islamic criteria. Claims and names are worthless! Most who use the word "salafi" don't even know what the word means, especially if they are a non-Muslim. The same goes for the word "Wahhabi", the vast majority of people in the world don't know what that word means either and will just say that it's strict extremist Islam promoted by Saudi Arabia.

The word "Wahhabi" was invented by the British disbelievers as a label for Muslims who correctly practiced Islam and waged jihad to liberate Muslim lands and establish Shariah in Arabia. The British invented the term because they wanted Muslims to get confused and think the Muslim scholar Muhammad ibn Abdul Wahhab had taught a new doctrine, so they wouldn't fight in jihad against the British. They also did this in order to change what the word Muslim meant. That scholar didn't come with anything new, he just quoted what the earlier Muslim scholars taught who were transmitting what the prophet pbuh taught. One should just follow the prophet Muhammad bin Abdullah ibn Abdul Muttalib pbuh the way the prophet said to. If someone is similar to another person who tried to follow the prophet pbuh then that doesn't make them a follower of that other person. Technically there is no such thing as a "Wahhabi" as people think there is because the guy himself told people not to follow him, but that people should follow the prophet Muhammad pbuh; as did other scholars such as Imam Abu Hanifa, Imam Malik, Imam ash-Shafi'i, Imam Hanbal and others. None of these scholars said to follow them and disregard all others, they all taught to follow the prophet pbuh and if you learn that something they taught goes against the teachings of the prophet pbuh then don't do what they taught and do what the prophet Muhammad pbuh taught instead. Muslims are those who submit to God in Islam and follow the final prophet Muhammad pbuh, we do not worship him or pray to him, we just try to follow his teachings and behavior. This is why disbelievers used to call Muslims "Muhammadeans" because they knew we followed Muhammad pbuh, but since Christians worship Christ the disbelievers called us Muhammadeans instead of Muslims in order to give Christians the wrong idea of what Islam was and what Muslims believed. Sometimes practicing Muslims get labeled "Wahhabi" because people want others to think that such Muslims aren't following the prophet Muhammad pbuh or Islam, but are following a certain scholar instead whose ancestor was named "Abdul-Wahhaab", which means the slave of Wahhaab. The term Wahhaabi was invented by enemies of Islam to make Muslims think that other Muslims were doing what they were doing because of what a particular scholar taught and that what Islam taught was different. Yet the word itself "Wahhaab" is actually an attribute of Allah that means, "*The One who continually bestows gifts, favors, mercy and success upon all of creation. The One who gives freely and endlessly without expectation of return. He gives without our earning it/working for it and His gifts are unmatchable. The Bestower who gives whatever He wills to whomsoever he wills."* So from a linguistic aspect if one thinks a "Wahhaabi" is one who follows "the Wahhaab" then every single Muslim would be a Wahhaabi. Yet that's not the name Allah gives us and it would be confusing to use such terms because Allah has many attributes and if one calls themselves a Wahhaabi then they could call themselves a Rahmaani, Raheemi, Kareemi, Jabbari, Salaami and even an Allahi, but again such terms aren't really proper. It would be like saying someone who believes in God is a Godi. Today disbelievers label Khawarij as "Wahhabis" and "Salafis", also giving those who practice Islam correctly the same label. This was done deliberately to make people think that extremists were the same as those whom they labeled "Wahhabi". It'd be like calling both poison and water "liquid X". Since people don't want to drink poison, because poison gets called "liquid X" it causes people to think everything called "liquid X" is poison even if in reality it's water. So if you presented water to someone who's dying of thirst, because they heard the TV define what was water as "liquid X" they would think you were trying to poison them and reject it. Thus violent extremists were given the same label by disbelievers as proper Muslims were who waged jihad against oppression, because it'd make people equate jihad with extremist criminal violence. In reality the disbelieving oppressors just wanted Muslims to stop jihad so they could commit oppression, so they labeled both groups the same even though they are really in different boats. As a result people who correctly try to sink the ship of the dangerous criminal extremists end up attacking the ship of the proper Muslims as well because they don't know the leaders of disbelievers gave both boats the same name and description; they think that the label has only been given to one boat and crew. Thus since the boat of the proper Muslims is described the same as the extremists' boat, ill-informed Muslims end up jumping off the ship of Islam thinking that it's the extremist ship, then they tell other Muslims to avoid that ship by labeling those on it who are trying to cast them a life raft as "Wahhabis" or "Salafis". Thereby aiding the enemies of Islam who started this inaccurate name-calling campaign in order to cause oppression throughout the land by eliminating Jihad. Today they are so confidant in their plot they have even come out into the open and are publicly labeling violent criminals as "Jihadis", thereby making people think Jihad is crime in the hopes that this second phase of their smear campaign will eliminate Jihad in its entirety. Then if Jihad is eliminated, Islam and the Muslims will be put on the chopping block. When that happens the disbelievers aren't going to care if someone calls themselves Salafi or tries to be a Salafi or not, every version of Muslim and anyone claiming to follow any type of Islam will be killed. This is what happens, and it happened as recently as the 1990s in Bosnia, is still happening in Chechnya, Kashmir, Palestine, Myanmar, China, Syria and other places. If you study those countries that's how it started, the governments said they only wanted to harm the "extremists" and after most of the good Muslims were gone then they said, "Well it turns out we actually should kill all the Muslims." Frequently there aren't even extremists at all but it's a manufactured political excuse that gets bought by taxpayers. A prime example is the former Russian FSB agent Alexander Litvinenko who co-authored a book revealing how in September 1999 CE Russian FSB agents planted explosives in Russian civilian buildings and deliberately blew them up killing innocent civilians in compliance with government orders. These attacks were then blamed on Muslims in Chechnya and were used as the pretext for the 2nd Chechen war and as political ammunition by Vladimir Putin to grant him the Russian presidency. Putin actually became president for killing his own countrymen and blaming it on the Muslims. The Russian agents themselves admit that they deliberately killed innocent people and blamed it on Muslims just so they could go kill Muslims stating their war was "only against extremists" but it was actually designed to exterminate Islam and all Muslims. Some of the most zealous enemies of Islam have already went on to the third phase of their plot by replacing the word "Jihadis" with "Muslims" and publicly making false claims that Islam equals violent criminal extremism, whilst the more devious will try to claim that one can be Muslim without Islam. Thereby making a two pronged attack where both are at war with Islam by painting it with the same brush as they do criminal violence, with one group saying to kill the people who follow the doctrine of Islam and the other saying to destroy the doctrine of Islam which Muslims follow. In reality both types want the destruction of Islam and Muslims and work together. The first type wages war on the battlefield getting support from violent or aggressive disbelievers, while the other wages war on the ideological field getting support from peaceful and passive disbelievers as well as ignorant and deviant Muslims. Some who do this know they're evil and deliberately distorting the truth while some don't and just believe/feel they are correct. One tactic used by enemies of Muslims is to say *"I'm not against Muslims, I'm just against Islam."* This is rarely said directly to Muslims, it is usually said to non-Muslims to make the speaker seem academic or justified for hating and condemning Islam instead of being a prejudiced bigot. If someone says such a statement then you should know they are a liar. You cannot love Muslims and hate Islam. Likewise you cannot hate drugs but love drug dealers, or hate Satanism but love Satanists. It is impossible to love a person who embodies and promotes what you hate. The reason enemies of Islam and Muslims make this claim is to change the definition of what being Muslim means. A Muslim is someone who believes in, practices and preaches Islam. To hate or oppose 1 is to hate and oppose both. Enemies of Islam want people to think Islam can be separated from being Muslim and they intend to make Muslim into an ethnicity or culture instead of being someone who believes certain things and lives a certain way.

Islamaphobes will say they love Muslims but hate Islam because if they said they hated both then people will scrutinize their reasons for hating people. This is because most humans care more about people's feelings than people's beliefs, which is why to insult someone's person usually causes a more hostile reaction than if you insulted their beliefs or ideas. Islamaphobes are reluctant to say they hate Muslims and Islam because they fear their reasons for hating Islam will be exposed as unjustified when scrutinized. Thus as long as enemies of Islam pretend it's not a hatred of people themselves the modern culture interprets such hatred almost as though it's humanitarian and sanctions it. Then non-Muslim people fail to see how such hatred for Islam is personal and applies to Muslim people as well, so then they fail to see the preachers of genocide until after masses of Muslims get killed; of which the biased media rarely even mentions nor connects the dots to implicate the non-Muslim culprits. Thereupon when Muslims explain that a literal war is being waged both theologically and physically against Muslims, the non-Muslim crowd thinks that's just "extremist talk to radicalize Muslims" said to disrupt the peace and "religious debates". Yet how can there be peace and "religious debates" when the kafirs are killing and imprisoning the Muslims all over the world? The non-Muslims imprison, kill and persecute our best and brightest debators because they really don't want to debate but destroy. It is not extreme to label your enemies as your enemies. Moses and Aaron pbut never pretended to be friends with Pharaoh or the Egyptian masses who believed in different religions than them. It's not extreme to admit a theological and physical war is going on, that's called honesty and shows a solution is desired. Getting labeled extreme can make one numb to the idea until eventually the person becomes extremely deviant one way or the other, if they don't remain firm and steadfast upon the truth. One can only practice the true religion and avoid extremes if they stop caring about what people say and think about them, instead focusing solely on pleasing their Creator. The religion of God is not extreme, but to disbelievers and extremists it will be considered extreme. Regardless if we consider hellfire and heaven, these are two extremes. One is extremely bad and one is extremely good. It is only natural that such extreme destinations would be reached through what seem to be extreme means. Either one is extremely good and goes to paradise or extremely bad and goes to hell. Either your belief is perfectly correct and complete, or totally false and wrong. God doesn't have a permanent place for the average person where they experience both pain and pleasure forever. It's one or the other, either eternal torture or eternal pleasure. The test of life has extremely high stakes, therefore in a sense the religion of God is extreme, it is extremely good and important. Just as the opinions of people should not be valued over the opinion of God, the opinions of illegitimate governments who don't rule by the law of God should also be devoid of influence over us. Rather than care if something is politically correct we should be concerned if something is religiously correct. Out of all the prophets I know of I don't know of any whom the disbelievers considered to be "politically correct". Pharaoh threatened the magicians who repented, reformed and followed Moses pbuh with a torturous death because they believed. Yet the believers were steadfast in doing what was right, worshipping God alone in the correct way. Thus

Pharaoh said he must kill them to protect the citizens, justifying his actions by saying he was terrified of their assault on the beliefs, values and way of life which the Egyptian people held dear for centuries. But pause. Most people will tell the story of Moses pbuh and Pharaoh in the course of a few minutes or hours, but keep in mind this interaction took place over the course of many years. Moses pbuh didn't enter Egypt, show his signs, get rejected and then flee across the Sea all in one day, his mission took years to finish. According to the Quran in chapter 10:87 Moses pbuh and the believers built masjids in Egypt and worshipped God while living there. Yet in the same chapter, in context Moses pbuh and the believers are described as being persecuted whilst living in Egypt. This is very important because people today will say, *"Muslims have masjids in this country and can pray there anytime they want, they're not being persecuted."* However Moses pbuh and the believers built masjids in Egypt and could pray there as well, yet they were still persecuted and Allah describes them as being persecuted despite them having places they could worship in. So a country letting Muslims build a masjid and pray there doesn't mean they aren't simultaneously persecuting

Muslims while they live there. At the same time Pharaoh was killing believing men and raping their women, you had the Jew Korah peacefully living in a mansion. Korah was a Jew living in Egypt during the time the believers were persecuted and he was one of the wealthiest people in the world of all time. Despite being Jewish living luxuriously in a mansion with slaves serving him, he wasn't robbed or persecuted by Pharaoh because he was "a good Egyptian citizen" who was a great benefit to Egyptian society. Korah publicly claimed to be a believer in Moses pbuh but he wasn't "strict or extreme" or anything like that. You know the type, there was your religion and then there's your work and then there's your nationality, they think religion is a separate issue that shouldn't cause any trouble with your politics or nation nor cause any friction in regards to your financial activities. He didn't see any problems with being a believer in Moses pbuh and a patriotic Egyptian taxpayer despite the Egyptian government butchering the believers. Moses pbuh then told this Korah to pay the obligatory zakat on his wealth in charity and Korah calculated it and refused to pay it, saying that God didn't make him rich it was because he was smart and worked hard and that God wasn't upset with him not paying charity because he kept getting richer every day. Now obviously Moses pbuh couldn't do anything to Korah in Egypt, and Pharaoh even wanted Moses pbuh executed himself. Since Moses pbuh couldn't legally physically punish Korah for his disobedience, God caused a special earthquake to occur that swallowed up Korah, his wealth and nothing else; thereby proving to all how he was detested by God and was a disbeliever despite his claims. Yet the fact remains Pharaoh never bothered Korah despite actively harming the believers in Egypt of whom Korah claimed to be one. Pharaoh considered Korah to be one of the "good Muslims" while Moses pbuh was labeled as a hateful, disrespectful dangerous radical extremist. You have to keep in mind Jews were in Egypt long before Moses pbuh became their prophet, so to Pharaoh and his government there was Moses' version of Islam and Korah's version. Pharaoh just thought that Korah's version of Islam was the right moderate one and that Moses pbuh was some Jewish extremist preaching something new that was purely political in motive. The enemies of Pharaoh and the state were just the "few extremists" who "took the teachings of Moses(pbuh) too literally or to extremes". Eventually those "extremists" who correctly followed Moses pbuh were labeled *"enemies of the state"* because they publicly said Pharaoh was not God, his government was illegitimate and they told the Egyptian people that they were going to burn in hell if they didn't change their religions and accept Moses pbuh as their prophet and political leader. Pharaoh got fed up with it and ramped his persecution up to the next level, when political moods made further persecution possible. You see Pharaoh couldn't just kill whoever he wanted whenever he wanted, he had to persuade his followers to do what he wanted and it took some time to persuade the Egyptian military to be willing to slaughter every believing man, woman and child on command. At first it was "just the extremists" getting imprisoned and killed and Pharaoh maintained he only had a problem with Moses' radical version, yet eventually all Jews even those who didn't follow Moses pbuh were officially on the kill list. These were real people just like people today are real people. It's well known how the Egyptian people ended up and the course of action Pharaoh eventually led them to take. Yet some of those people were true believers who were solely concerned with what their Creator thought about them, even if it meant having their hands and feet cut off on opposite sides being crucified to the trunks of palm trees by Pharaoh, which is what happened to the magicians immediately after they believed in Moses pbuh. Pharaoh even went so far as to kill his own wife Asiyah, because she was Muslim, and only God knows how many babies. Which again, I remind you Pharaoh didn't kill all these people in one day, it was just one part of his entire political policy. Just like any ruler who has ever killed their wife, they had to cajole the populace to take their side and support them in the deed, and those real people did. Do you know what the majority of people said about those killed by Pharaoh? The majority vilified them and said they were appalling, crazy, evil criminals. They thought killing them was a good deed. Yet Pharaoh and the pagan Egyptian citizens are the ones who will burn in hell and the believers will be in paradise. The point is that because the religion of God conflicts with unislamic government policies they will try to pressure people anyway they can to prevent them from practicing the religion of God. But we can't let them influence us. The police cannot put you in hell, the military cannot put you in hell, the kings, presidents and prime ministers cannot put you in hell, the U.N. can't put you in hell, even if all the humans, animals, jinn and aliens worked together to put you in hell they can't. They can't even cause you pain because Allah created the pain receptors and controls their functioning; nothing can activate your pain receptors only Allah can. They can't even cause pain! Not only do they have no ability to cause pain, but they can't cause pleasure either, nor can they bestow honor or cause disgrace. They can't even stop themselves from falling asleep or cause themselves to wakeup. How foolish can it be to fear something that sleeps or needs energy from other things to function? It's stupid to fear something that needs something and has no power to bestow anything. Nothing except the Creator of heaven and hell can put you in heaven or hell, so never fear anything except for the one being that can protect you from hell or prevent you from paradise. Likewise don't think anyone except the Creator of heaven can get you into heaven. God has given us the criteria so we know what to believe and do to get to where we want. So if anything or anyone is preventing us from taking that path, we can't turn around or stop traveling the road to paradise as a result. Since time keeps moving it means we are always moving on the road to paradise or the roads to hell. Most social pressure will either cause us to leave the road to paradise, shift gears on the road to paradise so we stay in the same place without moving while spinning our wheels wasting energy, or cause us to go in reverse on the road to paradise making us farther from our goal as time passes. You should not care what any of the creation says, writes or thinks about you while alive or dead. But in reality regardless of whether we let the negative social pressure affect us or not, there will be pressure. Therefore we should make sure that the pressure is positive and that the environment we are in motivates us and promotes us going to the finish line on the road to paradise. The solution for sinful environments is a government based on the religion of God. I don't think such a state will come about through revolutions or force. If it ever did it wouldn't last or be secure. The way to have a government structured by the laws of God is if people accept the authority of God and want to practice the religion of God, then demand a government that establishes the religion of God which protects them from sin. This requires human interaction and communication. Most people are ignorant and simply don't know what the true religion is, and not all who do know it practice it. If people practiced the true religion and shared it with others, it would flourish. This is what the prophets pbut did. Primarily we have to start with ourselves, how can you possibly be a happy citizen of a country governed by the laws of God if you personally disobey the laws of God publicly or privately? How can you live in a country where the laws of God are the laws of the land if the laws of God aren't obeyed within your own household? Fundamental steps are required. I must practice the true religion before I can share it with others. Then others must practice it before they can share it. Then many must practice it before it can be established throughout the land. You don't have to be sinless before you share Islam with others, else none would ever share it, but it is important to practice what one preaches and have knowledge about what one teaches. If you don't know, then say you don't know. If you don't practice a particular aspect then when telling others to do so keep in mind your ears are closer to your mouth than their ears are, so speak your words to yourself while directing them towards others. If many people practiced the true religion then it would peacefully become the model for a government system because even disbelievers would see the justice of it and want to live under the laws of God. This is how Muhammad pbuh established the Islamic State in Madinah. The prophet pbuh practiced Islam in Mecca and told some travelers from Madinah about it. Those travelers became Muslim and practiced Islam when they returned to Madinah. Eventually people in Madinah voluntarily became Muslims and practiced Islam. Later Muhammad pbuh was requested to come live in Madinah and be its leader by both Muslims and non-Muslims. This is the way Muhammad pbuh established an Islamic State, simply by practicing Islam and sharing it with others. The religion of Islam can never be forced upon people it must be voluntary. Although once the Islamic State was established in Medinah, Islam spread exponentially, especially after the conquest of Mecca because the world saw that Islam truly is the best thing for humanity. Islam has the best form of government, the best economic system, the best moral code, the best legal system, the best social system and the best attitude towards life. When Muslims conquered lands through jihad and disbelievers experienced an Islamic environment they saw that Islamic Shariah is how the world should be run, truly is God-given and voluntarily chose Islam as their way of life; though not all did but most did. Islamic Shariah ensures government is not corrupt, wasteful, extravagant, or spending on undesirable useless things. A Khilafah treasury is considered the wealth of all Muslims and it is sinful for it to be used irresponsibly. As a result it was the practice of the early Khalifahs to distribute the entire treasury to the people on a routine basis, sometimes monthly, sometimes daily because they didn't want to be held accountable in the afterlife for not spending it properly. The Khilafah was a welfare state, not a parasite state, but a welfare state in that the government had no money because it would spend all it's money on the people as soon as possible and rely on Allah for tomorrow. Under the Islamic fundraising method if governments were corrupt or wasteful then nobody would voluntarily give their money to the government. If the government project were ineffective, or undesired, the budget for it would remain unfunded. This is why an Islamic State has a small mandatory levy on disbelievers living in their country, called Jizya, it entitles them to certain advantages of citizenship. Otherwise it wouldn't be fair for a Muslim army to protect disbelievers who didn't contribute to the nation in any way and it would be unjust for Muslims to let disbelieving residents be slaughtered if enemies arrived. Therefore disbelievers who aren't poor are obligated to pay an Islamic State something whether they want an Islamic army to protect them or not. Yet there can be exemptions to Jizya and Khaalid bin Waleed even offered such a "Jizyah exemption" when conquering Hirah. Khaalid wrote saying: *"I write this to you: if any of you become old, poor or ill or his people have to donate to maintain his livelihood I will never ask Jizya of him. He will also receive a grant from the Bait ul-Maal (Treasury of the Islamic state). He and his children will be entitled to this as long as he resides in Dar ul-Hijrah and Dar al-Islam. If they go out (from this jurisdiction) then the Muslims are no longer obliged to provide anything for them."* In a sense the Jizya also was a forerunner of the social security and pension plan system, except it wasn't a scam with everyone being forced to pay and only those who needed money were given it. Sadly the non-Muslim governments learned about Jizya, corrupted it and then applied it to everybody calling it civilized and then they say Jizya is medieval. Well the medieval Jjizya is a lot better than the modern social security or pensions. The difference with Jizya and taxation is that it really is just for protection and this is why in 636 CE the

Jizya that had been collected from the city of Emessa, Syria was returned to the disbelievers by Abu Ubeidah because the Muslims were tactically withdrawing from the area and would not be able to protect the people from the oppression of the Romans. So the Muslims actually paid back 100% of the Jizya that was paid. The people of Emessa then said they would never let the Romans back in to oppress them again under unislamic laws and hoped the Muslims would return. Even though the majority of the people of Emessa were disbelieving non-Muslims they promised they'd fight the Romans themselves rather than let them be their rulers again. Thus the Roman disbelievers said they wanted Shariah over Roman laws and would rather fight against their own nation than become a part of it again. In comparison no unislamic nation has ever paid back 100% of the funds they collected because they "couldn't fulfill their duties the payment entailed". When the army led by Abu Ubeidah which consisted of 40,000 Muslims later defeated the Christian Byzantine/Roman army of 150,000-600,000 at the battle of Yarmuk (4,000 Muslims killed to about 105,000 Christian soldiers dead and 40,000 Christian soldiers taken as prisoners of war) the disbelievers of Emessa rejoiced at the return of the Muslims and gladly opened the city gates for them to implement the justice of Shariah once more. Whereas if you are familiar with military history you will know that such battle results are phenomenal and those numbers are the accurate numbers reported by Abu Ubeidah himself to Umar bin al Khattab who punished any who lied and Muhammad pbuh had called Abu Ubeidah the trustworthy man of the nation of Muhammad pbuh since he had killed his father in the battle of Badr and lost his two front teeth during the battle of Uhud extracting chain links that had penetrated the cheek of Muhammad pbuh. Most history buffs who learn of the Battle of Yarmuk would be flabbergasted as to why they didn't know of such a battle if it were really that spectacular and important. Well the simple reason is that it was explicitly religious and perhaps one of the most religious battles Muslims and Christians ever fought and the Muslims won and completely embarrassed the Christians, so the Christian world really doesn't want people to know about it especially since they said they would win because of their Chrisitan faith and superior technology and massive numbers. During the skirmishes before the battle of Yarmuk the famous Khalid bin Waleed took 60 Muslims to fight 60,000 Arab Christians led by Jabalah bin al-Ayham Al-Ghassani, Khaalid wanted to take just 30 but the Muslims persuaded him that was reckless and could be sinfully suicidal. Khaalid explicitly chose such a low number because he wanted to humiliate the Christians so that when they said how many Muslims were in the army that defeated them they would become a laughing stock. That skirmish of the 60,000 Christian Arabs vs. the 60 Muslims resulted in 5,000 dead Arab Christians with 10 Muslims killed and 5 Muslims taken captive. Yet clearly with the ancient adage of "Might is Right", during the most religious wars in Muslim vs. Christian history when you have 60 Muslims defeat 60,000 Arab Christians in battle then it's obvious as to why the people would surrender cities to the Muslims. Logistically these numbers sound crazy and I know they sound crazy but these are the historically authentic numbers regarding the battles of the Muslim conquests of the Christian middle east. The names of those 60 are known and later on the Christian commander Bannes freed the 5 Muslim captives because he was afraid when Khaalid and 100 other Muslims threatened to kill him and his entire army on the spot or be martyred in the process should Bannes behead the 5 Muslim prisoners as he threatened. People don't want Muslims and non-Muslims to know these historical facts because any rational person would logically conclude religion was the reason for such results, especially when technologically and numerically the Muslims were outmatched. Religion and Justice are truly the only reasons Muslims have ever conquered any place. Muhammad pbuh himself has said that an army of 12,000 true Believers will never be defeated by anything. So according to the prophet Muhammad pbuh Muslims only need 12,000 true believers to conquer the whole world. Yet it's not easy to meet Muhammad's criteria pbuh of a "true believer". Surely his definition of a "true believer" is a little different than the mainstream modern criteria. A famous conversion also took place during the battle of Yarmuk when the Christian General, named George, wanted to meet Khaalid during a time between the fighting. After meeting him and discussing the reasons the Muslims were fighting and what Islam was about George decided to become a Muslim, joined the Muslim army, then fought as a Muslim for the cause of Islam and died fighting against his former compatriots and coreligionists. So this was a famous epic battle wherein a leading general when speaking to the opposing general between the fighting ended up changing his religion and joining his enemy to fight against his former troops that he led to the battle. The city of Emessa is also not the only example of non-Muslim citizens siding with Muslims against governments who practice the same religion as them, many such examples exist. Another famous example is the city of Shayzar. The commander of the Muslim army sent a letter to Shayzar asking the people to surrender, their governor Niks asked the people their opinion and they wanted to surrender knowing they couldn't win by fighting and that the Muslims were just, so it behooved them to surrender peacefully rather than fight. Well the Shayzari governor Niks disagreed and so the army and the civilians fought each other while the Muslims waited outside. After awhile the civilians killed Niks and his soldiers and then came out to tell the Muslims about their actions and their decision. Then guess what happened? The Christians of Shayzar still remained Christians despite fighting for the Muslims to rule over them. So anyone claiming they weren't "real Christians" is wrong because they remained Christians, they just really wanted Islamic Shariah. Shayzar is just one example of Christians fighting and killing their own Christian rulers in order to live under Islamic Shariah. The cities of Aleppo, Azaz and Antioch are also remarkable examples with even greater stories that would be unjust for me to summarize. To think Muslims just came with the sword and forced Shariah upon the disbelievers is completely foolish. Maximillian Robespierre, considered by "counter-terrorism experts" to be the "father of terrorism" said: *"The most extravagant idea that can be born in the head of a political thinker is to believe that it suffices for people to enter, weapons in hand, among a foreign people and expect to have its laws and constitution embraced. No one loves armed missionaries; the first lesson of nature and prudence is to repulse them as enemies."* Yet it is a historical fact that is not what all the disbelievers did when Muslims came with Shariah. So either Robespierre was wrong about people not loving but repulsing armed missionaries or the justice of the legal system of the true religion is an exception to the rule. The Western non-Muslim world thinks Robespierre was right so they try to conquer the hearts and minds creating love for kufr and kafirs prior to invading. But Muslims don't work that way, when we wage Jihad we are armed missionaries on a mission to establish the Law of God on earth and nothing else. This works despite the non-Muslims never ever loving us because, notwithstanding their hate for Islamic theology, after learning about and experiencing Shariah they love to admit that politically/economically/socially Islam is the best governing force there is. This is why Christians never learn about how the Muslims conquered Christian Palestine, Egypt and Syria in the 600s CE because it shows only 3 stories. One is that of Christians joyfully surrendering to Muslims and choosing to live under Shariah. Another is one of masses of Christians becoming Muslim and betraying the other Christian soldiers, as Lawan and Luke and their soldiers did at Azaż and Falantius and his soldiers did in Antioch, Basil of Tyre, or Jonah of Damascus. While the third shows the staunch Byzantine Christians who sought help in the name of Jesus Christ, the Bible, the Cross and passionately waged a religious war more religious in nature than the crusades were 400 years later and lost in humiliating fashions time and again even though they themselves would pray God gives victory to those upon the true faith and the Christians had more numbers and better weapons. Logistically speaking the Muslims should've never been able to conquer the Byzantines or Persians, Islam was the only thing in their favor and that's the only thing Muslims need to be victorious. Seriously consider why do Christians tend to know more about the Crusades than they do about the initial Muslim conquests of Syria, Palestine and Egypt? Whereas while some Christians did choose to become Muslims after and during those conquests, many didn't because being Muslim is not a requirement to live under Shariah. Honestly if I wasn't Muslim I'd still want Shariah because it's the best legal system I've ever studied or heard of. Jizya mainly ensures non-Muslims don't exploit the Islamic State as a tax haven, because according to Islam for a government to impose taxes is a bigger sin than committing adultery.

This is why it should be the priority of Muslims today to reestablish a genuine Khilafah. That will prove with a real-life example which none could deny that Islamic Shariah is superior to Democracy, Libertarianism, Hedonism, Statism, Nationalism, Individualism, Freedom and everything else. For any who truly fear criminal violence from extremists, the Khilafah would deal with them. It is because we don't have a Khilafah today that extremists get support, because people are impatient and decide to follow the extremists who attempt to establish an Islamic State in unislamic ways. The ends don't justify the means, God judges us based on the means we use. Ending the murdering of innocents is just another benefit of a genuine Khilafah, a Khilafah wouldn't tolerate oppression anywhere on the planet. But unlike the USA or UN, a genuine Khilafah wouldn't kill innocents or violate human rights and it actually would solve the problem, instead of using it as an excuse to oppressively tax citizens. That's why wicked people are terrified of a genuine Khilafah. Maybe the modern criminally violent extremists will die out or be killed off, but others will take their place if a Khilafah isn't established. If you really want to end human terrorism throughout the world then you should know that only Islam can end it. This is because Islam teaches mankind to only fear the Creator of everything and nothing else. It is simply impossible for a Muslim to be terrified of anything except Allah. The word "terrorist" linguistically, literally and originally means someone whom you fear, so when Muslims are called terrorists it doesn't mean they commit acts of criminal violence it means people fear them because we preach Islam. It's because the evildoers know that Islam forbids all evil, establishes true justice and abolishes all falsehood that bad people are terrified of Islam and those who practice it. It's because the prophets completely proved without a doubt that they were sent by the Creator, that only he is to be worshipped and that hell awaits all those who reject the religion of Islam and choose another lifestyle, that many of them were considered terrorists. Pharaoh was terrified of Moses pbuh, the Pharisees were terrified of Jesus pbuh and Muhammad's enemies were terrified of him. When the 100% true religion is proven to you it's scary, because you come face to face with the choice of guaranteed hellfire if you choose not to practice it. As a result many people who don't want to change their lives for the better just hate the messengers who disrupted their dangerously blissful ignorance. I was terrified too when I learned Christianity leads to hell. This is why a proper Muslim is often labeled a terrorist by enemies of Islam because Islam frightens satanic people and institutions. That doesn't mean those labeled terrorists today are proper Muslims, murderous criminals are murderous criminals and should be called that instead. Murderous criminals have been mislabeled as terrorists by enemies of Islam to distort Islam and give disbelievers and hypocrites excuses to harm practicing Muslims on a global scale. A terrorist is simply a being you fear. When people say they killed a terrorist they are just saying they killed someone they feared, maybe they were violent criminals maybe not. The Creator is the only being who should ever be labeled a terrorist because no creature can do anything unless Allah decrees. It is completely absurd to fear a created being, unless you are a disbeliever, or you are opposing Allah's friends. When one knows the Creator and fears his displeasure and punishment there is no room in the human heart to fear anything or anyone else, whether it's poverty, illness, war, social rejection, labels, loneliness, imprisonment, torture or whatever. Seriously, if you fear anything other than Allah then you don't know God. But how can a Khilafah be established today?

According to the majority of Muslims Scholars the Muslims should consolidate in the Muslim lands to establish the Khilafah, because by having a Khilafah and practicing Islam there 100% the whole world will be unable to deny that Islam is the solution for everything. It is partly because Muslims are divided and disunited throughout the world that they have been oppressed. Since Muslims are being killed in Muslim lands at this very moment, I think they should be the priority rather than informing non-Muslims about Islam. First disbelievers must be prevented from killing Muslims, then we can talk about Islam. Yet the reason the non-Muslims will never stop fighting Muslims is because they know that a peaceful dialogue will destroy their false religions and ideologies. War is the only means they can use to prevent the spread of Islam, by physically reducing the number of Muslims and waging an ideological campaign of lies about Islam domestically and internationally to both disbelievers and Muslims. However despite their utmost efforts in doing so the number of Muslims is increasing. Although I think more concern should be given to focus on improving the quality of Muslims rather than increasing the quantity, even though both are important. For instance every year Muslims can say there is X% increase in the number of Muslims, but when have we ever been able to say we are X% closer to establishing a Khilafah? Also the low quality of Muslims actually hinders the quantity from increasing. Which is why the Muslims who aren't devout and knowledgeable about Islam shouldn't be in non-Muslim societies because they are misrepresenting Islam making it harder to spread the message. Honestly there are many

Muslims in America who in their attempt to spread Islam, they make it harder for Islam to spread. This is because they don't have knowledge about Islam and lack sincerity. In reality they are just spreading an idea about Muslims and Islam in order to make their own lives in America more comfortable. Muslims can't "go with the flow" inside unislamic non-Muslim societies. The "flow" of unislamic ideologies, cultures and systems are toxic, oppressive, immoral, lead towards the hellfire and are inferior to Islam as anyone who compares them objectively will realize. When we honestly compare Islamic Shariah to any other government system or legal code, every single time the people have agreed that their system has flaws in which Islamic Shariah is better and superior. One easy example is how Shariah law forbids government price controls while American law uses them. Such as in the 1930s when poverty was widespread in America, they got the idea to help farmers out by fixing prices making things expensive so that farmers got more money. How did they do this? They passed laws ordering agricultural products such as milk, food, cotton, animals etc. to be destroyed so as not to have an increase in the supply cause a drop in prices. Now Islam says this is sinful waste but

America did it and the effect was that prices indeed went up, however that made things worse because people could not afford to buy food since they were poorer and the supply was artificially reduced. This in turn made the farmers poorer too since they sold less for more which gave them less profit than if they had sold more for less; they also had to pay higher prices too. Thus American law in attempting to alleviate poverty actually created more poverty by destroying agricultural products while Shariah law forbid that during the time of Muhammad pbuh. Whereas America still does this today, they call it subsidies where the US government uses tax dollars to pay farmers for their food assuring they will get a certain profit, then when stuck with all that food in order to not cause the market price to drop the government destroys that food they can't sell without having market prices drop as a result. In 1980 CE for instance the USDA destroyed 50 million lemons, 100 million pounds of raisins and 1 billion oranges, all because they didn't want the prices of those products to decrease because that could theoretically mean less profit for American farmers which could mean less tax revenue. But in reality everyone had to pay extra for food, especially Americans all the while people are starving. Why didn't they just give that food away? Well if they gave it away, it would cost money to give via transportation costs, then people would eat it and not buy as much food globally which would cause prices to decrease globally and reduce the income taxes the government collects by taxing the income of farmers selling food. Basically the US government deems that it is financially beneficial for some Americans if they destroy billions of pounds of food, even though it causes global starvation. This is called "protecting American jobs". So according to American law it is better for the US economy to destroy food and let people starve than to give it away in charity, even if they were to only give it to Americans to eat. Yes, believe it or not the US government believes that feeding the American poor and homeless with free food will hurt America and cause people to lose their jobs and profits. Therefore American law facilitates tax dollars being used to buy food just so it can be destroyed. That is what democracy does to the world, and yes this is democracy's fault because this policy of destroying food was voted for and approved "by the majority of the people". The fundamental problem and cause of much modern oppression is voting and deeming the choice with the largest number of votes in support of it to be right. Voting cause starvation, for decades the majority have voted that the minority should starve. Shariah law says that's a sinful crime which governments cannot do, while American law calls it, *"protecting America's economic interests"*. The US government destroying food is actually a matter of "national security" and a way of protecting the American lifestyle of it's citizens. This is also a part of free-market capitalism, in that a free-market means farmers can freely choose to destroy their food to raise prices. Seriously that is what a free market means, it is considered a "sacred right" that Americans can choose to destroy billions of pounds of food per year for the sake of money and to disagree is to disagree with freedom and be against freedom, democracy and capitalism. To say or believe that Americans cannot be allowed to destroy metric tons of food every year is to want to take away their freedom. Freedom in 1 nation causes global starvation. Democracy has no mercy, Freedom has no mercy and Equality means there is no mercy for anybody. The USA still subsidizes industries, making Americans and everyone else pay more than they should be for most things. So which legal code is better? American law or

Shariah law? Democracy or Shariah? Freedom or Shariah? The answer is obvious and it's like this across the board for every single aspect. Furthermore anything good about any unislamic legal code was copied from the Islamic Shariah and it's a proven fact, not just a claim. Even colonial America incorporated Islamic Shariah into the American Law, but they didn't want to publicly say they copied it. Yet in the Supreme Court they have a engraving allegedly depicting Muhammad pbuh because of his positive influence on American law. Muslims and non-Muslims in America both want this engraving destroyed, for different reasons, but it doesn't get destroyed because the Court insists they want to acknowledge his beneficial influence on American law or rather the fact that they copied parts of Shariah law but don't say so. Those who oppose Shariah law don't even know what it is except for the famous penalties for apostasy(treason), adultery or theft. Although why would someone who doesn't steal or commit adultery have a problem with Shariah's laws regarding the treatment of thieves or adulterers? Really if they aren't thieves or adulterers then even if they hate the notion of adulterers or thieves being sternly punished under Shariah it will never happen to them so they don't have to worry about it. As they always say to Muslims, "*If you got nothing to hide and aren't a terrorist then why worry about surveillance?*" So one can pose this same type of question to opponents of Shariah for almost every aspect of it they oppose. For example if they aren't sodomites then it shouldn't matter to them that Shariah punishes sodomy and if they aren't sinful people then Shariah will never harm them in any way. The problem is that Shariah does legally forbid certain popular vices, like gambling, cheating, lying, slandering, smoking, buying/selling intoxicants, fornicating. Within Shariah violent corporal punishments only amount to maybe 2-5% of Shariah law and they are rarely applied, just as the death penalty is rarely applied in secular states today. Yet how many who disagree with the death penalty also demand the country's entire legal code be abolished because of that one tiny legal aspect of criminal law which they might dislike? Nobody, they acknowledge that's just one tiny thread of a whole tapestry. So even if there was something a non-Muslim doesn't like about Shariah, first of all it most likely will never effect them and secondly no entire system can be rejected just because of 1 aspect of that system. If an entire legal code is to be rejected then there must be a fundamental reason to reject it all, but never can a tiny aspect of something be a valid reason to condemn the entirety of it. Just as 1 bad apple doesn't ruin the bunch, 1 bad law doesn't invalidate a legal system. Now I'm not saying Shariah has any bad laws, I don't believe it does but what I am saying is that you can't delegitimize any system based on bits and pieces of it. The apple analogy is appropriate. The reason the unislamic legal systems are condemned is not necessarily because a few apples(laws) are toxic or a few bad branches of government exist, or due to a few bad leaves(politicians), but because the apples were grown from the tree Allah has forbidden us to utilize and the foundational seeds(doctrines) are satanic in their origin. So when the seed from which a government is planted is sinful then the government that grows upon those principles will be a sinful tree resulting in poisonous consequences with the roots ruining the earth and the growth of the tree blocking out the light of Allah spreading devilish darkness where light once was. It is a christian concept that "you will know them by the fruits they produce", Islam decrees that the fruits can reveal much about the tree but fundamentally you study the seeds which planted the tree and ignore the tree basing your decision on whether to keep the tree or not based on the seed it grew from not the fruits it produces or it's appearance or the strength of it's roots or popularity throughout the land. Sadly most non-Muslims judge governments solely by their fruits and only the famous fruits rather than all the fruits and they think new leaves will fix the problems the various branches of government are responsible for. Democracy basically teaches that leaves can cure or corrupt an entire tree. One problem non-Muslims have with Shariah is that they've never tasted any of its fruits directly from the tree and only hear of the taste of the notorious fruits which to them seem bitter because their tastebuds are attuned to thinking injustice tastes sweet. Yet Shariah produces many fruits and not everyone will taste them all since it is impossible to do since certain laws only apply to certain people in certain situations. Thus the problem with the kuffar is they desire the fruits of the trees that grew from seeds planted by Satan and as such fear the taste of trees from the seeds planted by God and his prophets. In reality nobody ever tastes all the fruits of a legal system so their judgements are based on theories and prejudices, which is fine if the decisions were made based on the seeds. Yet unfortunately their decisions are based on the fruits of which they haven't tasted from both trees so they always will make the wrong decision until they taste Shariah or learn more about it. Those who do learn more than 5 things about Shariah law say it's great. They find it fascinating how just and modernly applicable it is for being around for over 1400 years. Some people even go so far as to say that they want to live under Islamic Shariah and they aren't even Muslims. The well-informed non-Muslims actually support Shariah law, but typically since after becoming informed they become Muslim then their opinion, desire and reasoning gets discounted by most of the non-Muslims. One time a foreign business partner wrote me in regards to banking that, "*I am a Christian at heart but would never deal with a institution that does not practise Shariah law.*" Thus as a non-Muslim who can choose other than Shariah, he still freely chooses Shariah law regarding banking simply because to him, despite his religious beliefs, Shariah compliant institutions are better than all the rest. So this is where any Muslims who assimilate within unislamic environments are actually degrading Islam. There is nothing about Islam that Muslims can be ashamed of, rather it's the non-Muslims and the unislamic Muslims who feel shame when they genuinely compare their beliefs and ways with Islam. The very definition of assimilation is sinful for any and all Muslims to do, at any time, for all time. Assimilation is officially defined as: *"when a conquered people adopt the conqueror's culture before or at the same time they adopt the conqueror's religion."* Assimilation is literally a policy by which a nation forces or encourages a conquered nation to adopt it's customs, cultures and creeds. Hence to assimilate and/or "blend in" is to socially convert in practice to another religion. To assimilate is to apostate in practice but not necessarily in the heart, but most of the time if assimilation is voluntary then the heart has also assimilated as well; even if the person claims or thinks otherwise. That's why Muslim Fundamentalists actually want an ID card that says we're Muslim, as long as it doesn't have pictures of animate beings or unislamic nationalistic stuff. We have nothing to hide and it'd probably make non-Muslims feel safer if we wore ID cards, so that's a good thing, and it would help stimulate public religious dialogues. Under an Islamic government all Muslims would have Muslim ID cards anyways, so the government knows to collect Zakat from us and not Jizya. It's a badge of honor to be labeled Muslim and it would actually help Muslims because then nobody could hide their Islam and would be legally forced to share it with others even if it's just by publicly identifying themselves as Muslim. It would actually force Muslims in the West to publicly practice Islam, apostate or break the law. Although we should go even further and have those Muslim ID cards have tracking chips in them with the data available on a live stream app whenever a Muslim leaves their home to go out in public.(of course with safeguards so guys can't lookup girls to ambush/stalk and vice versa) This way any Muslims in need of help could be helped by nearby Muslims and we would come closer together as a community if we knew who and where we could find a Muslim to spend time with. Also if any disbeliever ever wanted to discuss or learn about Islam, with tracking chips on our Muslim ID cards they would easily be able to find a Muslim to learn from whenever they wanted to chat. The only trouble with government issued "Muslim ID" cards, especially in the West, is that they might give someone a "Muslim ID" who might not actually be a Muslim according to Islam and that would cause problems if a unislamic government of non-Muslims had authority to declare who was legally a Muslim and who isn't. Muslim Scholars would have to be in charge of setting up the system and criteria of issuing/revoking Muslim IDs. Muslim Scholars should also be the only ones labeling people as Muslim extremists too, for the same reasons. This raises an important point in that most people would think American politicians forcing Muslims to wear a special ID is bad and think that by denouncing or preventing such legislation they are helping Muslims. They'd likely assume that just because the policy comes from an enemy of Islam then Muslims must hate it, but that's not the case at all. Believe it or not some policies people think are anti-Islamic actually help Islam and Muslims while some seemingly pro-Islam legislation actually harms Muslims and Islam. So that's where it's frustrating in America when people think Muslims are being helped unfairly when it actually hurts us. Sometimes even ignorant Muslims advocate policies that hurt Muslims and Islam because they have a combo disease of ignorance with kafirphobia, and if they have influence then it triggers a spiritual plague. Case in point is if the anti-Muslim politicians advocating a national Muslim ID learned practicing Muslims actually want one, they'd probably stop advocating it saying how it's wrong to single Muslims out because everyone is equal regardless of religion. Whereas the Quran teaches that there's Muslims and then non-Muslims and they are not equal. That's why so many U.S. politicians oppose a Muslim ID, it's not because they like Muslims but because they hate us and don't want us to practice Islam or take pride in Islam. Whereas the Muslims who oppose such measures that publicly identify them as Muslims are simply ignorant afflicted with kafirphobia and not really practicing Islam. That's why they oppose such policies because they want to play on both sides of the fence, in reality they tend to belong to neither side and are hypocritical.

Today, as always, many Pharaoh's are persecuting Muslims and waging war against Islam. Although instead of Muslims following their faith as they did in Egypt under Moses pbuh, they are preaching Pharaoh's religion using his very own phrases as their mottos and platforms saying and even believing that its Islam. Hence its worse than it was for the believers living under Moses pbuh because under Moses pbuh there was only the true version of Islam being preached or practiced. Today many types of Kufr, Shirk and Bida are called Islamic so its a theological and intellectual persecution being waged unlike it has ever been waged before. Most of the non-Muslims likely won't call any further wars against Islam or Muslims a crusade ever again. Whether it's for Nationalism, Democracy, Freedom, Equality, Liberty, Capitalism, Globalism, Interfaith Tolerance, is irrelevent. Kafirs will probably one day even have the gall to call their war against practicing Islamic Muslims a "Jihad" and get Muslims to kill Muslims because of them practicing Islam correctly. This has been the American/Christian policy for centuries since Abraham Lincoln, a supporter of proto-Israel said, *"When the conduct of men is designed to be influenced, persuasion, kind unassuming persuasion, should ever be adopted. It is an old and true maxim that 'a drop of honey catches more flies than a gallon of gall.' So with men. If you would win a man to your cause, first convince him that you are his sincere friend. Therein is a drop of honey that catches his heart, which, say what he will, is the great highroad to his reason, and which, once gained, you will find but little trouble in convincing him of the justice of your cause,"* That's the history of the *"catch more flies with honey than with vinegar(gall)"* line. Many think it is about getting friends and it is, but to do what with them? Smarter people realize one "catches flies" typically to kill them, but those who lead with the interfaith "let's be friends" doctrine do so with the intention of having those "flies" kill the rest of their species and that's what Muslims are financially doing by paying taxes in the non-Muslim dar al-harb West. Next they get Muslims to vote to kill Muslims via elections and emotionally connect to the enemies of Muslims until eventually Muslims will kill Muslims on behalf of non-Muslims for the sake of religions other than Islam. Since a vote is an allegiance to a politician elections are Lincoln's conversion method put into practice. "Muslims" can say all they want about *"I vote but I don't believe in democracy."* yet even if that were true the elections are the honey which the preachers of democracy use to catch people and convert them to democracy. By voting in elections you are eating the democratic honey and they caught ya, and eventually all voters believe in democracy; to vote is nearly proof of belief(in democracy/kufr). Yet as Lincoln taught "after they're caught they can be convinced to agree with your cause" and that's what happens with the voters even before they vote. People vote because they agree X policy by X politician is better, so in reality they already believe in the cause and love the politician. Voting just seals their allegiance but they fool themselves into thinking they haven't become a slave of the politician. The flaw behind man-made laws is that the politicians have no authority to invent laws regarding most matters, since God has already given us a perfected law. Thus for you to believe X politician's policy is better than Y politician's is to believe that X's policy is more valid when in reality both are invalid and such beliefs about some man-made laws being more valid than other man-made laws indicates disbelief in God's laws. Voting is loyalty, a Muslim's loyalty is to the Creator and the believers. Having loyalty to God means not voting for disbelief or disbelievers. One votes for God's laws by not voting in democratic elections. Voting is an act of worship and only God can dictate if we vote as God tells us how/when to worship. And the Jews asked God if they could vote instead of have Saul rule them and God said "*No you can't vote for your leaders or laws.*" Voting is an act of friendship and Muslims never ever befriend non-Muslims, especially in such an intimate type of friendship as voting entails because voting is a friendship unlike any other. If non-Muslims want to be friends with Muslims then become Muslim and practice Islam with sincerity without hypocrisy. When people don't share the same faith there is no friendship. Those who are friends with the angels aren't friends with devils or the friends of the devils. If you want to be a friend of God then you cannot be friends with one who worships a false god. You select your friends only based on who God's friends are. Enemies should be determined based on who God's enemies are, not based on how they treat you or what they say to you. If you are a slave of God, then God picks your friends and your enemies. The super strict sincere Islamic believing friend of God is never left with "only God" as their friend either even if no humans are, because angels are the friends of the friends of God, as are the sinless Muslim plants and Muslim animals. Likewise even if they are in the most sinful environment of all without any good human companions or living role models to interact with, the friend of God is never left without positive influences. Because they spend time at their best friend's house with angels. Sinners also spend time in the masjid, to get away from devils.

     Because of the present situation and perpetual reality I'm not going to sugarcoat Islam for you. It's hypocrites who remove spices and ingredients changing the recipe of Islam to make it taste less salty or add sugar, artificial flavoring and food coloring thinking that makes the taste of Islam better. It's a great struggle to practice Islam in America or the West, or on earth for that matter and the modern human "Muslims" don't always help and sometimes they make it harder to practice Islam; but because of all this the great hardships mean greater reward. It's never been easy to be a practicing believer, and personally I don't find it easy to be one in America. If others think it is then I guess they are better than me. The vast majority of Muslims who weren't born in the West don't have a valid Islamic reason for living in the West and shouldn't be. They may have a legitimate Islamic reason to not live in their home countries, but that's different than having a valid Islamic reason to live in the West. People who do and say it's easy really don't know what they are talking about, it's not. Strategically Muslims must prioritize on where Dawah is needed most and focus there. If we try to hit every target all at once then we will miss them all. Whenever considering circumstances and problems the first thing to take into account is location. If you aren't in the right spot to solve the problems you won't solve the problems and if you are in the wrong spot then you will cause extra problems, even if you have and try to implement the correct solutions. So your location itself is either part of the problem or part of the solution. To me it seems hypocritical for Muslims to preach Islam in disbelieving lands while Muslims are being murdered, oppressed and impoverished in Muslim lands. I don't think any prophet if they were on earth today would abandon the believers getting killed throughout the world or wallowing in ignorance, in order to preach to the disbelievers in the West. So #1 Muslims are not physically in the right location to solve the problems of the Muslim world. Many Muslims in the west just plan to stay in the west and pay taxes until the middle eastern Muslims fix their problems all by themselves. However Muslim masses are not designed to live in the jungle of Satan. Non-Muslim governments just want Muslims to live in their lands to weaken the Muslim countries, disunite and isolate Muslims, pay taxes to them and because they fear Allah will destroy them for their crimes if there are no Muslims in their lands just as Sodom wasn't destroyed until Lot pbuh left. While just as Pharoah didn't want the Muslims to take Egyptian gold with them when they left, modern western governments don't want Muslims to leave with anything either; even with our religion. So Muslims living in the non-Muslim lands is a problem itself and them staying their acting as they have been is probably not going to solve any problems but cause more and larger problems for Muslims in general and each one individually. Non-Muslim governments use Muslim residents as an excuse to say because they have "Muslims" in their country then it's impossible for them to be at war against Islam or Muslims, just as a racist(colorist) says they can't possibly be racist(colorist) because they are "friends" or "neighbors" with a person of another skin color. Yet it's obvious that across the world governments are ideologically at war with Islam and physically at war with practicing Muslims. Obviously the non-Muslim governments would never let Muslims know if they were fighting against genuine good Muslims at any time, in any place, because then every Muslim would be obligated to leave and side with the Muslims against the Western governments and stop paying taxes. The non-Muslim governments will never ever tell Muslims that it's sinful for those Muslims to live in their lands and it puts them at spiritual risk both in this life and the next.

The situation today was unimaginable to classical Muslim scholars where you would have Muslims in the U.S. praying in a masjid while at the same time the U.S. government is killing Muslims in multiple countries as well as imprisoning them and torturing them in places like Guantanomo bay wherein to date of the 780 people held prisoner during America's war on terror 732 have been released without ever even having a trial or charges brought against them. Classical Muslim Scholars couldn't conceive of a country who would do such things and allow Muslims to live there in safety, nor could they conceive of Muslims who would live in such a place voluntarily, let alone pay taxes that support the military that kills Muslims. It's preposterous! Muslims paying taxes to people harming Muslims is hypocritical at the least and potentially disbelief. Therefore Muslim scholars throughout the world and in America itself have said that the majority of the Muslims in America should leave because few have a legitimate reason to be there and the taxes paid go to kill innocents, but the government locks those scholars up on false charges and people condemn them as anti-American extremists. Thus few Imams in America will preach this publicly, Allah knows best why.

While extremists use their silence to say they're hypocrites, puppets or disbelievers; which might not be inaccurate to say regarding some of them. By Muslims in America being cautious of offending the government and/or disbelievers it only supports violent extremists and makes them seem correct. Think about it, if you know paying taxes to kill innocent people is wrong and you only learn of one group denouncing it then your brain will logically think that one group must be the only one that's good and right. If America really wants safety from violent Muslim extremists they have to stop committing extreme acts of war against Islam and Muslims. Muslims are one nation, if you harm one of us, we all have a problem with it; the same policy applies to innocents. Or rather it's unwise for me to say "one nation" because the word nation as understood today does not convey the meaning I intend when I say "one nation". A better example given is that given by Muhammad pbuh himself as related in the authentic collection of hadith known as Sahih Muslim, which in english Muhammad pbuh taught what means: *"The example of the believers in their mutual love, their mutual mercy, their mutual kindness is that of one body. If one limb complains the whole body cries out for it in sleeplessness and fever."* Note that the example of the Muslims is "one body", Muhammad pbuh didn't say we were all one family or one tribe but one body. This is significant because members of a family or tribe can break apart, stop loving each other, abandon each other, or even become enemies and fight each other. In short family and tribe members have choices in how they deal with their fellow members. Although *"one body"* doesn't have a choice. If a single tiny part of the body gets hurt or attacked then the whole body feels the pain and impetus to take defensive action. "One body" can never ignore a wound to any body part no matter where or what it is, even if it tried. When 1 body part is attacked then 100% of the body reacts as if 100% of the body had been attacked because the body is the part and the parts are the body. There is no such thing as attacking part of a body without becoming an enemy of the entire body. Thus any nation who wages war on a single Muslim wages war on us all and it doesn't matter who or where we or they are. The concept of being at war with Muslims in X country but not in other countries does not exist. The connections Muslims have are stronger than family. We love each other more than we love ourselves, even if we never met.

So why is it that Muslims are scattered and living amongst disbelievers letting the Muslims be slaughtered paying taxes to their kafir killers? The prophet Muhammad pbuh foretold that a time would come when Muslims would be numerous and yet butchered by all others. He explained the reason was because Muslims will fear death and love this worldly life. Whereas that's the main reason most Muslim migrants give for living amongst disbelievers, because they fear death in their homeland or want material benefits like money or "education" or "freedom". Yet such fears/desires determining one's geographical location contradicts core Islamic values. A Muslim loves death and can't wait for it because it means getting to meet Allah and being rewarded. A Muslim hates this worldly life because it distracts them from worshipping Allah and may lead them to sin. A Muslim would rather die young and poor as a Muslim than grow old and rich living in the land of the kuffar. This is because when you are on the road to paradise, it doesn't matter how good life is, you would rather be in paradise. Even if Muslims are oppressed by "Muslim rulers" Muhammad pbuh taught that if anyone comes to a Muslim to harm or rob them and they fight back and die in the process they'd be a martyr. So Muslims who "flee oppression" from Muslim majority lands are practically running away from paradise to come to the West. Prophet Muhammad pbuh also told us that Muslims won't remain oppressed forever and that Islam will rule this entire planet before the end of time. Whether an unislamic ruler will repent and reform, as some of the Mongol rulers did, or a Muslim country will repair it's foundation, or a state of disbelievers will be guided to Islam first, I do not know. Although it is important to remember that Muslims only started living amongst disbelievers on a largescale after a titular "Khilafah" was abdicated in 1924 CE, by Mustafa Kamal Ataturk, but theologically that Khilafah ceased in 1839 CE when secularization began and the Shariah was supplanted. Yet even before that despite there being nominal Khilafah's they weren't quite ruled by Khalifahs but Kings. The position of Khalifh is not a hereditary position, so those leaders of the Khilafah's who came to power through their lineage were technically Kings from a Shariah aspect and not Khalifhs even though history books may claim otherwise. So that is also something to consider in that the past Khilafah's were not all ruled by Khalifhs and thus they had problems because of such fundamental mistakes in how leadership was bestowed. An Islamic Khilafah is not dynastic. Thus when discussing a Khilafah Muslims should not be looking at the Ottomon Khilafah as an example because they had kings, not Khalifhs, instead the Khilafahs which had Khalifhs should be the blueprint. When a Khilafah exists Muslims live together. If disbelievers want us out of their countries then they actually want a Khilafah based on the Islam of Muhammad pbuh. And perhaps the greatest misconception among Muslims regarding a Khilafah is that it must encompass 100% of Muslim territory. That's not the case at all and there are examples of the Abbasid Khalifah existing in the middle east while the Ummayad Khilafah existed in Spain or the Ottomon Khalifah existing at the same time as the Africa Sokoto Khalifah. A Khalifah is just a state it doesn't have to be the only state of Muslims even though the original Khilafah was. Anyways its because Muslims aren't living together as a nation of brothers and sisters practicing Islam correctly that we have become disunited. If Muslims do suffer/risk life in the lands of non-Muslim majorities then they should congregate together and make "*Muslim Towns*". If Muslims in the West united and made cities and regions where the majority were Islamic Muslims they could create near Islamic societies within unislamic countries. Without using force, just by having a city with a majority of Islamic Muslims it would provide a glimpse of what Islamic society is. For instance there wouldn't be drugs, prostitution, crime, casinos or alcohol in Muslim Towns because there wouldn't be a market for such things and it would be uneconomical. Peacefully an Islamic society without legal authority could demonstrate and prove to non-Muslims in their own country that an Islamic State is the only good type of State there is, because the Islamic system comes from God and really is the only true religion. Since Muslim majority Islamic cities in the West would be the best and most moral, it would inspire Western people to study Islam to see why such cities are superior to all the rest. This is the manner in which Muslims should live in non-Muslim majority countries if they do so. However non-Muslims fear this and don't want Muslims in their country making Muslim majority Islamic communities and if Muslims did this they might get exterminated as a result. Similar to how Americans destroyed Black Wall Street in Tulsa, Oklahoma on June 1st, 1921

CE. "Black Wall Street" was an affluent black community and racist whites bombarded it killing thousands of black Americans and destroying 600 black businesses, 21 churches, 21 restaurants, 30 grocery stores, 2 movie theatres, a hospital, a bank, a post office, libraries, schools, law offices and a bus system. Black citizens proved to Americans they weren't inferior and were equal to and actually better than whites at doing certain things, and America decided to blow up "Negrotown" lest such ideas of black equality spread; none of the whites who lived there were harmed while they watched the massacre of the blacks. If that's what America did to "Negrotown", or Black Wall Street, proving racism was nonsense, what do you think Americans would do to Muslim Towns proving Islam is true and superior? Would America follow Trump's plan, aka the "Winslow Plan", aka the Reagan plan, aka the Andrew Jackson plan, aka the Thomas Jefferson plan, aka the Christopher Columbus plan, aka the Pope Urban II plan, aka the Heraclius plan, aka Pharaoh's plan, aka the antichrist's plan? Most certainly they will, eventually, unless they decided to embrace Islam. But we must be realistic. Another reason this "Muslim Town" plan is impractical is because many Muslims living within non-Muslim lands are infected with kafirphobia have fallen into disbelief due to falling in love with disbelievers and prefer living amongst disbelievers instead of Muslims. Most Western Muslims don't want Muslim Towns because that would mean they'd have to act more like Muslims and wouldn't be able to use their environment as an excuse to sin or act unislamically. Which is why the majority of Muslim scholars say most Muslims should leave the non-Muslim lands, because it's easier and quicker to make Islamic communities in Muslim majority lands, where such lands will likely have legal authority and ability to implement Islamic Shariah before the lands where disbelievers are the majority do. Also to protect oneself from kafirphobia leading one into kufr without one even realizing it. Muslim majority lands have a cracked foundation that needs to be repaired, while non-Muslim majority lands have institutions which need to be demolished before an Islamic foundation can be laid and built upon. Also logistically the language of arabic plays a role. For example if we say there is no Islamic country in the world today, as western Muslims always say because if there were they know they have no excuse to stay in the West, then which place is most likely to become an Islamic country populated by Muslims? A non-Muslim non-Arabic nation or a Muslim majority Arabic speaking nation? Since arabic greatly helps one to understand Islam and some types of islamic knowledge require one to know arabic, then on an individual level to be the best possible Muslim arabic would be needed to reach one's full potential. Now this doesn't mean a non-arabic speaking Muslim is automatically on a lower level, because in this day and age many Muslims who don't know arabic are better than those who do. However in principle a Muslim who knows arabic has higher potential than one who doesn't. Therefore since most of the people in non-Muslim countries don't know arabic they inherently have less potential as a nation if being great Muslims is the goal. This is because for non-arabic nations the arabic language means there is a cap on just how Muslim or islamic the people and nation can become. Whereas countries with arabic don't have that linguistic limitation and have a higher potential without having to spend the time and effort in learning a language. Thus logistically to create an Islamic Muslim nation a place where they know arabic has greater potential over places where the people don't. Of course other factors play a role, but at the end of the day it is a simple fact that it's far likelier that an Islamic nation will arise from a land which knows arabic than from a land which doesn't. So Muslim lands where arabic is known should be given priorities for those seeking to establish an islamic political system. Realistically in the long term an arabic speaking Muslimish population is more likely to establish Islamic laws and government sooner than a non-Muslim non-arabic speaking population. There are many other reasons, Quran verses and sahih hadith about the importance of Hijrah but this is more of a military history book and once again it's a thing in which different rulings apply to different people in different places at different times. I'm not qualified to write in depth of the important and delicate subject of Hijrah so I won't. Yet all the prophets such as Adam, Noah, Hud, Salih, Abraham, Ishmael, Lot, Shuaib, Moses, Aaron, Ezra, Elijah, John, Jesus and Muhammad pbut made hijrah. Generally the principle is that if a Muslim feels or thinks their life, family, ability to practice Islam, or their property are endangered or restricted in a certain place, it is their personal obligation to either migrate to a place where these will be protected; for example, from a hostile redneck country town to a large city with a major Muslim population, or if there is no such place in the land where these will be protected, they should migrate to a Dar al-Islam or the land of the Muslims.

In the past for thousands of years Muslims were forbidden to remain in countries where Islamic Shariah had no legal authority, except when they were able to freely practice their religion and observe it without impediment without any fear at all that their presence or activities there could damage them in any way. When this is not the case, they were/are obligated to migrate to a better place where the authority of Islam is of some legal account; the more the better. Scholars were unanimous that if they refused to migrate from dar al-kufr to dar al-islam while able, then they would have no further way to claim to be Muslims. Afterall in Sahih Muslim hadith 4294 it is reported on the authority of Sulayman bin Buraydah that his father said, "*Yaazid Bin Hussaib Al-Aslami reported that whenever the Messenger Muhammad sent an expedition he would elect an Ameer (and then would advise them), 'If you appoint someone for an army or an expedition first fear Allah and treat all the Muslims who are with him well, raid and fight in the name of Allah, those who disbelieve in Allah. Do not take the booty and do not be traitors; do not mutilate nor torture. Do not kill children. If you see your enemy from the disbelievers, invite them to one of (the following) three and if they accept your offer do not fight them further: Invite them to Islam and if they accept ask them to relocate from Dar al-Kufr to Dar al-Islam, inform them that if they do so they will take similar to what the Muhajireen took. If they move to Dar ul-Muhajireen they will be eligible for this, otherwise they will be like the Muslim Bedouins living outside of Dar al-Islam and will get nothing from the Fai or the booty. (The final offer) if they reject to become Muslims is to ask them to pay Jizya. If they respond and pay, accept it from them and do not fight them. Otherwise have full reliance in Allah and fight them.'"*

Muhammad pbuh is also reported to have said to his companions in authentic hadiths what means: "*I am not responsible for any Muslim who stays among polytheists.*" They asked: '*Why, Messenger of Allah?*' Muhammad pbuh said: '*Their fires should not be visible to one another.*', and he said, "*Who joins the polytheists and lives with them then he is like them*" and he said: "*Migration will not end until repentance ends, and repentance will not end until the sun rises in the west*(which will happen near the end of time)." The key to understanding this in context is that it was in reference to dar al-harb (a land at war with

Muslims) and there are special rare exceptions that can still allow a Muslim to live in dar al harb and still be a Muslim as well as dar al-kufr. As proven by Umair bin Wahb getting permission to migrate to Mecca to do hateful dawah despite it being dar al-harb, so it's not automatically disbelief to be in dar al-harb there are variables. Although the bit about "joining" the kufar is forbidden under all circumstances, in all places even dar al-islam. A Muslim can live with or amongst non-Muslims under certain circumstances if their relationships fulfill a certain Islamic criteria, which I'll mention later, but Muslims can never "join them" emotionally, ideologically, politically, militarily, or in their sinful activities. This is because Muhammad pbuh expressly said in dozens of authentic letters which he wrote to new Muslims when they became Muslim that they must "*sever ties with the polytheists*" or they aren't Muslims. Many Muslims don't read the authentic letters Muhammad pbuh dictated so they are uninformed that Muhammad pbuh equated "severing ties with the polytheists" to be just as important as praying 5 times a day or paying zakat. But the Quran says it's forbidden to "sever ties with kin" and new Muslims obviously had non-Muslim relatives so what does

Muhammad pbuh mean when he says "sever ties with polytheists (non-Muslims)"? It means you sever the ties of religion, love, friendship, nationalism, tribalism, sectarianism, nepotism, racism, and other aspects of a co-religionist relationship. Those who don't sever these ties of love, affection, mentalities with non-Muslims and live amongst non-Muslims, even if they are living in dar al-islam with non-Muslim neighbors, have this hadith apply to them. From personal experience knowing some people who claim to be Muslims and love non-Muslims or don't hate them, I can attest they are "just like them" and personally I have nothing to do with them unless we are praying together or they seek my assistance in matters of religion, because in such matters the Quran states its obligatory for a Muslim to aid such "Muslims" in matters of religion despite them failing to sever certain ties regarding their relationships with the kuffar. The problem is that some ignorant extremists automatically equate living with joining and forget the hadith says "joins...and lives" which is a multi part criteria. Staying amongst kuffar, while it can and does apply to geographical location also more importantly refers to mentality, ideology and emotionality. If one physically migrates but their heart still stays with the kuffar then that's sinful. Likewise if one's opinion is an opinion among the non-Muslims instead of an opinion among the Muslims (ie. they preach democracy, equality, freedom, interfaith pluralism instead of Islam) then this is forbidden as well. A Muslim practicing Islam has to spiritually, emotionally and mentally migrate away from the kuffar so that spiritually, emotionally and mentally they are in dar al-islam and not dar al-kufar even if geographically they are in dar al-kufr or dar al-harb. As it's said *"home is where the heart is"*, if your heart is with the non-Muslims Kufr doctrines then you aren't a Muslim but if it's with the Muslims and Islam then it's where it's supposed to be and soon the body should follow, and if it doesn't in this life then it will in the next. This is why oftentimes at a generic get-together with my family, frequently a relative will tell me "It's like you're here physically but you're not here at the same time." This is because while physically I can be with them at some events in the same location, mentally, emotionally and spiritually I'm far from them. Or as they'd say, "It's like you're living on another planet." Yet don't misunderstand my explanation to be a distortion of the standard interpretation, in general, the hadith is mentioning physical locations and physical emigration but I'm simply adding the element of spiritual, mental and emotional "joining" and "staying" so Godwilling a fuller in depth understanding supplements the apparent meaning. The hadith is about physically moving away from non-Muslims, but that's not all that the hadith is about and if someone just physically migrates they may still have the hadith apply to them if the physical emigration is the only one which they made. Also it is important to stress staying and joining is different than growing up and living while hoping to emigrate. Joining geographically refers to immigration and staying means to refuse to emigrate. Simply being there already is different and in all cases ability and intentions must be taken into account. Those who want to emigrate but truly cannot find a way to do so have a legitimate excuse with Allah and would only be sinful if they don't practice Islam as it has to be practiced when Muslims are living amongst non-Muslims or in unislamic nations. And that last bit is something which many Muslims forget is necessary for them to be a Muslim without emigrating. Being a Muslim is a lot more than mere physical location. You have to be on the road to paradise no matter what land you are in, and being on the road to paradise requires deeds as well as beliefs. Don't think having a valid excuse to not do 1% of Islam gives one an excuse to neglect 99%, or that doing 99% gives one an excuse to neglect doing 1%. Allah knows best if what I'm saying is correct or makes sense but I think to simplify and limit the meaning of Muhammad pbuh in this hadith on emigration to just the physical location is a mistake, he did mean it physically but I think he meant more as well. Unfortunately some simplify the hadith to only physicality or simplify the teaching itself and restrict it to a certain time period, both of which are wrong. Just because a Dar Al-Kufr may be safe for Muslims to live in, does not mean it is permissible for them to live there nor does it mean that land cannot have war declared against it by Muslims. Every country is different and has a different ruling as does every person. Although it's important to note that the scholar Ibn Hazm stated that: *"Whoever joins the 'land of war and disbelief',(Dar Al-Harb) of his own freewill and in defiance of whoever amongst the Muslims calls him to his side, is by virtue of this act an apostate, by all the laws of apostasy, in Islam. But whoever flees to the 'land of war' for fear of oppression, who neither opposes the Muslims in anything nor bears any malice towards them, and who was not able to find any refuge among the Muslims, is free of any guilt since he was compelled to leave."* Basically if Muslims in a Muslim or Islamic country ask you to live with them and you say no, then you are a disbeliever if you voluntarily choose to live in Dar Al-Harb. Later on you could repent and change your mind and then not have the opportunity and be a Muslim, but to refuse to emigrate from dar al-harb when invited to do so is an act of major disbelief. But if there are no Muslims who invite you to live in their country, and you have no opportunity to live in a Muslim land or Dar Al-Islam then you are still a Muslim "as long as you don't oppose the Muslims in anything or bear malice towards them". Also that last caveat is widely interpreted, some say that paying taxes to governments who kill Muslims counts as opposition and malice, thus they say if you pay taxes to an enemy of Islam or a nation of Dar Al-Harb then that's disbelief, but there is a difference of opinion over the issue of taxation and the types of taxation and the logistics of the modern era of global taxation when so many governments kill Muslims with taxpayer dollars. So a Muslim going to live in a land at war with Muslims can have different rulings depending on the individual, which could make him a disbeliever or not. There are also different rulings for whether one was a native non-Muslim born in Dar Al-Harb versus a Muslim born elsewhere who moved to Dar Al-Harb. Those who changed their religion to Islam have different rulings apply to them than those who have always been Muslims. However remember every government in the world is not killing Muslims with taxpayer dollars, and not every citizen or resident in countries who do kill Muslims has to pay taxes for the army. So one cannot just use the excuse that because so many countries kill Muslims or innocents then that must mean it's okay for Muslims to pay taxes to anybody no matter where they live, that ruling cannot be derived. Likewise one cannot say as the extremists do that paying any and all types of taxes is tantamount to disbelief. That's the anarchist doctrine, not the Islamic doctrine. However one who takes the Muslims as enemies, offering help and service to disbelievers who are at war with Islam/Muslims, is a disbeliever by all accounts. Meaning Muslims cannot join the American military and fight Muslims, nor the Israeli military and fight Muslims or else they would be disbelievers in Islam. That might sound extreme, but it's actually common sense, it'd be like someone who claimed to follow

David pbuh moving to live with Goliath and joining Goliath's army while claiming they believe in and practice the same religion as David pbuh. Anyone would understand such a person claiming to be a member of David's faith would not be. Yet if say a believer left persecution in China to live in Goliath's country and had more safety there than in China, then that would be different than the one who left David pbuh in Jerusalem to live under Goliath and fight with him, as long as the Chinese believer didn't fight with Goliath against Muslims. However those who emigrate to non-Muslim lands in search of wealth or prosperity to live under kafir protection, while they were able to go to live amongst the Muslims in the Muslim land, but still do not withdraw themselves from the disbelievers; such people are not far from the fold of disbelief. Only a scholar could say whether they were Muslim or not based on individual cases and circumstances. This is because if the option to live under David pbuh amongst believers were available and the Chinese believer chose to live under Goliath and rejected the opportunity to live under David pbuh something would be very wrong with that individual, even if they didn't fight with Goliath against David pbuh. If he just wanted to live under

Goliath because Goliath's state was richer or had better technology this would not be a legitimate excuse. To make it easier to understand, the Muslim scholar Hamad Ibn Ateeq, divided Muslims in non- Islamic countries into three groups. So if you are curious to know of the 3 types of "Muslims" living in Dar Al-Harb (country where non-Muslim unislamic government is at war with Muslims anywhere on the planet) these are they:

"**The first group:** *stays amongst the disbelievers by choice and inclination, they praise and commend them, and happily disassociate themselves from the Muslims. They help the disbelievers in their struggle against the Muslims in anyway they can, physically, morally, and financially. Such people are disbelievers, their position is actively and deliberately opposed to religion.*

So this first type of "Muslims" living in the Western nations that are at war with Muslims are really not Muslims if they are actively fighting in the army and supporting their war against Islam and Muslims in others ways. Now the tricky thing is "What does 'support' entail?" Extremists and the likes say that taxes equals support and so they make takfir of western taxpayers. Even if somehow it wasn't sinful for Muslims to pay taxes for anti-islamic militaries, fundamentally it's dumb and not okay. It's just natural to know it's wrong. However there are also other ways of waging war against Muslims which some can fall into as well, such as spreading various anti-islamic or anti-Muslim media if say a Muslim worked in a non-Muslim media outlet delivering newspapers that advocated war against Muslims or slander against Islam. Aiding enemy propaganda is treason in most nations, as it is in Islam, whereas many Muslims can fall into this trap, sometimes even doing so thinking they are helping Islam or Muslims but due to ignorance they are waging war against Islam by lying about what it teaches. An example of this could be promoting democracy, interfaith events/doctrines or waving the Israeli or U.S. flag to show support for a country of dar al-harb or dar al-kufr. Most disbelievers consider this to be patriotism/assimilation and it's exactly how most disbelievers want Muslims to be like. An American priest wrote on refugees coming to America saying *"the problem in Syria is that poverty causes terrorism"*, then sentences later the same priest wrote he wants Muslims from Syria to come to America because *"they are highly skilled laborers who work hard and pay taxes which helps our country prosper"*. Thus even according to the priest's false diagnosis of the problem of terrorism allegedly caused by poverty, the priest's advice to Muslims helps to contribute to the very problems he says exist in the Muslim world, and his "solution" also exposes Muslims to unislamic environments/pressure while they pay taxes to fund the armies that kill Muslims in the middle east. Why would American Christian priests want Muslims to come to America? The answer to that is in the following statement from American census data: "*The number of Muslims in North America is in dispute: estimates range from under 3 million to over 6 million. The main cause of the disagreement appears to be over how many Muslim immigrants have converted to Christianity since they arrived in the US.*" That's what the American statisticians say, "*We don't know how many Muslims there actually are over here because about 50% of Muslims who immigrate to America end up becoming Christians, or their kids or grandkids do.*" Muslims however are oblivious to this because they don't realize the long-term trend and tend to be the 1st or 2nd generation themselves so they have no accurate long-term Muslim-made statistics because the earlier American Muslim immigrants do not have modern Muslim descendants in America today. Instead Muslims frequently use short-term data with over-optimistic projections for the future which have little basis in reality. The Christians can clearly see the effect of Muslim immigrants coming to the West and see how most eventually convert after enough consistent anti-islamic social, political and economic pressure is applied. As much as Muslims may hate to hear it, their population surge in the non-Muslim lands is primarily due to reproduction and immigration not conversions as they wish. That's not to say non-Muslims aren't becoming Muslims but the problem is the immigrant Muslims and their kids convert to Americanism or Christianity, then the revert's descendants soon do the same if they remain. Hence the Muslims always see increasing numbers as if it's a trend not realizing that the immigration and reproduction numbers have increased more than the % of the Muslim population has. So Muslims should have higher totals than the record shows, because of increased immigration and birthrates but because many lose their faith here it's the non-Muslims who become Muslims that are pulling the extra statistical weight making up for the losses to give the impression of growth when it's actually negative growth. More are leaving Islam in the West than are joining but the statistics get manipulated because Muslim immigrants keep flooding in at increased rates. It's like there is a hole in a bottle while you are trying to fill it which is getting bigger over time but because you turn the faucet, so more water enters the bottle faster, it appears as though the bottle is filling up to the naked eye; yet in reality the bottle is leaking and eventually it will be empty once the external influx ceases. Meaning once the immigration stops increasing, the Muslim populations in non-Muslim countries will most likely drop. I hope I'm wrong but that's the conclusion I've come to. This doesn't determine whether Islam is true or false, because the same can be sad about Christians or Americanists in Muslim lands their populations end up changing their religion to Islam. It's just that statistically Muslims who live in non-Muslim lands end up disbelieving in Islam more often than not. Then when there is consistent genuine growth, not based on immigration or reproduction but non-Muslim masses accepting Islam, then non-Muslim lands start getting more religious and go to war and sometimes the Muslims are explicitly killed off such as in Spain, Bosnia or Croatia or something like WWI or WWII happens where so many people die non-Muslim history "forgets" to record the Muslim casulties and then the game starts again until either the Muslims wage Jihad to conquer the non-Muslim lands or the non-Muslims conquer the Muslim lands by force or guile. So these disbelievers know exactly what they are doing by bombing Muslims into moving to them, directly causing the conditions for Muslim immigration, so they pay taxes that help them bomb more so more Muslims move in; all the while those Muslims get brainwashed while living amongst disbelievers until they become disbelievers openly or their descendants do. The problem stopping the global decrease in the Muslim population is the high rate of reproduction in the Muslim lands, but that's not going to last forever; especially the way things are looking today. If not for the non-Muslims using contraception and abortion the trends would likely be reversed. I've read material written by alleged apostates from Islam where they openly say the way to eliminate, or as they say "reform Islam", is to trick the Muslims into disbelieving/discarding 5 points of their 1400+ year old faith. 1. The Quran's infallibility and Muhammad's status of absolute authority regarding religious matters, they say the hadith must be discredited and rejected before the Quran is. Then the Quran must be rejected as a man-made book not from God as it claims. 2. The investment in life after death being more important than investing in this worldly life before death. 3. Shariah as being the best and only legal system allowed by God and the idea that it is ordained by God or for the modern age. 4. The empowering of individuals to encourage good and forbid evil, by both tongue and hand. 5. The imperative to wage Jihad. Those are the 5 points alleged apostates from Islam say will destroy the Muslims if they adopt all or any of them. I say alleged apostate because the individual who proposed these 5 points to "reform Islam" claims they were raised as a Muslim who apostated. However they never fasted in Ramadan, and they didn't start praying until they were 16 when they started practicing Shiism. So Islamically speaking they were not a Muslim, then became a Shiite then apostated from Shiism and today go around claiming they are a Muslim apostate denouncing Islam telling people how to destroy it; or as they say "reform" or "rennovate" it. They explicitly use these terms because they know if they say destroy then it will never work as their plan involves getting Muslims to destroy it. The 5 points are what they list in their book written for disbelievers to read in order to hate/reject Islam and join the "reformation efforts". Later in the same book they explain how to get Muslims to adopt and practice the 5 points so as to destroy Islam without them even knowing it. When "Muslim reformers" are preaching the 5 points to destroy Islam, or non-Muslims pressure Muslims to adopt the 5 points, they are never to tell the 5 points explicitly for what they are but use the following points which are identical in meaning but camoflauged via language. The enemies of Islam say that to get Muslims to destroy Islam Muslims should: 1. Ensure that Muhammad pbuh and the Quran are open to interpretation and criticism. 2. Give priority to this life, *along with* the next one. Basically you have to focus on the here and now more than the afterlife, live in the real world in the present and work for it. 3. *Reconcile* Shariah with unislamic laws and dispel the notion that Shariah is superior to every other type of law. Muslims must learn to *adapt* Shariah with unislamic laws *and compromise* on things. Shariah must become flexible and adapt to the times as well as non-Muslims' political systems. 4. End the practice of "commanding right and forbidding wrong" on the individual level. Make it a institutional responsibility. Also stress that people have the freedom to believe and do whatever they want and nobody has a right to judge them or treat them differently or negatively based on their beliefs, speech or actions. Freedom and Equality means you have to keep your opinions about right/wrong to yourself, respect people's privacy and avoid judging them according to Islamic values but view and treat everybody as equals. Love the sinners, don't judge them or criticize them, or try to get people to change. Muslims have to learn to tolerate different religious beliefs and cannot just dismiss them as invalid because they are unislamic. They teach that interfaith is the key to destroying the Islamic faith. This is because Christians and Jews have learned they cannot effectively coerce someone to convert if they haven't cooperated with them beforehand becoming emotionally and socially dependent or intertwined. Christians/Jews get you to love Christians/Jews first before Christianity/Judaism because nobody can ever voluntarily love or adopt their faiths without having love for Christians/Jews first. Thus hate for non-Muslim people is the preventative factor between Muslims converting to other faiths. Therefore the enemies of Islam preach that "love all, hate none" doctrine that I hate so much. 5. Abandon the call to Jihad. First stress Jihad is only defensive. Then teach that Jihad as only a spiritual struggle, violence is never justified and offensive Jihad is unislamic/sinful. Lastly teach that Jihad was historically useful but in the modern age of freedom and democracy it is extreme, obsolete and incompatible with civilized morality. Essentially the final step is to persuade Muslims that the prophets would never have fought anybody if they could have voted in elections. Now I paraphrased the points a little but in essence those are the points proffered by the enemies of Islam to get Muslims to destroy Islam. Whereas if you go to America or other countries, this is exactly the stuff disbelievers pressure Muslims to believe, practice and preach. It's also exactly what the misguided sects and innovators teach Muslims to believe in and practice in this modern day and age. You have the enemies of Islam preaching one message to "reform(destroy) Islam" and then some people come to a masjid and teach the same exact message but say they are Muslims and/or Islamic. Then Muslims hear that anti-Islamic message and go around telling everybody that's what Islam teaches and they actually think by doing so they are teaching Islam to people just as Muhammad pbuh taught it. So when a rule about Muslims not waging war against Islam if they live in non-Muslim countries exists, one must consider all the different elements and aspects of a war; including the political, economic, social, moral, verbal and ideological aspects. Not every warrior gets their hands bloody or physically fights. Some "Muslims" in dar al-kufr could be ideologically or methodologically at war with Islam. While being "financially at war with Islam" is something I won't define. Yet if you consider the enemies of Islam and their 5 points to be a war strategy then some Muslims in the West who preach such stuff could Islamically speaking be considered spiritual enemies of Islam. The extremists say they should be killed for that. I don't, but think that they should be properly peacefully educated and if they refuse to change or desist then refuted, denounced and prevented from preaching in the name of Islam or advertising in masjids or to Muslims. It is important to know how an individual Muslim need not be on the military battlefield to be "at war with Islam". They could be a theological warrior against Islam while claiming to be Muslims due to ignorance. That is the danger of living in Dar Al-Kufr that could make one a disbeliever and that danger is even greater in Dar Al-Harb. Yet sadly many Muslims are unaware of these dangers and thus fall into the danger zone unknowingly, then label those strict Muslims who stress how important it is to live in Dar Al-Islam as extremists or unrealistic. Some Muslims don't even think their nation is Dar Al-Kufr or Dar Al-Harb at all, I've even spoken to Imams in America who ignorantly say where they live is Dar Al-Islam. While others refuse to call the USA Dar Al-Harb.

<u>The second group:</u> are those who remain amongst the disbelievers because of money, family or homeland. He does not demonstrate a strong attachment to his religion (Islam), nor does he emigrate. He does not support the disbelievers against the Muslims, whether in word or deed. His heart is not bound to them, nor does he speak on their behalf. Such a person is not considered a disbeliever merely because he continues to live among the disbelievers, but many would say that he has disobeyed Allah and His Messenger by not going to live among the Muslims, even though he may secretly hate the disbelievers.

Many Muslims hope to be in this category but it is currently unknown whether they are due to the tax issue, it depends on what taxes they pay and on what is in the heart and whether they are "strong Muslims not attached to non-Muslims". Modern Scholars have not given a unanimous opinion on the tax issue, yet, because of the logistical, economic and political implications. However their delay then allows violent Khariji extremists to take the spotlight on the issue and seem correct due to their early simplistic blanket ruling. Note that group 2 "secretly hates the disbelievers", this is because if they had zero hate they would not be Muslims, unless they were ignorant, insane or posessed. Unfortunately some preach that hatred is not part of Islam thus teaching kufr in the name of Islam. They are called Zindiqs, which are people who openly and publicly commit disbelief but claim they don't. In recent times the Zindiqs have multiplied under the guise of "fighting extremism" when they are the extremists themselves. The disbelievers love the Zindiqs because they mold Muslims into being in group 1 without Muslims even knowing or intending it. The Zindiqs are the ones who get the spotlight and government funding to preach the 5 points and other anti-Islamic points as well. The sad part is that such groups even expose the Islamaphobes. I have personally read materials distributed by Muslims who specifically condemn the inventor of the 5 point plan to destroy Islam from the inside, and label them as one of the #1 enemies of Muslims and Islam yet on the very same packet the "Muslim group" preached the same exact

5 points the "enemy of Islam" teaches in their book but they said that's how Islam teaches Muslims to live. The specific name of the group that did that is MPAC but many "Muslim groups" teach the 5 points to destroy Islam in the guise of Islam and gullible foolish Muslims fall for this trick. So the anti-Islamaphobes are preaching the exact points the Islamaphobes want them to preach, but most Muslims don't know this and fall into the trap thinking these groups against Islamaphobia are Islamic Muslims when they really have kafirphobia and are following the plan of the enemies of Islam. The Islamaphobes and Kafirphobes are working together but the kafirphobes are too stupid to realize it. I won't name the names of such groups because they change their names and new groups form, but if you've read this far you should be able to identify such groups regardless of what names they may decide to use for themselves. It's not their name, it's their game, their goals, organizational structures and religious beliefs. Some people could call themselves "Club Sinful" and be islamic while a group claiming to be an "Islamic Society" or "Islamic State" could be working for Satan promoting sins, shirk, kufr and bida.

The third group: *are those who may remain among the disbelievers without impediment, and they are two categories:*

1. *Those who are openly able to proclaim their religion and dissociate themselves from disbelief.* **When they are able, they clearly disassociate themselves from the disbelievers and tell them openly that they are far from truth, and that they are wrong.** *This is what is known as 'Izhar ad-Din' or 'assertion of Islam'.* <u>This is what exonerates a person from the obligation to emigrate.</u> *Muhammad was commanded to tell the disbelievers of their clear disbelief and that their religion was not the same, nor was their worship, nor what they worshipped. That* <u>they could not be in the service of Allah, so long as they remained in the service of falsehood</u>*. He was commanded to express his satisfaction with Islam as his religion and his denial of the faith of the disbelievers. Therefore, Whoever does this is not obliged to emigrate.* <u>Asserting one's religion does not mean that you simply leave people to worship whatever they please without comment</u>*, like the Christians and the Jews do.* <u>It means that you must</u> **clearly and plainly disapprove** <u>of what they worship,</u> **and show enmity** <u>towards the disbelievers;</u> *failing this there is no assertion of Islam.*

2. *Those who live amongst the disbelievers, and have not the means to leave nor the strength to assert themselves,* *have a license to remain. Allah says, But the exemption comes after a promise to those who remain among the disbelievers. It is an exemption to those who could not devise a plan nor find any other way out.*

I am more likely of this 2nd type of the 3rd group. Realistically I am somewhere between group 2 and 3.1 and 3.2 wishing I'm not of group 1 and can emigrate before my death. Many reverts to Islam as well as born and raised Western Muslims hope to fall into this category of not having the means to leave, thus their failure to assert Islam in public in dar al-kufr or dar al-harb would be excused. Yet some might have the means and just choose not to leave making them fall into group 2, or they might be supporting the war against Islam and fall into group 1. Again the tax question is a very big one that I can't answer. Yet at the end of the day I think we can agree that paying taxes to those who kill innocents or good people is not what leads you to paradise but would more likely lead to hell. Of course the governments who collect those taxes don't want you to know that, so they'd label those forbidding taxes as evil. No government will say paying them taxes can lead you to hell. Thus they like the preachers who don't teach that honest truth. Now keep in mind just because paying taxes to killers can lead to hell doesn't mean it's disbelief, I'm just saying it's a big sin. It's not okay to pay for killing innocents, whether that's a personal expenditure you choose to pay to a hired assassin, or a popular tax that you are coerced to pay to your government. Another important element of being able to assert Islam and practice includes the Islamic dresscode such as beard or niqab and other parts of the Islamic uniform regarding fashion options. Now a Muslim doesn't have to wear "middle eastern clothing" but there is a Islamic way to dress for whatever clothing style one wears and some styles and items cannot be worn by Muslims; ironically some Muslims who occasionally wear "middle eastern clothing" violate the Islamic dress code the way they wear it. So don't misunderstand me thinking I'm limiting the Islamic dress code to "middle eastern attire", I'm just saying whatever the attire there is a dress code that should make one known as a Muslim. Middle eastern clothing itself is not technically islamic, it's only Islamic because the Islamic prophets wore it because that's the region they were from, the kafirs in the middle east wore it too but the way Muslims wear it is different, or at least the way they are supposed to wear it is supposed to be different so you can tell a middle eastern attired Muslim apart from a middle eastern attired non-Muslim. Several years ago a Muslim scholar in the West was asked *"What if a Muslim can't dress Islamically in a non-Muslim society because it will cause them to suffer socially, or politically, or economically and possibly physically?"* The scholar said if you are ever in such a situation that means you are in Dar Al-Harb and it is time for you to leave that country if you can't dress Islamically and visually establish a distinct Islamic identity. He wasn't kidding either. Really why would any Muslim ever choose to live in a country where they don't feel comfortable dressing Islamically? I guarantee that if a Muslim isn't dressing Islamically then they aren't acting or living Islamically, because if they were they'd be dressing Islamically. The only valid reason a Muslim could have to not publicly dress Islamically while in dar al-kufr is if they'd be killed for doing so, can't afford it, can't move and have an extreme fear/extreme circumstances that prevent them being a Muslim in public, or if they were undercover on a secretive Islamic military mission, or if they are ignorant. If only Muslims in the West knew this and either dressed the part or decided to depart. Sadly many who are ignorant of this, dress themselves in garments of ignorance. It is a type of love/allegiance to dress like your spiritual enemy. Everyone dresses like those whom they love and want to imitate.

Those are the 3, technically 4 groups, of "Muslims" living in non-Muslim lands who wage war against Muslims, which currently includes most of Europe, the Americas, Austrailia, India, Russia, China and some African nations. However it seems South America isn't actively at war with Muslims, but oddly not many Muslims want to live in South America so they make excuses to live in those other countries which may or may not be valid. However when comparing warfare personally I think that South America is a much better type of dar-al kufr than the Austro-Euro-Asia-merica region. Yet what about Muslims traveling to countries at war with Muslims for business reasons and not to live there? Scholars have taught based on Abu Bakr traveling to Syria during the time of Muhammad pbuh, while Syria was at war with the Muslims, that if you are able to assert your Islamic faith (see group 3.1) not do any sinful business transactions, while also not supporting the disbelievers' military war machine, then such business is permitted. Which is another fine point many Muslim businessmen fail to understand. For instance most like to cite how Indonesia peacefully got so many Muslims because of Muslim businessmen trading with them, or they'll cite how the Sahabah went all the way to China for business/dawah but then they jump to the incorrect conclusion to say thus as a result that means Muslims can and should live in America. Whereas that can't be deduced based on the facts that business is different than residence and most importantly one cannot do sinful transactions anywhere, while if business is done in/with nations at war with Muslims one must be sure they don't help the war effort as a result of their business. Which due to the taxes and unislamic economics of today may not be possible with Western nations. So one must keep in mind modern Europe and America is very different than the China, Europe or Africa of the time of the Sahabah. They were not doing sinful transactions or paying any taxes, and they were doing their dawah in dar al kufr whereas America and Europe is a type of dar al-harb. Also the excuse many Muslims use by saying Muhammad pbuh said "Seek knowledge even if you must go to China" as meaning it's okay to go to dar Al-Kufr or dar al-harb to get a college education is false, because Muhammad pbuh never said that statement and it is a fabricated hadith. Likewise Islam forbids interest, even if an interest loan helps pay for college. Muhammad pbuh never taught *"Interest is sinful and prohibited, unless you need to pay it to go to college."* Such a loophole does not exist, even if some ignorant Imams say it's okay or allow it. A college education is not a requirement for life. A good job is not a requirement for life either. Avoiding poverty is also not a requirement for life. Thus interest is not a requirement for life. Although such sins somehow get justified by many because of the laxity Muslims have by saying they live in unislamic lands. Those Muslims who live in non-Muslim lands are ignorant by evidence of their location. And that's what's almost funny about the usage of the fabricated hadith "Seek knowledge even if in China." that's used to live in dar al-kufr in that those who use this hadith don't seek Islamic knowledge so even if it were true, which it's completely fabricated and false they still shouldn't be in China or dar al-kufr because you can't get knowledge there since the people there don't have Islamic knowledge. This lack of knowledge then leads to many falling into major sins, bida or even kufr/shirk. Especially when the ignorant tend to use more fabricated hadith to justify their beliefs/deeds than they do authentic. Another popular fabricated hadith modernists will use is "Love for one's country is part of faith." and then they use that to justify patriotism. Yet that hadith is a fabrication and contradicts the Quran and authentic hadith of Muhammad pbuh. So it's not as though Muslims in dar al-kufr lack information about their religion, it's that they have an abundance of misinformation camoflauged as Islamic when it's false information, or misinterpreted in the name of Islam for the sake of satanic interests, with taqleed of Imams just because they got a beard and a turban with a Bachelor's degree from a diploma mill perpetuating the whole anti-islamic system built and operated in dar al-kufr in the name of Islam and Muslims when in reality it is the biggest threat to Islam and Muslims. It's actually safer religiously speaking to live in middle eastern warzones than the peaceful lands of dar al-kufr because in the Muslim lands your life may be endangered but in the non-Muslim lands your faith is hanging by a thread of the rope of Allah. Muslims are supposed to "hold fast and firm to the rope of Allah" as the Quran teaches but in dar al-kufr Muslims struggle just to grasp 1 thread of the rope. Whereas that's why Islamically speaking a country like America is not a place where Muslims should live because they fall into so many sins as a result and are pressured to compromise their faith in order to exist or live comfortably. Yet again politics, economics and logistics have caused modern Muslim scholars to delay and hesitate in making rulings about boycotting entire nations or emigrating en masse, although some have issued fatwas telling Muslims to boycott America and Israel, but logistically that's tricky to do especially if they live there like I do. However there is a fatwa by the knowledgeable scholar Ibn Taymiyya which he gave concerning the region of Mardin in the 14th century. This region called Mardin in what is modern day Turkey actually included Ibn Taymiyya's hometown of Harran where he was born. When the non-Muslim Mongols conquered Mardin his family left the city of Harran, Mardin when he was 7 years old. Other Muslims didn't leave Mardin and continued to live there despite the Mongols implementing their own unislamic legal system. So at that time Mardin was a formerly islamic region in all regards that was occupied by unislamic non-Muslim rulers who employed Muslims in their army and fought against Muslims in neighboring Muslim lands but allowed the Muslims of Mardin to live in peace and practice Islam therein. So Mardin was much like how Afghanistan was when the Americans came and conquered, established unislamic laws and fought Muslims but allow Muslims to live and pray in Afghanistan without killing them all wholesale. The people of Mardin wrote to Ibn Taymiyya asking: "*Is it a land of war (Dar al harb) or a land of peace (dar al silm)? Does a Muslim resident therein have a duty to emigrate to the lands of Islam or not? If emigration is obligatory for him and he does not emigrate, and he gives assistance to the enemies of the Muslims with his person or his goods, is he sinning in so doing? And one who accuses him of hypocrisy and insults him (by calling him a hypocrite), is he sinning or not?*" Now while his reply is meant specifically for the people of Mardin it provides a useful scholarly precedent of what Islamic Scholars have said Muslims should do regarding such living conditions which we may be able to apply in our modern situations. Also keep in mind this was not just some scholar writing about something he didn't know or care about, his hometown was in Mardin and he personally knew people who still lived there. So Ibn Taymiyya knew the reality of the region and the people and the living conditions, he knew it was peaceful for the inhabitants and that they could pray and practice and preach Islam there despite being ruled by unislamic laws and kafir rulers. Another important point to note when reading his reply is that the majority of the population of the region were Muslims, so this ruling isn't something that necessarily applies to Muslims who are living in lands of a non-Muslim majority. Some things could apply but it's still important to remember this was a Muslim majority region(not just a city, it was a region/province/state) ruled by a unislamic government that let Muslims live under them but fought Muslims in foreign nations. So this fatwa was written for Muslims living amongst Muslims in a Muslim land but living under unislamic laws and ruled by non-Muslims. Ibn Taymiyya replied: "*All praise is due to Allah! There is an interdiction against (muharram) [any assault on] the lives and property of Muslims wherever they may be, in Mardin or anywhere else. To give assistance to those who depart from the Way/Law of the religion of Islam (Shariah) is also forbidden, whether it be the people of Mardin or others. If the one resident is disabled from putting his religion into effect, it is obligatory for him to emigrate. If that is not the case, it remains preferable but is not obligatory. That [these people] give assistance to the enemy of the*

Muslims with their persons or their property is forbidden to them, and they must abstain therefrom by all the means possible to them-evading, equivocating, compromising. When it is not possible for them to do this (not assist enemies of Muslims via person or property) except by emigrating, (emigrating) is incumbant on every single one of them. It is not lawful to insult them in a general manner, nor to accuse them of hypocrisy [hiding unbelief]. Rather, insulting and accusing of hypocrisy is to be done in respect of the specific characteristics mentioned in the Quran and Sunnah. Now this concerns the people of Mardin and others also. Is [Mardin] a domain of war or of peace? It is a composite (murakkab), in which both the things signified [by those terms are to be found]. It is not in the situation of a domain of peace in which the institutions (ahkam) of Islam are implemented because its army (jund) is [compose of] Muslims. Nor is it in the situation of a domain of war, whose inhabitants are (all) disbelievers. Rather, it constitutes a third type, in which the Muslim shall be treated as he merits, in which those living there who depart from the Way/Law of Islam (apostate intentionally or unintentionally) outside of the authority of Islamic Law should be treated as each merits and combated." Since this fatwa is misinterpreted by many I will attempt to summarize for you in plain terms 4 principles that can be derived from Ibn Taymiyya's fatwa about Mardin:

1. The lives and property of the Muslims living in a mixed state are inviolable. Their living under the subjugation of the unislamic non-Muslim rulers does not compromise any of their rights, nor can they be maligned verbally or accused of major hypocrisy(disbelief). Neither the Muslims of Mardin nor the non-Muslim civilians of Mardin could be harmed despite their unislamic government being actively at war with Muslims.

2. As long as the inhabitants of Mardin(or places like it) are able to practice Islam <u>in full</u>, they are not obliged to emigrate.

3. Muslims must not give assistance to non-Muslims who are fighting against any Muslims in any place, even if they are forced to flatter them, be evasive, lie or absent themselves; aid cannot be given to any non-Muslim enemies. It is forbidden for Muslims to aid the enemies of Muslims/ Islam in any of their war efforts. <u>If ever a Muslim in any land is unable to avoid aiding the enemies of Muslims via their person and/or via their property then that means they cannot practice Islam</u> in that land. In such a scenario it becomes obligatory for all the Muslims in

that land (who are able) to emigrate to another land where they can avoid aiding the enemies of Muslims. Meaning if by living in a country they have to pay taxes that go to a non-Muslim military that kills Muslims, every single one of them has to emigrate from that land or risk hellfire if they have no valid Islamic excuse that prevents them from emigrating. But even if they can't emigrate its still a major sin to financially aid the non-Muslim militaries against Muslims. Adultery is less of a sin than a Muslim supporting a kafir army.

4. The mixed territory is neither wholly a part of the Muslim world, since it is under the domination of the disbelievers and/or unislamic law, nor is it part of the non-Muslim world since the majority of it's people were Muslim. Such a land is a composite type. The Muslims living therein should be treated according to their rights as Muslims, while the non-Muslims living there outside of the authority of Islamic Law should be treated according to their rights. While people living in such a state should not be denounced as major hypocrites (disbelievers) due to them living there the Quran and Sunnah itself should be the standard by which major hypocrisy(disbelief of one claiming to be Muslim) is declared. The population shouldn't be labeled en

masse as major hypocrites just because they live in such a place, but takfir of them requires a case by case analysis of each individual to be done by those qualified to make takfir. Nontheless despite it being an unislamic land those who depart from Islam should be combated according to how their level of deviancy merits. For example some major hypocrites may be combatted by the tongue, others by the hand and others by the sword(if possible should the situation of such a major hypocrite merit it and circumstances allow violence, as in the case of those who join the non-Muslim army and betray/sabotage/risk the safety of Muslims). Yet in such a scenario a Muslim may not be able to fully combat the major hypocrites as they deserve since/if they cannot fully practice Islam. Also the combatting whether peacefully or violently of hypocrite apostates in such a mixed state should be done by those qualified to do the combatting correctly and effectively, not just any and every true Muslim. Likewise since/if violence against such hypocrites/apostates would result in greater evil than non-violence then violence should not be used against such persons in such scenarios.

The fatwa continues for several pages wherein the Islamic proofs for his ruling are listed but since there are so many I have not included the proofs as I was only including this fatwa to show what Muslim scholars in the past have said Muslims who live in peace and can allegedly practice Islam under non-Muslims and unislamic governments should do. Because people sometimes say no scholars have said anything because it's a modern situation but it's not a modern situation and scholars have issued rulings on these situations in the past. Although sadly both types of extremists misuse this fatwa to teach unislamic things with some mistranslating it by saying the translation I typed is mistranslated when it's not but they claim it is because they don't like the word "combat" so they lie about it being mistranslated because it refers to combating hypocrites. In 2010 CE there was even a conference about this fatwa where they claimed it didn't say combat but referred to non-Muslims being treated according to how the unislamic law says they should be instead of hypocrites/apostates. However after the conference the leading sheikh who claimed and ruled that it was mistranslated admitted that it does indeed say/mean to combat hypocrites, but he didn't want to say it said that because many violent extremists and non-Muslims wouldn't understand what that meant. Hence I elaborated on point 4 so you don't misunderstand it. I did that because violent extremists may say the fatwa means everyone should violently fight hypocrites of all types both major (disbelief) and minor(sinful). Unfortunately modernists then use such false claims of mistranslation to then straightaway tell non-Muslims that entire methodologies and views are based on a mistranslated fatwa when they have nothing to do with the fatwa and the fatwa isn't even mistranslated. In reality the fatwa says what it says and it means what it says. The 4 principles I listed are the correct meanings Ibn Taymiyya intended as far as I can deduce and Allah knows best. Regardless of the controversy over the last line of the fatwa, in it's proscribed treatment of those Muslims who depart from the way/laws of Islam while living in such a state, the default big picture relevant ruling is that it's preferable for Muslims in such a situation to move to lands ruled by Muslims and Islamic laws, with it being obligatory for the individual if they are unable to fully practice Islam including expressing public enmity and disavowal of kufr and kafirs. Now most Muslims in the world today agree with that, although some may misunderstand the hatred and disavowal bit.

However most don't know that it is forbidden for any Muslim to assist enemies of Muslims via their person or property and they must avoid doing so by all means available. If the Muslims cannot avoid supporting enemies of Muslims via their person <u>OR property</u>(ie. paying taxes to a military that harms Muslims either domestically or abroad) then it is obligatory for all the Muslims in that region to emigrate away from that land so that they are not guilty of supporting the enemies of Muslims. Keep in mind Ibn Taymiyya wrote this to an entire region where the majority of people were Muslims, it wasn't a non-Muslim land ruled by unislamic laws it was a Muslim land ruled by unislamic laws by non-Muslim Mongols. So in practice Ibn Taymiyya was advising the Muslims that if they couldn't avoid paying taxes to the disbelieving Mongol military then they all had to leave which would thereby make it a 100% non-Muslim region. Muslims were told by scholars they were supposed to emigrate to the lands where the law was Islam and the rulers were Muslims and then those Islamic Muslim governments would return to liberate the land via Jihad from the non-Muslim Mongols. So if that is the ruling for a land that was ruled by Shariah for a long time and the majority of the population were Muslims where Muslims were able to practice Islam in peace then what do you think the ruling would be for a land like America where Shariah has never been applied and the majority of the population is not Muslim and you can't really practice Islam fully nor with respect? If it's obligatory for all the Muslims to move away from Muslim majority lands if living there means supporting the military of the enemies of Muslims then surely we can deduce an even stricter ruling would apply to Muslims in non-Muslim unislamic lands today. The only difference is that Shariah may not be implemented 100% by Muslim rulers in any land today while it was in Ibn Taymiyya's time. Yet still the basic principle in that it's obligatory to avoid supporting the enemies of Muslims remains, even if one is living in peace under non-Muslim rule amongst a Muslim majority. It's not a question of whether Muslims in certain non-Muslim countries should emigrate, they should emigrate, it's just a question of where is the best place for them to go. It's been the consensus of the Muslims for thousands of years that Muslims have to move away from the non-Muslim unislamic governments and live in the lands of Muslims so as to live under Shariah. But alas today as with the fatwa of

Mardin, not everyone does what Islam teaches even when Muslim scholars tell them what Islam teaches providing proofs. Frequently sinful people do what they want or what is easiest. Although traditionally the Islamic rules are crystal clear, in the past there was no valid difference of opinion about emigration. That doesn't mean there was no other opinion, there was but it was wrong. During the Crusades there were some "scholars" who said Muslims shouldn't fight the Christian Crusaders but just coexist in peace under Christian rulers and Christian laws. Some scholars even suggested Muslims during the crusades should ally with the Christian crusaders to fight other Muslims and they did. Yet those scholars' unislamic opinion was wrong and history has proven that opinion was wrong. Likewise more recently in the 1980s CE some Muslim Scholars inside and outside of Afghanistan said Muslims shouldn't fight the Soviet Union who was trying to establish Communism. Islam taught that the Muslims should've fought the Russian Communists or leave Afghanistan to move into Pakistan and Pakistan should've invaded to expel the Communists. Instead Afghan Muslims fought back for many years keeping what territory they could while non-Afghan Muslims helped them in person and property. Eventually the Soviets were driven out by the Muslims, and the Muslim world rejoiced agreeing that Jihad was the right response afterall and those who said to peacefully live under Communism and pay the Soviets were wrong. Then America invaded Afghanistan but Pakistan and the world acted differently. Islam still said that the Muslims should've fought the invasion and/or left to go to Pakistan whereupon Pakistan islamically should've then invaded Afghanistan to drive out the non-Muslim American invaders and establish Shariah. But Pakistan didn't do that, they picked the wrong side. Which one could justify by saying they didn't have the means to win the fight but in such a circumstance they still should not have helped the non-Muslim anti-Islamic coalition. So today is similar to how it was during the Soviet invasion except there is significantly less support for the Muslims fighting for Shariah because the opposing faith is different and the flags of the unislamic non-Muslim enemies are different colors. But history repeats itself. Of course today Muslims might say that *"Well the Crusaders or Soviets were ruthless and didn't allow Muslims to live in their lands but today it's different, now Muslims have democracy and freedom to practice Islam in safety in non-Muslim lands under unislamic laws."* Whereas they are wrong about that. Muslims have lived in Russia since it was a Muslim country many centuries ago and they lived in Russia throughout it's wars with Muslim States and through it's genocides as well. Muslims in Russia stayed even while they were hunted down and killed. They also stayed while they paid the Russian military who killed Muslims in other lands, as Russia is doing in Syria while I write with millions of Muslims living in Russia. As I write Muslims in Russia are praying for the Syrian Muslims to live/win while paying the Russians taxes so they can bomb the Syrian Muslims. Thus Muslims are praying for victory while paying for defeat. But that's not what Islam teaches them to do, not now and not in the past either. Yet Muslims haven't just done this in the present but have done this in the past as well. During the era popularly known as the crusading era, from 1050-1650 CE, Muslims lived in Europe. Thousands of Muslims lived in medieval Europe while the Crusades were going on. The same exact time England, France and Germany sent armies to fight Yusuf ibn Ayubi there where Muslims living in those countries paying money to the Christian governments which was spent on the Crusader armies. Or to "pay to pave the roads" which the crusading armies used to walk on to get to the holy land to kill people. Yet "Muslim scholars" in Europe said it was perfectly fine for Muslims to do that and pay for the Crusades because they lived in Europe and it was their duty as a European. Muslims in Europe paid for the Christians to go on the Crusades to the Holy Land to kill Muslims. During the crusades thousands of years ago the Muslims in Europe were told to just "ride out the hostility" and keep preaching Islam since soon Europe will become Islamic voluntarily without any need for Jihad. The Muslims did that and what was the result? Did Europe become Islamic and peacefully implement Shariah like the medieval Muslims were told would happen? No. This is because the majority of people on earth do not and will not sincerely care about religion. Many just go with the religious flow of their environment and will never consider choosing or changing their religion until they can no longer politically, socially and economically afford to delay choosing a religion. Most will stick with whatever faith they grew up with unless they have worldly reasons to consider a change. Most people don't care about the afterlife and won't choose their religion based upon proof or concerns for the afterlife. To change a religion the majority of people don't need proof that their faith is wrong and another is more right or true, they need some material real world reason that forces them to commit to a religious choice one way or the other. That's why offensive Jihad is legislated at certain times, because peaceful preaching has a limit to how many converts it can result in. No religion in the world has ever become popular among the masses via peaceful methods. That doesn't mean it can't happen but when the majority of people have no worldly pressure to make a conscious wholehearted decision regarding religion then they won't. Most will just live how they want or however they legally can and follow the religious ideas of the crowd they are influenced by most. Islam is different because it doesn't allow people to not choose a religion. Islam provides real worldly consequences and incentive to choose a religion. Other religions either don't require everyone to make a choice so most never choose or choose many, or the other religions only allow people 1 option, convert or die. Islam forces non-Muslims to choose Islam or something else because that way everyone makes the choice regarding Islam. People don't have to become a Muslim, but Islam teaches they have to choose whether to become a Muslim or not. While today non-Muslim lands allow for this choice in theory, they don't promote or require this choice. Islamic nations do require people to choose Islam or something else. One cannot live under shariah without making a choice to be a Muslim or not, but one can live under something else other than Shariah without making such a choice. Thus while the difference in choice availability is slight the difference in results is big. This is because when people realize they have to research Islam and choose it or reject it as a political/economic/social act, then many end up choosing Islam because they did the research and felt they had to make a choice due to the worldly consequences and pressures to make a choice regarding Islam. A perfect example of this is Mecca. Regardless of whether you agree with me in the prophetic dawah in Mecca being hate preaching or disagree and think it was love preaching, the fact is that whatever it was it didn't work to convert the city to Islam. Mecca became a Muslim city with a Muslim majority as a result of Jihad and military conquest which then forced the non-Muslims to feel real material pressure to make up their minds and choose Islam or not. All that preaching didn't do the job, but the pressure that came about after Shariah was implemented via

Jihad did. That's why Jihad will always exist because most people won't respond to any kind of preaching unless they feel pressure which makes their choice of religion an important decision with material consequences. There is "no compulsion in religion" but there is compulsion in the fact that you have to make a decision about whether to accept the Islamic religion. People should not have the option to say "*I have my own religion so I don't need to choose Islam or reject it, I already got one.*" or "*I don't have the time to think about becoming a Muslim or learning about Islam, I'm too busy.*" or "*My faith shouldn't effect how I get treated.*" or "*They're all the same, the religion I believe in or practice doesn't matter.*" Such religious beliefs about not having to learn something about Islam and decide to accept/adopt it or disbelieve and reject it are not valid from a Muslim perspective. People talk about "freedom of choice" and that's what Muslims fight for, we fight peacefully and violently so everyone has freedom to choose Islam or Kufr and chooses. Having the opportunity to choose Islam as your religion is not the same as making the choice. The cliche "freedom of choice" does not exist if you never make the choice. Nobody can claim to have freedom of choice if they never make an educated choice as to whether they accept Islam or not. It is the right of every person to be given the choice to go to paradise. Having freedom to choose is not the same as being given the choice, because if people don't feel pressure to examine the road to paradise (Islam) then they won't choose to travel it and as a result may burn in hell forever for making the wrong choice due to not choosing Islam since they had no compulsion of choice. Islam teaches that one's choice of religion is up to them but not making a conscious decision about Islam is unacceptable. Muslims simply want everyone to make the choice, not just have the theoretical option to make the choice if by random chance special circumstances dictate they decide of their own freewill to make a decision to learn about and choose or reject Islam. For disbelievers to choose Islam or not is compulsory, having the option to choose is not enough, they all have to choose. Nobody should live life without being directly faced with having to make the choice of Islam or disbelief. For a country to exist without this choice being a legal requirement is tantamount to religious oppression. The tyrants today have oppressed people by taking their choice away in the name of freedom of religion and have thereby prevented them from making the choice through both peaceful and violent means, both overt and subliminal. How can people get told they have to choose which politicians to vote for, but not get told they have to pick Islam or something else? They compel people to use voting to decide everything except the one thing that is important. If people have freedom of choice in these "free countries" why is there never a religious ballot where people choose their religion? It's because the governments never want them to have the option to choose and by giving the theoretical loophole to choose they take away the motivation to choose so the choice is never freely made. By governments not pressuring their population to choose a religion they are in effect pressuring them to not choose any traditional religion. Without pressure to make a decision about a religion people decide not to believe in or practice religions. Fundamentally contrary beliefs, like truth and falsehood, cannot come in contact without seeking to annihilate each other, as soon as one side feels capable of dominating/destroying the other. Religious tolerance is only ever possible with polytheistic people who have weak religious beliefs they don't care much about. Monotheists or Kafir Absolutists cannot have religious tolerance. One side or the other, or both will apply pressure and if ever neither do it's because everyone is polytheistic or believes the same thing. Any belief that is held as a "absolute truth", or as Americanists would say "self-evident truth", is necessarily intolerant because both the real and imagined truth can never tolerate anything but itself. Religious tolerance is a symptom of a lack of religious faith and a diluted polytheistic belief system. It is a fact that not a single religious/political/economic/social belief in the history of humanity has ever been destroyed by refutation alone. Do the research, you will not find a single example where simple dialogue led one belief to go extinct. Even the people of Jonah pbuh did not have their false faith vanish as a result of mere refutation, God applied pressure and they then adopted the truth 100%. So peaceful preaching has a limit, no type of idolatry has ever ended simply because of conversations alone. I'm not saying violence gets the world to 100% unanimity, it might it might not, but one thing is certain in that some type of pressure need be applied that discourages evil falsehood and encourages the truth and goodness. Prophets literally came with divine miracles and people still rejected the truth and clung to falsehood until further pressure was applied. Prophets who effectively abolished falsehood didn't just preach, they created environments to facilitate their preaching and put pressure on people to choose a religion, and as such when people are pressured to make a decision more often than not they make the right decision because pressure increases focus. When I say pressure to pick Islam or not, I don't mean a sword on the neck, peaceful pressure could do the job but preaching without pressure on the masses can never finish the job. The key is to apply prophetic pressure that pleases the Creator. We must keep in mind Satan is always going to exert pressure for people to disbelieve, meaning that if the pressure to believe and obey God isn't equal to or stronger than Satan's pressure to disbelieve or disobey God then Satan will always have some followers. Satan may always have some followers in falsehood but if we are going to fight a theological war against Satan, then we have to plan for total victory because that's what God wants us to intend to achieve even though we may never do so, due to God's own wise plans for the world which we don't fully know. For either side to win the war the winner will have to apply pressure and Satan's has never stopped applying pressure, nor will he ever. Therefore at some point in time, for the believers to ever win the theological war against Satan and falsehood pressure will have to come into play. Today such conditions or pressures promoting people to choose theistic religions, particularly Islam, don't exist in most places so most don't do the research nor make the choice regarding Islam, even if they get preached to, because they lack a non-religious reason to make a choice. The majority of the non-religious masses won't become Muslims without a having a non-religious incentive to research and choose Islam. Most are too busy living life to even do research about their own faith of kufr. On top of that humans are inherently resistant to changing their beliefs or the status quo. That's why peaceful preaching doesn't affect non-Muslim masses in unislamic lands because unislamic governments do not give non-religious reasons for people to choose Islam or reject it. People vote because they are pressured to believe they must make a choice and the choice will affect their worldly lives. When religion doesn't matter in politics, economics or society(relationships) people tend not to care to change faiths regardless of whether they are preached to or not. For peaceful preaching of Islam to result in more Muslims, typically religion has to play an important role in the preached to person's life. If they don't care about religion they won't care to adopt Islam as their religion. For most of the masses to become Muslim the masses need a reason to do so and being the true religion is not enough of a reason for the masses to embrace that religion. People need pressure to choose a religion, because without pressure to choose the truth the pressure from Satan and their own desires will overwhelm them and they will choose falsehood. Notice I said pressure to choose "a religion" not "the true religion" because I have faith in humanity that pressure to simply choose a faith will result in people choosing the correct one. I could be wrong to have faith in humanity, and they may need pressure to choose the truth and mere pressure to choose is not enough, but unlike with politics God helps people choose the right religion if they are sincere and naturally all things being equal the truth will always be chosen over falsehood. God sent prophets to earth to put pressure on people so they believe in and practice the religion they are supposed to. All prophets pressured people to believe or disbelieve. They weren't violent about it, and we don't have to be violent and probably shouldn't be violent about it in most instances, but all of God's prophets did force people to make a religious choice about their prophetic religion. All who the prophets interacted with either had to accept it or reject it, there was no ignoring it or not making a decision about it. Nobody who interacted with a prophet went away thinking they didn't have to make a decision about accepting the prophetic faith. So that is one condition for the choice people must be pressured to make, the choice of the prophetic religion must be available. The difference between the way we preach today and the way the prophets preached is that they applied theological pressure and few of us apply theological pressure the way the prophets did or the way God wants us to. Typically regarding the masses in the days without prophets on earth, the pressures from Shariah and Jihad are the primary reasons why people bother to research Islam and choose. Without Shariah or Jihad most people don't make a choice about Islam no matter how much peaceful preaching is done to them. Meanwhile Muslims living in lands without Shariah are the ones who face the pressure to choose or disbelieve in Islam. So in times of peace under unislamic law, Muslims face worldly pressure to choose kufr and shirk everyday. Sometimes Muslims face peaceful pressure and sometimes violent, in the long-term in unislamic non-Muslim lands the Muslims either get converted to kufr or get killed. If you disagree then I simply ask you this, did the non-Muslim European masses convert to Islam after thousands of years of preaching? Or did the Inquisition happen and the Muslims got killed? Or did the Catholic vs. Protestant wars happen and Muslims got killed? Or did the world wars happen and Muslims got killed? Or did I just make them up and Muslims were never in Europe until after the world wars and "freedom" flourished? No, it's a proven historical fact that Muslims have lived in non-Muslim unislamic Europe for thousands of years, it's just that history books hide this fact because the non-Muslims want to keep the Muslims there in perpetuity to keep up the pressure to eliminate Islam and the Muslims while disuniting Muslims so they can kill them in the Muslims' own lands. It's much easier to do that if people think that Muslims living in non-Muslim lands is a new trend. If Muslims living in Europe learned the history of Muslims in Europe being a disrespected minority who repeatedly gets wiped out as religiosity rises and falls over the centuries then they would see the pattern and decide to leave, or do something different that past Muslim generations didn't do in order to break the cycle. If the history being taught accurately informed people that Muslims lived in Europe during the papal Crusades and have been in Europe as a religious minority for thousands of years, it would become public knowledge that Muslims end up converting to other religions through the course of a few generations due to constant unislamic social pressures and finally the Muslims in unislamic lands end up being forced to convert via violence once Muslim political threats arise domestically or internationally. While ironically if you ask Muslim scholars today what the ruling would be regarding Muslims living thousands of years ago in Europe during the Crusades they all agree that it was dar al-harb and all the Muslims living there who were able should've emigrated to the Muslim lands since it was obligatory for them to do so. This is what even non-scholarly Muslims today say, yet few who say this actually do the historical research and know that Muslims lived in and practiced Islam in Europe during the Crusades. These same Muslims will say they can personally live in non-Muslim lands but if they were living in Europe during the Crusades they'd leave for sure. However during the era in which Muslims today say they'd leave Europe and that it was forbidden for Muslims to live there, Muslims were in Europe who said they could stay for the same exact reasons Muslims today in Europe use to justify living under unislamic law among non-Muslims while supporting the armies that kill Muslims in the Muslim lands. Over time the situation hasn't changed much, presently Muslims simply have more visibility in non-Muslim lands than they had before and now it's harder for historians to hide their existence there. The difference today is the vocabulary, technology, geo-political and economic situations and the religions/morality of the kuffar. Today as in the past, Muslims shouldn't live in the non-Muslim unislamic lands supporting enemies of Muslims and the same argument continues with fake "moderate" scholars saying it's okay for Muslims to live in non-Muslim lands while the Muslim fundamentalists say Muslims can't and shouldn't. The correct ruling has always been the same, in that Muslims should live under Shariah among Muslims and are generally forbidden to live in unislamic and/or non-Muslim lands and are obligated to move away from such lands if they cannot practice Islam OR if in living there they cannot avoid supporting the enemies of Muslims via person, or property. There have always been ignorant people who ignore or argue against the 2nd clause of it being forbidden to live in lands if one supports the enemies of Muslims. The end results for people living in such lands today will be the same as it was for those in the past, both on earth and in the afterlife. It's just that today things are extra complicated regarding emigration since Muslims are more widely scattered and the world is deeply interconnected politically and economically. The world is turning into Dar Al-Americanism and the hands of oppressors have greater reach than they did in the past. So while Muslim scholars will still issue rulings about Muslim emigration, there still haven't been rulings accepted unanimously by all Muslims. But in all of history there never has been unanimity regarding Muslim emigration, even during the time of Moses and Muhammad pbuh people differed despite it being 100% obligatory for Muslims to emigrate. It took many miracles for Muslims to get the political ability to leave and even then many didn't want to leave Egypt with Moses pbuh and they were literal slaves just like people today are taxslaves. They thought slavery would be their lot everywhere just like today they say you gotta pay taxes everywhere. They didn't forsee that they needed to leave to improve their conditions and that God while helping them needed them to take some steps for themselves. God tends to help with the hardship not before it. Some "Muslims" in Egypt told Moses pbuh they can peacefully practice Islam in Egypt as slaves and don't need to leave to believe and then when they did leave and got told to fight they told Moses pbuh to fight with God helping him while they remain peaceful and pray for victory. I imagine during the time of the antichrist there will be "Muslims" claiming they can live in the lands of the antichrist and practice Islam fully without having to emigrate or fight. Of course that last example might be an exaggeration but realistically it is easier for Muslims to emigrate today than it will be on that day. The differences over the obligation of Muslim emigration today exists mainly because if the scholars say and prove that all of the Muslims have to leave the unislamic non-Muslim lands, then they have to enter some other country somewhere and which country is willing to open their doors to hundreds of millions of Muslims? So if Scholars say Muslims of X country all have to emigrate then Muslims will ask where they should go and currently Muslim

Scholars can't answer that. Therefore to avoid backlash and uproar from not having an easy answer to the follow-up question, the specific ruling for the Muslim masses of X country to emigrate isn't made due to political difficulties. The scholars say this too, in that the answer is to emigrate but currently few can emigrate because of X, Y and Z. Therefore since the right answer involves more work few tend to ask the question or accept that the right answer still says they should emigrate even though it doesn't say where to. I'll admit it's a half-answer but it is still the right answer and Muslim scholars in the past and present have publicly given it. Sadly we are living in a scholastic dark age because Muslim scholars are given less respect than leaders and there are many ignorant or corrupt people posing as scholars. Scholars should be able to tell the Muslim leaders of nations that Islam says they have to let Muslims live in their country if they want to and immediately the leaders should open the borders and give every Muslim the rights of citizenship and establish Shariah. Unfortunately when some true scholars dare to suggest such things, they get locked up, threatened and tortured. It used to be that leaders feared the scholars, today that is not the case because they know the people don't care about the knowledge or advice the scholars have. Thus today the Muslim scholars can get tortured without any reprisal but TV shows or sporting events can't be cancelled without a revolution. In the past Muslim leaders would seek the companionship and advice of the Muslim scholars in the masjids and would implement their recommendations, while the rich people avoided the Muslim leaders fearing they would command them to be charitable or forbid a certain business practice which they profited from due to the leaders listening to the scholars and implementing Islamic law in every aspect of the community. Today it's the opposite where leaders avoid the scholars and the masjids out of fear the scholars will forbid them from something and the leaders flock to the rich seeking their advice and companionship while the leaders implement all the recommendations of the wealthy. However true scholars still do give the correct rulings and make the importance of emigration known because it's sinful for them to conceal the knowledge, but they admit that currently reality prevents the implementation of the ideal for many but not all. So despite the general ruling remaining the same forever, for an individual to act upon the Islamic ruling it is complicated in our day and age and complications means customization and sadly customization leads many to corruption and rejection of the correct answers and confusion. Before people can accept the right answer they have to be ready to accept it and act upon it, otherwise giving the right answer could cause them to reject what is right due to their unpreparedness to do what is right. Hence some scholars don't preach emigration or the full message of Islam and how to solve the world problems because the corrupt masses can't handle it at this time. As a result the mainstream remain ignorant but the reason that is dangerous is because the popular religion today teaches that the opinion of the majority or the masses is correct. So that's why I'm sharing this even though to know it can make life difficult, because whether you act upon it or not, it's good to know for when you are able to act upon it. One can be rewarded for the intention even if the action doesn't happen. Muhammad himself pbuh taught that the Muslim who intends to do a good deed has 1 good deed written in their book of deeds, when they do it then they get the reward for 10-700 good deeds written in the book of deeds or even more reward than that. Thus while I fear some Muslims who read this won't emigrate or be able to, they should still know the importance and obligation of it regardless so they can have the intention and at least be rewarded for that. Having the ability to emigrate has nothing to do with a person having the intention and having the intention could save oneself from punishment in hell. For example there is a famous incident of a believer who killed 99 people and asked if God could forgive him. The people of the town he lived in told him to go ask a pious hermit his question and the hermit said God wouldn't forgive him, so the murderer got upset and made the pious hermit his 100th victim. Later the murderer felt like repenting and this time he went to a Scholar and asked if God could forgive him for killing 100 people. The Scholar said, "*Yes, what could possibly come between you and repentance? Go to such-and-such a town, for in it there are people who worship Allah. Go and worship with them, and do not go back to your own town, for it is a bad place.*" The man then repented and traveled to the suggested town but died on the way and the angels disputed on whether he should be counted as one who repented or not, so they asked God. God told them to measure the distance between the 2 towns and see which he was closer to. In reality the man was closer to the town which the scholar described as a "bad place". Yet it is reported in sahih hadith that "*Allah commanded (the evil town) to move away, and (the righteous town) to move closer, and said: 'Measure the distance between them,' and they found him to be a hand-span closer to the righteous town, so he was forgiven.*" So despite the reality of the man being physically closer, due to his spiritual distance and intention to be in the righteous town God forgave all his sins. Many Muslims are aware of this hadith and cite it as an example of how forgiving God is. Yet one must keep in mind the scholar did not know the man would die when telling him to move and really when you think about it, God is so merciful he could've forgiven someone for murdering 100 people without them moving to another town. Afterall murder isn't really something you can totally blame on your environment. So why did the scholar tell the murderer if he wanted to be forgiven he had to move when God could just forgive him if he stopped killing and repented? Did the scholar not know God could just forgive him? No, the scholar knew that but he also knew the people of the town the murderer lived in, while not killers themselves, were ignorant and not righteous worshippers of God. Therefore the Scholar realized the problem was partially social in that because the murderer lived amongst religiously ignorant people he didn't have righteous companions to help him do good and avoid evil, so no matter how much he tried to repent from murder without righteous companions and knowledgeable people to learn from the murderer would likely continue to sin. Or it could've been that the land was dar al-harb or dar-al kufr and emigration was obligatory. Yet based on what is apparent both towns were full of believers except one town was ignorant and unrighteous and the other was righteous and knowledgeable. Hence because the murderer intended to be among the righteous and knowledgeable and never again commit the sins he did, God forgave him despite not physically being able to get any closer to the land of the righteous and knowledgeable believers before he died. Therefore what we can learn from this report is that to repent from some sins and never do them again, it helps to have righteous companions and knowledgeable environments. Some will never stop sinning because they have foolish unislamic companions and/or lack righteous knowledgable islamic human companions, and this is why Muslims in dar al-kufr tend to be more sinful or find it harder to permanently repent from sins than Muslims in Muslim territories do, sinful as they may be. We can also deduce from this that the intention of emigration was what earned paradise for the man who killed 100 people. It's not just "God is so merciful", God was so merciful because the man intended to emigrate to a more Islamic town. The man didn't fully emigrate before his death, but his sincere intention to emigrate to a better more Islamic location merited him getting the forgiveness of Allah and eternal paradise. This shows how important having the intention to emigrate is for Muslims and shows how some people will never be able to stop sinning until they emigrate to dar al-islam, thereby showing the danger of living in dar al-kufr amongst ignorant Muslims. And that's one thing Muslims lose in non-Muslim nations, they lose access to righteous knowledgeable companions because so few Muslims in non-Muslim nations are knowledgeable and even fewer are righteous. This is why Muhammad pbuh stressfully ordered Muslims living in non-Muslim nations to emigrate because many will not be able to stop sinning without an Islamic environment. I'm not saying it's impossible to repent in dar al-kufr from all sins, but realistically it is much harder to do. God wants Muslims to have the intention to emigrate, by people not informing Muslims of the obligatory intention they must have to live in the lands of the Muslims (and under Shariah) then they miss out on rewards and the love of God. Having the intention to emigrate away from dar al-kufr could cause a sinful Muslim to go to paradise when they die. By Muslims not having intentions to emigrate which are obligatory for them to have they are sinful and can suffer punishment in both this life and the next. Learning and teaching the knowledge is beneficial even if one doesn't implement it, because knowledge cleans, benefits and corrects the heart. This is something many fail to understand regarding knowledge about religion. Maybe when learning religious knowledge you learn nothing but that you are more sinful than you thought. How can that be good to know when it feels so bad? Well first it makes you humble which makes you a better person and second it helps to create good intentions within yourself so that instead of being a foolish sinner without regret one becomes a conflicted sinner who plans to change. While our hearts must change before we can and we must improve before the world does. Knowledge can also influence your actions because just as knowing you will die helps you act better, knowing you should do something helps you act better and different even if you don't do it. Learning religious knowledge is also something God loves for you to do and that's why it's obligatory. If the knowledge about obligations like emigration isn't taught to Muslims correctly then unislamic extremists will teach it and use the lack of teaching it as a means to mislead people. Contrary to popular belief ignorance about religion equals vulnerability not safety. So to not know is dangerous, it can be better to know and fail to implement than to not know and not implement. Plus how can the next generation know what they need to know if you don't tell them? Maybe you can't emigrate but perhaps your kids can, and knowing that they should will help you to better position them in life so they are able to do that. For example it is known where the safe zones will be when the antichrist goes on his rampage. Now today you might not be able to live there but you could get closer and better positioned so maybe your kids could get closer and their kids get closer so that way when the antichrist does come maybe your descendants will be in the safe zone and won't have to suffer under his tyranny or be tempted to worship him. Therefore religious knowledge helps you provide a better and safer future for your family. Since nobody wants their descendants to worship the antichrist we learn it not only for our own sake but so that we can teach the important knowledge to the next generation so they can act upon it while we get rewarded by God for passing along the knowledge even though we didn't act upon it ourselves. To not learn due to lack of ability to implement is to deprive your kids of knowledge and endanger the future of your family. As a result of the lack of teaching about the conditions making Muslim emigration an individual obligation, violent extremists try to make it all simple and choose violence to be the solution to fix everything instead of teaching a complicated half-answer. Which honestly violence might be the cause of the solution in the end, BUT the extremists then use unislamic violence to achieve their semi-Islamic goals. Violent extremists basically say, *"Well all Muslims have to leave in order to stop funding the enemies of Muslims but no Muslim country is willing to let them all move in and become citizens. So let's make our own country and Muslims will have to come to us, and then with them we'll conquer all those Muslim countries who closed their doors, fight Muslims or don't implement Shariah."* which by itself isn't necessarily unislamic but the way they fight is and then they easily go to extremes making takfir of all who don't join them, or agree with them, or pay any type of taxes to non-Muslims or unislamic governments whatsoever. Thus they start out with a noble good idea but are just too dumb to do it the right way and the logistics may not be favorable, especially if they are sinful and/or have unislamic doctrines. Also to make a country out of scratch you typically have to carve chunks out of other countries to do that, since most territory is already occupied and people logistically aren't yet able to build a country out in the ocean. Whereas Islamically one cannot just take someone's land and Antartica isn't really inhabitable; plus Antartica is already claimed anyways. There are priorities in Islam and sometimes obligations like doing Hajj or reestablishing a Khilafah can be postponed if there is an important valid Islamic reason for it. For example the famous Yusuf ibn Ayubi, who reconquered Jerusalem from the Christian Crusaders, never made the Hajj because Scholars told him that the Muslims needed him to stay doing his daily duties. Yusuf ibn Ayubi, wanted to go on Hajj but he didn't because there was a priority and need for him to do other things first. So while the Khilafah is an obligation, as is Hajj, there are other needs too that take priority before a Khilafah can be established. If you just look at the prophet Muhammad pbuh and the first building he built in Medinah it shows how to build an Islamic State. Likewise after he built that first building the things it was used for also show how the time of the Muslims should be spent as well as what percentage of Muslims were doing activities in that building. Then one can look at the second building Muhammad pbuh built in Medinah and how many Muslims used it and what it was for to see the priorities Muslims today should have. The Quran tells Muslims how to create an Islamic State repeatedly by commanding one to have Taqwa, and وَأَقِيمُوا الصَّلَاةَ وَآتُوا الزَّكَاةَ. That is how one fuels the Khilafah, if all the Muslims sincerely did that as it should be done then we would have a full-fledged Khilafah, in spirit, mind, practice and purse. Other conditions of a Khilafah include Muslims who وَعَمِلُوا ٱلصَّٰلِحَٰتِ وَتَوَاصَوْا۟ بِٱلْحَقِّ وَتَوَاصَوْا۟ بِٱلصَّبْرِ. A Khilafah comes whenever and wherever Muslims fulfill the conditions of it. Just like a legitimate healthy baby comes if/when Allah wills when enough people fulfill the conditions for it. However the very first step Muhammad pbuh took in establishing the Khilafah in Medinah is often forgotten entirely. The first step Muhammad pbuh took to establish a

Khilafah was to step out of his house to leave Mecca (dar al-kufr/dar al-harb) when making the Hijra. But that was the Khilafah, what were Muhammad's first steps taken to establish Islam? They were actually taken before he even became a prophet and they also led out of his house in Mecca (Dar al-Kufr) towards a different location away from sinful environments. Even the construction of Mecca itself occurred as a result of Ishmael pbuh and Hagar taking the steps to leave a comfortable hospitable home in exchange for a desolate "wasteland" without material wealth, nice weather or nice people; but it was where God wanted them to go and live. But does this mean to establish Islam and a Khilafah that Muslims shouldn't spend time in houses? No, but it does show which type of house or lands they should be spending time in, especially if one considers the first 2 buildings Muhammad pbuh built in Medinah and what they were used for. Thus the prophetic steps to build a Khilafah are known, the footprints have been made. Yet most Muslims haven't yet bothered to put their socks on, let alone their walking shoes, and they don't even know how to run. The prophetic path is the one to follow, Moses pbuh had a similar path before prophethood, before dawah, before warfare and establishing a state. The first step Moses pbuh took to create a Khilafah, that David and Solomon pbut later ruled, was not to conquer Jerusalem. That moment came much later and when it did the majority of his people failed their test and disobeyed despite yearning for a Khilafah for centuries. This was because as a majority they had never taken the small steps along with Moses pbuh, but just let him lead while they followed half-heartedly without sincerity or knowledge or pleasure in every step on the road to paradise.

The point is that Muslim Fundamentalists actually agree with Islamophobes in that it's a good idea for Muslims to get out of non-Muslim majority lands, except the Islamophobes want Muslims to leave so we don't liberate those brainwashed by falsehood and so that they can kill all the Muslims in one place. Although since if Muslims leave the West we will be better able to defend ourselves and establish Islam, the Islamophobes don't really want us to leave and actually just want us to stop practicing Islam altogether. Thus they pretend they want us to leave so as to make us feel uncomfortable pressure to convert/conform. Yet since most won't say that publicly, they try to redefine Islam similar to how Saul/Paul redefined

Christianity when he found he couldn't destroy the religion of Jesus from the outside he changed tactics. The trouble is that if all the practicing Muslims leave the West then the West will be left with nothing but deviant people claiming to be Muslims who will give them an incorrect view of Islam. Then just as Paul's doctrine which developed in Rome and Greece went back to replace the religion of Jesus pbuh in the holy land, the deviant Westernized self-proclaimed "Muslims" may try to conquer the Islamic lands and impose their falsehood thinking the proper Muslims are deviant. That's where I actually want to leave America, but because of the local Muslims living in America not practicing Islam it frightens me to think what would happen if I left. Especially in regards to my family, because realistically they don't need me to practice Islam; only God can help someone. Yet I'd be afraid of them becoming a Muslim then going to the local American masjid and being taught something that's not Islam yet believing that it was Islam. So then they'd think they were Muslims when they were practicing something other than Islam and that would make family interactions even more difficult and distressing. Fortunately it's not like that at every masjid in America but that just so happens to be the case at some masjids in some places in America. Most of the Muslims have a dangerous disease called kafirphobia. It's a self-inflicted disease usually brought on by an unislamic attempt to counter Islamophobia. It can be contagious if people don't learn Islam or practice Islam. Some symptoms of kafirphobia are: diluting Islam, making friends with disbelievers, not letting disbelievers know you think their religion is false and abhorrant, and thinking Muslims who practice Islam are "too strict", "radical" or "extremists".

The sad thing is that I can easily imagine a situation where if anyone in my family became Muslim they would go to a masjid and get told by Muslims in America that I'm some kind of radical extremist. In fact it's happened before, I took my non-Muslim mom to a masjid so she could see what it's like and where I spend time at and she said some Muslim lady told her after just a few minutes of talking about me that, "*He sounds like an extremist.*" I was stunned because I don't even know this lady and she doesn't know me, yet she labels me like this to my mother. I still struggle to understand why they would say that even if they thought that. What benefit did they think would come from saying that to my mom? In America too of all places. A Muslim labeling someone they don't even know nor met as a Muslim extremist in America isn't exactly a very smart idea, especially when they're saying that to a non-Muslim. What's worse is people might even believe it because of the grandfather clause in that people think if their family has been Muslims for generations or that if they're from or been to a Muslim country they think they know Islam. Only arrogant fools ask: "*How could a white American who's only been Muslim X years possibly know more about Islam than people born overseas into Muslim families who've been Muslims longer?*" Your family, skin color and travel log have nothing to do with whether you know Islam or practice Islam. Also time spent being Muslim doesn't mean you know or practice Islam either. Just as being born in Italy, of Italian descent, knowing Latin and going to Church every week doesn't mean such a person knows and/or practices Catholicism even if they claim to have been a Catholic since birth. However the reason the lady told my mom I sound like an extremist is probably because of how I get portrayed by my mother to other Muslims. For example once my mother said she reconnected with her childhood friend who had a daughter that married a Muslim guy and he was visiting the area for an event my mother was also attending. She said this guy was the "Muslim Archbishop of New York City" and I told her "There is no such thing as a Muslim Archbishop. In Islam there are no archbishops." Yet not trusting me she said "Well maybe you just don't Islam and are some extremist." and she decided to meet and ask this "Muslim Archbishop" to see if he thinks I'm extreme. So I told her again there are no archbishops in Islam, so this "Muslim Archbishop" is probably an extremist or deviant so he will likely tell you I'm an extremist because he is an extremist and his extremist doctrine would teach that the true Islam is an extreme form. (In my mind I feared this "Muslim Archbishop" was a Shia or something, who would poison my mom's mind and soul with heretical Shia doctrines.) After my mother met this Muslim guy and his Muslim wife, she told me she told them that I was a Shia Muslim and they gave her a weird look. I was upset and shocked my mother could say such an evil false thing about me to some Muslim strangers who don't know anything about me. Then she said as they talked she remembered I was a Sunni when they told her they were Sunnis. My mother also said that in her discussion they confirmed there were no Muslim Archbishops, and she doesn't know where she got the notion they were an archbishop. When I expressed my shock at her advertising me as a Shia she said she clarified to them she meant to say I was a "Shariah Muslim". Whereas there is no such thing as a "Shariah Muslim" so again this was another unislamic label invented by my non-Muslim mom when describing me to Muslims. The reason my mom thinks there is a special type of "Shariah Muslim" is because she thinks the Muslims who live in America and Canada believe in democracy/freedom and doesn't know what Islam teaches about those things and that it's a requirement of Islam for all Muslims to believe in Shariah while expressing hatred for and rejecting all other political systems. As a direct result of how other Muslims in America and Canada seem to her, since many don't publicly reject democracy and freedom or hatepreach like I do, she thinks I'm the only one in all of North America who believes in Shariah. Thus she thinks I'm a "Shariah Muslim" and that it's some type of sect or special denomination of Islam hence she tried to explain to "normal moderate Sunni Muslims" that I'm a "Shariah Muslim", but she said "Shia Muslim" by mistake. Her ignorance was hilarious but depressing as well, because I've explained Islam to her in depth. Yet because of the Western Muslims she meets being so friendly and "westernized" they make her think that my beliefs are particular to me and that I'm extreme or something and they don't even understand how they misinform/misguide her by trying to be friendly and tolerant. I told my mom how the way she presented me was inaccurate and made me sound extreme, wrong and unislamic. She thought I was extreme because she thinks differently and so by trying to make me seem non-extreme in her opinion she unwittingly presented me as an extremist. Then I realized due to the way my mom described this other Muslim guy, I thought he was extreme/deviant and then she had the same effect on him when describing me. This is exactly why Muslims get blacklisted, imprisoned and tortured, because of people presenting a distorted version of someone that inevitably makes someone appear extreme because what they learn of as "truth" is a extreme distortion of the real truth about a person. This is exactly how Jesus pbuh got presented as a satanic magician to the Jews because those who talked about him didn't give people the full picture. I mean honestly if you met Jesus pbuh nobody would ever think he was a crazy satanic magician, yet if you met the Jews who met Jesus pbuh and they told you about him then you would be inclined to think that about him because you got their version of Jesus pbuh and not Jesus'. Likewise the same applies to Christians, in that if you met Jesus pbuh you would never think he was God in the flesh or a son of God because that's not how he acted. However if someone else like Saul/Paul told you about Jesus pbuh then you might get such an extreme opinion of Jesus pbuh and think he taught such extreme things. I've learned that non-Muslims cannot help themselves from mislabeling practicing Muslims extreme and disuniting Muslims due to their mislabeling. Some do this intentionally but my mom wasn't trying to do so, it's just that kafirs genuinely don't know enough about Islam or Muslims to correctly talk about either to anybody. Just as scientists are the ones to discuss and label scientists, Muslims are the one's who are to label Muslims and extremists, likewise scholars are the ones to label who scholars are. One must present the full 100% truth in order to prevent others from thinking people are extreme incorrectly. That my Christian mother wanted to "*make sure that her Muslim son believed in the right stuff*" is a farcical notion. If my mother thinks Jesus is God or the son of God and Muslims don't then it doesn't matter whether I'm a Muslim extremist or not because to her all types of Muslims would be believing the "wrong stuff" about Jesus pbuh and God. So I asked my mom what she really meant in wanting to make sure I believed the right stuff? Since if I believe the right stuff then it would mean she believed the wrong stuff, and if she believed the right stuff then me being a non-extremist Muslim would still be wrong for me and make me extreme anyways for being wrong if Muslims were wrong. In short my mom was fundamentally trying to assure herself I *"had the right kind of wrong religion"*. After I explained this to her she laughed because she saw how ridiculous it was to care whether her Muslim son is an "extreme Muslim" or not, if Muslims themselves believe something extremely different than Christianity. All types of Muslims will be extremists from a disbeliever's point of view and vice versa. So anyone who doesn't believe what the prophets taught and doesn't act accordingly is an extremist by default. The correct opinion regarding religious beliefs is that if you have the right beliefs then everyone else who believes something different than you, must be an extremist who is wrong and on the road to hell. Although keep in mind I'm talking about beliefs here, not differences of opinion regarding jurisprudence which can validly exist within a religious faith. One logically can never "be okay with someone being a disbeliever as long as they aren't an extreme one". Hence this global talk about non-Muslims only fighting extremists, is complete nonsense, by definition every non-Muslim must view every Muslim as an extremist because Islam/truth is extremely different than falsehood. Disbelievers never champion the orthodoxy of another faith, if they did they wouldn't be disbelievers. My mother's concern wasn't really about me being an "extreme non-Christian" because her primary religion isn't Christianity, even though she claims it is, if Christianity were her primary religion she'd have a problem with me being any type of non-Christian at all. Yet her real concern wasn't that I was a non-Christian or a Muslim, but that I was a "Shariah Muslim", as she put it. This detail reveals her true religion is Americanism and that's why she was concerned over me believing in Shariah and not concerned over me being Muslim. This is because to her any Muslim who doesn't believe in Shariah and believes in Democracy,

Freedom, Equality etc isn't really a "disbeliever" in her religion, but the ones who don't believe in Americanism get the disbeliever treatment except they don't call them disbelievers today but extremists. To Americanists the word "extremist" means heretic/disbeliever because their theology is made up of secular terminology. The Americanist label of "extremist" today is the equivalent of being labeled an apostate in the past. Hence those who thoroughly believe in any type of Americanism usually are more concerned about "extremists" than they are over people believing in other traditional religions, since their primary religious loyalty is to Americanism rather than a traditional theology. The Americanists will have no problems at all with Americanist Christian/Jew/Hindu/Buddhist/etc, but they will have a very direct problem with any non-Americanist of any faith. Most people today know so little about religion they don't even understand what religion they belong to so they think their "tolerance" might be taught by X religion which they claim to believe in, when in reality they are only "tolerant" because their religion is Y religion and they are only intolerant of those which Y religion says to be intolerant of. That's why the ignorant Jews and Christians today who do interfaith are able to do it without apparently malicious intentions to convert Muslims to Judaism or Christianity. Those ignorant interfaith Jews/Christians aren't really Jews or Christians but Americanists or Pluralists trying to convert Muslims to Americanism or Pluralism. And the worst part about that is how they preach Americanism or Pluralism in the name of "Abrahamic faiths". Abraham pbuh had nothing to do with Freedom, nothing to do with Equality nothing to do with Democracy (the F.E.D.) and Abraham pbuh had nothing to do with "*interfaith tolerance/unity*". In reality ignorant Americanists are preaching Americanism in the name of Abraham pbuh, of which Zionists are co-religionists with Americanists hence the Zionist-American alliance. Meanwhile the true Christian and Jews are exploiting the Americanism taught in the name of Abraham pbuh simply to weaken the Muslim resistance to Christianity and Judaism knowing that most Muslims will never ever convert to Christianity or Judaism but if they convert to Americanism then their kids will likely apostate from Islam and then their kids will convert later. Most of the non-Americanist missionary Christians and Jews view Americanism as a gateway faith which can eventually lead Muslims to Christianity or Judaism. Some Christians and Jews are so devious that that they are willing to preach Americanism today if it helps them preach their own faith in the future. This is because Christianity and Judaism can never seem better than Islam and Christian missionaries have learned this, but both those false faiths are better than Americanism. Hence the clever Christians and Jews today never bother trying to convert a Muslim but try to convert an Americanist who thinks they are Muslim. Their goal is to convert Muslims into being Americanists so they can eventually convert those Americanists (claiming to be Muslims) to Christianity or Judaism. Their basic plan is to get Muslims to give up Islam in practice but not in belief (except for the belief in hate and Shariah, since that contradicts Americanism/interfaith). That is the reason why my mother was concerned I might be a "Shariah Muslim". Because even though she is ignorant regarding Christianity and Americanism, every Americanist internally knows how to and actively does preach their religion to others even if they don't consciously try to do so. This is why when my mom goes to the masjid she frequently tells an Imam if she meets one that "*My son needs to assimilate to the American culture. Can you help him understand he needs to assimilate? I'm not telling him to disbelieve in Islam or anything like that, I have no problem with him being a Muslim. But he just has to assimilate with the American way of life in order to live. So can you help him assimilate like all the rest of the Muslims here have done?"* (Keep in mind assimilation is defined as: *when a conquered people adopt the conqueror's culture before or at the same time they adopt the conqueror's religion.* Ironically my mother is trying to use other Muslims to convert me to Americanism, sadly sometimes they try to do so in the name of "combatting extremist ideas or tendencies".) Yet to this day my mom still insists she is entirely tolerant of Islam and isn't trying to get me to convert to her religion, despite publicly on multiple occasions asking Muslims in masjids to help me "assimilate". So that's where my mom thinks she is tolerant when in reality she is highly intolerant, the main difference that causes her to be mistaken about herself is that she is ignorant of her own religion and thinks it's Christianity instead of Americanism + others and isn't aware of when she is preaching, because she does it automatically in ways which to her seem secular. It's simply impossible to not preach your religious doctrines to others. Even fools preach their faiths despite doing it foolishly by default. For example if you believe in fiction then you will preach fiction, if you believe in hedonism you will preach hedonism, if one believes in the tolerant globalist interfaith Americanist movement then they will preach that even if they do so in the name of other religions. While the person who stresses they "don't want to talk about religion" is preaching secularism. The secularist converts you to their faith by getting you to "not talk about religion" or make religion out to be something of social/public relevance. Secularists are the worst types when it comes to public social interactions, because they get everyone to submit to their religious views making them think it's polite to avoid religious discussions when in reality the secularist just won the field and everyone else ended up practicing social secularism on demand. If any secularist ever tries that "Please let's not talk about religion." line with you then tell them you don't want to not talk about religion because the religion of secularism teaches people not to talk about religion and you aren't a secularist and would appreciate them being more honest when they try to convert you to secularism with their secularist preaching in the name of not preaching religions, because that's how secularists believe religious conversations should go and you refuse to convert and converse in a secular manner. Secularists believe there shouldn't be religious argumentation. So politely explain to them that if they really believed in what they said about "not talking about religion" then they wouldn't have preached secularism with that request/desire, but because secularism is so blatantly false the only way it can survive is if no other religions are discussed. Then you can inform the secularist that you are going to continue to talk about religion and are wondering whether they are willing to discuss religion politely as mature adults or are they going to act like a fanatical secular bigot who refuses to discuss religion because of their religious intolerance and fear of religious disagreements? With every conversation a religion is being preached, you are either preaching a religion or a religion is getting preached to you. If you are talking then it's a religious conversation and if you are communicating with anything then it's a religiously themed communication. There is no such thing as "non-religious" thoughts, speech or actions. Everything everyone is doing at any given time in the Universe is a religious activity whether they know it or not or intend it to be a religious activity or not. That's why God judges us according to everything. There is not a second of time which God has given you where God will say *"Well this second of time that I gave, which you spent living, was a second that had nothing at all to do with religion. So I won't judge you for what you did during that time in life, that was secular free time."* Know that every second has to do with religion and that's why Satan is working every single second because he knows that every second you have is spent on religion whether you know it or not. Satan doesn't take a second off, so if he doesn't then how can we if we are defeating him? In sports coaches tell their players, to never take a second off until the game is over. Well with religion we cannot afford to take a second off until the test of life is over. That is the truth regarding time, religion and the test of life. This is what the prophets taught and this is what the people who go to paradise for eternity believe. Most don't think this way about time or religion. So even if disbelievers don't think you are extreme just for having a different religion than them(which they will, even if they don't think they do, or know how to tell you, or intend to tell you) the believers themselves might think you are extreme even if you both profess the same religion because of the different levels people who follow the prophetic religion are on. Simply put the era we live in today is an era where if you are someone who is going to paradise then you will be labeled as extreme. It has always been that way ever since the beginning, the "normal people" burn in hell for eternity. The "normal people" fail the test of life. The goal is not to be normal but to be a friend of God who passes the test of life and dwells forever in the highest levels of paradise amongst the prophets of God. That is not normal. That is an extremely good eternal ending and you don't get that by being average/normal.

Today, as it always has been, it's not about whether people become Muslims, it's about whether they truly know Islam and practice Islam correctly the way the prophets pbut taught them to; which sometimes is different than the way some modern Muslims teach. In reality it actually is about whether a person becomes a Muslim or not, but I make this technical distinction because people have misunderstood what the fundamental definition of a Muslim is. The situation is such that I can't even focus on teaching Islam to non-Muslims because I turn around to find Muslims violating Islam and even advertising for evil religions and things. Many "Muslims" are preaching Americanism without knowing it, or at least I hope they don't know they are preaching Americanism of a Christianized and Secularist flavor. Although it's possible for Americanists to feign ignorance in order to keep preaching without condemnation. Islamically the position of the Muslim is to assume another Muslim is just foolish rather than suspect them of being an undercover hypocrite or disbeliever, since sometimes suspicious can be sins. Yet regardless of whether the preachers of Americanism are ignorant Muslims, hypocrites or full-fledged Americanists who are cognizant of it or not do you honestly think their type of preaching and activism is going to establish Islam and Shariah law in America leading the masses to become Muslims rejecting Christianity, democracy, freedom, equality, secularism and Americanism? That's what the "Muslims" in America tell me. I use the word "Muslim" because technically many actions and beliefs Muslims do in America nullify their Islam but because of ignorance they are not necessarily disbelievers. Of course to them I might seem extreme, but this is well known throughout the Muslim world and globally Muslims even have a name for "American Islam" and tell horror stories about the "Muslims" in America who preach stuff akin to what I've witnessed and been horrified with myself. I mention this because sometimes not caring what people think can lead to extremely dangerous situations, where you could do something sinful like takfir when the conditions haven't been fufilled, but if you keep the prophetic guidance as your manual for life and care about living as God wants then Godwilling you will come to know the right thing and how to do it the right way; eventually. Having the right belief and right intention is not enough, one must also do things the prophetic way which is not always the convenient or conventional way. One can have the right beliefs but do the wrong actions because of crazy misunderstandings. The point is that many "Muslims" in America simply don't know Islam and they believe/preach unislamic doctrines like Americanism due to ignorance or ignorance in how to communicate. Whether the Muslims who preach unislamic doctrines are disbelievers is not my job to say, the Muslim scholars should do that; but I do tell the Muslims in such situations when they teach such doctrines that what they are upon and teaching is not Islamic. It's possible for a Muslim to believe unislamic doctrines and preach unislamic doctrines and still be a Muslim due to extreme ignorance, and in my personal experience I've learned that <u>it's possible to mistakenly think a fellow Muslim is a disbeliever and not ignorant because you are ignorant of how they are ignorant</u>. That's the danger many semi-knowledgeable Muslims fall into, they get a little knowledge and then think those who don't have that knowledge or preach messages that contradict their knowledge must be hypocrites or disbelievers when in reality they are just ignorant, and the semi-knowledgeable Muslim is ignorant of how their fellow ignorant Muslims are ignorant. They don't know how such "Muslims" could not know Islam or not understand Islam when the proof of the correct position is provided to them. They forget to make every excuse they can for their Muslim brother or sister to keep them in Islam and avoid takfir. It's always best to assume a Muslim who believes/preaches anti-islamic things is a completely ignorant fool whom you need to struggle to kindly teach rather than assume they are a disbelieving hypocrite. Sometimes you really have to struggle to convince yourself they are stupid and don't know better in order to avoid labeling them a disbeliever which will just make them embrace their error even more and refuse to learn from you. Hence when I hear anti-islamic doctrines now from people I just try extra hard to assume they are ignorant and try to correct them. Rather than go to takfir I blame myself for not being able to teach them Islam gently and correctly so they come to have the correct beliefs. If someone else is stupid and/or wrong, then that's my fault for allowing them to be stupid/wrong and not correctly teaching them in a way so they understand what's right and wrong and accept it. For example it can actually amount to disbelief if a Muslim doesn't do their 5 daily prayers. With that in mind a questioner once asked the Muslim Scholar Al-Ghazali, *"What is the ruling of the one who left prayer?"* To which Al-Ghazali replied, *"The ruling is for you to take them along with you to the masjid."* Al-Ghazali also said "*Half of disbelief in God in the world is caused by people who made religion look ugly due to their bad conduct and ignorance.*" I'm not saying takfir is haram, it's not. Its an important obligatory currently neglected part of Islam, but lots of Muslims today don't know Islam so the conditions for takfir are different today than they were in the past because the ignorance levels today are different. Of course many peaceful people who I'd label "dangerously ignorant" think I'm extreme but I denounce violent extremists just the same, extremism must be opposed even if the extremists are peaceful preaching love in masjids in the USA. Either one fights and defeats 100% of extremism or 0%, there is no such thing as somebody defeating 99% of extremist beliefs. Fundamentally all the extremist beliefs must vanish for any extremist belief to vanish. That's the true Jihad, to denounce any and all deviation and extremism <u>correctly</u> even when it's socially unpopular to do so. Sometimes denouncing is done by the tongue or the pen and sometimes by the hand or the sword, but the tongue and pen are the types that truly win the theological wars even though the hand or sword can be effective and necessary. Whereas what may shock most is how the whole fallacy that preaching Islam as a total package or with enmity won't work in America, is that I asked one Imam who preaches the "Islam is peace, Muslims and non-Muslims can tolerantly coexist and love each other in America" if he had a plan for turning America into a Muslim country with Shariah. Which is the fundamental point peaceful extremists make, in that their dawah supposedly guides nations to Islam. I asked him and he told me that he has no plan but just personally plans to leave when it gets too hard to practice Islam in the US. Seriously he has no plan at all to establish Shariah in America. So that's where this Imam publicly preaches love, integration and even promotes voting in the elections and Muslim activism yet behind the scenes he plans on leaving, meanwhile I'm here telling people to leave or stay to establish Shariah while they tell me to stay and preach what the Imam is preaching since "he knows best because he's the Imam and you should stay in America like he says we should". Thus lots of the Imams in the West are hollow and phony when they publicly preach this moderate tolerant "Islam is peace" stuff. Most aren't sincere, have no plans to convert the West and are just basically living life and some might not even be Muslims. If any ever tell you "Islam is peace" then tell them what they are teaching is not Islam but tiny pieces of the full piece of the prophetic religion called Islam. Tell them to keep Islam in one piece without picking and choosing the peaceful aspects and ignoring the hateful, intolerant or violent aspects; because if they teach "Islam is peace" then they are turning Islam into pieces and you don't go to paradise with "just a piece" of the prophetic religion. You need to believe in the full piece of Islam not just the peace. Ask them for a single quote from the Quran or authentic hadith that says "Islam is peace", and they'll never give you one piece of information to corroborate their diluted "Islam is peace" salespitch. They'll say "Islam comes from word Salam which means peace in Arabic, thus Islam is peace" yet never did Muhammad pbuh in Arabic say "Islam is Salam". It's frustrating and sad but I mention this so that when the genocide does happen in America, then perhaps Muslims who wonder *"What the hell were Muslims in America doing before they got slaughtered?"* might read this and learn so they don't repeat the mistakes that were made in America. Wherein Islam was diluted, corrupted and lost in nearly all but the name and the "Muslims" themselves stopped and hindered those trying to revive and spread Islam. Honestly the greatest obstacle for me preaching Islam to people in America has come from Muslims themselves. These broadcasts where people say how all these foreign Muslims coming from overseas are trying to spread Islam, seem mainly false to me. From my perspective, generally it's native disbelievers who become Muslim who try to spread Islam while the foreign Muslims come to the West in order to get money, educations or safety and many of them thwart the spread of Islam in the West because of their own ignorance, fears, self-interests, habits, indifference, lack of confidence and misconceptions. Then the foreign Muslims, or born and raised western Muslims descended from foreign Muslims, chastisingly tell us reverts that there are no Islamic Shariah compliant Muslim countries in the world today, so we just have to deal with it, accept it and adapt to unislamic standards and preach how they preach because my style of preaching is "too harsh/insulting" and won't work; even though it's the only way that does work and turn males into men and females into women. So then I ask them which Muslim country I should go to then to practice Islam 100% and they say I should just stay in America and establish Islam here because I'm native and as a former disbeliever know how to talk to people, but don't push for Shariah or denounce kufr, kafirs or kafir systems. They tell me to stay in America because I know how to tell people about Islam and they don't, but then they tell me that I don't know how to tell people about Islam and I should do as they do and just "don't be too strict or go too deep into things". However legally in theory Islamic Shariah can become the law in the Western world even if the people aren't Muslims. For example there are legal loopholes to establish Shariah in America without any compromise whatsoever. I'm talking 100% shariah in American states is legally and peacefully a real possibility, but not with the attitude Muslims have today nor with the types of speeches they are giving to disbelievers nor believers. While even if the loopholes get closed, with a man-made system men can always choose to abolish that system. They can't change it, but they can abandon or abolish it. In my opinion this disheartening westernized Muslims' attitude of "We're here deal with it." must be replaced with "We're here, dominate it." or emigrate from it. That's what reverts are in the West to do. Many reverts want to live under Shariah, but born and raised Muslims as well as foreign Muslims tell us briskly that there is no Shariah so play the game of democracy just like nearly every other religious group is doing but somehow the Muslims are going to win that game in the non-Muslim land when even the kuffar can't win that game. Most born and raised Muslims have never been a non-Muslim so they have no clue what they think or how to preach to them yet their arrogance leads them to chastise the true prophetic preaching as unislamic, unwise or wrong. Meanwhile Muslim countries don't really want western reverts who want to establish shariah in their countries. Thus what does a revert do? Either they fight for somebody like ISIS trying to sinfully fight Shariah into place, or they try to turn their native land into an islamic country, or they leave their native land and move to a Muslim country and try to turn it into an islamic environment. Or they just go crazy and leave Islam altogether. The problem is the foreign Muslims really don't want to see the West implement Shariah. Honestly do you really think the Muslims who came to the Western world for business and school would be pleased if Shariah were implemented here and all the sinful stuff became illegal? Or would they move to escape Islam like they did when they came to the West because their Muslim countries were too Islamic for them? For Muslim reverts we're either going to implement Shariah in our native lands or we will leave, so they should either find us a country to move to or let us refute the kafir system and reform our own people. The big issue is that the Muslim reverts want to change their countries but the other Muslims just want to fit in with the unislamic Western system and live comfortably. The reverts want to fit in with Islam and change their countries just like they changed themselves, but the other group wants to fit in with kufr and kafirs and are changing Islam to do so. As a message to all Muslims, if you are in a non-Muslim land then you are there to change it and guide it to Islam, you are not there to improve the Muslim image; every person is created to spread Islam throughout the land even though the disbelievers hate it and yes the disbelievers hate it because Allah said so, thus if they don't hate the Islam you are presenting either they are on the road towards Islam or you aren't teaching the truth of Islam but a distorted version which they like but God hates. As they say the truth will set you free, well legally the truth with Allah's aid will make Islam the law in Western non-Muslim lands and abolish freedoms. The key is that such pure Islamic truth must not be compromised and must be fearless. Islam does not achieve victory if Muslims fear any other than Allah. Muslims should reject the falsehood, they must not "learn to live with it". A minority is powerless only when they conform to the majority, because whenever a minority conforms it is no longer a minority but converted. In reality Imperialistic colonization was just conformity of the majority to the minority Imperialists. Had the Imperialists conformed to the majority they would have been powerless. There is no difference between conforming and converting, it's just terminology in that conforming is a social/economic or political transformation and converting is a transformation which is theological/intellectual/emotional. Regarding religion some types of conformity qualify as religiously converting. The road of Muslims conforming to Kafir principles/society is both the equivalent to and the eventual road to converting to Kufr. In this religious war between Islam and Kufr you either confront or you conform. Which did the prophets teach God's slaves to do? I don't care about the insides, I'm stating the external reality. The correct choice is easy to identify but Satan confuses many. The road to paradise leads to a direct confrontation with the devil himself. If you can't be confrontational with people then the devil's job is easy and the believers will never win this war, in this world. But God has promised victory for the believers in advance. So the only question is if when you are playing your position on God's team, will you have a winning season or will you conform to the devil's playbook, lose the competition and risk God firing you forever for a poor performance in the arena. God has put you on the battlefield at this time in the theological war and expects results from you. What are you going to do with your life to win this war? What makes your test of life special? It is up to you to turn the tide of this war in God's favor. God has given you a mission, and the time you have left is short. You cannot afford to conform to the desires of yourself or Satan.. *"How then are we supposed to live with kuffar?"* That is a question a Muslim doesn't ask. The question they should be asking is "How can we make this country a Muslim country who chooses to reject freedom, equality, secularism, democracy and every other form of Kufr, Shirk and Bida and submit to Islam?" Our goal is not to fit in with the kafir status quo, we are here to change the world and fix their affairs. You can only fix their affairs if you let them know they got some problems that Islam solves. It's already known how Muslims live with disbelievers from the examples of the persecution Muslims suffered under unislamic rule in Mecca or in Egypt between Joseph and Moses pbut, how they lived in peace in unislamic rule in Abyssinia where the king became Muslim protecting the Muslims from every harm whether physical or verbal and put down a rebellion of Christian citizens who wanted to kill the Muslims, and from the peace non-Muslims experienced wherever Shariah has been implemented. I'm not saying Muslims can't live with disbelievers peacefully but what I am saying is that the goal of a Muslim is to live under Islamic laws amongst Muslims and not under kafir laws or kufr systems or with any non-Muslim majority. Scholars have even stated that Muslims cannot have all non-Muslim neighbors, and if they don't have Muslim neighbors then they should either move so they have at least 1 Muslim neighbor, or actively preach Islam until their neighbors become Muslim or move. Rather than Western Muslims wondering about how the non-Muslims view them, they should worry about conveying the message of Islam to them, so they stop being disbelievers and can become believers in God. The non-Muslims should be adjusting themselves in order to live with us not the other way around. The thing is I hated Muslims and wanted them all dead and made plans to exterminate them for many years, but then I became a Muslim so then Muslims no longer had to worry about me. Whereas if Muslims had focused on trying to make me tolerate and like them I probably would never have embraced Islam and burned in hell after death. Yet because I learned my religion was false and found Islam to be true it lead to the disappearance of the problem I was for Muslims and their concerns of living with me in peace in America. The difference between Muslims today and the Sahabah is that almost every companion of Muhammad pbuh was a revert to Islam and most of them knew and lived a life as a disbeliever before Islam. Born and raised Muslims don't know what that's like and that's the difference between the companions of Muhammad pbuh and many modern Muslims. Thus simple confrontational dawah is the solution to this whole dilemma, as it was in the past, is now and always will be and then the world will end and we get our scores on the test of life. Freedom is the problem in America, not the solution. If you want to improve the image of Muslims then do prophetic dawah and have our enemies become Muslims. That's what really hurts me about the attitude of some Muslims in America, they automatically think Americans won't become Muslims. I was the biggest enemy of Islam I knew of and I became a Muslim, so if I became a Muslim everyone can become a Muslim. Muslims in the non-Muslim lands should know that Allah did not send them there to defend Islam or the Muslims. If that is why you are here/there then please leave. Allah has sent us to America to establish Islam and reject all falsehood like freedom/democracy.

America needs us, we don't need them nor their approval or support. They are slaves of Satan and we aren't even telling them they are enslaved/oppressed. Muslims must free the kafir world from freedom, not congratulate and support them in their sins/transgression. It's expected that some nations will react in nasty or violent ways if Muslims refute their false religions and actively try to spread Islam with earnest sincerity; as if people's eternal destination truly depended on it. When that happens Muslims will leave, but currently we don't have any 100% Islamic Muslim country to easily go to that will accommodate us all. We want one but don't have one and the Muslim countries are getting bombed by non-Muslim countries so some Muslims think they are better off trying to peacefully spread Islam in the West, but sadly many just want to live a comfortable life and get money or a degree and don't truly care to actively spread Islam. That's how Muslims went from being dignitaries in Egypt when Yusuf was alive to slaves by the time of Moses pbut. In that trap many become sinful and fall out of Islam without even knowing it. Thereupon they start preaching things that are contrary to Islam claiming to be Muslims teaching Islam to non-Muslims. So it's a big mess that took centuries to develop and may take more than a few days to fix. This is not the first time after Muhammad pbuh where Muslims have been without a Khilafah. It happened before when the Mongols killed the Abbasid Khalifah in 1258 CE. When that Khilafah ended in 1258 CE it wasn't until 1517 CE that another Khilafah became recognized by all Muslims. Of which a fascinating phenomenon is that in 1453 CE there was no Khilafah when Muslims conquered Constantinople but there was a Khilafah when the Muslims lost Jerusalem to the Crusaders. The point is that a Khilafah is not necessary for nor indicative of military dominance. Also when you consider it took 259 solar years for Muslims to reestablish the Khilafah in the past, the current struggle to reestablish Islam and a Khilafah in the world may still be in it's early stages. Only Allah knows how and when change will happen, but the help of Allah is always near; as is our own death. Whereas sometimes it's better not to see the successful end because the winning team might celebrate in sinful ways once the victory does come and we don't want to be sinful or ungrateful winners. So dying before dominating can be better for people than if they live to become prominent. In the end the only question is whether you and I will be Muslim, practice and support Islam thus entering paradise, or oppose or disbelive in Islam thereby choosing the hellfire. I'm not going to hide the fact of Islamic world domination and think that by publicizing my idea of how to reestablish the Khilafah it would be jeopardized in anyway. This has already been decreed by Allah. In fact the planets and each animal, plant and mineral are already all Muslims, it's only people and jinn who aren't. The key to success isn't in planning or executing the plan, but in total submission to the Creator of everything. The plan we should have is to totally devote ourselves to our Creator and believe, think and do what he wants every moment regardless of anyone's opinions or actions. This includes ourself and we should value what our Creator wants over our personal desires, fears, ego, urges, habits, dreams and feelings. When you follow God's plan you have no problems, even if the rest of the world thinks and says you have problems I guarantee that you won't. That is the fundamental blueprint. The Quran and Sunnah also teaches the technical blueprint as well, but to learn the technicals of the problem solving blueprint one must have the knowledge and follow the steps of the fundamental blueprint first. Once you know the fundamental blueprint you will know exactly where the technical blueprint is and what is needed to fulfill it and obtain the means to fulfill it. Thereupon you'll fulfill it. I will give you a hint, the fundamental blueprint and the technical blueprint combine as the blueprint for your journey to paradise. Many talk the talk in public and private, loudly and softly, but few will walk the walk over the siraat, or talk the talk when they are asked the 3 questions in the grave by angels Munkar and Nakir.

    The emergency excuse Muslims try to give to justify preaching unislamic doctrines or living unislamic lifestyles is that Allah allows one to speak a word of disbelief if they are in danger, thus they say since preaching the truth or living Islamically is dangerous and can cause difficulties then they use this loophole to justify whatever it is they are doing. However Muslim Scholars explained there are 4 conditions for compulsion to be genuine to warrant making a statement of kufr. Also know that this is just for statements of disbelief, actions of disbelief are not allowed except in a extremely rare circumstance such as a Muslim spy infiltrating the ranks of an enemy army as a stategem of military warfare, not theological.

1. The compeller is actually able to perform that which he is threatening to do and the compelled one, who is commanded is unable to repel that even by fleeing.

2. That your assumption is certain that if you refuse then the compeller will fulfill the threat.

3. The threat is immediate and will be fulfilled on the spot.

4. Nothing indicates the excessiveness of the one compelled in giving into demands. Meaning only the minimum to remove the trial/danger/threat may be done. For example if someone is torturing you to say kufr/shirk then you can only say the absolute minimum that is needed to stop the torture, not a single unislamic syllable more.

In fact this loophole that allows Muslims to on extreme occasions say something unislamic or pro-kufr and pro-kafir was allowed by Allah due to the case of Ammar bin Yasir. Ammar's parents got killed by disbelievers because they were Muslims. When Ammar was then walking by some disbelievers in Mecca he heard them cursing Muhammad pbuh so he forbid them from doing that. They basically said "*This is a non-Muslim land with a non-Muslim majority, I got freedom of speech. Who do you think you are to forbid me from cursing Muhammad? We will hurt you for daring to forbid our freedom and preach the religion of Islam to us.*" then the disbelievers seized him and tortured him attempting to get him to disbelieve in Islam. Thus to escape torture he said a word of disbelief, then he went to Muhammad pbuh in tears that he cracked under life-threatening torture. When asked about his belief in Islam Ammar said he truly believed but just couldn't bear the pain of the moment and lost control of his own tongue due to his body trying to preserve his life. Thus Allah made it known that Ammar was still a believer and in such situations of genuine compulsion then a Muslim can be permitted to say such unislamic things that contradict Islamic doctrines/teachings. Also this only refers to uttering words of disbelief, under the genuine and immediate fear of death, not fear of embarrassment or displeasure or dislike and even still this allowance is only regarding words and not actions of disbelief. Remember it's permitted, it's not obligatory and there is reward for not making use of the compulsion allowance. Abbas bin Abdul Muttalib and Bilal are examples of not using this to escape torture and they were rewarded by God as a result. Another important thing is this allowance to utter words of disbelief when compelled does not allow becoming friends with non-Muslims or alliances. The allowance under the 4 conditions of compulsion is just a permission to disguise enmity, not to preach love or friendship. One can't say "*I voted for X because X said they'd kill me if I didn't.*" because even in such a situation, them killing you still doesn't give them the vote they wanted. So realistically they wouldn't even kill you for not voting for them, if they did it would be because of not participating in the democratic religious ritual of voting, not because of not voting for them. Yet voting for a kafir is an action, so it doesn't come under the allowance of the 4 conditions when compelled. But when the 4 conditions are met a Muslim is allowed to verbally say anti-islamic things. This is called Taqiyyah, which is that infamous notorious principle where "Muslims can lie to non-Muslims about their religion." Seriously this is that famous "Islam teaches Muslims lie to us" doctrine. It's only allowed under true fear of death when a sword is at your neck but the Islamaphobic enemies of Islam would make people think it's a obligatory way of life instead of just an emergency allowance that's permissible but disliked anyways.

But then why if the Islamaphobes are peaceful would they stress that you can't trust Muslims because of Taqiyyah since Islam says Muslims can lie when threatened with death? This is because those enemies of Islam know enough about Islam to realize this Taqiyyah means you can't give Muslims a choice of "convert or die" and have them convert via the tongue with it being genuine. Thus by preaching "you can't trust what any Muslims say because of Taqiyyah" they are truly preaching to an audience that only exists after Muslims have a literal gun to their head. Since they have planned for mass Muslim genocide they are pre-programming people to not hesitate to kill Muslims even if we pretend to say we disbelieve in Islam when threatened to convert. Meaning the Islamaphobes don't even want conversions, they just want the Muslim blood so rather than say Muslims might lie when coerced to convert via force they automatically train killers to kill on sight without even offering to convert Muslims by force. Yet many Muslims today foolishly think they will be given the choice of convert or die when the kuffar get violent, however the non-Muslims already learned that doesn't really work. Muslims won't be given the option to convert once the violence starts in the non-Muslim lands. The Islamaphobes fundamentally tell people *"Islam is an evil religion and Muslims are untrustworthy because when you put a gun to their head and tell them to convert to your religion then their religion says they can lie to non-Muslims and pretend to convert while still being Muslims in their heart."* How does that make Islam and Muslims bad and evil? This is because other religions don't allow that, and that's how Christianity was able to achieve success with it's "convert or die" method in pagan lands because they knew the conversions via the sword were mostly genuine. Although since Muslims can verbally fake it, the Jews, Christians, Americanists and others have developed new methods to convert the Muslims since their patented sword conversions can't work effectively. Sadly though their semi-peaceful methods of converting Muslims are working on many fools. For example how many Muslims today are tortured? Rather how many living in the non-Muslim countries are tortured? How many truly fear that they will die on the spot if they don't say X words? How many are even verbally threatened? Only an extreme minority. (Note verbal threats alone don't constitute genuine compulsion to excuse verbal disbelief.) So this whole Taqiyyah loophole truly doesn't apply to most Muslims and is forbidden in the majority of cases in the majority of places in the world. Many are just psychological cowards who fear their own paranoid feelings of inferiority and differentness. Many Muslims are afraid to face the worldly consequences of practicing Islam correctly in the prophetic manner. They subconsiously expect the test of life is supposed to be easy entertainment. Many Muslims are afraid to be feared so they say unislamic things because they are afraid kuffar might be scared or react like the devils they are. Now truly that is the epitome of being terrorized, to be afraid that others are afraid of you or your religion. Lots of "Muslims" are terrified that they'll be thought of as terrorists. They'd rather dance with the smiling human devils than have uncomfortable hostility between them, or have the human devils dislike them or disparage them or dare to harm them for practicing Islam. Note I said "practicing Islam" because most devils will always "let you believe in Islam". This is because they know a religion is not just belief but practice as well, so to the anti-islamic devils you don't really believe in Islam if you aren't practicing it. The devil doesn't mind the "believers" he just hates practicers. It's a good thing Moses pbuh wasn't afraid of having Pharaoh fear him. Moses pbuh was legitimately concerned about a death sentence because he committed manslaughter, but he still preached the confrontational truth of Islam to the entire pagan Egyptian nation right to Pharaoh's face, eye to eye, mouth to ear. Today the vast majority of Muslims have no legitimate excuse to verbalize unislamic statements promoting freedom, democracy, secularism, equality, patriotism, nationalism, interfaith, and "love" for non-Muslims. Those who say such things without genuine compulsion that fits the 4 conditions of compulsion are hypocrites, or ignorant at best and possibly disbelievers depending on each individual and the situation. Also if one must utter words of disbelief due to true compulsion then it should only be done in private, never publicly if one need not do so, and if a public declaration of disbelief is needed to live then other rulings can apply that may make it forbidden to publicly declare kufr depending on the circumstances.

Notwithstanding the unjust way Muslims have been treated, that does not give any Muslim the right to do injustice to non-Muslims, no matter how bad the treatment is no matter for how long. Unjust actions are still unjust and sinful, even if it is a reaction to injustice and oppression. This is something many fail to understand Muslim and non-Muslim alike, but this is what Islam teaches. Sometimes malicious war crimes are committed, even though self-defense is allowed the victims justly retaliating can easily be led to extremes by Satan and commit war crimes themselves, making the Good vs. Evil scenario turn into Evil vs. Evil. This only adds fuel to the fire which will result in all involved being added as fuel to the hellfire, despite one side being good and correct in the beginning. It is better to forgive. Those quickest to forgive will be the quickest to enter paradise and will be shaded on the Day of Judgment when the sun is a mile away and people are drowning in sweat. However while it is better to forgive, sometimes forgiveness will exasperate the problem and cause it to continue if not worsen. In such a case everyone who retaliates must be conscious of not exceeding the limits of justice because this is exactly what Satan wants to happen as a result. If the bounds are overstepped and the oppressors are oppressed, then they will seek revenge and feel justified oppressing again and the cycle of oppression will continue to continue as it has throughout human history. Patience and forgiveness are important to remember as well as self-restraint.

I don't intend to paint Muslims as the victims of history. I'm making the case that history has a pattern of ostracizing Muslims which continues until modern times. Since Satan has always been against the believers, if history shows that one faith has constantly been attacked throughout history from all others, then that could be an indication in and of itself that perhaps Satan is the enemy of this faith because it leads to paradise and is what God wants from humans. At the least it should make one consider that there must be something very special about this particular religion that has constantly united humans against it throughout time. The lives of the Prophets pbut shows that most of mankind has always opposed the unique religion of God. The history of the world in regards to Muslims should make someone interested to find out why they have been treated as they have been. Of course everyone can make their own religious group out to be the victim, but those arguments are weaker when compared to Muslim persecution. Of course because I'm Muslim I'm not entirely unbiased, you can decide for yourself whether I'm just pulling theories out of thin air or if there is evidence to support my claims. God gave you a brain, heart and the innate ability to determine truth from falsehood, even if we have become rusty and are not used to frequently discerning.

All hope for humanity is not lost, the truth is still available and the Creator can guide people to it if they desire guidance. Don't despair, we just have to take things more seriously, see the big picture and what the long term causes and effects are. In the long term, all the lies will be exposed when everyone is judged by the Creator. As it relates to you, the important thing is whether you will be among those who lived and acted according to the truth and justice for the pleasure of God, or if you lived and acted according to falsehood for other reasons. In our era it is not easy to oppose falsehood and stand up for truth and justice, it never has been, it was even harder during the time of the prophets pbut. Although there are simple things we can do. First we have to start with ourselves, then our family, then our friends, then the public at large. However the most important thing is that we ourselves hold fast to the truth, because it may be that the world will reject you for being truthful, all your friends, family, and fellow humans may all be against you and say you are crazy. People said the same about the prophets pbut. It is unlikely we will ever be tested so severely, but even if that is the case if we remember death, the dark dirty grave and the questions we will be asked, the hellfire and paradise, then we will see how this life is very short and temporary. Any hardship we encounter doing a good deed will pass yet the deed will be credited to us, likewise any temptation to do a bad deed will pass and the deed will be credited to us, these deeds will be on our records long after they have been experienced. All we have to do is be patient for a few seconds. This is the reality of life which is forgotten by the masses who don't know, don't care and won't be cared for in the eternal afterlife. We have the opportunity today to separate ourselves from falsehood and sin, we don't have to be like everyone else, we can achieve a status of being someone whom the Creator of everything loves. This is what all should strive for. Whenever you discover a lie, don't despair or be judgmental, be grateful that you now know the truth so that you are no longer amongst the deceived. Thank your Maker for letting you recognize a lie as a lie and guiding you to the truth instead of allowing you to fall for another lie, as most people do arrogantly thinking they could never be fooled more than once by Satan. Don't let that make you arrogant though, because emotions are what lead us to believe satanic lies in the first place. After reading such information you might be experiencing an emotional outrage whether you're Muslim, Catholic, Christian or just another human that feels the embarrassment of having believed a lie(s) all their lives. It is very important not to let those emotional reactions to information have too much control over your behavior. Most of this stuff happened in the past. That doesn't mean it's not important, but many of these oppressive transgressors are dead now and will be recompensed for all eternity. On a personal level we cannot hold a grudge against people living today as a result of what their ancestors or organizations which they belong to have done in the past, including the past of yesterday. Of course justice must be pursued, but if our emotions control us then it's easy for Satan to manipulate us and cause further oppression and transgression which we will then regret the consequences of. I shared this information so that you can gain an appreciation for why some Muslims might feel that they have historically been attacked by non-Muslim society. Muslims are entirely justified in feeling this way and history supports this position. Unfortunately this persecution is not just historical, it is happening in many places of the world today. Jews are oppressing Muslims in Palestine, Buddhists are boycotting, burning, raping and killing Muslims in Burma/Myannmar, Hindus are oppressing Muslims in India, Christians are killing Muslims in Kenya, Chinese are oppressing Muslims in China forcefeeding them during Ramadan preventing them from fasting, Russians have been oppressing Muslims since the days they took Russian land from the Muslims, Christians are killing Muslims in Somalia, Bodos are killing Muslims in Assam, Buddhists are killing Muslims in Sri Lanka, Shia are killing Muslims in Lebanon, Hindus are killing Muslims in Bangladesh, Christians are killing Muslims in Nigeria, nearly everyone has been killing, raping and robbing Muslims in Iraq, Secularists around the world ban female students from wearing niqabs and hijabs. In the Central African Republic Christians have been killing Muslims since 2013 CE forcing them to make a choice of *"become Christian or die"*, destroying 417 of the country's 436 masjids as of March 2015 CE (that's 95%), Shia and nearly everyone else is killing and raping Muslims in Syria, French are killing

Muslims in Mali, Shia are killing Muslims in Yemen, Secularists are killing Muslims in Egypt, Christians are killing Muslims in Liberia, Christians are oppressing Muslims in Eritrea, the Shia regime in Iran has been oppressing Muslims for decades, Christians are oppressing Muslims in South Sudan and there are too many crimes to list them all. With all this injustice and oppression that is happening to Muslims worldwide, how does the international media portray Muslims? Are Muslims depicted as the victims of the world? Last time I checked Islam and Muslims were the punching bags for international media outlets, which should make everybody suspicious of the integrity and reliability of such sources of information. Several places I've listed, where Muslims are being killed for being Muslim, are not reported by the mainstream media so you might never have even heard Muslims were being persecuted there, or even lived there. But you can be certain that once Muslims fight back in those countries and non-Muslims die, the mainstream media will be all over it pointing the finger at Islam and Muslims. In many other places Muslims are being murdered simply because they are Muslim, but I only listed the organized mass murders that I know of which are taking place as I write. On the continuing Christian oppression, as a former Christian I feel something must be clarified. Oftentimes Christians hear that it's the Muslims who are killing Christians in Africa rather than the other way around. Many times what happens is that there may be Christian missionaries or preachers forcing Christianity upon people, or inciting Christian congregations to violence. Then when Muslims get killed they fight back and kill Christians, but it is only after the Christians get killed in retaliation that churches in the west will say something about it and give a false impression without telling the full story of what is going on. To be fair the same thing happens the other way too and some Muslims might disobey the religion of Islam and commit unjust atrocities on Christians undeservedly and then Christians retaliate, but then Muslims are not informed of who started killing who first, so both sides see themselves as victims. What makes it even worse is that frequently when both sides retaliate they end up seeking revenge on the wrong people by mistake. In trying to get even innocent people are oppressed and the original oppressors get away while the new victims seek rectification. This conflates to create problems of massive proportions. Usually we don't know the full side of the story and let our desires selectively process the information we receive to come to conclusions we already believe in, even if they are a distortion of the facts that we may or may not know of. Some of these persecutions of Muslims are making headlines around the world and some are not. It is incredible that Jews, Christians, Communists, Capitalists, Atheists, Secularists, Hindus, Buddhists, Shia, Nationalists and Internationalists are all simultaneously fighting Muslims in different parts of the world. If you gathered these various groups together for a meeting they wouldn't even be able to agree on what to eat for lunch. Yet all these groups are killing Muslims as I write. Despite Muslims being the most killed religious group today, the numbers of Muslims in the world is increasing. Muslims have the smallest sword in the world today yet Islam is the fastest growing religion, clearly Islam is not a religion that is spread by the sword. What is it about Islam that makes it so unique and different from all the other ideologies that unites the entire world against Muslims? It has already been established that there can only be one true religion, that the majority of people will not be upon it and that Satan will use any and all means available to oppose it. Could it be because Islam is the truth that is why the world oppresses Muslims? But if Islam is the true religion and Muslims are believers, then why would God allow the believers to be abused so much? This is an important question but easy to know the answer to if we remember the reality of life. Life is a test, it's not an easy test it is a hard test. Everyone would agree that the prophets pbut were believers and loved by God, yet they suffered some of the worst persecutions imaginable. Although God loved the prophets, so why would those God loves suffer? Suffering is a means of humbling and causes one to seek relief. There is no better reliever than the Creator, so suffering draws people closer to God because we tend to worship more when we need help than we do when life is easy. Any pain that befalls a believer is a means of expiation for their sins and is pain they will not have to suffer in the afterlife. Suffering purifies a believer similar to how gold is purified in fire to remove the impurities. It's as the widely popular saying goes: *"no pain, no gain"*. Sadly many Muslims today do not practice Islam correctly nor wholeheartedly, culture and innovations have crept in with some Muslims thinking that these practices are part of the religion. As a result there are many impurities that need to be removed, perhaps this suffering will lead people to the true pure Islam. Since Muslims are 1 nation the sins of 1 Muslim can affect the whole Muslim body, when 1 part of the body is hurt, even if it's via their sins, it hurts us all. Also if Allah loves a person and wants them to have a high rank in paradise that they can't get through their deeds, then calamity will be brought down upon them in order to elevate their station in the afterlife. Suffering also tests the patience and gratitude of a believer like how Job pbuh was tested to see whether he would be steadfast through hardship as he was through ease. The prophets were so severely tested that it would reach a point were even they would ask, "*when will the help of Allah come?*" and they were prophets. This was to see whether they would believe no matter how much pain and suffering befell them. Therefore suffering can be a good thing that brings us closer to Allah as well as separate the true believers from the hypocrites. Many a times towns would reject their prophet and then Allah made life easy for them increasing their wealth and children, purposely giving them the ability to do more sins, so that they would be even more deserving of the punishment when they were destroyed. Ease in life is actually a harder test because it is easier to sin and to be ungrateful when life is easy. Yet the suffering of others in the world should make one better. For example if others are poor, unhealthy, oppressed, abused, and have all types of hardships which I don't experience then personally how can I possibly contemplate doing sins when God has blessed with all the things which I have that others don't. How can I learn about current events and starving people in other countries who are not doing sins and then turn around and do sins that are worse than those people would even dream of doing? Since God has given me more and favored me in many respects over others, then I have to be doing more good deeds than the others and most certainly I must refrain from doing sins. Since those who have less aren't doing the sins, I have no excuse for my sins. What will it be like on the day of Judgement when those poor persecuted sinless people come and are besides me with my life of luxury and evil sins? Without even saying anything by default everyone will know those poor oppressed people will be better off than me, since they were better with less and I was worse with more. Thus today we may be thankful that we aren't tested with hardship but it might be better for us in the next life if we were. You cannot have both this world and the next, you could have neither, but you cannot enjoy yourself to the fullest in both, one must be sacrificed to obtain the other. You can't expect to be with Moses pbuh in paradise if you're living the lifestyle of Pharaoh. If Satan cannot brainwash your mind, poison your soul or corrupt your heart, then he will try to punish your body using his soldiers and followers to do so. The better you are the more strongly and frequently Satan will attack you, directly and indirectly in disguise and subtlety. Satan doesn't bother those who are already on his team. The oppression befalling Muslims today is an opportunity to see who will help the oppressed and fight injustice, even though it is unpopular and/or difficult to do so. For instance a 10 year old Palestinian Muslim boy throwing a rock at an Israeli tank that just crushed his home is called a terrorist, while the Jewish sniper who shoots that young boy in the head killing him gets called a hero and given a parade. We are living in a strange time where good guys are called bad guys and bad guys are called great guys, all depending on which source of information you get your news from. These drastically different perspectives mean that someone is very wrong and misled by Satan, unfortunately in our time both sides could be wrong. One of Satan's biggest deceptions is making us think every conflict is between Good vs. Evil. Sometimes it can be Evil vs. Evil, Good vs. Good, or perhaps it is Evil vs. Good and we may be on the side of evil and not realize it. Real life is not like the cartoons where the bad guys say they are evil, in real life the bad guys say that they are good guys and trick many into believing them, supporting them, loving them, killing for them and sometimes even dying for them. Thereby effectively causing people to live as a friend of Satan and enemy of God, without them knowing it until after the angel of death extracts their soul. So choose to be a slave of Allah so as to defeat Satan. Your entire life until your death is a religious war between you vs. your desires + satan and his army. However remember satan's allies can at any time repent and stop fighting for satan by submitting to Allah in Islam as Muslims. Thus the Muslim side will always extend the peace branch of forgiveness should any of satan's allies wish to join Allah's team. In such a case we must love and forgive them as members and fellow co-religionists. This has most recently been embodied by the display of forgiveness the Taliban showed to its military opponents from the puppet Afghan National Army. The open arms of welcoming brotherhood always existed since the time the confederation of anti-terror crusaders led by the USA invaded Afghanistan in 2001 under flimsy illegal pretenses. Throughout the war many would repent from fighting the Muslims and join the Taliban in their Jihad to liberate Afghanistan, and some prisoners of war even embraced Islam voluntarily yet no Muslim prisoners captured by the crusaders and illegally tortured in Guantanomo Bay ever apostated. While even a non-Muslim guard at Guantanomo Bay called Terry Holdbrooks embraced Islam. So when one side doesn't apostate and the other side has their lead torturers repentfully embracing the religion they were fighting against it really tells the story between truth and falsehood. While the mercy of the Muslims during Jihad throughout history is famously known to those who study, from the bloodless conquest of Jerusalem by Umar bin Khattab and again the bloodless conquest of Jerusalem by Salahuddin both of whom were following the example of Prophet Muhammad's conquest of Mecca, the overwhelming historical lesson is Muslims will always readily forgive their enemy combatant once sincere repentance and/or cessation of hostilities are made. Lest it be lost to history I shall include the English translation of the eid al adha message from the leader of the Taliban Hibatullah Akhunzada in July 2021 while the 20 year war against the puppet unislamic democratic afghan regime was still ongoing. Within 1 month of this message the vast majority of the 300,000 soldiers of the Afghan National Army surrendered peacefully and even joined the Taliban government thereby ending the war with minimal bloodshed.

In the name of Allah, the Most Compassionate, the Most Merciful

Allah is the Greatest, Allah is the Greatest, there is no God but Allah, Allah is the Greatest, Allah is the Greatest, and all praise be to Allah.

All praise be to Allah. We praise Him and seek His help and forgiveness. We also seek His refuge from the evils of our inner selves and from our wicked deeds. Whoever is guided by Allah, there is none to mislead him and whoever is left by Allah in error, there will be none as guide for him (except Allah). I testify there is no God but Allah. Alone is He and has no associate, who honored his soldiers, helped His servant and defeated the confederates. And I testify that Muhammad is His Servant and Messenger, may peace and blessings be upon him, his family, and his companions.

Verily, We have given you a manifest victory. That Allah may forgive your sins of the past and future, and complete His Favor on you, and guide you on a Straight Path. And that Allah may aid you with a mighty victory. (Quran Surah Al-Fath, verse 1-3)

Verily, We have granted you Al-Khauthar. So turn in prayer to your Lord and sacrifice [to Him alone]. Indeed, your enemy is the one cut-off [from all goodness]. (Quran Surah Al-Kauthar; verse 1-3)

Say, "Indeed, my prayer, my sacrifice, my living and my dying are for Allah, the Lord of 'Alamin (all that exists). He has no partner. And of this I have been commanded, and I am the first of the Muslims". (Quran Surah Al-An'am; verse 162-163)

To the Muslim and valiant people of Afghanistan, courageous Mujahideen and entire Muslim Ummah!

May peace and blessing of Allah be upon you all!

- I extend my felicitation to you all on the occasion of Eid-ul-Adha, and may Allah accept all your sacrifices, Hajj pilgrimage, charity, prayers and good deeds.

I also sincerely congratulate all our compatriots, Mujahideen, the displaced, families of martyrs, prisoners, widows and orphans on the near complete withdrawal of foreign forces as well as the recent conquests and advancements. May Allah accept all the sacrifices, hardships and travails endured by all strata in pursuit of freedom, establishment of pure Islamic system and raising high the Word of Allah, Amen O' Lord of the 'Alamin (all that exists).

Dear Compatriots!

We are celebrating this Eid at a time when majority of American and other foreign forces – by the grace and mercy of Almighty Allah– have evacuated our country and the remaining are following suit, numerous districts and large regions of our homeland have attained comprehensive security, and the Mujahideen, with the Help of Allah, have become stronger, better organized, well-equipped and more robust compared to past.

This success is not for the Islamic Emirate and vanguard Mujahideen alone, rather it is a shared triumph of the entire nation who have mutually endured every hardship with us over the course of two-decade Jihad so that our fellow compatriots are freed from foreign occupation.

- In spite of the military gains and advances, the Islamic Emirate strenuously favors a political settlement in the country, and every opportunity for the establishment of an

Islamic system, peace and security that presents itself will be made use of by the Islamic Emirate, Allah willing.

We have opened a Political Office for ease of negotiations and political track, have appointed an authoritative negotiations team and are committed to finding a resolution through talks on our part, but unfortunately, the opposition parties are still wasting time. Our message remains that instead of relying on foreigners, let us resolve our issues among ourselves and rescue our homeland from the prevailing crisis.

- We seek good and strong diplomatic, economic and political relations in the framework of reciprocal interaction and mutual agreements with all world countries including America following the withdrawal of all foreign forces, and consider such beneficial for all sides.

- We fully assure neighboring, regional and world countries that Afghanistan will not permit anyone to pose a security threat to any other country using our soil.

And we similarly urge other countries to refrain from all interference in our own internal affairs.

- We assure all foreign diplomats, embassies, consulates, humanitarian organizations and investors that they will not face any problems from our side, rather we will exert all efforts for their protection and security. Their presence is a need of our country that cannot be ignored hence they

should continue their work with a peace of mind and not feel a sense of apprehension from the advances and rule of Mujahideen.

- We call on all internal parties that we are not looking for enmity with anyone and our arms remain open for all. Afghanistan is our shared home and if they accept our demand for a pure Islamic system, we will also accept all their rights and lawful demands, and will make good use of their capabilities in the rehabilitation of the homeland.

- Our message to soldiers and various new military formations standing in opposition ranks is to cease fighting and resistance, to join us akin to the thousands of other soldiers who made use of the opening provided by the Islamic Emirate and experienced dignified treatment, so that you may also be safeguarded from dangers of this world and the hereafter, and no longer be a cause for the destruction of our country.

The amalgamation of thousands of Kabul administration troops in various provinces and districts across the country with the Mujahideen in a fraternal atmosphere is a step worth commending. We hope that all those pushed towards war and ensnared in enmity with their own kin also awaken and utilize the available amnesty offer to return to peaceful lives. The Islamic Emirate will arduously fulfill its commitments made to troops that have joined us, will protect their lives, property and honor, and will not allow anyone to oppress or do them harm.

- As the amalgamation process of opposition fighter with the Islamic Emirate is proceeding, I instruct the Military Commission to give special attention to the protection and safe return to homes of those soldiers.

- We call on circles encouraging and exploiting individuals for war under the name of uprisings to learn lessons from past experiences. When you failed to gain anything with the support of tens of thousands of foreign forces, aircrafts and advanced weaponry and technology, you will similarly fail to do anything by yourself, Allah willing. Therefore, it is better you end hostilities and instead support the establishment of an Islamic system.

- None should have reservations about the future. The Islamic Emirate as a representative of its nation is well aware of the problems afflicting our people. Our foremost efforts and priority are geared towards finding a resolution through dialogue and understanding for all outstanding matters, and our belief remains that the general public will no doubt continue to robustly back the Islamic Emirate. The steps of those scholars, tribal elders and sincere figures are commendable whose effective intermediation and acuity led to a large number of opposition troops and fighters defecting to our side. We urge these leaders to continue their efforts and assist the Islamic Emirate in establishing peace and security.

- People play a pivotal role in shaping governments and developing nations. The Islamic Emirate will also provide an opportunity for its people to play an equivalent positive role so that we can build our war-torn homeland together and live in harmony and prosperity under the shade of an Islamic government.

- The Islamic Emirate gives significant attention to literacy programs. If our nation fails to improve educationally, we will fail to advance both socially and economically. Keeping educational institutes operational for economic independence and self-sufficiency, training our children in all educational fields, and especially teaching and training them in religious affairs and advancing in modern sciences are elements the importance of which the Islamic Emirate acknowledges and strives to promote.

Our instruction to the Mujahideen in this regard is to place special focus on religious and scientific programs in areas under the control of Islamic Emirate, to keep madrasas, schools, high schools and universities functional, to help make things easier, to respect teachers of modern sciences, university lecturers and learnt individuals alongside religious scholars, to understand their vital role in society and to assist them in meeting their needs to the best of your abilities.

- Concentrate even more on (protecting) civilian lives during clashes and firefights. The Islamic Emirate has assigned duties to a designated commission so that no one faces harm from Mujahideen during fighting. The Islamic Emirate pays special attention in this regard and stresses to all Mujahideen to continue cooperating with the Commission for Prevention of Civilian Casualties and to take particular care of civilian lives.

- The Islamic Emirate also has a Department for Complaints Registration within the structure of Commission for Prevention of Civilian Casualties. If any fellow compatriot, God forbid, were to face injustice, they may contact this department and lodge a complaint. Moreover, the workers of Complaints Registration are instructed to closely monitor every complaint, to follow up on each case, and to address and resolve it. And if there arises any need for further action, you may seek assistance from the Supreme Court and Military Commission.

- Providing health services within the available resources is also the duty of the Islamic Emirate for which the Health Commission has been assigned. Our instruction to them is to keep all clinics and health centers operational in all possible localities specifically in the newly liberated areas, to broaden and focus on health-related issues, to keep in constant touch with international health NGOs and organizations, and to exert extra efforts in expanding health capabilities and providing additional services for your compatriots.

- Noble religious scholars across the country should focus on cooperating with the Commission for Preaching and Guidance to spread awareness, understanding and character reformation. Every nation and country can only *taste dignity and true peace and prosperity when they stop disobeying and rebelling against Allah. Alas, the duty of spreading Islamic awareness and reform has been bestowed upon the noble scholars, and they are required to fulfill their obligation in the best manner possible, to strive in reforming and enlightening people in mosques, gatherings, media and through other mediums, and to become a guiding light for them.*

- With regards to rights of citizens, the Islamic Emirate is committed to granting all compatriots their rights because Islam commands us to safeguard and give everyone their due rights. Additionally, the Islamic Emirate will pay particular attention to and strive to create an appropriate environment for female education within the framework of sublime Islamic law.

The Islamic Emirate is committed to freedom of speech within the limits of Shariah and national interests. Journalists should continue their activities while keeping in mind these two important factors and adhering to the principles of journalism.

- All skilled and professional strata, scholars, teachers, doctors, scientists, engineers and educated cadres along with national traders and investors should rest assured that they will not face any harm with the advent of the Islamic Emirate. Our homeland is in dire need of their expertise, advice and work, and the future government shall hold them in high esteem. Similarly, our fellow

countrymen should not head abroad, rather all of us need to participate in the establishment of an Islamic government and through it, rebuilding our battered country. The Islamic Emirate wants to reassure everyone in this regard.

- The Mujahideen should pay close attention to their daily activities, integrity, purity of intentions in Jihad, obedience to superiors and good conduct with people, and must avoid arrogance and pride at all cost so that the Help of Allah may continue to descend and not be lifted.

Maintenance and care for public treasury needs attention from us all, especially newly seized weaponry, military gear, equipment, government buildings, national assets and everything else related to the treasury is a public trust. No one has the right to damage, move outside the country, waste or take possession of it without acquiring permission from their superiors.

Moreover, it is our duty to duly safeguard documents, archives of identification and tribal registers along with other essential material left behind by the enemy in districts and other government buildings. The opposition must also desist from damaging these documents and archives during evacuation.

- Every effort must be made to address the needs of the indigent, orphans, disabled, families of prisoners and other needy people in the country. The Islamic Emirate has a *assigned a special commission for this stratum and has instructed it to give assistance within the available means to the indigent, families of the orphans and widows, and to other people in need. The entire nation also bears responsibility in this regard – to making assistance to the needy and indigent a focal point in these dire economic times. And especially in these blessed days of Eid, our wealthy compatriots and brotherly businessmen must also particularly focus on lending a supporting hand to these people.*

To end, I once again extend my felicitation to our fellow compatriots on the occasion of Eid-ul-Adha and hope that they will celebrate these joyous days of Eid in a reassuring atmosphere.

Anyone who isn't foolish can see the Taliban were never the "bloodthirsty terrorists" their enemies portrayed them to be and neither are true Jihadis though Satan's lies of inciting war against Islam are spread nonstop. There will be future wars against Muslims and Islam in various disguises, perhaps less easily detected than those covered in this book. However those whom Allah guides will know and react accordingly so as to earn paradise avoiding hellfire. Which in reality is the purpose of the wars, the true war is over our souls and where they will end up forever. May Allah bless the Muslims and guide all to the 1 true prophetic religion of Islam, even if they've fought for Satan in the past. Allah is oft-forgiving and readily forgives former enemies.

Narrated Thawban: *The Prophet said: The people will soon summon one another to attack you as people when eating invite others to share their dish. Someone asked: Will that be because of our small numbers at that time? He replied: No, you will be numerous at that time: but you will be scum and rubbish like that carried down by a torrent, and Allah will take fear of you from the breasts of your enemy and cast enervation into your hearts. Someone asked: What is wahn (enervation). Messenger of Allah? He replied: Love of the world and dislike of death.*

Sunan Abi Dawud 4297 Grade: Sahih

Tamim al-Dari reported: *The Messenger of Allah, peace and blessings be upon him, said, "This matter will certainly reach every place touched by the night and day. Allah will not leave a house or residence but that Allah will cause this religion to enter it, by which the honorable will be honored and the disgraceful will be disgraced. Allah will honor the honorable with Islam and he will disgrace the disgraceful with unbelief."*

Musnad Aḥmad 16957 Grade: Sahih

Abu Umamah reported: *The Messenger of Allah, peace and blessings be upon him, said, "A group of my nation will continue to be victorious upon the religion, overpowering their enemies. None who oppose them will harm them, except what afflicts them of difficult circumstances, until Allah brings his command while they are like so."*

Musnad Aḥmad 22320 Grade: Sahih li ghayrihi

Al Numan bin Bashir reported: *"We were sitting in the mosque of the Messenger of Allah (saw), and Bashir was a man who did not speak much, so Abu Tha'labah Al-Khashnee came and said: 'Oh, Bashir bin Sa'ad, have you memorized the words of the Messenger of Allah regarding the rulers?' Huthayfah replied, 'I have memorized his words'. So Abu Tha'labah sat down and Huthayfah said, 'The Messenger of Allah said 'Prophet-hood will be amongst you as long as Allah wishes, then He will lift it up when He wishes to lift it up. Then there will be a Khilafah on the way of the Prophet, and it will be as long as Allah wishes it to be, then Allah will lift it up when He wishes to lift it up. Then there will be an inheritance rule, and it will last as long as Allah wishes it to, then Allah will lift it up when He wishes to lift it up. Then there will be a coercive rule, and it will last as long as Allah wishes it to be, then Allah will lift it up when He wishes to lift it up. Then there will be a Khilafah on the way of Prophet-hood.' Then he was silent."*

Musnad Ahmed 18430 Grade: Sahih by Albani

Quran 24:55

Allâh has promised those among you who believe, and do righteous good deeds, that He will certainly grant them succession to (the present rulers) in the land, as He granted it to those before them, and that He will grant them the authority to practice their religion, which He has chosen for them (i.e. Islâm). And He will surely give them in exchange a safe security after their fear (provided) they (believers) worship Me and do not associate anything (in worship) with Me. But whoever disbelieves after this, they are the Fâsiqûn (rebellious, disobedient to Allâh). (55)

Quran 41:34

The good deed and the evil deed cannot be equal. Repel (the evil) with one which is better, then verily! he, between whom and you there was enmity, (will become) as though he was a close friend. (34)

Quran 33:22

And when the believers saw Al¬Ahzâb (the Confederate armies), they said: "This is what Allâh and His Messenger (Muhammad) had promised us, and Allâh and His Messenger (Muhammad) had spoken the truth, And it only added to their faith and to their submissiveness (to Allâh). (22)

www.ingramcontent.com/pod-product-compliance
Lightning Source LLC
Chambersburg PA
CBHW050254010526
44107CB00003B/317